£57-99

ADVANCES IN CULTURE, TOURISM AND HOSPITALITY RESEARCH

ADVANCES IN CULTURE, TOURISM AND HOSPITALITY RESEARCH

Series Editor: Arch G. Woodside

ADVANCES IN CULTURE, TOURISM AND HOSPITALITY RESEARCH

EDITED BY

ARCH G. WOODSIDE

Carroll School of Management, Boston College, USA

ELSEVIER
JAI

Amsterdam – Boston – Heidelberg – London – New York – Oxford
Paris – San Diego – San Francisco – Singapore – Sydney – Tokyo
JAI Press is an imprint of Elsevier

JAI Press is an imprint of Elsevier
The Boulevard, Langford Lane, Kidlington, Oxford OX5 1GB, UK
Radarweg 29, PO Box 211, 1000 AE Amsterdam, The Netherlands
525 B Street, Suite 1900, San Diego, CA 92101-4495, USA

First edition 2007

Notice
No responsibility is assumed by the publisher for any injury and/or damage to persons
or property as a matter of products liability, negligence or otherwise, or from any use
or operation of any methods, products, instructions or ideas contained in the material
herein. Because of rapid advances in the medical sciences, in particular, independent
verification of diagnoses and drug dosages should be made

British Library Cataloguing in Publication Data
A catalogue record for this book is available from the British Library

ISBN-13: 978-0-7623-1257-3
ISBN-10: 0-7623-1257-2
ISSN: 1871-3173 (Series)

For information on all JAI Press publications
visit our website at books.elsevier.com

Printed and bound in the United Kingdom

07 08 09 10 11 10 9 8 7 6 5 4 3 2 1

Working together to grow
libraries in developing countries
www.elsevier.com | www.bookaid.org | www.sabre.org

ELSEVIER   BOOK AID International   Sabre Foundation

CONTENTS

LIST OF CONTRIBUTORS

David Airey	School of Management, University of Surrey, Surrey, UK
Aloys Borgers	Eindhoven University of Technology, Eindhoven, The Netherlands
Joseph Boughey	School of the Built Environment, Liverpool John Moores University, Liverpool, UK
Marylouise Caldwell	H69-Economics and Business Building, The University of Sydney, NSW, Australia
Jenny Cave	Department of Tourism Management, University of Waikato Management School, University of Waikato, Hamilton, New Zealand
Sara Dolnicar	School of Management & Marketing, Marketing Research Innovation Centre (MRIC), University of Wollongong, Australia
Elspeth Frew	School of Sport, Tourism and Hospitality Management, La Trobe University, Bundoora, Australia
Rich Harrill	Department of Hotel, Restaurant & Tourism Management, University of South Carolina, Columbia, SC, USA
Jun-Ying Huang	Graduate School of Management, I-Shou University, Kaohsiung County, Taiwan

Shoji Iijima	Department of Commerce, Faculty of Commerce, Okayama Shoka University, Okayama, Japan
Erdogan Koc	Department of Business Administration, Dogus University, Istanbul, Turkey
Yu-Shan Lin	Department of Business Management, National Sun Yat-Sen University, Kaohsiung, Taiwan
Roger March	School of Marketing, University of New South Wales, Sydney, Australia
Taketo Naoi	Department of Commerce, Faculty of Commerce, Okayama Shoka University, Okayama, Japan
Outi Niininen	Department of Management and Marketing, School of Business, Faculty of Law and Management, La Trobe University, Bundoora, Australia
Chris Ryan	Department of Tourism Management, University of Waikato, Hamilton, New Zealand
Harry Timmermans	Eindhoven University of Technology, Eindhoven, The Netherlands
J. M. Trapp-Fallon	Welsh Centre for Tourism Research, University of Wales Institute Cardiff, Cardiff, UK
Peter van der Waerden	Eindhoven University of Technology, Eindhoven, The Netherlands
Arch G. Woodside	Boston College, Carroll School of Management, Department of Marketing, Chestnut Hill, MA, USA

EDITORIAL ADVISORY BOARD

PREFACE: ADVANCING CULTURE, TOURISM, AND HOSPITALITY THEORY, RESEARCH, AND PRACTICE

Advances in Culture, Tourism, and Hospitality Research (*ACTHR*) is a new book series that provides a forum for scholarly contributions offering both broad and deep reports of progress in theory, research, and practice in relating the fields of culture, tourism and hospitality. *ACTHR* welcomes long papers that delve deeply into antecedents, behaviors, and consequences of topics related to culture, tourism, and hospitality.

Similar to issues of scholarly journals, paper submissions to *ACTHR* are double-blind reviewed – members of the *ACTHR* Editorial Board provide extensive suggestions to authors for revising submissions during the review process. Unlike most journals, the *ACTHR* has no page limits; possibly one or two lengthy papers will constitute an entire future volume in this series. The aim is to encourage authors to ponder and report on how their papers contribute to building an interdisciplinary theory of human behavior beyond the borders of psychology, sociology, marketing, management, tourism, geography, hospitality, and other fields in the behavioral sciences.

This preface champions the view that weak cultural and psychological ties both stimulate and inhibit tourism and hospitality behavior. Many of these ties are held unconsciously by consumers, and some ties may be retrievable automatically when thinking about a tourism-related activity. In most cases the presence of any one weak tie is necessary, but not sufficient to result in a specific stream of tourism behavior; the conjunctive presence of three or more antecedent events are observable in different streams of behavior relating to tourism and hospitality experiences.

In his article aptly entitled, *Tourism is All about Consumption*, Hoch (2002, p. 1) emphasizes,

... consumption behavior is a more salient aspect of touristical pursuits that it is of everyday life. I think that this is especially the case when traveling to places where you don't speak the language, don't quite understand the currency and what it buys you, and when one travels solo. I remember visiting Japan several years ago on business and I have to say that my biggest sense of accomplishment each day came from successfully figuring how to buy three meals a day without very going back to the same restaurant.

Thus, developments in knowledge, theory, and practice of tourism and hospitality behavior may benefit from examining the consumer psychology occurring in planning and doing such behaviors. Such an examination includes, but is not limited to, acquiring knowledge of how consumer think consciously and unconsciously (see Zaltman, 2003) about alternative leisure destinations, hospitality options, leisure activities, and whether or not to travel, stay home, or forego leisure time as much as possible.

This logic is worth nurturing in the study of tourism and hospitality behavior if several psychologists, sociologists, and psychiatrists are correct

In actuality, consumers have far less access to their own mental activities than marketers give them credit for. Ninety-five percent of thinking takes place in our unconscious minds – that wonderful, if messy stew of memories, emotions, thoughts, and other cognitive processes we're not aware of or that we can't articulate (Zaltman, 2003, p. 9).

Consequently, consumers are only vaguely aware, if at all, of the conjunctive combination of the multiple events and below conscious thoughts that were antecedent to their tourism plans and behaviors.

Some tourist behavior involves overcoming culture shock – becoming aware that alternative cultures to one's own culture have unique sets of values, rituals, folkways, mores, rites-of-passage, and views relating to sacred and profane consumption experience. The *ACTHR* explicitly seeks to contributions that call attention, describe, and interpret culture and cross-cultural influences relating to tourism and hospitality. Solomon (2004) both defines and explains the need to focusing on culture in behavioral research.

Culture, a concept crucial to the understanding of consumer behavior, may be thought of as a society's personality. It includes both abstract ideas, such as values, and ethics, and material objects and services, such as automobiles, clothing, food, art, and sports that are produced or valued by a society. Put another way, culture is the accumulation is the accumulation of shared meanings, rituals, norms, and traditions among the members of an organization or society. ... Culture is the "lens" through which people view products [services, and experiences]. Ironically, the effects of culture on consumer behavior are so powerful and far-reaching that their importance is sometimes difficult to grasp. Like a fish immersed in water, we do not always appreciate this power until we encounter a different environment. (Solomon, 2004, p. 526)

The irony of culture's powerful, yet unrecognized, influence strikes home in a very personal way. The following is a brief story of culture shock that Solomon's thoughts bring automatically to my mind.

I was 20 years old traveling home in July on a weekend pass from an Army base with a group of three other Reserve Officer Training Corps (ROTC) candidates. Before being dropped-off at my house, we stopped at house of one of the other candidate's house in the Squirrel Hill district of Pittsburgh, PA – a lower-upper class neighborhood. I vividly remember standing in the living room of this house – shocked at the beauty of the furniture, books, magazines, chess set, window treatments, and mahogany woodwork. "Wow, Jesus!" These unspoken words are the ones that I almost said aloud at that moment. The first half of my youth was spent in an upper-lower class neighborhood in the Southside district of Pittsburgh – my family lived in the bottom floor of a two-bedroom rental unit of a house and I shared a bedroom with my two sisters until I was 8 years-old. We moved on my birthday in 1951 to a lower middle-class neighborhood in the Carrick district of Pittsburgh to a house with two-floors including a bedroom just for me. My family moved again on my 16th birthday to an upper-middle class neighborhood in the South Hills of Pittsburgh but I never consciously thought about social-class cultural differences before entering my fellow ROTC candidate's house in July 1963. For the first time I realized **how** other people lived differently than the way my family lived. I recall the moment to be a humbling experience for me – my parents had made great strides in improving their (and children's) standard-of-living; I had not consciously realized the vast range in social class differences until that moment in July 1963. Reflecting a later age in 2007, thoughts again of amazement come-to-mind of how my parents lifted themselves away from poverty – given that both achieved less that fourth-grade educations in their childhoods. "Wow, Jesus!" captures the conscious view that follows this subjective personal introspection of my own and my parents' upbringing.

This story of traveling and experiencing another environment includes an example of how such cross-environment behavior awakens interpreting and understanding of cultural influences. Such awakening – conscious thinking – is likely to occur when traveling from Canada to the United States, the United States to Italy, northern Italy to southern Italy, China to Australia, and from the Southside of Pittsburgh to Squirrel Hill. The story also serves to illustrate the influence of cultural antecedents – a family or nation's level of formal education affects its way-of-living and thinking. Cultural antecedents are worthy of attention in culture, tourism, and hospitality research because specific streams of antecedent conditions lead to (or prevent) behaviors that include or exclude tourism and hospitality behavior. Let's now consider two examples at the national level.

CONJUNCTIVE EVENTS AND THOUGHTS CAUSING CONSUMER PLANS AND BEHAVIORS: BRANDING BRITAIN FOR GERMANS AND VICE VERSA

Weak psychological ties stimulate or inhibit tourism behavior. Many of these ties are held unconsciously (e.g., Bargh, Chen, & Burrows, 1996), and some ties may be retrievable automatically when thinking about a tourism-related proposal. Exhibit 1 illustrates the previous two sentences.

Exhibit 1 is a causal map (see Huff & Jenkins, 2002) that includes a characteristic in the national character of Germans (box 2) that affects the automatic image retrieval of the tourist brand, Britain, by Germans – the positive, multiple-surface, image of Britain helps to stimulate lots of holiday visits to Britain by Germans. The actions of ZDF (box 5) nurture this image as well as help keep the brand easily retrievable (box 4) among Germans. Note that three separate nodes appear that help stimulate leisure trips to Britain by Germans – nodes 2, 3, and 5.

Exhibit 1. Tourism Exporting Behavior of Germans Visiting Britain. *Note:* thick arrows indicate dominant influence.

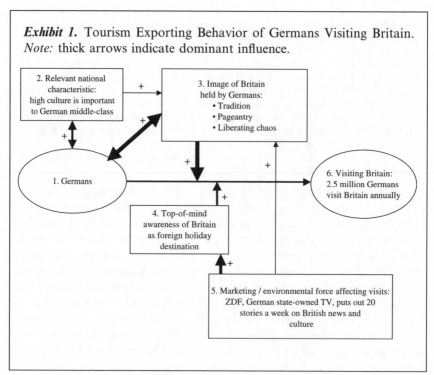

The impact of national character is one of those background factors that often go unnoticed in identifying inhibitors and drivers affecting tourism behavior. For example, the *Economist* (2003, p. 49) points out that the British "don't mind the BMWs, the Volkswagens, and Miele dishwashers, but they are not much interested in the high culture so important to the German middle class."

In comparison, the causal map of the British thinking about a holiday trip to Germany is discouraging. (see Exhibit 2). The automatic thoughts about the brand, Germany, among the British still include "Hitler, WWII, and emotional darkness" (box 2 in Exhibit 2). This automatically retrieved image is nurtured by three environmental forces (box 6) and the much lower interest in high culture by the British middle class compared to the Germans (box 3). This national character trait among the British negatively affects the attempts to build a new, positive, cultural image of Germany

Exhibit 2. Tourism Exporting Behavior of British Visiting Germany. *Note:* thick arrows indicate dominant influence.

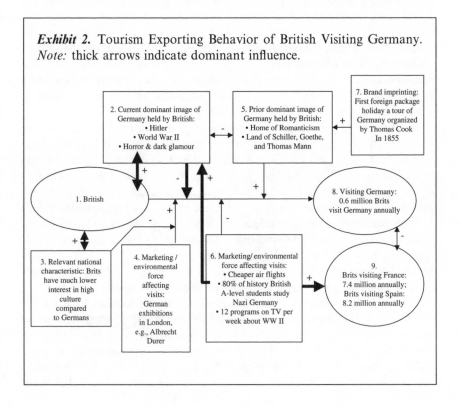

(box 4 and arrow from box 3). The *Economist* concludes, "Selling Germany in Britain will be a tough slog."

Such mapping of strategic knowledge is helpful for identifying what needs to be done for affecting cultural and psychological changes among tourists. (e.g., eliminating the continuing focus in British TV and schooling on Nazi Germany and World War II is a necessary pre-condition – change in a cultural antecedent relating to tourism behavior). Such mapping is helpful for identifying the unique and valuable benefits of a tourism brand; for example, Germans' experiencing British pageantry and liberating chaos.

Developing and studying causal maps provides a gestalt view of what is happening and why it is happening in the minds of leisure travelers and nontravelers. Such mapping helps us consider a case research approach rather than relying only on a variable-by-variable analysis of tourism psychology and behavior. Unconscious–conscious mapping research suggests the need to identify unconscious thoughts that consumers may be unaware and unable to report on as influences on their leisure travel behavior as well as listening to their verbal answers to researchers' questions.

Consequently, culture, tourism, and hospitality researchers need an eclectic toolkit (see Woodside, 2006) that permits research on the unconscious and conscious thoughts and actions of humans when focusing on tourism-related plans and behaviors. The contributors and editors intention is that Volume 1 of *ACTHR* serves in stimulating your creative energy to contribute useful applications using such a toolkit.

Exhibit 3 attempts to generalize several propositions that relate to the German and British case studies and culture, tourism, and hospitality research in general. Exhibit 3 emphasizes that tourism and hospitality do not occur in cultural vacuums. Cultures provided crucial grounding that influence both tourism–hospitality behavior and the interpretation of such behavior – cultures affect unconscious and conscious interpretations of both tourists and researchers. Consequently, while useful, variable-based positivistic empirical research is inadequate for achieving full, rich, understandings of tourism behavior. Research needs to embrace holistic case study tools that include both emic (tourist own) and etic (researcher) thick descriptions and sense-making reports of tourism behavior.

Exhibit 3 illustrates several propositions. P_1: export tourism behavior for culture B (A–B inbound tourism) is substantially larger than export tourism behavior for Culture A, i.e., absolute and relative sizes of export tourism vary substantially among cultures – the impact of tourism varies substantially among different cultures in different time periods. P_2: outbound and domestic tourism behavior competes with non-tourism leisure behavior.

Exhibit 3. Culture, Tourism and Hospitality Research. *Notes:* Two cultures in Exhibit 1 may be nation states (e.g., France and Canada) or two cultural regions in one country (e.g., U.S. South and North). The exhibit illustrates several propositions. P_1: export tourism behavior in culture B (A–B inbound tourism) is substantially larger than export tourism behavior in Culture A that is absolute and relative sizes of export tourism vary substantially among cultures. P2: outbound and domestic tourism leisure behavior. P3: hospitality behavior varies for domestic versus inbound visitors and in non-tourism contexts. P4: cultural antecedents affecting tourism and hospitality differ substantially for A and B. Hospitality research includes studying customer behavior relating to airlines, beverages, cruise ships, foodservice, golf, gambling, lodging, skiing, real estate, theme parks and attractions, time share, vehicle rentals, meetings and conventions.

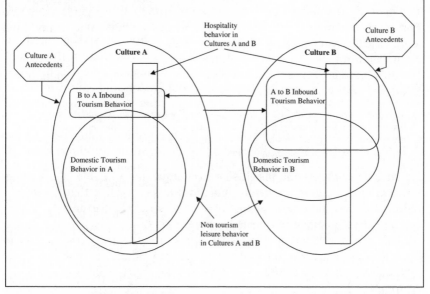

P_3: hospitality behavior varies for domestic versus inbound visitors and in non-tourism contexts. P_4: cultural antecedents affecting tourism and hospitality differ substantially for A and B. Hospitality research includes studying customer behavior relating to airlines, beverages, cruise ships, foodservice, golf, gambling, lodging, skiing, real estate, theme parks and attractions, time share, vehicle rentals, meetings and conventions. P_5 hospitality research always includes but extends beyond describing and interpreting aspects of tourism behavior – hospitality research deepens, broadens, and enriches the study of how culture influences tourism behavior.

The coverage of contributions in Volume 1 probes these and additional propositions. The following discussion provides an introduction and a brief assessment of the value in reading these 11 papers.

THE UNIQUE AND VALUABLE CONTRIBUTIONS OF THE PAPERS IN VOLUME 1 OVERCOMING GHETTO TOURISM

While not using the expression, ghetto tourism may come-to-mind when reading Chapter 1, *Fables of the Reconstruction or Reconstruction of the Fables? Pragmatic Aesthetics for Advancing Tourism, Culture, Place, and Community.* The failure of a tourist (me) visiting the Algarve (southern Portugal) to experience the spirit of a Portugal culture came to my mind automatically while reading of this contribution by Rich Harrill – views of clean, beautiful, and antiseptic city streets are my memories of the Algarve. Harrill's message has profound implications for managing/designing places to attract first-time and repeat visitors to a destination.

> The reconstruction of the fables dictates that any design or policy preference used for place and community are pieces of a much larger puzzle, including people, place, and myth. Over the last two decades, professionals offer a grand design without considering the organic nature of these elements in place.

Harrill's descriptions and insights are so unique and valuable in describing interactions of culture, tourism, and hospitality practice that Chapter 1 reflects the core rationale for this new book series. Unfortunately, appreciating Harrill's conclusions usually only occurs during the second half of a reader's lifetime. If you are under 40, don't miss this early opportunity to learn how aesthetics are integral components in culture, tourism, and hospitality. Older readers are likely to submit to the urge to read Harrill without a prompt.

Explaining Why People Do Not Travel

Understanding why some people do not travel was a motivation behind the research study leading up to Chapter 2. See Australia Ltd. provided a grant to Woodside and Caldwell to conduct a study to help explain the decrease in domestic travel by Australians. Chapter 2 builds from ecological systems theory in an attempt to uncover both unconscious and conscious explanations resulting in travel and non-tourism behavior. Chapter goes beyond reason – why explanations of tourism behavior in building a cultural contingency based model of facilitating and inhibiting contingencies leading to, or preventing, travel.

The Power of the Web and TV Miniseries: Why Greece is Attracting an Increasing Number of Taiwanese and Why South Korea Attracts Overseas Asian Visitors

In Chapter 3, Yu-Shan Lin and Jun-Ying offer rich descriptions of how web log entries and television miniseries influence tourism behavior. If you are unfamiliar with Flickr, PhotoFlix, Shuttfly, Pixnet, and Webshots, let these authors introduce you to these important communication tools. The indirect influence on Taiwanese tourism to South Korea resulting from the exporting of South Korean TV miniseries to Taiwan is a 21st Century trend that is going to be repeated among other countries. Read Chapter 3 for details.

Beyond Studs Terkel: Oral History Interview Analysis

Studs Terkel's *Working* offers a classic report in oral history interview analysis (Terkel, 1997). Trapp-Fallon and Joseph Boughey describe the value of this tool in case study research in tourism behavior in Chapter 4. The authors provide a valuable survey of the oral history literature; Chapter 4 serves as a unique and valuable introduction to applying oral history methods in tourism and hospitality behavior. Take time to read Studs Terkel's classic work as well.

Accepted Standards Undermining the Validity of Tourism Research

In Chapter 5, Sara Dolnicar focuses on three accepted standards in empirical tourism research, which may often serve to undermine the validity of findings. The three standards include:

- the uncritical use of ordinal multi-category answer formats,
- derivation of cross-cultural comparisons that do not consider cultural response biases resulting from response styles, and
- standard step-wise procedure used in data-driven market segmentation.

This paper describes the potential dangers of these standard approaches and makes recommendations for researchers on how to apply tools that overcome their limitations.

Gender in Backpacking and Adventure Tourism

In Chapter 6, Jenny Cave and Chris Ryan examine gender differences in perceptions of the backpacking experience and illustrate how mixed research methods aid in deriving richer understandings of a social phenomenon. Reading this paper helps brings to consciousness implicit attitudes about how females and males attend and interpret information and experiences. This chapter offers important insights about the nuances of seeing tourism and hospitality experiences through the lens of both genders.

Spatially Differentiated Utility Functions for Urban Greenspace

In Chapter 7, Borgers, Timmermans, and Van der Waerden demonstrate the contextual affects on consumer preferences. This contribution offers a remarkably useful breakthrough for improving conjoint analysis for designing urban parks and other leisure environments.

Advancing Theory on Consumer Plans, Actions, and How Marketing Information Affects Both

In Chapter 8, Roger March and Arch G. Woodside use two sets of data from visitors to Prince Edward Island, Canada, to describe how visitor plans differ dramatically from their reported behaviors. Chapter 8 shows how both sets of data provide useful evidence on the effectiveness of marketing information in crafting plans and influencing behavior that would not have occurred otherwise.

The Serious Face of Humor

In Chapter 9, Elspeth Frew provides an excellent literature review of humor in tourism marketing, and behavior. Humor can have both substantial positive as well as negative consequences. The benefits and pervasiveness of humor make a compelling case of its application in developing tourism management programs but only after learning about the risks that relate to its use. A big mistake is in thinking, you know a lot about humor without reading Frew's contribution.

Assessing All-Inclusive Pricing from the Perspective of the Main Stakeholders in the Turkish Tourism Industry

In Chapter 10, Erdogan Koc provides strong evidence that a viable share of international visitors prefer all-inclusive pricing. Reading this paper provides knowledge in the nuances for success and avoiding failure in all-inclusive pricing strategies. One price does not fit all is a key lesson that Koc advocates.

How Visitors Assess Historical Districts

In Chapter 11, Taketo Naoi, David Airey, Shoji Iijima, and Outi Niininen use a combination of repertory grid analysis and laddering analysis to elicit relationships in visitors' minds fro-historical districts concepts, benefits, and their own values. "How to make complex mental processes clear" would make an apt subtitle for this paper. This chapter provides excellent training for how to apply repertory grid and laddering techniques in tourism research.

A Note of Appreciation and Call for Papers

The *Advances in Culture, Tourism, and Hospitality Research* Associate Editors, Rich Harrill and John Crotts, and I appreciate the services of the members of the Editorial Board for the series as well as the willingness of the authors in sharing their expertise and contributing to this cross-disciplinary field of study. We invite readers to share their thoughts on this first volume and to contribute a paper for publication consideration in future volumes in the series.

REFERENCES

Bargh, J. A., Chen, M., & Burrows, L. (1996). Automaticity of social behavior: Direct effects of trait construct and stereotype activation on action. *Journal of Personality and Social Psychology, 71*(2), 230–244.

Economist (2003). Germany and Britain: Bringing back the romance, *Economist, 368*(8331), 49.

Hoch, S. J. (2002). News from the President: Tourism is all about consumption. *ACR News*, Winter, *27*, 1–4.

Huff, A. S., & Jenkins, M. (2002). *Mapping strategic knowledge*. London: Sage.

Solomon, M. (2004). *Consumer behavior*. Upper Saddle River, NJ: Pearson Prentice Hall.

Terkel, S. (1997). *Working*. New York: New Press.

Woodside, A. G. (2006). Overcoming the illusion of will and self-fabrication: Going beyond naïve subjective personal introspection to an unconscious/conscious theory of behavior explanation. *Psychology & Marketing*, *23*(3), 257–272.

Zaltman, G. (2003). *How customers think*. Cambridge, MA: Harvard Business School Press.

Arch G. Woodside
Editor

CHAPTER 1

FABLES OF THE RECONSTRUCTION OR RECONSTRUCTION OF THE FABLES? PRAGMATIC AESTHETICS FOR ADVANCING TOURISM, CULTURE, PLACE, AND COMMUNITY

Rich Harrill

ABSTRACT

Culture, place, and community are major themes in international tourism and destination management. Responses to the perceived loss or lack of these ideals include neo-traditional design and communitarian policy. However, although these movements offer practical solutions, they fail to address the social and political conditions underlying sprawl and place-lessness. This theoretical essay contends that discussions of place and community locate within a context of pragmatic action for transforming old and creating new institutions. Specifically, this paper argues for a pragmatism that is communicative and critical as well as institutionally experimental. Such an approach requires a redefinition of place and community as people, space, and myth. Through these reflections, the

Advances in Culture, Tourism and Hospitality Research, Volume 1, 1–16
Copyright © 2007 by Elsevier Ltd.
ISSN: 1871-3173/doi:10.1016/S1871-3173(06)01001-9

paper recounts a few fables of the reconstruction regarding place and community, and then initiating "reconstruction" drawing upon examples from planning theory and history. The result aims for vibrant, authentic places and communities for both hosts and guests.

Repeating a common southern American epigram, visitors and residents experience increasing difficulties in getting from there to here. Humans disconnect from place, and if connection is not entirely absent, little continuity exists among communities. Place and community are central to tourism and destination management, linking the industry intimately with public sentiment and imagination. Dreams and aspirations for family and work, as well as travel and tourism, depend heavily upon subjective appraisals of local social, economic, and environmental conditions. For example, Chattanooga, Tennessee, had little tourism when it was regarded in 1969 by none other than Walter Cronkite as, "America's Dirtiest City." By the 1990s, this brand image has changed completely with a complete revitalization of its riverfront and downtown.

To satiate the desire for place and community as a prerequisite for good tourism, humans tell fables of how they lost these ideals, why recovery is necessary, and how to carry out reconstructive programs. A small cottage industry has grown up around the rhetoric of construction. Yet the fables of place and community have drifted into intellectual doldrums, offering little innovation regarding tourism planning and design. This century requires a new destination design ethic for place and community.

Place and community are distinct concepts. For example, in virtual communities it is possible to have social relationships without physical space. Increasingly, these virtual communities – such as virtualtourist.com – are used to exchange information about destinations. Conversely, humans can identify many places in which social relationships are weak or non-existent. Increasingly, a "smart or sustainable" community is where place and community converge and is appealing to both visitors and residents. Yet, how do we cultivate place and community for the benefit of tourism? How do we reconcile these concepts with social and political equity? In this theoretical essay, I contend that we locate our discussions of place and community within a context of pragmatic action for transforming old and creating new social and political institutions. Specifically, this paper argues for a "prophetic" (Cornel West's term) tourism planning approach that is theoretically communicative and critical and links local and global destinations. Such an approach requires a redefinition of place and community as people, space, and myth. Through these reflections, this paper recounts a few fables of the reconstruction regarding place and community and then initiates reconstruction drawing examples from tourism planning theory and history.

FABLES OF THE RECONSTRUCTION

Much of the recent debates concerning place and community in the United States and Europe has revolved around the New Urban or "neo-traditional" design movement, which at its best combines elements of traditional, human scale architecture and smart growth practices. Ultimately, downtowns are revitalized for tourism by reproducing a pedestrian-oriented, small-town environment with sport, entertainment, and retail. For example, the towns of Seaside and Celebration – both in Florida – were originally built as residential communities but are now tourism attractions in their own right. The New Urban movement promotes place and community through historical planning and design prototypes found in, for example, heritage tourism destinations such as Charleston, New Orleans, and many European cities. The fable told by New Urbanists is that the reconstruction of place and community begins with a return to "functional" urban forms through the revision or elimination of outdated planning and architectural codes.

For Kunstler (1996), the bugaboo is zoning: inefficient, zoning-driven planning leads to the dysfunctional separation of public (and tourist) spaces, such as the separation of residential and commercial zones resulting in automobile over-dependence. In response, Duany and Plater-Zyberk (2003, 2005) single-handedly attempted to reinvent community design through elaborate code, while Calthorpe (1995) sought to relieve automobile dependence through transportation-oriented development (TODs).

Criticism of the New Urban movement is not new. However, problem identification and enumeration of planning and design solutions, such as mixed uses and density adjustments, is an end in themselves for many neo-traditionalists. Lacking a critique of underlying conditions that create sprawl and "bad" tourism places, the literature is frequently superficial. Who would disagree that some types of sprawl expand ecological footprints (defined by Wackernagel & Rees (1996) as the land and water supporting a defined human population and material standard indefinitely) and undermines livability? A more fruitful inquiry begins with the social, economic, and political conditions that divorce guests and hosts from place. For example, many New Urbanists fail to address the origins of zoning by class and race. As Hall (1988, p. 58) pointed out, American land use zoning apparently originated to control Chinese laundries in California, first in Modesto and then San Francisco in the 1880s. In 1916, New York City adopted a comprehensive zoning ordinance combining land use and height zoning as a response, in part, to concerns that immigrant garment workers would destroy the exclusive character of businesses thus threatening property values (ibid., p. 59). Few tourists realize the darker history underlying their favorite destinations.

This lack of critique reflects New Urbanism's own language, absconding the social and political implications of its design preferences and biases. For example, terms like "syntactical coherence," "valid urban form," and "permanent authority," take on caste-like connotations with the design templates used by New Urbanists. According to Linder (1993, p. 21), this tautological logic, known as "this is this," presents design values as self-evident without public debate. Much like the explosion of aquariums and triple-A baseball clubs, this design is unabashedly promoted as good for tourism. By its terminology, the New Urbanism drifts from better planning and design toward association with gated communities. Although integrated into the urban fabric, New Urban codes and ordinances restrict social and physical dialogue between the project and surrounding neighborhoods. Thus, erected is a verbal boundary as insurmountable as a gate. This closed development becomes a world within itself, devoid of social and political experimentation. With little doubt, New Orleans will emerge from Hurricane Katrina as a vastly improved destination, but at what cost in social and cultural dialogue that made the city a tourism attraction in the first place?

The creation of generic places is the real issue for tourism and destination management. Through its strict adherence to code and architectural conformity, the New Urbanism threatens to create a uniform small-town experience that denies visitors the sense of discovery and exploration – hidden alleys and winding paths – that make community tourism so appealing. Ironically, many of the destination cities used as models for neo-traditional design exhibit a combination of irregular design and architectural formalism that makes them so interesting.

Ultimately, the problem of place for New Urbanists is that they derive their perspectives from urban aesthetic theory, not from rigorous studies about place and community. From Ebenezer Howard, father of the Garden City, and Patrick Geddes, father of the Regional Survey, the theoretical lineage diverges uneasily and with much overlap into two groups. Raymond Unwin, Barry Parker, and Fredric Osborn emphasize design over the social and political ecology of human settlements. New Urbanists frequently cite Unwin's *Town Planning in Practice* (Unwin, 1911) as an inspiration for their work. Invaluable to contemporary sustainable building, this work complements a more comprehensive approach of the Regional Planning Association of America (RPAA) of the 1930s and 1940s. For Lewis Mumford and Benton MacKaye, planning begins with a local inventory of social, economic, and environmental resources and ended with the collective, sustainable use of these resources within and between regional communities. Human scale, aesthetically pleasing environments are then fit constructively within a regional framework.

Much in the same way, contemporary tourism planners start with a local inventory of attractions and assets, both developed and undeveloped, and ending with recommendations for their improvement or development. What is often missing, however, are recommendations for collective, sustainable resource use between communities. Thus, a community may end up with a sustainable tourism product that is not grounded in a sustainable community. Sustainable regional tourism is defined in this way as no more than regional product development.

COMPETING STORY LINES

If the New Urban design ethic alone is inadequate for the recovery of place and community, then where shall we begin? Arguably, neither place nor community exists without people to build, inhabit, and breathe life into space. Place as people, has a long pedigree in the sociological theories of Toennies, Simmel, and Wirth. These theorists argued that social pathologies affecting human populations result from urbanization and industrialization. Loss of place results in *anomie* or normlessness. Park and Burgess of the Chicago School later theorized that community attachment and solidarity persisted despite modernization. Recent sociological theory conceives community as either network relationships, exchange relationships, or embedded within rational choices. The tourism literature is heavily indebted to this tradition, employing community attachment (Harrill & Potts, 2003; Jurowski, 1998; Jurowski, Uysal, & Williams, 1997; McCool & Martin, 1994; Um & Crompton, 1987) and social exchange theory (Ap, 1992; Getz, 1994; Jurowski et al., 1997; Madrigal, 1993; Perdue, Long, & Allen, 1990). However, these theories are relevant to the notion of sustainable community development that supports tourism development in that we are again discussing the toll of "placelessness" on individual and social health.

However, like the New Urbanism, these theoretical perspectives inadequately address explicit connections between people – whether visitors or residents – and place.

Conservative-liberal policies embrace sociological and economic theories as "neutral" explanations of place and community. For example, the late Peter Drucker lamented in *The New Realities* (Drucker, 1989) that the modern welfare state overextends its management capabilities. Reflecting the rhetoric of the Reagan/Thatcher era, he called for the private sector assignment of functions that government should not or cannot perform. For Drucker, government expansion weakens communities through favoritism and paternalism. Conversely, Thurow in *The Future of Capitalism* (Thurow, 1996) argued that privatization means a withdrawal from the public domain and consequently, a withdrawal from community. As economists and storytellers (see McCloskey, 1990), both authors argue for a role of government suitable for community and destination development.

Arguably, however, place and community depend upon both conservative and liberal values, rather than a sweeping, comprehensive platform. For example, Friedman in *The World is Flat* (Friedman, 2005) argues government must operate effectively in a world without borders. Striking a balance between Druker and Thurow, Friedman argues that safety nets for communities as borders open and jobs are restructured. Yet at the global scale it can be very difficult to discern specific local, regional, and even national interactions between tourism, place, and community. Employment issues may vary significantly from destination-to-destination, making tourism planning and marketing extremely difficult.

The contemporary communitarian movement also locates community between the right and left, addressing such issues as health, education, marriage and divorce, crime, and the preservation of public space. Communitarians "favor strong democracy ... we seek to make government more representative, more participatory, and more responsive to all members of the community" (Etzioni, 1998, p. xxvii). For communitarians, however, "community" exists between the extremes in public policy, as loosely bound initiatives rather than a coherent movement for the reconstruction of place. By simply occupying discursive space between conservatism and liberalism, communitarians neither challenge the assumptions of these traditions nor call for progressive institutional reform. Thus, the movement poorly defends threats against representation and participation or responds to social and political change. Like New Urbanists, communitarians successfully frame problems and suggest solutions; however, absent is an in-depth analysis of conditions that hinder the development of place and community, and in turn, tourism and destination development.

PLACE AS PEOPLE

Social and political theory helps define place as people. For example, according to the philosophy of pragmatism, truth relies upon a relatively free interplay of opinions and ideas among people in society. This philosophy is found frequently in arguments for tourism, as it is frequently noted that there is a high correlation between free societies and international tourism.

Pragmatism has long influenced planning theory (Friedmann, 1987), with theorists over the last three decades attending to the communicative side of the philosophy. In this context, understanding depends upon "the person and the situation of the speaker as well as the words heard, when we listen we explore intended and contextual meaning as well as literal meaning" (Forester, 1989, pp. 111–112). However, pragmatism also concerns the human agency and solidarity to remove constrictive social and political conditions (Rorty, 1982). This critical side of pragmatism emphasizes the relationships between political and institutional economics, material conditions, and the social and political requirements for community. Pragmatism in planning should emphasize both communicative and "critical" explanations of the influences that facilitate or retard place and community.

Pragmatic philosopher John Dewey emphasized the revitalization of community, basing his notion of the "Great Community" upon face-to-face public interaction and neighborly dialogue to emerge out of mass society. Dewey argued for the renewal of community of place contrasting with communities of interest (Blanco, 1994). Importantly, Dewey tempered his community of ideal dialogue with realistic assessments of American politics and economics affecting democratic intelligence. In sum, Dewey would temper argument that tourism opens societies with the realization that tourism is often used as a powerful political and economic tool for a city's or region's elite.

Lewis Mumford conceives a sustainable relationship between cities and regions as depending upon regional exploration, an expanded version of Dewey's learning by doing precept (Friedmann, 1987, pp. 197–200).

However, Dewey's dialectical influence is also evident in Mumford's definition of urban development:

> Out of the ritual and dramatic action, in all their forms, something even more important emerged [in the historical city]: nothing less than human dialogue. Perhaps the best

definition of the city in its higher aspects is to say that it is a place designed to offer the
widest facilities of significant conversation. (Mumford, 1961, p. 116)

Mumford's conception of the city contradicts New Urban and communitarian sensibilities: design must remain open to the possibilities offered
through social and physical means. In addition, political life must remain
democratic so that the urban form reflects human hopes and aspirations.
Extending Dewey and Mumford's metaphor, the good city should aspire to
Forester's (1989, p. 144) criteria for mutual understanding, including com-
prehensibility, sincerity, legitimacy, and truth. It is little wonder that the
world's greatest destination cities are also some of the most democratic and
open to constant dialogue among residents and tourists.

Prophetic pragmatism challenges tourism planners and destination
managers to make connections between urban design, institutions, and
issues of class, race, and gender. West (1989) challenges us to take action in
word and deed. Increasingly, globalization and environmental consciousness define this action. The local institutions created to deliver sustainability
must serve an experimental purpose regarding the construction of new
national and international institutions. In this way, it may be possible to
position tourism as having a much larger role in urban and community
development – tourism can inform the way democratic institutions are
created and operated.

Social and political theorist Roberto Mangabeira Unger provides a neo-
pragmatic bridge between the North and South. In his groundbreaking
three-volume *Politics*, Unger (1987a, 1987b, 1987c) develops a social theory
of human empowerment and social experimentation that avoids the iron-
clad laws of positivism, capitalism, and other "deep-logic" theories.
According to Unger, these social theories reproduce context-preserving
routines that hinder imaginative institutional development. Interestingly,
Unger claims that developing countries have been the most successful at
creating new institutions and alternative government. Unger argues that
non-Western countries have long begun to combine Western-style technology or non-Western varieties of work organization with different ways of
social organization. Thus, South has new institutions, which might develop
with the capacity to deliver sustainable tourism and development. For
example, in Unger's native Brazil, the city of Curtiba has won international
recognition as an ecocity featuring an efficient bus network, green spaces and
parks, a 24-hour downtown pedestrian district, and innovative social services.
Although such efforts are no replacement for international social and
economic reform, they anticipate the reconstruction of place and community

on a global basis, rather than the exportation of sustainable development, and therefore sustainable tourism, from the North to the South.

PLACE AS SPACE

The interaction between people and environment is relatively simple to articulate but hard to visualize and even harder to realize in research and practice. What is it *exactly* when we speak of the interaction between people and physical space. In "Barn Raising," from *Community and the Politics of Place*, Kemmis (1990, p. 79) captures the interaction between people and space:

> It is concrete in the actual things or events – the barns, the barn dances – which the actual practices of cooperation produce. But it is also concrete in the actual, specific places within which those practices and cooperation take place. Clearly, the practices of frontier families did not appear out of thin air; they grew out of the one thing those people had in common: the effort to survive in hard country. And when the effort to survive comes to rely upon shared and repeat practices like barn raising, survival itself is transformed; it become inhabitation. To inhabit a place is to dwell there in a practiced way, in a way which relies upon certain regular, trust habits of behavior.

People and environments interact to create place through collective habits and practices. Some of the best tourism places are those in which the visitor experiences that physical place carved out of by repeat practices, but also gains an appreciation and understanding of the habits that inhabit or formerly inhabited that place. This is the core of "authenticity," an important ingredient in destination building. This view is consistent with pragmatism, as Dewey (quoted in Johnson, 1949, p. 59) remarked that the "foundation of democracy is faith … in human intelligence and in the power of pooled and cooperative experience". Tourism planners and architects should encourage collectivity as a necessary stage toward effective destination development and design. Increasingly, this collectivity should reflect an emerging international culture from which new habits and practices of human settlement arise.

Leisure and tourism scholarship is filled with references to the interaction between people and place, resulting in measurable attitudes and preferences. According to Kaplan and Kaplan (1989, p. 51), people prefer, "circumstances that require them to expand their horizons, or at least circumstances where enrichment is a possibility." Concurrent with pragmatism, the authors contend that exploration is a primary need in physical environments and that it is an important factor in accumulating experience. Kaplan and

Kaplan (1989, pp. 50–57) noted four factors that influence environmental preference: coherence, complexity, legibility, and mystery. Coherence facilitates a sense of order and directs attention. Complexity is the number of visual elements in a scene. Legibility includes the centrality of orientation and the ability to construct a cognitive map. Mystery is the promise of further information. Over the course of their careers, the authors found mystery and coherence as important factors in explaining environmental preferences. Not coincidentally, these attributes are common to the most visited destinations.

If coherence, complexity, legibility, and mystery are important environmental attributes then we should begin with a tourism design ethic that includes the element of chance with order, maintaining interest without inducing bewilderment. These rules of thumb are consistent with Kevin Lynch's *The Image of the City* (Lynch, 1960). Lynch's (ibid., p. 9) *imagability* includes elements of legibility and coherence: it is the quality in a physical object that gives it a high probability of evoking a strong image in an observer. Lynch's classic design methodology includes interviews with residents regarding their environmental images and an examination of images evoked by design professionals in the field (ibid., pp. 140–159).

The work of environmental psychologists such as Kaplan and Kaplan (1989) and urban theorists such as Mumford, Lynch, and Jane Jacobs support a neo-pragmatic tourism design theory. Humans interact with environments through exploration and experimentation. Place is never inert space, providing an optimal problem-solving environment. Similarly, the urban landscape is active space: paths, edges, and landmarks regulate a highly fluid destination, providing clues that residents and visitors require when moving through the urban form. Along the way, residents and visitors confirm or eliminate design choices through choice of action.

This process is the basis for Mumford's (1961, p. 302) urban theory and the process is useful as a theory of destination development:

> Organic planning does not begin with a preconceived goal: it moves from need to need, from opportunity to opportunity, in a series of adaptations that themselves become increasingly coherent and purposeful, so that they generate a complex, final design, hardly less unified than a pre-formed geometric pattern.

Tourism planners and architects should encourage this calculus of choice through expanded participation and experiential learning rather than a narrow technical approach stifling organic destination development. However, critics charge that sprawl is also "organic development." Yet destination development referred to as "sprawl" is not necessarily bad or unsustainable, but can become so without proper institutional guidance and integration into existing land uses. Sprawl results from institutions that emphasize growth over development, that are unable or unwilling to respond to demographic or economic change, and that perpetuate factionalism over democracy.

PLACE AS MYTH

Anthropology, philosophy (as in transcendental interpretations of nature), psychology, and theology (particularly the Jungian varieties) describe place as myth. However, many tourism planners and architects fail to consider the role of religion in the cognitive mapping and the interpretation of space. An excellent mediator of ideas and concepts about place and community, myth should become important in this century as well engage in international myth-making. Modified to unique people and places, many well-known myths such as John Henry and Johnny Appleseed help to hew English, Spanish, French, and Native American cultural traditions into contemporary rules and definitions of place and community. With a healthy respect for local customs and traditions, the integration of myth into tourism planning is critical if we are to understand place and community as "sacred places."

Mircea Eliade's *The Sacred and the Profane* (1957) provides a starting point for an inquiry into place as myth. For Eliade, the solidarity between culture and geography is the experience or feeling of belonging to the place. Place and community create an experience greater than people or environmental attributes:

> Life is not possible without an opening toward the transcendent; in other words, human beings cannot live in chaos. Once contact with the transcendent is lost, existence in the world ceases to be possible. (Eliade, 1957, p. 34)

Shared history, religion, or mythology creates a social world through the interaction of people and environment. Place is people along with space and myth. For example, many cultures recount an "origins" story confirming the designation of place and the establishment of community:

> In extremely varied cultural contexts, we constantly find the same cosmological schema and the same ritual scenario: settling in a territory is equivalent to founding a world. (Eliade, 1957, p. 47)

In much the same way, a tourist engages in myth-building when visits a new destination; there is the same feeling of founding a world therefore, expanding inner horizons. Considered that the mythical often contradicts pragmatic sensibilities, we find many action metaphors in Eliade's description of place as myth, including founding and settling. Place as myth becomes an action in that residents and visitors create and recreate community out of "chaotic" relationships, interactions, and environments.

Place as myth is relatively easy to integrate into a tourism-planning methodology. While planning for the coastal town of Manteo, North Carolina, Hester (1993) develops a plan that would induce economic prosperity without sacrificing valued landscapes. Following a method similar to Lynch, the author and his team maps local behavior in various locations. They then construct a list of places through to be important to the town's social fabric, "places where community and psychological values were concretized in the landscape" (Hester, 1993, p. 275). Finally, the researchers provide residents with a survey asking for a ranking of local places with significance. The final list, dubbed the "sacred structure" of Manteo, includes a drugstore, a statue, and a local restaurant. Overlooking many places if simply designated by social function or environmental attributes, this structure embodied place as myth. In this case, mythology proved as important to place as people or space, resulting in a ordering of spaces that can then be protected for residents or shared with tourists.

RECONSTRUCTION OF THE FABLES

With a new definition of place, building from people, space, and myth, we must reconstruct the fables of place and community for the future. This new narrative should be broad enough to capture people, space, and myth as critical elements of tourism planning and destination development. The *fifth migration* provides such a narrative. According to Hall (1988, pp. 150–151), Mumford and his colleagues conceived regional planning in response to "four migrations." The first migration was the original settlement of the United States. The second migration was the country's industry development. The third migration was the birth of regional cities. Finally, the fourth migration was the movement into the suburbs and the birth of Clarence Stein's dinosaur's cities. Because of the pre-World War II rejection of regional planning, we now struggle to redress the effects of this last migration. However, as we attempt to address sprawl as an artifact of the fourth migration, we are well into the fifth migration. The fifth migration includes the movement from the suburbs to the exurbs (areas outside the suburbs), the growth of edge cities and suburbs, and the continued decay of some urban centers without appeal to affluent gentrifiers. No longer exclusively White flight, the fifth migration includes young African, Hispanic, and Asian-American families moving to the suburbs and exurbs in increasing numbers. The tourism balance of this migration shows that some destinations (especially coastal) lose, while retirement and quality-of-life locations such as Asheville, North Carolina, gain regional market share.

As an unfortunate consequence of the fourth migration, many commentators now blame sprawl and placelessness on ineffective urban planning and design. They believe that an antidote for these effects is to reduce the regulatory power of planning and zoning, allowing development to take its "natural" course toward human scale and functionality. However, such a reactionary position only considers the fourth migration without addressing exurban, interregional, and international demographic and economic shifts. If we abandon planning in the face of the fifth migration, we can expect the unsustainable development of peripheral areas that will further unbalance regional towns, cities, and destinations. *Required is a different type of planning, not less.* Noting the striking ethnic and class dimensions of the fifth migration, this planning must encourage human solidarity through communicative and critical means, as well as commit to institutional experimentation. Reconsidering local planning and design, controls remain critical in support of planning and design at county, regional, and destination levels. Ironically, if planning and architectural controls are eradicated, neo-traditional development will likely be swallowed by the fifth migration as anachronistic reminders of the late twentieth century attempt to turn back the hands of time.

When speaking of design, most observers come to expect a set of principles or a specific physical vision. What would a pragmatic tourism design look like? What rules would this ethic follow? In response, the point of such an ethic is to avoid the iron-clad principles touted by the New Urbanism and competing fables quickly corrupted by geography, history, or accident. Instead, seismic shifts such as the fifth migration are used only as a context for imagining new procedures and institutions. We can start with the ubiquitous environmental preferences uncovered by psychologists and designers, although much more cross-cultural research is required. Analysis of the historical record of urban experimentation from Mojendaro to Mexico City is possible. From these basic themes and motifs, we must rebuild our notions of place and community linking reconstruction with new institutions and markets, with society and ecology, and most importantly, tourism and destination development. This nascent design theory will combine universal aspirations for empowerment with local architectural and planning idioms.

The ethic must be flexible enough to absorb new values such as sustainability and to accommodate technology innovation. Always, resulting plans and design must be subject to communicative and critical interpretation. Neither left nor right, and avoiding the excesses of ecological, technological or architectural utopias, this ethic includes elements of these approaches while remaining open to those to come.

However, in forsaking ideological arguments and utopian dreams, pragmatic planning and design can fail to inspire practitioners and fuel the popular imagination. For example, neo-traditional architecture provides residents and visitors with a visible, concrete promise for a better life. Similarly, communitarian policy appeals to those weary of gridlock politics. Conservative, centrist, and liberal traditions provide familiarity and comfort. Thus, a major shortcoming of any pragmatic proposal lies with its futuristic orientation and lack of specific strategies and solutions that planners rely upon when interacting with the public. People want alternatives they can see, feel, and touch. Business persons want a vision for place and community they can invest in and politicians want a vision that they can promote or take responsibility for if already achieved. Ultimately, however, the difference between the City Beautiful and the City Pragmatic lies with the rhythms of economic fortunes. Most economic sectors in North America and Europe during the 1990s, neo-traditionalism and sustainable development reflect this optimism. However, after the recessionary 2000s, the search is on for alternative settlements and destinations and perhaps even alternatives to sustainable development as defined by the North.

CONCLUSIONS

Culture, place, and community must not be static and fixed historically or aesthetically, but consist of a democratic process of experimentation in which new settlement practices emerge. In some cases these habits and practices may prove to be temporarily bad or wrong, giving way to new settlements and conflict between models. However, over 100 years of planning experience bears out the virtues of flexibility and experimentalism over fixity and dogma. In the new global frontier, new urban development prototypes will surface, including conventional, sustainable, and indigenous alternatives. Adherence to one particular design or policy ethic would rob planners and architects of an opportunistic period in urban design history. However, with these new opportunities will come challenges. The severe social, economic, and ecological disparities between regional, national, and international communities will call for a more political informed view of place, especially in context when, perhaps, the most contested type of economic development is involved – tourism.

The reconstruction of the fables dictates that any design or policy preference used for place and community are pieces of a much larger puzzle, including people, place, and myth. Over the last two decades, professionals offer a grand design without considering the organic nature of these elements in place. Further, research has yet to look deeply into the question of why tourists seem to prefer organic destinations. Grand designs quickly lose their problem-solving capabilities if conceived as panaceas for bad planning. These grand narratives lose explanatory force as new details no longer fit the old story. Planning for the fifth migration will require planners to quickly adapt problem-solving strategies to new contexts and situations. Fortunately, a wealth of international knowledge exists to match the increasing magnitude of some planning problems. Conversion of this knowledge, into tools and strategies, must occur to get planners and the public from here to there. A pragmatic approach to tourism, culture, place, and community emphasizing experimentation helps planners shape action from knowledge, when surfacing information from myth, historicism, and an understanding of unconscious assumptions about life, the world, and everything.

REFERENCES

Ap, J. (1992). Residents' perceptions on tourism impacts. *Annals of Tourism Research, 19*(4), 665–690.

Blanco, H. (1994). *How to think about social problems: American pragmatism and the idea of planning.* Westport, CN: Greenwood Press.

Calthorpe, P. (1995). *The next American metropolis: Ecology, community, and the American dream.* New York: Princeton Architectural Press.

Drucker, P. F. (1989). *The new realities.* New York: Harper and Row Publishers.

Duany, A., & Plater-Zyberk, E. (2003). *New civic art: Elements of town planning.* New York: Rizzoli.

Duany, A., & Plater-Zyberk, E. (2005). *Smart growth manual.* New York: McGraw Hill.

Eliade, M. (1957). *The sacred and the profane: The nature of religion.* New York: Harcourt, Brace & World, Inc.

Etzioni, A. (Ed.) (1998). *The essential communitarian reader.* New York: Rowan & Littlefield Publishers, Inc.

Forester, J. (1989). *Planning in the face of power.* Berkeley, CA: University of California Press.

Friedmann, J. (1987). *Planning in the public domain: From knowledge to action.* Princeton, NJ: Princeton University Press.

Friedman, T. L. (2005). *The world is flat: A brief history of the twenty-first century.* New York: Farrar, Straus, and Giroux.

Getz, D. (1994). Residents' attitudes towards tourism: A longitudinal study of Spey Valley, Scotland. *Tourism Management, 20*(4), 685–700.

Hall, P. (1988). *Cities of tomorrow*. Oxford: Blackwell Publishers.

Harrill, R., & Potts, T. (2003). Tourism planning in historic districts: Attitudes toward tourism development in Charleston. *Journal of the American Planning Association, 69*(3), 233–244.

Hester, R. T., Jr. (1993). Sacred structures and everyday life: A return to Manteo, North Carolina. In: D. Seamon (Ed.), *Dwelling, seeing, and designing: Toward a phenomenological ecology* (pp. 271–297). Albany, NY: State University of New York Press.

Johnson, A. H. (1949). *The wit and wisdom of John Dewey*. Boston: Beacon Press.

Jurowski, C. (1998). A study of community sentiments in relation to attitudes toward tourism development. *Tourism Analysis, 3*, 17–34.

Jurowski, C., Uysal, M., & Williams, D. R. (1997). A theoretical analysis of host community resident reactions to tourism. *Journal of Travel Research, 36*(2), 3–11.

Kaplan, R., & Kaplan, S. (1989). *The experience of nature: A psychological perspective*. New York: Cambridge University Press.

Kemmis, D. (1990). *Community and the politics of place*. Norman, OK: University of Oklahoma Press.

Kunstler, J. H. (1996). Home from nowhere. *Atlantic Monthly, 278*(3), 43–66.

Linder, M. (1993). This is this. *Architecture New York, 1*, 20–21.

Lynch, K. (1960). *The image of the city*. Cambridge, MA: MIT Press.

Madrigal, R. (1993). A tale of two cities. *Annals of Tourism Research, 20*(2), 336–353.

McCloskey, D. N. (1990). *If you're so smart: The narrative of economic expertise*. Chicago: The University of Chicago Press.

McCool, S. F., & Martin, S. R. (1994). Community attachment and attitudes toward tourism development. *Journal of Travel Research, 32*(2), 29–34.

Mumford, L. (1961). *The city in history*. New York: Harcourt Brace Jovanovich Publishers.

Perdue, R., Long, P., & Allen, L. (1990). Resident support for tourism development. *Annals of Tourism Research, 17*(4), 586–599.

Rorty, R. (1982). *Consequences of pragmatism*. Minneapolis, MN: University of Minnesota Press.

Thurow, L. C. (1996). *The future of capitalism*. New York: William Morrow and Company, Inc.

Um, S., & Crompton, J. L. (1987). Measuring resident's attachment levels in a host community. *Journal of Travel Research, 26*(1), 27–29.

Unger, R. M. (1987a). *Social theory, its situation and its task: A critical introduction to politics – A work in reconstructive social theory*. Cambridge: Cambridge University Press.

Unger, R. M. (1987b). *False necessity: Anti-necessitarian social theory in service of radical democracy: Part I of politics – a work in reconstructive social theory*. Cambridge: Cambridge University Press.

Unger, R. M. (1987c). *Plasticity into power: Comparative-historical studies on the institutional conditions of economic and military success: Variations on themes of politics – a work in reconstructive social theory*. Cambridge: Cambridge University Press.

Unwin, R. (1911). *Town planning in practice*. London: T. Fisher Unwin.

Wackernagel, M., & Rees, W. (1996). *Our ecological footprint: Reducing human impact on the earth*. Philadelphia, PA: New Society Publishers.

West, C. (1989). *The American evasion of philosophy: A genealogy of pragmatism*. Madison, WI: University of Wisconsin Press.

CHAPTER 2

LIVED EXPERIENCE THEORY IN TRAVEL AND TOURISM RESEARCH

Arch G. Woodside and Marylouise Caldwell

ABSTRACT

Lived experience theory and research focuses on describing and explaining the thoughts and actions of individuals and groups within specific contexts of their lives. This article applies lived experience theory to examine the contextual facilitating and constraining factors in the thoughts and actions of individuals regarding work, leisure, and travel alternatives. The article presents the results of a case research study of seven Australian households with thought protocol data on these households' lived experiences in work, leisure, and travel and learning how they compare "noncomparable" leisure expenditure options; the discussion leads to advancing macro- and micro-lived experience theory in leisure travel behavior. The article includes suggestions for future research and implications for tourism marketing strategy.

ADVANCING LIVED EXPERIENCE THEORY IN LIFESTYLE, LEISURE, AND TRAVEL RESEARCH

Lived experience or ecological systems theory (e.g., Bronfenbrenner, 1986, 1992; Raymore, 2002) states that an individual's thoughts and actions can be

Advances in Culture, Tourism and Hospitality Research, Volume 1, 17–66
ISSN: 1871-3173/doi:10.1016/S1871-3173(06)01002-0

explained and described accurately only by understanding the micro- and macrosystem of the person's environment. "An ecological perspective of human development is concerned with understanding the contexts in which an individual exists, and incorporates the interactions between the individual, other individuals, and the social structures of society to explain human development" (Raymore, 2002, pp. 41–42). Microsystems include past and present roles, individuals and activities a person has experienced in his or her interactions, while a macro system includes belief systems regarding societal conceptions of ethnicity (i.e., a cultural mental model of correct behavioral practices for members of a particular society), socioeconomic status, gender, as well as best practices for structuring society and institutions.

This article advances lived experience theory in examining individuals' lived experiences and choices in lifestyle, leisure, and travel behaviors. The focus here is more limited than attempting to describe and understand "turning points" in a person's path through life from being with friends, marriage, career choice, job search and selection, decisions related to having and raising children, divorce, search and selection of housing, and hundreds of additional major and minor thoughts and actions occurring in life. Rather, the focus here is on how travel and leisure pursuits occurs or do not occur from an individual-lived experience perspective. This article confirms the usefulness of the facilitators–constraints interaction proposition (see Phillip, 1998; Raymore, 2002) for understanding and describing the combinations of factors resulting in travel, as well as nontravel, behaviors.

One of the objectives of conducting the study was to provide information and insights useful for planning effective marketing strategies by Australian national and regional government and near government organizations (NGOs) to stimulate domestic leisure travel among Australians. Consequently, this article concludes with specific marketing strategy implications that follow from the case study research data used for examining the lived experience framework as applied to leisure behavior.

The facilitators–constraints interaction proposition is that specific combinations of facilitating and constraining factors create paths leading to, versus preventing, certain outcomes (e.g., overnight travel or no travel during available leisure time periods). The proposition matches with the comparative method perspective in sociology (see Ragin, 1987) that multiple paths of events occur that lead to one outcome versus its opposite (e.g., revolutions versus peaceful transformations). In defining facilitators Raymore (2002, p. 39) adapts Jackson's (1997) definition of constraints: "Facilitators to leisure are factors that are assumed by researchers and perceived or experienced by individuals to enable or promote the formation

of leisure preferences and to encourage or enhance participation."
For Jackson's constraints definition, substitute "limit," "inhibit," and
"prohibit" for "enable," "promote," "encourage," and "enhance" into the
previous sentence.

Raymore (2002) crafts three levels of facilitator and constraint factors:
intrapersonal (i.e., individual characteristics, traits, and beliefs), interpersonal facilitators (i.e., other individuals and groups), and structural (i.e.,
social and physical institutions, organizations, or belief systems of a society
that operate external to the individual to promote or restrain leisure
preferences and participation. The present article serves to examine how
interactions across the three facilitator-constraint levels affect individuals'
current thinking and behavior.

MICRO- AND MACROSYSTEMS

Microsystems of individuals' lives include past and present roles and actions
that often affect both subconscious and conscious thinking (cf. Wilson,
2002). This microsystem proposal rests on several tenants: (1) most thinking
occurs unconsciously (for reviews, see Bargh, 2002; Zaltman, 2003); (2) individuals and organizations make sense of their actions retrospectively
(Weick, 1995); (3) individuals tend to find themselves in contexts – situations
in their lives – that they had not planned consciously to experience; (4) in any
one context multiple facilitators and constraints interact to push, pull, block,
and prevent both thoughts and actions; (5) individuals exhibit a volitional
bias, that is, they tend to report that they decided to engage in a leisure
behavior, and planned actions required to complete such behavior, without
seeking information or help from others – they tend to become aware of the
sequence of contextual facilitators and constraints affecting their thinking
and actions only through guided self-examination and reflection (Woodside,
2005).

The following context illustrates the interaction of facilitators and constraints in one individual's microsystem and its impact on not engaging in a
behavior – that is, one more rewrite on a manuscript:

Slowly an analysis takes shape and a paper develops. We may even reach a final
delusional state where we think that with perhaps one more rewrite, the paper will rise
from mere perfection to beatitude and the representation will at last correspond to the
world out there. But because of some wicked editor's deadline, classes that must be
taught, the demands of a new project, the family vacation, the illness of a child, the visit
of out-of-state friends, or the five minutes we have left to catch a plane, the form and

content of the paper freeze. We know that our analysis is not finished, only over. (Van Maanen, 1988, p. 120)

Macrosystem facilitating and constraining factors include money, ethnicity, gender, social class, institutions, and culture (see Floyd, Shinew, McGuire, & Noe, 1994; Raymore, 2002). Rhoads (2002) provides several illustrations of macrosystem factors facilitating and constraining leisure, for example, in 2002 France extended its three-year-old law reducing the work week to 35 hours from 39. "The far-reaching measure now includes companies with fewer than 20 employees. Parents in Sweden just got another 30 days of parental leave, at 80% of their salary. That brings the total to 480 working days per couple for each child – almost a threefold increase since the 1970s" (Rhoads, 2002, p. 1).

Juliet Schor (1991) found that Americans were overworked, working an average of 163 hours more per year in 1990 than in 1970. "The result is less adult free time per family than before, hence more stress on each adult from juggling household duties, and jobs" (Beatty & Torbert, 2003, p. 240). Early in the 21st century the average German adult spends 1,400 at work versus 1,800 for adult Americans.

> About 52% of Italians between the ages of 20 and 34 live at home with parents, an arrangement that provides not only warm meals and free laundry service but the opportunity not to work. That's a steady rise since the late 1980s …. The differing work habits of the two continents stem in part from a choice on how to use the gains from prosperity. Europeans opted for more free time; Americans for more money and consumption, surveys show. From the perspective of many Europeans, it's the hard working Americans who have it wrong, at a heavy price to society. (Rhoads, 2002, p. A6)

DEFINING AND MEASURING WORK AND LEISURE

Applying lived experience theory to human behavior research suggests the need for defining and measuring both work and leisure within the same research context. Beatty and Torbert (2003) inform this need in their essay, "The False Duality of Work and Leisure." In reviewing the literature, Beatty and Torbert report that work and leisure are commonly viewed as dichotomous and antithetical and argue that this conceptual duality in unreflective of reality and confounds the meaning of each concept. They report three common approaches for defining leisure: (1) the time-based approach (how much time are people not working?), (2) the activity-based approach (what do people do when they are not working?), and (3) the intention-based approach (what kind of intention is the intent to act in a leisurely manner?)

Beatty and Torbert (2003) "support the third approach as primary and advocate a definition of leisure *as the experiential quality of our time when we engage voluntarily and intentionally in awareness-expanding inquiry, which in turn generates ongoing, transforming development throughout adulthood"* (original italics).

While sharing Beatty and Torbert's (2003) view that between the poles of pure work (e.g., assembly-line labor done for money and as the boss requires) and pure leisure (e.g., meditating by oneself or producing works of arts for which there is no preexisting market) are many hybrid states, we advocate the activity-based approach for defining and measuring work, leisure, and additional behavior. The activity-based approach is useful in particular because of the core tenants of analyzing microsystems, especially the tenant that most thinking occurs unconsciously. Also, intention, volition, awareness-expanding inquiry, and "ongoing, transforming development throughout adulthood" are not necessary or sufficient for leisure experiences; an individual may engage in a leisure activity with little prior thought, no planning, with no freedom (e.g., required to perform the leisure activity by a spouse or medical doctor), and without committing to an awareness-expanding inquiry.

We advocate the view that leisure refers to an activity context (e.g., thinking, playing, and, socializing) unrelated to a job, employment, trade, profession or to maintaining life. Work represents an activity done in the context of a job, employment, a trade, or profession, whether or not such activity is necessary for livelihood; this view of work is similar to, but distinct from, Ransome's (1996, p. 23) definition that work "is a purposeful expedient activity requiring mental and/or physical exertion, carried out in the public domain in exchange for wages." Purpose, expediency, exertion, public domain, and wages are not necessary or sufficient for work.

Beatty and Torbert (2003, p. 244) emphasize that "distinguishing work from leisure is not easy. There are many examples of activities that conjoin both freedom and necessity [implying that leisure equals freedom and work equals necessity], muddying the distinction between pure work and leisure." Work can transform into leisure and vice versa (cf. Stebbins, 1992, 1997). Daydreaming in the office about being on the beach is an example of conjoining leisure and work contexts.

Similarly, Cotte, Ratneshwar, and Mick (2004, p. 334) describe the difficulty in respondents' abilities to report only on their leisure behavior, "We initially set out to study the consumption of leisure, but our informants frequently shifted their thoughts from leisure per se to talk in detail about the role and meaning of time as they experienced it in everyday life."

Consequently, the results of their study contributes mostly within the time-based approach to examining leisure and timestyles (i.e., the customary ways in which people perceive and use time, see Bergadaà, 1990; Feldman & Hornik, 1981; Hall, 1983; Hirschman, 1987; Lewis & Weigert, 1981; McGrath & Kelly, 1986; Zerubavel, 1981). Cotte et al. (2004) and Cotte and Ratneshwar (2001) describe "four key dimensions of timestyle":

(1) Social orientation dimension: approaching and categorizing units of time as either "time for me" or "time with (or for) others."
(2) Temporal orientation dimension: focusing on the past, present, or future.
(3) Planning orientation dimension: how the individual approaches time management.
(4) Polychronic orientation dimension: tendency toward monochronic or one-thing-at-a-time style to a polychronic, multitasking style.

From a grounded theory perspective, advancing a lived experience theory of lifestyle, leisure, and tourism benefits by identifying four conjoining activity contexts within present time as well as identifying additional behaviors (e.g., planning activities and actions done that a consumer would undo if she could). The possible existence of four present activities and their combinations include work, leisure, life maintenance, and resting/sleeping (see Exhibit 1). While resting/sleeping is part of life maintenance, Exhibit 1 illustrates this activity uniquely because of its ubiquitous nature and the substantial daily time commitment involved (e.g., for most humans, 6–12 hours of resting/sleeping depending on age and additional facilitating and constraining factors).

Life maintenance frequently includes such activities of eating, maintaining normal body temperature, urinating/defecating, doing the laundry, driving the kids to soccer practice, the dentist, and to/from school (nurturing), sexual intercourse, and taking actions to stay out of harms way (e.g., buckling a safety belt before driving). Note that Exhibit 1 depicts some portion of life maintenance activities conjoining with work, leisure, and resting/sleeping activities. For example, alternative life maintenance activities sometimes occur while traveling overseas by airline (e.g., eating, sleeping, and urinating) on a combined vacation/work related trip (i.e., the ABCD space in Exhibit 1). Recognizing the possibilities in life contexts of conjoining two or more activities, Exhibit 1 includes all two-way, three-way, as well as the four-way combinations of work, leisure, life maintenance, and resting/sleeping.

Exhibit 1 includes three additional areas that relate to contexts in life: E, F, and G. Area E indicates nonactivity – life contexts that an individual does not engage in or planned to engage in but she or he sometimes thinks about, or activities confronting the individual from time-to-time in life, or a special

Exhibit 1. Total Lived Experience by Household Member.

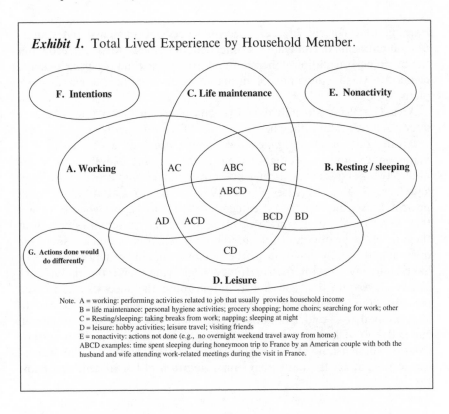

Note. A = working: performing activities related to job that usually provides household income
B = life maintenance: personal hygiene activities; grocery shopping; home choirs; searching for work; other
C = Resting/sleeping: taking breaks from work; napping; sleeping at night
D = leisure: hobby activities; leisure travel; visiting friends
E = nonactivity: actions not done (e.g., no overnight weekend travel away from home)
ABCD examples: time spent sleeping during honeymoon trip to France by an American couple with both the husband and wife attending work-related meetings during the visit in France.

area of interest by a researcher brought up for discussion with a respondent (e.g., learning why the individual does not engage in domestic travel). Area E recognizes the possibilities of unplanned and undone activities that sometimes in an individual's life space and asks the questions:

- What thoughts first come-to-mind about doing such an activity?
- What might you do in such a circumstance?
- What would the likely outcome for you from doing such a behavior?

See March and Woodside (2005) for further discussion on unplanned and undone behavior.

Area F indicates intentions related to work, leisure, life maintenance, and/or resting/sleeping. Work and leisure researchers often focus on examining the contents and degrees of commitment of an individual's intentions toward activities such as leisure and planned travel behavior and on learning how current life activities influences the contents and degrees of commitment of individual's intended activities. Area F recognizes the planning orientation dimension and asks what thinking processes and facilitators versus constraints occur in informants' specific near and far-term plans.

Area G reflects an individual's (unconscious and conscious) thinking about activities done that he or she would do differently, or not at all, regarding one or more single or conjoined areas of work, leisure, life maintenance, and/or resting/sleeping. Some amount of reflection occurs naturally among humans as they attempt to make sense of recent or long-ago events in their lives (see Weick, 1987). Reflections about activities in prior contexts include several categories depending upon whether or not they were actually done, the recognition of alternative activities now or at the time of the prior context, the individual's beliefs about the causes of the done activity and evaluation of the outcome of the activity done versus likely outcomes of alternative foregone activities, and the individual's ability to retrieve and consciously think about the specifics steps taken regarding the activity done. The contents of such reflections likely influence individuals' understanding of the activities that they engage in currently, as well as their intentions. Area G recognizes the temporal orientation dimension of timestyle and asks, in particular, how past experiences affect the individual's interpretation of the present and plans for the future.

PROBING THE FACILITATORS–CONSTRAINTS INTERACTION PROPOSITION

To probe how facilitator and constraint factors may combine to form contingency routes leading to engaging in some leisure activities while preventing others from occurring, the long interview method (McCracken, 1988) was applied in a national study of Australian households. The long interview method includes the use of face-to-face one-to-three hour interviews to permit interviewer probing for learning about informant reflections on the antecedents, consequences, as well as descriptions associated with lived experiences. The main objective of the interviews was having the informants describe and explain behaviors done: (1) today; yesterday evening; (2) the most recent past weekend; (3) last summer; this fall and coming winter and spring. The data were collected during the early fall in 2000.

Survey Instrument

A 44-page survey questionnaire was used. The questionnaire includes both open- and close-end items. The first 26 pages of the questionnaire (Sections 1–3) include mostly open-ended questions asking the respondent to describe the details of activities done or being planned as well as the antecedents leading up to these activities.

Section 3 asks the respondent to put "a tick next to all that apply" among 240 possible leisure activities that she or he has done or plan on doing in 2000. Section 3 also asks the respondent to "please underline the activities in the list that you did three or more times this year." The 240-listed activities were complied from several sources and include the following, among others:

- reading a lightweight paperback
- having a dinner party
- playing golf
- making love
- playing with children
- going camping
- going to a sing-along
- fixing a car
- walking the dog
- watching a TV sitcom
- taking a nap
- taking a bubble bath
- going to the casino
- going to the races/trots
- surfing the Internet
- dining at a casual restaurant
- visiting friends
- hanging out with mates.

Because the way choice problems are framed affects decision makers' thinking and choice processes (e.g., Tversky & Kahneman, 1984; Woodside & Chebat, 1997), Section 4 asks the informant consider activity options for two scenarios and to talk about each option as you are thinking about different ways of spending your time and money. "Each scenario has several different options for you to consider. Please comment on each option presented in the scenario." The first scenario included ten alternative options.

After commenting on each option and making a choice of an option for the first scenario, the informant was asked to consider a second scenario having twenty options. Each respondent was given one of two versions for the second scenario; the twenty options were identical for each of the two alternative versions of the second scenario. Thus, three scenarios were created for the survey but only two were covered per informant to keep the interview time under two hours. The following stories describe each scenario (see Exhibits 2 and 3):

> Scenario 1: You have a good bit of money set aside for paying for one or two big purchases that you are thinking about making within the next few months. Here are possibilities that you are thinking about or someone has mentioned to you. [Ten options presented; see Exhibit 2.]

> Scenario 2a: You have the opportunity to sign-up for a new credit card offering a low interest rate of any unpaid balance plus no interest charges on any balance during the first six months of purchase. You decide to sign-up for the new credit card and consider using the new card to pay for one of the following options. You say to yourself, "I might splurge for once in my life!" [Twenty options presented; see Exhibit 3. Note: some informants refused to consider any options; they reported that they would never sign-up for another credit card.]

> Scenario 2b: You have set aside some "mad money" to pay for something you always wanted to have or do even if some people say, "it was a frivolous thing to do." Here are some possibilities that you are thinking about or someone has mentioned to you. [Twenty options presented – the same options as used for scenario 2; see Exhibit 3.]

All respondents were asked to provide comments on each option available for Scenarios 1 and 2a or 2b. The set of options was created to include both nontravel and domestic travel alternatives to provide insights in informants top-of-mind thoughts and decisions on how well domestic travel alternatives compete against other ways to spend available funds.

Scenario 2a was crafted to gain insights into the ways some informants might use a new, low cost, line of credit presented to them. One aim of the study was to learn if such easy credit availability is likely to increase interest in domestic and/or overseas travel options. Scenario 2b was created to gain insights into ways some informants might spend money in situations framed to be high in personal freedom (i.e., spending "mad money"); the aim here is to learn the nuances in evaluating options and making choices that include domestic and international trips versus nontravel options.

The study includes data collection on consumer analysis of scenarios for two reasons. First, the decision-making and consumer psychology literature reports that individuals both tend to think, prefer, and are more influenced by a narration (i.e., a story) compared to processing product descriptions

---

Exhibit 2. Framing of First Scenario and Ten Options.

Scenario 1. You have a good bit of money set aside for paying for one or two big purchases that you are thinking about making within the next few months. Here are some possibilities that you are thinking about or someone has mentioned to you.

- Option U: getting a used car to get to work easier than sharing one car with a family member, partner
- Option R: for a few days–going to a really good hotel on the beach in South East Queensland with your spouse/partner; enjoying some great meals and the international ambience
- Option K: getting new kitchen cabinets because you hate the appearance of your current kitchen
- Option B: renovating your bathroom–the bathroom that is all pink and you hate pink bathrooms
- Option F: visiting and staying with family members (parent, child, uncle, aunt, or cousin) out-of-town; you really like these family members and you might visit theme parks, zoos, amusement parks, go to the beach, go shopping
- Option S: buying some shares of stock in a company that you think is going places
- Option H: using the money for a house payment or to pay-down the principal on a house mortgage
- Option D: buying a used car to have a second fun car to drive
- Option W: taking a wine tasting tour in South Australia with a family member/partner and maybe spend about half to two-thirds of the funds you have set aside
- Option G: spending a week in Adelaide going to art galleries, theatre, performing arts, dinning out, shopping and maybe some wine tasting

---

(see Adaval & Wyer, 1998). Tversky and Kahneman (1984) report, "The construction and evaluation of scenarios of future events are not only a favorite pastime of reporters, analysts, and news watchers .... It is of interest, then, to evaluate whether or not the forecasting or reconstruction of real-life events is subject to conjunction errors. Our analysis suggests that a scenario that includes a possible cause and an outcome could appear more

Exhibit 3. The Alternative Two Frames Used for the Second Scenario and Twenty Options.

Scenario 2[a]. You have the opportunity to sign-up for a new credit card offering a low interest rate on any unpaid balance plus no interest charges on any balance during the first six months of purchase. You decide to sign-up for the new credit card and consider using the new card to pay for one of the following options. You say to yourself, "I might splurge once in my life!"

Scenario 2[b]. You have set aside some "mad money" to pay for something you always wanted to have or do even if some people might say, "it was a frivolous thing to do". Here are some possibilities that you are thinking about or someone has mentioned to you.

- Option R: for a few days–going to a really good hotel on the beach in South East Queensland with your spouse/partner; enjoying some great meals and the international ambience
- Option W: taking a wine tasting tour in South Australia with a family member/partner and maybe spend about half to two-thirds of the funds you have set aside
- Option D: buying a used car to have a second fun car to drive
- Option G: spending a week in Adelaide going to art galleries, theatre, performing arts, dinning out, shopping and maybe some wine tasting
- Option C: buy new clothes just for you–a whole new wardrobe
- Option P: go to France and tour Paris, the wine region, and maybe French Riviera
- Option Y: go to the United States, visit friends and/or go to San Francisco; New York, or other cities or places
- Option J: go to Japan and really experience the local culture
- Option E: buy some new, really great, furniture for my home
- Option Q: have some second thoughts about opportunity [mad money] and end-up giving the money to my favorite charity, or a family member, or investing it for my retirement
- Option M: your own credit card ["mad money"] option, please briefly describe here: _____
- Option H: do things in Perth and maybe travel around Western Australia to see natural beauty
- Option I: do things I really want to do in Sydney and maybe attend some special events in and around Sydney

> - Option B: do things I really want to do in Brisbane and maybe attend some special events in and around Brisbane
> - Option N: do things I really want to do in Melbourne and maybe attend some special events in and around Melbourne
> - Option A: go to Alice Springs, maybe Ayers Rock, and maybe tour central Northern Territory and see unspoiled natural beauty
> - Option S: visit Cairns, coastal Queensland and Islands, maybe to do some snorkeling or scuba diving
> - Option D: visit Darwin, do some 4-wheel driving, and maybe some fishing and/or camping
> - Option X: travel around Canberra and attend a great special event or educational/learning experience
> - Option Z: visit Tasmania including Hobart, see unspoiled beauty, enjoy peace and solitude

probable than the outcome on its own." A conjunctive error is predicting higher probability for the combination of two events (i.e., events A and B both occurring) than one of the two events occurring (i.e., B). For example, subjects in one study gave higher probability estimates to following first scenario, joining together earthquake and flood, than subjects gave to the second scenario (flood only).

Scenario 1: An earthquake in California sometime in 1983, causing a flood in which more than 1,000 people drown.

Scenario 2: A massive flood somewhere in North America in 1983, in which more than 1,000 people drown.

Thus, the scenarios frame story lines (i.e., contexts) that possibly legitimize the consideration of alternative use of time and money. Important issues here include the consumer's perception of the likelihood each option in a given scenario and the consumer's preferred option for the given scenario.

The second reason for crafting scenarios with several options was to learn individuals' thinking processes when "comparing noncomparable alternatives" (Johnson, 1984), that is, learning how individuals make comparisons and choices when evaluating products and services in different categories that cannot be compared on concrete attributes. Thus, the first scenario asks the informant to consider domestic-travel options, renovating their bathroom, buying shares in a company, and additional options (see Exhibit 2). The literature includes two relevant findings on making such noncomparable comparisons. First, subjects tend not to use the lowest level of comparison possible when making their choices; people focus their comparisons at the levels that are most relevant to their ultimate satisfaction with their choices. Subjects who are less interested tend to use more abstract comparisons – as more abstract comparisons are easier to make, this finding suggests that less-interested subjects are less motivated to exert the effort necessary for more concrete comparisons (Corfman, 1991; Johnson, 1888, 1989).

Section 5 asked a number of demographic questions (e.g., age, gender, occupation, weekly and annual income using ten range categories), use of the Internet, frequent flyer club memberships, use of specific credit cards, and media behavior.

Procedure

The service of a professional research firm was used to select households that were representative theoretically of most Australian households. An objective for the study was to include all combinations of the following factors in identifying households for inclusion in the study:

(1) martial status: single (never married adults), married, separated/divorced;
(2) age: <30; 30–50; >50;
(3) city/state locations in proportion to populations of each with a 20 percent over sampling of small towns and the Outback (15 areas in total including Brisbane, Queensland other than Brisbane, Sydney, New South Wales other than Sydney, Melbourne, Victoria other than Melbourne, Hobart, Tasmania other than Hobart, Adelaide, South Australia other than Adelaide, Perth, Western Australia other than Perth, Darwin, Northern Territory other than Darwin, Australian Capital Territory);
(4) equal shares of nonovernight travelers, domestic only, and domestic and overseas travelers.

Following a telephone screening procedure, each qualified informant agreeing to participate in the study was sent a letter confirming their participation, time, and place for the interview. More than 90 percent of the interviews were conducted in the informants' homes. Each informant was informed by telephone and letter that she or he would receive a $70 (AUD) payment for their participation. The $70 payment was made by check at the close of each interview.

After extensive training that included completing two practice interviews by each interviewer, seven interviewers collected the data for the study. Each interview was done primarily with one interviewer and one informant; however, pairs of informants participated in answering questions for 86 interviews. All interviews were completed in face-to-face settings. The field study includes complete data for interviews from 184 households.

To provide gestalt views of informants' reports of lived experiences and the interactions of facilitators and constraints regarding their leisure behavior, the findings section of this article presents detailed results of an interpretive analysis of seven households. The choice of the seven households for this report was based on income, age, and current domestic and international leisure travel behavior with aim of achieving substantial diversity. Where discussed, the general conclusions found across the seven households also apply for the total households in the sample.

FINDINGS

The findings include descriptions of ecological micro- and macrosystems of seven households that succinctly and tellingly reflect the combinations of factors resulting in travel, as well as nontravel, behaviors. Two key points are worth noting here. First, the facilitators–constraints interaction proposition that specific combinations of facilitating and constraining factors create paths leading to, versus preventing, certain outcomes (e.g., overnight travel or no travel during available leisure time periods) implies that no one "main effect" (e.g., employment status) is necessary or sufficient in explaining a specific work/leisure/travel outcome. However, the combination of specific states or levels of a limited number (i.e., 3–6) variables is sufficient for explaining and describing the observed outcome – even if other possible combinations (paths) also exist for the same case study that also are sufficient for explaining the same behavioral outcome. Second, the claim is not made that the following case study reports describe the only sufficient paths leading to the observed behavioral outcomes – the claim is made that the reported path of events for each case is starkly observable in the data and sufficient in leading to the reported behavioral outcome.

Andy Hill: Staying Home Despite the Money and Time Available for
Leisure Travel

Exhibit 4 summarizes Andy Hill's very comfortable, home-centered, life. Note that Andy intends to travel both domestically and overseas but that his

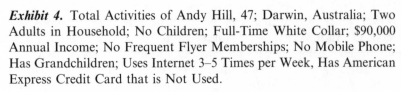

Exhibit 4. Total Activities of Andy Hill, 47; Darwin, Australia; Two Adults in Household; No Children; Full-Time White Collar; $90,000 Annual Income; No Frequent Flyer Memberships; No Mobile Phone; Has Grandchildren; Uses Internet 3–5 Times per Week, Has American Express Credit Card that is Not Used.

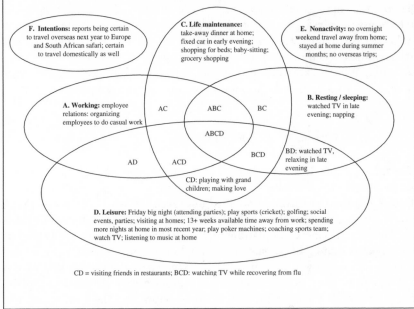

F. Intentions: reports being certain to travel overseas next year to Europe and South African safari; certain to travel domestically as well

C. Life maintenance: take-away dinner at home; fixed car in early evening; shopping for beds; baby-sitting; grocery shopping

E. Nonactivity: no overnight weekend travel away from home; stayed at home during summer months; no overseas trips;

A. Working: employee relations: organizing employees to do casual work

AC   ABC   BC

B. Resting / sleeping: watched TV in late evening; napping

ABCD

AD   ACD

BCD

BD: watched TV, relaxing in late evening

CD: playing with grand children; making love

D. Leisure: Friday big night (attending parties); play sports (cricket); golfing; social events, parties; visiting at homes; 13+ weeks available time away from work; spending more nights at home in most recent year; play poker machines; coaching sports team; watch TV; listening to music at home

CD = visiting friends in restaurants; BCD: watching TV while recovering from flu

lived experience includes infrequent leisure travel. Work, grandchildren, skill in fixing cars and in sports, parties with friends, and other local-area activities dominate his life.

Exhibit 5 illustrates a parsimonious path of work-grandchildren-coaching that is a dominating combination resulting in facilitating and constraining his life toward a local-centered nontravel lifestyle. Exhibit 6 summarizes Andy's responses to the first scenario exercise; note that Andy reports that the beach on the ocean option (R) to be a "possibility" but his comments about this option reflects its dormant unconscious state in Andy's mind. None of the travel-related options compete successfully for Andy's final selection in Scenario 1.

Andy's comments about each option in the first scenario support the very abstract processing level for noncomparable alternatives that Corfman

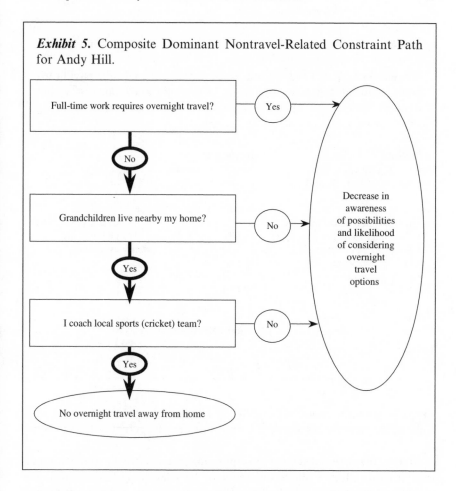

Exhibit 5. Composite Dominant Nontravel-Related Constraint Path for Andy Hill.

(1991) and Johnson (1984, 1988, 1989) describe in their studies. Andy's comments center on mental processes that provide answers to two questions:

(1) Is this option relevant in my life (an ecological issue)?
(2) Do I like or dislike the option globally (an affect-referral simplifying heuristic, see Wright, 1975)?

The comment, "It's not pink," regarding the bathroom remodeling option reflects relevancy. "Not OK with me," reflects the global attitude strategy of "affect referral" (Wright, 1975). Certainly, relevancy and affection are nonorthogonal issues that reflect a behavioral imprinting influence on affection.

Exhibit 6. Responses of Andy Hill to First Scenario and Ten Options.

Scenario 1. You have a good bit of money set aside for paying for one or two big purchases that you are thinking about making within the next few months. Here are some possibilities that you are thinking about or someone has mentioned to you.

Option:	**Response:**
• U: used car for work	Not OK. I just purchased a new car.
• R: hotel, beach, South East Queensland	Possible, have been thinking of this for some time.
• K: new kitchen cabinets	Possible, needs working on.
• B: renovating pink bathroom	It's not pink.
• F: visiting with family members	Don't do this too often. They only visit me.
• S: buying shares of stock	Possible. High on my priority list of things to do.
• H: a house payment	Not OK with me.
• D: used car for fun	Not OK; just bought a new car.
• W: wine tasting tour in South Australia	Not OK.
• G: week in Adelaide	Not OK.

Final selection:
S. I need to get money working for me so that I may reward myself with R and K.

The following rule captures this influence: my behavior indicates to me what I like to do, and by implication, I must not like the activities that I do not do.

Andy refused to participate in responding to Scenario 2a, the new credit card opportunity, "I am never going to have another credit card." His statement reflects both a lack of relevancy and affection toward using credit cars. The lack of use of his only credit card (American Express) is further evidence of his anti credit card stance.

Strategy Implications
Andy Hill's lived experiences and thinking processes strongly reflect a home-centered lifestyle. The implication of such a lifestyle and household ecological system for Australian national marketing strategies to stimulate domestic travel might be to ask, what are the lifestyles alternative to Andy Hill's lived experiences that indicate higher likelihood of favorable response to such strategies – investing in marketing actions to stimulate Andy Hill to

travel domestically is less likely to be influential than stimulating alternative focal consumers whose lives and thinking are more ready to accept domestic leisure travel opportunities.

Vera Kellie: Domestic Travel by a Low Income, Retired Older Person Living Alone

Exhibit 7 summarizes Vera Kellie's activities in her life. Note that Vera is retired from work and engaged in no job-related activities; consequently, Exhibit 7 does not include an oval related to work.

Vera's life is separated from her husband, lives alone with a cat, and has a very limited annual income. Yet Vera's life is enriched by her bridge hobby

Exhibit 7. Total Activities of Vera Kellie, 67, Sydney, Separated, No Children at Home; Retired; $13,000 Annual Income; No Internet Use; No Frequent Flyer Memberships; Does Have Mobile Phone; Has Visa Credit Card that is Not Used.

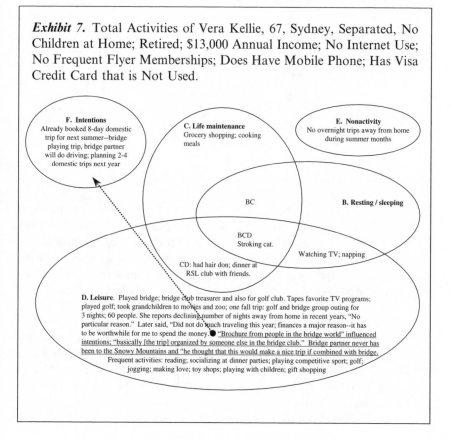

F. Intentions
Already booked 8-day domestic trip for next summer--bridge playing trip, bridge partner will do driving; planning 2-4 domestic trips next year

C. Life maintenance
Grocery shopping; cooking meals

E. Nonactivity
No overnight trips away from home during summer months

BC

B. Resting / sleeping

BCD
Stroking cat.

Watching TV; napping

CD: had hair don; dinner at RSL club with friends.

D. Leisure. Played bridge; bridge club treasurer and also for golf club. Tapes favorite TV programs; played golf; took grandchildren to movies and zoo; one fall trip: golf and bridge group outing for 3 nights; 60 people. She reports declining number of nights away from home in recent years, "No particular reason." Later said, "Did not do much traveling this year; finances a major reason--it has to be worthwhile for me to spend the money. "Brochure from people in the bridge world" influenced intentions; "basically [the trip] organized by someone else in the bridge club." Bridge partner never has been to the Snowy Mountains and "he thought that this would make a nice trip if combined with bridge. Frequent activities: reading; socializing at dinner parties; playing competitive sport; golf; jogging; making love; toy shops; playing with children; gift shopping

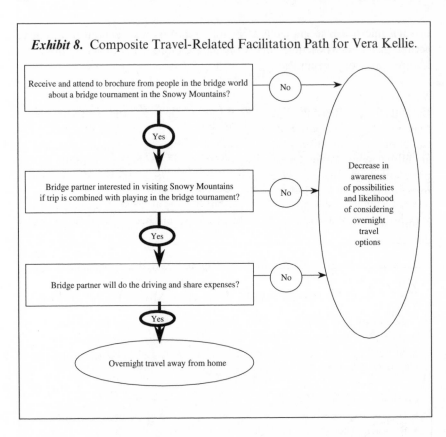

Exhibit 8. Composite Travel-Related Facilitation Path for Vera Kellie.

and companionship with her bridge partner; this hobby affects her frequent domestic-travel behavior. Note that the path through the travel-facilitating variables in Exhibit 8 includes attending to a brochure promoting an event-specific leisure trip (e.g., a bridge tournament) as well as trip-nurturing events by her bridge partner. This combination of domestic-travel facilitating factors supports the view that stimulating domestic travel effectively may need to include several lifestyle-specific marketing campaigns rather than a general image campaign.

For example, rather than spending $5 million for a national image advertising campaign to stimulate domestic travel, a national tourism NGO might test the strategy of providing relatively small grants (e.g., average of grant of $50,000 to national hobby organizations with the grants earmarked for promoting regional and national meetings and membership expansion programs. Both the immediate and long-term (say, over ten years) influence of such micro-marketing campaigns might be more influential in affecting actual travel behavior than image-only advertising.

Strategy Implications

Exhibits 9 and 10 include Vera's responses to the two choice scenarios. Note that both sets of responses imply that Vera does like the idea of some of the travel options but this affection is unlikely to morph into high intention or actual behavior – remodeling a bathroom or investing options dominate her preferences. Travel options must fit like a glove in Vera's ecological system to be considered and acted upon. The interaction of Vera's dedication to playing bridge and resulting bridge tournaments coupled with her bridge–companion relationship represents a facilitating route for generating domestic travel.

Exhibit 9. Responses of Vera Kellie to First Scenario and Ten Options.

Scenario 1. You have a good bit of money set aside for paying for one or two big purchases that you are thinking about makingwithin the next few months. Here are some possibilities that you are thinking about or someone has mentioned to you.

Option:	Response:
• U: used car for work	I would never buy a used car.
• R: hotel, beach, South East Queensland	Love to.
• K: new kitchen cabinets	No, I love my kitchen.
• B: renovating pink bathroom	That would be great.
• F: visiting with family members	I would love to visit but would not like to stay with them.
• S: buying shares of stock	Yes.
• H: a house payment	I have no mortgage so this would not interest me.
• D: used car for fun	I don't like used cars.
• W: wine tasting tour in South Australia	No way..
• G: week in Adelaide	That would be nice
	Final selection:
	B. My bathroom is functional but I would like to update it if I had the money.

Exhibit 10. Vera Kellie's Responses to "Mad Money" Second Scenario.

Scenario 2[b]. You have set aside some "mad money" to pay for something you always wanted to have or do even if some people might say, "it was a frivolous thing to do". Here are some possibilities that you are thinking about or someone has mentioned to you.

Option:	Response:
• R: hotel, beach, South East Queensland	Love it!
• W: wine tasting, South Australia	No.
• D: fun used car	No. I don't like used cars.
• G: week in Adelaide	That would be interesting.
• C: buy new clothes just for you	I would love that.
• P: go to France, tour Paris, wine region	I've already been there. [No.]
• Y: United States, visit friends, cities	I've always wanted to go there.
• J: Japan, the local culture	My husband always wanted to go there.
• E: new, really great, furniture	I am too old [for new furniture].
• Q: second thoughts, give or invest	Yes, investing in my retirement.
• M: own mad money option, describe here	Give it to my children.
• H: do things in Perth, Western Australia	Not interested.
• I: Sydney, special events	I would prefer that.
• B: Brisbane, some special events	I have been there. [No.]
• N: Melbourne, special events	Yes, I would.
• A: Alice Springs, Ayers Rock, tour	I did that. [Would not do again.]
• S: Cairns, coastal Queensland and Islands	I did that too. Loved it. [Would not do again.]
• D: Darwin, 4-wheel driving, fishing, camping	Too hot. [No.]
• X: Canberra, educational/learning experience	Traveling in Canberra is a nightmare. [No.]
• Z: Tasmania, Hobart, unspoiled beauty.	I did that many years ago. [No.]

Final selection:

Q. I am a sensible person and having money in retirement is important.

Bonnie Moss: Combining Pleasure with Work-Related Travel

Exhibit 11 summarizes the busy conflicted life of Bonnie Moss. Bonnie's work as a university academic/administrator requires frequent overnight domestic trips as well as overseas trips annually; she tries to squeeze in some leisure-related activities on some of these trips. Bonnie is also a single parent of a

Exhibit 11. Total Activities by Bonnie Moss, 42, Darwin, Divorced, One Teenager at Home, $65,000 Income, Use Internet < 1 per Month, Member of Four Frequent Flyer Clubs, Diners and MasterCard User, Has Mobile Phone.

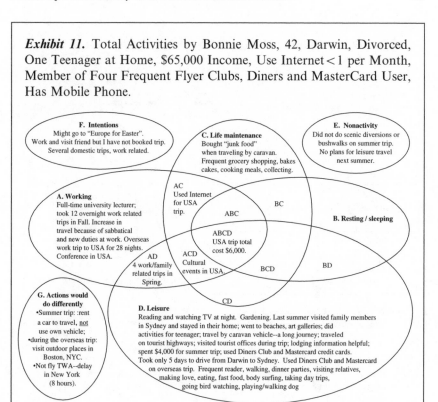

teenager and her leisure-time lived experiences center on localized activities (e.g., gardening, visiting friends and the local beach, local activities with child). When Bonnie does domestic leisure-only travel, she is a budget-oriented traveler: does long-haul traveler by personal caravan vehicle, eats low-price junk food along the way, and stays with relatives when ever possible.

Exhibit 12 displays a conflicted ecological microenvironment: Bonnie's lived-work reality requires trips away from home but her single-parenting requirements along with personal lived experience behaviors lead to infrequent leisure travel. The resulting travel experiences are low in satisfaction for Bonnie and she does appear to be unable to successfully combine work and leisure-related travel.

While some individual may be able to combine work with leisure travel, such persons are less likely to have lived experience that include single

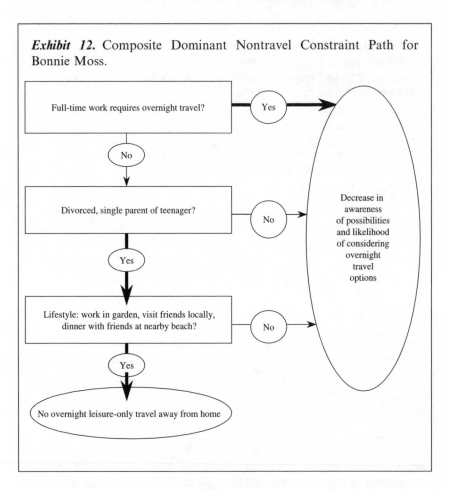

Exhibit 12. Composite Dominant Nontravel Constraint Path for Bonnie Moss.

parent commitments with heavy additional commitments to home-centered activities (e.g., note the dog walking activity in Exhibit 11). Bonnie's life reflects Scitovsky's (1992) description of living in a "joyless economy."

Part of the solution of enabling more joy to enter Bonnie's life (and possibly increase her domestic leisure travel) may include suggesting that she reframe her work lifestyle to include *less* travel – a "take time to smell the roses and really connect with loved ones" image campaign. However, Exhibits 13 and 14 include results that indicate that such a campaign is unlikely to be successful. Bonnie's choice of options indicates that for Bonnie, travel-related options cannot stand up to the attractions of

Exhibit 13. Responses of Bonnie Moss to First Scenario and Ten Options.

Scenario 1. You have a good bit of money set aside for paying for one or two big purchases that you are thinking about making within the next few months. Here are some possibilities that you are thinking about or someone has mentioned to you.

Option:	**Response:**
• U: used car for work	No. Never share a car; it causes too many problems.
• R: hotel, beach, South East Queensland	I would have to be really selective–a boutique, not too large hotel only–maybe from *Gourmet Traveler*
• K: new kitchen cabinets	Quite in line with my priorities. I did it last year. [No.]
• B: renovating pink bathroom	Absolutely–give me $5,000 now. Our present one is old; has mould.
• F: visiting with family members	A good way to keep in towels but not too many activities. They make me exhausted.
• S: buying shares of stock	I would need advice to make a real sure buy.
• H: a house payment	Not for me. Too boring.
• D: used car for fun	As long as it's better than my $2,000 one [20 years old].
• W: wine tasting tour in South Australia	Not with the kides in the car.
• G: week in Adelaide	Great! I would love to stay at a small boutique hotel and do the festival.

Final selection:
D. My family car is now on its last legs and we never buy new cars so I would use $5 to $7,000 for a second hand one

noncomparable alternatives. Life maintenance requirements felt by Bonnie take precedence over her attraction felt toward domestic-travel options.

Strategy Implications

Bonnie's ecological (environment and thinking) profile indicates a low response to domestic-travel marketing campaigns attempting to increase trip frequency. However, Bonnie does rely on tourist offices while traveling. Supporting the work of tourist offices serves to facilitate domestic leisure travel by households similar to Bonnie's profile. Bonnie's domestic-leisure travel behavior indicates the continuing need to offer information at tourist offices that such travelers find useful.

Exhibit 14. Bonnie Moss's Responses to New Credit Card Second Scenario.

Scenario 2[a]. You have the opportunity to sign-up for a new credit card offering a low interest rate on any unpaid balance plus no interest charges on any balance during the first six months of purchase. You decide to sign-up for the new credit card and consider using the new card to pay for one of the following options. You say to yourself, "I might splurge once in my life!"

Option:	Response:
• R: hotel, beach, ,South East Queensland	No way! Not for credit.
• W: wine tasting, South Australia	Not my idea of fun.
• D: fun used car	A good sound choice for me at this moment.
• G: week in Adelaide	Would not be bad; I would rationalize and do this.
• C: buy new clothes just for you	No way! Not on credit.
• P: go to France, tour Paris, wine region	If it maybe was lotto, not me paying; too expensive!
• Y: United States, visit friends, cities	If it was organized with work for a visit to another institution.
• J: Japan, the local culture	Would be loved by my son who is a martial arts zen person–would be fun.
• E: new, really great, furniture	Would make me feel better about being at home.
• Q: second thoughts, give or invest	A great idea, but which to choose? Maybe a friend who is really sick.
• M: own mad money option, describe here	Buy a reliable second hand car.
• H: do things in Perth, Western Australia	Needs too much time and we have gone to WA two years ago.
• I: Sydney, special events	Would be good but not unique enough.
• B: Brisbane, some special events	No way!
• N: Melbourne, special events	Would be good if I can stay with friends.
• A: Alice Springs, Ayers Rock, tour	Spent 12 years there already–couldn't recommend it more highly!
• S: Cairns, coastal Queensland and Islands	Great fun and especially if we had four weeks to go to the Cape and Capetown.
• D: Darwin, 4-wheel driving, fishing, camping	[No response.]
• X: Canberra, educational/ learning experience	I go every year; it is where I would move to if I left Darwin.
• Z: Tasmania, Hobart, unspoiled beauty	One of the most beautiful and uncluttered environments.

Final selection:
M. I would want to make a sensible choice; no
choice for me really. Scenario is not realistic for
me; I am a single parent. I have to be real with
money and try to keep down credit
commitments or I will sink!

Richard Mills: High Income Guy Seeking a "Good Deal" When Traveling

Richard Mills is retired from working and has a high-annual income from
investments. He is recently married. He often includes domestic and overseas travel in his life but seeks to get a "good deal" for both trip categories.
Exhibit 15 summarizes his leisure-oriented life.

Note in Exhibit 15 that his home life includes playing with grandchildren,
a dog, and a cat along with going to sport events and many other local
activities. Still, Richard and his new wife are rich in time in comparison to
other informants. Being retired with a comparably high-annual income enables engaging in a wide variety of local and travel-related activities.

He often crafts a good deal into his domestic and overseas trips. He stays
overnight in friends homes and bought an airline-accommodations-break-
fasts package for his recent overseas honeymoon trip. Richard is responsive
to credit card deals that enable him to acquire points on his frequent flyer
airline memberships.

Exhibit 16 shows the combination of macro- and microsystem facilitating
factors influencing Richard's travel decisions. The interaction of money,
time, and deal responsiveness stimulates domestic travel; lengthening the
path to include a macrosystem development (i.e., honeymoon) stimulates
overseas travel.

Exhibits 17 and 18 report Richard's responses to the two choice scenarios.
Notice that how the framing of the scenarios affects his final selections. The
first scenario about money set aside for paying for one or two big purchases
enables consideration of a wide variety of options ranging from very sensible
to highly frivolous; Richard chooses a very sensible, nontravel, option. In
framing a mad money context, the second scenario is more biased toward
carefree options than the first scenario; Richard chooses an exotic option – a
second visit to Japan. However, the note in Exhibit 18 indicates that
Richard quickly reports second thoughts about such a trip; he is willing to
consider his wife's preferences and substitute a cruise for the trip to Japan –
again illustrating a complex combination of macro- and microsystem factors
leading to behavioral outcomes.

Exhibit 15. Total Activities by Richard Mills, 57, Sydney, Married, $150,000 Annual Income, Retired, Use Internet Daily, Member of Three Frequent Flyer Clubs, Diners Club and MasterCard, Has Mobile Phone.

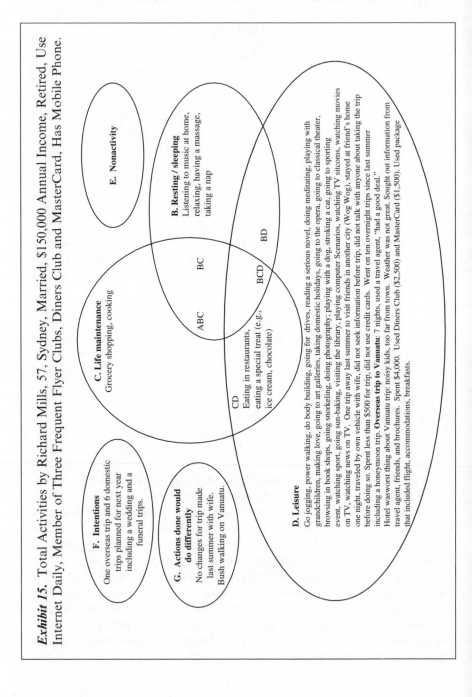

F. Intentions
One overseas trip and 6 domestic trips planned for next year including a wedding and a funeral trips.

G. Actions done would do differently
No changes for trip made last summer with wife.
Bush walking on Vanuatu.

C. Life maintenance
Grocery shopping, cooking

E. Nonactivity

B. Resting / sleeping
Listening to music at home, relaxing, having a massage, taking a nap

ABC

BC

CD

BCD

BD

Eating in restaurants, eating a special treat (e.g., ice cream, chocolate)

D. Leisure
Go jogging, power walking, do body building, going for drives, reading a serious novel, doing meditating, playing with grandchildren, making love, going to art galleries, taking domestic holidays, going to the opera, going to classical theater, browsing in book shops, going snorkeling, doing photography; playing with a dog, stroking a cat, going to sporting event, watching sport, going sun-baking, visiting the library, playing computer Scenarios, watching TV sitcoms, watching movies on TV, watching news on TV. One trip away last summer to visit friends in another city (Wog Wog), stayed at friend's home one night, traveled by own vehicle with wife, did not seek information before trip, did not talk with anyone about taking the trip before doing so. Spent less than $500 for trip, did not use credit cards. Went on ten overnight trips since last summer including a honeymoon trip. **Overseas trip to Vanuatu:** 7 nights, used a travel agent, "had a good deal." Hotel was worst thing about Vanuatu trip: noisy kids, too far from town. Weather was not great. Sought out information from travel agent, friends, and brochures. Spent $4,000. Used Diners Club ($2,500) and MasterCard ($1,500). Used package that included flight, accommodations, breakfasts.

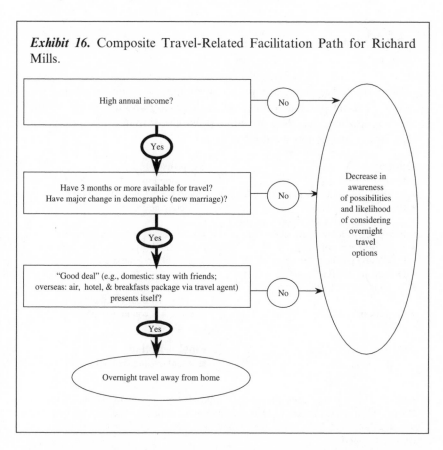

Exhibit 16. Composite Travel-Related Facilitation Path for Richard Mills.

With the exception of remarrying, Richard's lifestyle, leisure, and tourism behavior matches closely with Stanley and Danko's (1996) "millionaire next door" (e.g., such millionaires live well below their means). Richard is ready to spend money on leisure activities but wants to save money while spending it.

Strategy Implications
When thinking about who buys packaged travel deals, Richard might not represent most marketers' first-to-mind prototype. However, Richard's ecological travel-related profile supports the view that offering upscale air-line-accommodation-meal deals are likely to be effective in promoting both domestic as well as overseas leisure trips. Designing travel packages that enable thoughts of saving money and achieving a good deal among wealthy households may be more effective in travel marketing than designing budget

---

Exhibit 17. Responses of Richard Mills to First Scenario and Ten Options.

Scenario 1. You have a good bit of money set aside for paying for one or two big purchases that you are thinking about making within the next few months. Here are some possibilities that you are thinking about or someone has mentioned to you

Option:	Response:
• U: used car for work	Not an option.
• R: hotel, beach, South East Queensland	Sound like a whole lot of fun.
• K: new kitchen cabinets	Definitely not.
• B: renovating pink bathroom	No.
• F: visiting with family members	Would always contemplate [doing].
• S: buying shares of stock	I don't think I need to.
• H: a house payment	Sounds like a good idea.
• D: used car for fun	No.
• W: wine tasting tour in South Australia	My wife has connections in the Baroon Valley. I would definitely do it.
• G: week in Adelaide	My wife has connections there too– would do it.

Final selection:
H. Fundamental economic–get rid in one bump.

Note: Mr. Mills Moves from "Sounds Like a Whole Lot of Fun" to "Definitely Would Do It" When a Destination Includes "Connections" with the Possibility of Free Accommodations; Mr. Mills Looks for a Good Deal Occurring Before Increasing His Intention to Travel

---

packages for middle and low-income households – where noncomparable alternatives often have a dominating presence.

Lynn Hale: Domestic Travel by a Single, Low Income, House Cleaner

Exhibit 19 includes domestic travel in Lynn Hale's lived experience but highly restricted plans for such travel. Lynn's lifestyle includes hard manual work and the expressed need for domestic "resort" travel to rest and be pampered.

Exhibit 18. Richard Mills' Responses to "Mad Money" Second Scenario.

Scenario 2[b]. You have set aside some "mad money" to pay for something you always wanted to have or do even if some people might say, "it was a frivolous thing to do". Here are some possibilities that you are thinking about or someone has mentioned to you.

Option:	Response:
• R: hotel, beach, South East Queensland	Definitely.
• W: wine tasting, South Australia	Yes.
• D: fun used car	No. I would rather take a holiday [trip].
• G: week in Adelaide	Yes.
• C: buy new clothes just for you	Me? No.
• P: go to France, tour Paris, wine region	Always. It's great over there.
• Y: United States, visit friends, cities	Not interested in the U.S.
• J: Japan, the local culture	Definitely! But my wife wouldn't.
• E: new, really great, furniture	No.
• Q: second thoughts, give or invest	No.
• M: own mad money option, describe here	I would like to take a long cruise and travel in luxury.
• H: do things in Perth, Western Australia	Perth is too far [away].
• I: Sydney, special events	Always.
• B: Brisbane, some special events	Brisbane is not an exciting place.
• N: Melbourne, special events	Melbourne is not an exciting place.
• A: Alice Springs, Ayers Rock, tour	Yes, that would be interesting.
• S: Cairns, coastal Queensland and Islands	I love to snorkel; I've been there and it was great.
• D: Darwin, 4-wheel driving, fishing, camping	No.
• X: Canberra, educational/learning experience	I lived in Canberra for five years–no thanks!]
• Z: Tasmania, Hobart, unspoiled beauty	I'd like the hiking in the wilderness–not Hobart itself.

Final selection:
J. Fascinating for 14 years. History, culture, language challenge, interesting. Went there in 1969; a great time. Art, religion.

Note: Based on Responses to Both Scenarios, If "Good Deals" Comes to Mr. Mills' Attention, Travel is More Likely Than Other Options; Overseas Travel More Likely Than Domestic; Luxury Cruise May be More Likely Than Visit to Japan Because His New Wife "Wouldn't" [Go to Japan] and No Objection by Wife was Mentioned About the Cruise Option

Exhibit 19. Total Activities by Lynn Hale, 52, Cairns, Female, Single, Works Full Time: Cleans Houses, $12,000 Annual Income, Has Visa Credit Card, Member of One Frequent Flyer Club, Never Uses the Internet, No Mobile Phone, No Children at Home.

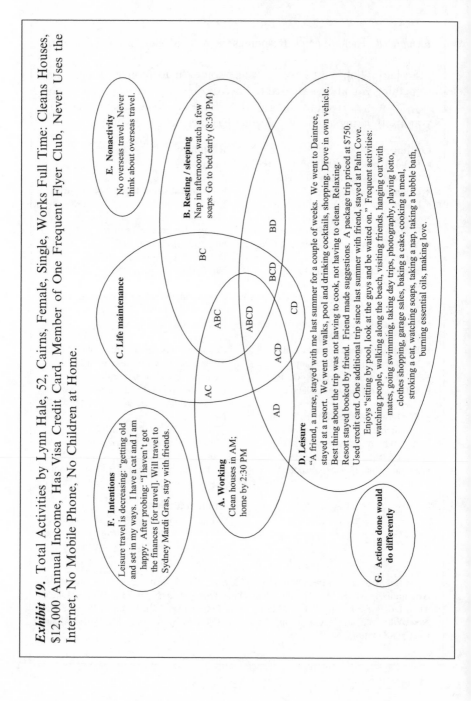

Lynn intends to decrease the frequency of her leisure travel next year due to the combination of her self-awareness of "getting older, having a cat, and limited finances." Lynn's current leisure travel behavior runs counter to intuitive thoughts that the poor cannot afford to stay in moderately priced resorts. The combination of sharing expenses with a friend and buying a travel package facilitates Lynn's felt need for "resort" travel that includes sitting by the pool, being waited on, and watching people.

Exhibit 20 summarizes the combination of facilitating factors enabling Lynn to attend Mardi Gras in Sydney. For such a distant trip from her hometown, Lynn requires free accommodations and consequently she stays with friends in Sydney. Lynn's perception that she is time rich overcomes her felt financial constraint for such a trip. Visiting friends in Sydney alone is not sufficient to stimulate the trip; the Sydney Mardi Gras alone is not

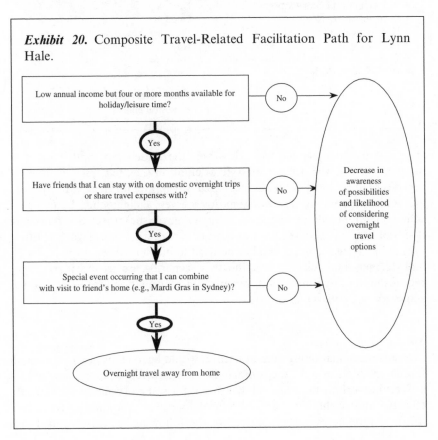

Exhibit 20. Composite Travel-Related Facilitation Path for Lynn Hale.

Exhibit 21. Responses of Lynn Hale to First Scenario and Ten Options.

Scenario 1. You have a good bit of money set aside for paying for one or two big purchases that you are thinking about making within the next few months. Here are some possibilities that you are thinking about or someone has mentioned to you.

Option: **Response:**
- U: used car for work   Got car. [No.]
- R: hotel, beach, South East Queensland   Great!.
- K: new kitchen cabinets   Have new kitchen cabinets [now].
- B: renovating pink bathroom   No.
- F: visiting with family members   No.
- S: buying shares of stock   Good idea.
- H: a house payment   I'd rather rent.
- D: used car for fun   No.
- W: wine tasting tour in South Australia   Great idea!
- G: week in Adelaide   Sounds nice.

Final selection:
R. Restful holiday.

sufficient to stimulate the trip. However, the presence of both factors is necessary along with Lynn's lifestyle orientation (i.e., felt time availability and desire to get away from her local area way of life) for the trip to Sydney.

Lynn's responses to the two scenarios are very enlightening. Lynn's way of life does not facilitate savings and encourages leisure travel. She rents and does not own a house; she has not need to buy down a mortgage. She often uses public transportation and has no need to buy a used car. In Exhibits 21 and 22, her final selections in the two scenarios are leisure trips. Rest, relaxation, and by implication, reward and rejuvenation are the end states achieved by Lynn via leisure travel.

Strategy Implications
The mistake in marketing domestic travel would be to ignore Lynn Hale and similar residents as a focal customer. Domestic-travel packages designed to attract the working poor and fill their needs for rest and renewal are likely to effective and profitable – and beneficial for these customers. Visual and word positioning messages that reflect the following benefits are likely to

Exhibit 22. Lynn Hale's Responses to New Credit Card Second Scenario.

Scenario 2[a]. You have the opportunity to sign-up for a new credit card offering a low interest rate on any unpaid balance plus no interest charges on any balance during the first six months of purchase. You decide to sign-up for the new credit card and consider using the new card to pay for one of the following options. You say to yourself, "I might splurge once in my life!"

Option:	Response:
• R: hotel, beach, South East Queensland	Good idea.
• W: wine tasting, South Australia	No.
• D: fun used car	No.
• G: week in Adelaide	No.
• C: buy new clothes just for you	[Okay.] Why not.
• P: go to France, tour Paris, wine region	No.
• Y: United States, visit friends, cities	Yes.
• J: Japan, the local culture	No.
• E: new, really great, furniture	No.
• Q: second thoughts, give or invest	Not a good idea.
• M: own mad money option, describe here	Clear my credit card.
• H: do things in Perth, Western Australia	Yes.
• I: Sydney, special events	Yes.
• B: Brisbane, some special events	No.
• N: Melbourne, special events	No.
• A: Alice Springs, Ayers Rock, tour	No.
• S: Cairns, coastal Queensland and Islands	Live in Cairns.
• D: Darwin, 4-wheel driving, fishing, camping	No.
• X: Canberra, educational/learning experience	No.
• Z: Tasmania, Hobart, unspoiled beauty	Would be nice.

Final selection:
Y. To visit friends.
Scenario 2 is realistic
for me.

Note: Ms. Hale Only Travels Domestically and Shares Expenses with a Friend When She Does Travel. She Does Use Her Credit Card to Borrow Money (Pays Monthly Interest Charges). She Prefers to Travel to a Resort and Sit by a Pool and be Waited on When Traveling match the unconscious–conscious thoughts about travel generated by these customers' macro-micro ecological system: "Come to us – rest, relax, and be pampered – you've earned it."

Aiden Blechynden: The Good Life for Generation X Includes Travel

Exhibit 23 summarizes travel and local area behavior in Aiden Blechynden's life. His work as an accountant does not require overnight travel; he does engage extensively in domestic leisure. Aiden is 27, married, with limited financial obligations and feels time wealthy now that he has completed part-time postgraduate training in accounting. Aiden plans to reward himself and wife for completing his postgraduate accounting training with a trip to Europe – indicating that a travel destination unique from destinations experienced on an annual basis may signify a major epiphany to oneself and others.

Aiden engages in automatic-habitual leisure travel annually; such travel includes his ten-day camping holiday with male friends is taken every year as well as visit to his parents and to his wife's parents. Aiden also engages in two or more "purely holiday trips" taken annually as well. Exhibit 24 reflects both types of holiday travel by Aiden.

Aiden's responses to the two scenarios show his preoccupation with his upcoming trip to Europe. Exhibits 25 and 26 indicate that domestic destinations per se do not motivate Aiden's domestic-travel behavior. His domestic-travel decisions focus on friends and family events in his life – promoting travel to see, experience a particular destination is not going to impact Aiden.

Strategy Implications
Maintaining and nurturing camaraderie and family bonds reflect the lived experience outcomes of Aiden's travel behavior. "Seen that, done that" are not thoughts that are relevant for Aiden's domestic-travel experiences. Similar to the experiences portrayed in the movie, *The Big Chill*, domestic travel for reunions, weddings, and funerals to be with close friends and family members fit closely into Aiden's ecological system. Positional messages reinforcing the nurturing of close bonds with friends and family are more likely to be effective in promoting domestic travel among such generation X members.

Michelle Ciccolella: Travel by a Middle-Income Married Couple with Children

Exhibit 27 illustrates how young children can partially constrain domestic-travel behavior. Michelle reports that her children are now reaching a travel

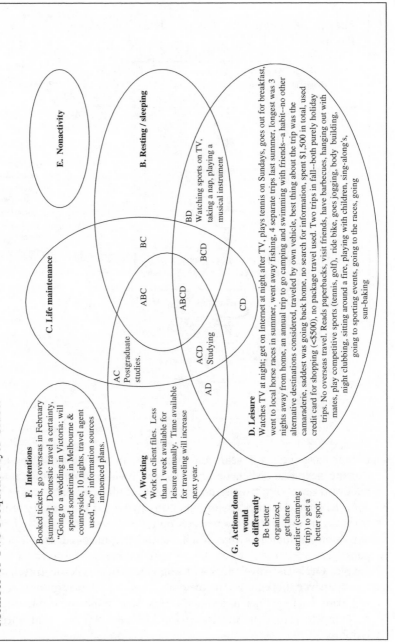

Exhibit 23. Total Activities Aiden Blechynden, Perth, 27, Male, Married, No Children, Works Full Time, Accountant, $65,000 Annual Income, Has Visa Credit Card, No Mobile Phone, Uses Internet Everyday, Member of Two Frequent Flyer Clubs.

F. Intentions
Booked tickets, go overseas in February [summer]. Domestic travel a certainty, "Going to a wedding in Victoria; will spend sometime in Melbourne & countryside, 10 nights, travel agent used, "no" information sources influenced plans.

G. Actions done would do differently
Be better organized, get there earlier (camping trip) to get a better spot.

A. Working
Work on client files. Less than 1 week available for leisure annually. Time available for traveling will increase next year.

E. Nonactivity

C. Life maintenance

B. Resting / sleeping

AC
Postgraduate studies.

ABC

BC

ACD
Studying

ABCD

BCD

AD

CD

BD
Watching sports on TV, taking a nap, playing a musical instrument

D. Leisure
Watches TV at night; get on Internet at night after TV, plays tennis on Sundays, goes out for breakfast, went to local horse races in summer, went away fishing, 4 separate trips last summer, longest was 3 nights away from home, an annual trip to go camping and swimming with friends--a habit--no other alternative destinations considered, traveled by own vehicle, best thing about the trip was the camaraderie, saddest was going back home, no search for information, spent $1,500 in total, used credit card for shopping (<$500), no package travel used. Two trips in fall--both purely holiday trips. No overseas travel. Reads paperbacks, visit friends, have barbecues, hanging out with mates, play competitive sports (tennis, golf), ride bike, goes jogging, body building, night clubbing, sitting around a fire, playing with children, sing-along's, going to sporting events, going to the races, going sun-baking

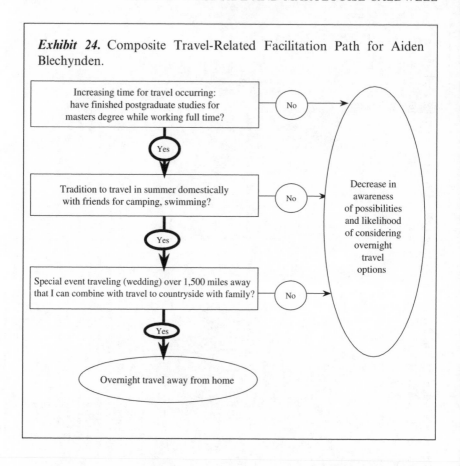

Exhibit 24. Composite Travel-Related Facilitation Path for Aiden Blechynden.

friendly age (i.e., > 7 years old) and that more frequent trips are likely starting next year. Michelle and husband own a house with a pool in the backyard and "don't really go anywhere." Still, they did manage to travel with the kids to Sydney (two hours away by highway) twice last summer for three nights away from home each time.

Exhibit 28 indicates that Michelle and her husband are influenced by package travel offers when they can combine such travel with another couple. Overseas travel does not compete with domestic travel; Michelle reports never thinking about overseas travel and her responses to the two scenarios back up her assessment. However, noncomparable alternatives do compete with domestic travel for Michelle. See her final selections in Exhibits 29,30.

Exhibit 25. Responses of Aiden Blechynden to First Scenario and Ten Options.

Scenario 1. You have a good bit of money set aside for paying for one or two big purchases that you are thinking about making within the next few months. Here are some possibilities that you are thinking about or someone has mentioned to you.

Option:
- U:used car for work
- R: hotel, beach, South East Queensland
- K: new kitchen cabinets
- B: renovating pink bathroom
- F: visiting with family members
- S: buying shares of stock
- H: a house payment

- D: used car for fun
- W: wine tasting tour in South Australia
- G: week in Adelaide

Response:
No. Not practical for us to have two cars
No. Have plans to go to Europe.
No. Don't own a house yet.
No. Don't own a house.
No. Plans are set to go to Europe.
Yes.
No, but if not going to Europe, would be an option.

No.
No–not that fanatical about wine.
No.

Final selection:
Europe [my real choice]. But H of the options mentioned above: H is most appealing considering my present circumstances.

Michelle's choices of leisure activities are fluid and depend on the ease of mental availability of competing options. When Michelle stops and thinks about comparing noncomparable alternatives, domestic-travel options are not ones finally selected. However, in real life, Michelle and her husband do not usually make such comparisons.

Strategy Implications
Designing travel packages that include adult and child activities (e.g., casino and beach experiences) are likely to be attractive to middle-income married couples with children older than six years, as represented by Michelle and family. Such guests likely represent substantial total room sales and profits for hotels and casinos even though such revenues and profits are below average per customer visit. Because of the substantial number of households in this population segment and the segments responsiveness to promotional

Exhibit 26. Aiden Blechynden's Responses to "Mad Money" Second Scenario.

Scenario 2[b]. You have set aside some "mad money" to pay for something you always wanted to have or do even if some people might say, "it was a frivolous thing to do". Here are some possibilities that you are thinking about or someone has mentioned to you.

Option:	Response:
• R: hotel, beach, South East Queensland	I would be interested, perhaps concerned about cost.
• W: wine tasting, South Australia	Not quite excited enough about wine. [No.]
• D: fun used car	Not interested.
• G: week in Adelaide	Would not interest me.
• C: buy new clothes just for you	I am not overly interested in clothes.
• P: go to France, tour Paris, wine region	This option is quite appealing.
• Y: United States, visit friends, cities	Sounds great.
• J: Japan, the local culture	Would be interested.
• E: new, really great, furniture	Do not have a home.
• Q: second thoughts, give or invest	None of these options appeal to me.
• M: own mad money option, describe here	Go to Europe and tour for six months.
• H: do things in Perth, Western Australia	Would not be an option.
• I: Sydney, special events	Not that appealing.
• B: Brisbane, some special events	Not interested in Brisbane.
• N: Melbourne, special events	Would be interested because family is over there.
• A: Alice Springs, Ayers Rock, tour	Not at this stage in my life.
• S: Cairns, coastal Queensland and Islands	Scuba diving sounds appealing.
• D: Darwin, 4-wheel driving, fishing, camping	This would be great.
• X: Canberra, educational/learning experience	I've heard that Canberra is quite boring.
• Z: Tasmania, Hobart, unspoiled beauty	Maybe later in life.

Final selection:
M. It was easy to make this choice as it was my own idea and not one of the generic options. Europe is the most appealing option at present.

Note: Domestic Travel Trigger Includes a Conjunction of Friends or Family Times Along with Outdoor Activities; Cities are in the Reject Set of Options; Overseas, Holiday/Vacation, Travel Plans to Europe are Completed

Exhibit 27. Total Activities by Michelle Ciccolella, 33, Female, Wollongong, $70,000 Annual Household Income, Wife, Husband and Two Children in Household, Never Uses Internet, Has a Mobile Phone, Visa Card, One Frequent Flyer Membership, Michelle Works Part Time as a "Casual Sales Assistant".

F. Intentions

Visit sister 3 times a year; 6 domestic trips planned; more trips next year than this year because "kids are getting older." One trip to Sydney--staying in casino; have brochure--just need to book holiday package--1 mile to beach; no travel agent; trip planned with another couple.

A. Working

Works 3 to 5 hours per day: casual sales assistant; waits on customers, works cash register

G. Actions done would do differently

None.

C. Life maintenance

Home activities involving raising two children both less than 10 years old.

E. Nonactivity

No overseas travel and no interest in overseas travel

B. Resting / sleeping

BD
Napping, facials, manicures
TV watching

AC
ABC
BC
AD
ABCD
ACD
BCD

CD: gardening, baking cakes, clothes shopping

D. Leisure

Spend summer leisure "mainly swimming in pool in backyard, going to the park, picnics. Don't really go anywhere." Made two trips last summer to Sydney, 3 nights each, "the kids are so small, so particular where we went." Traveled just to see friends; stayed in friends home. Traveled by own vehicle. A good trip. "Always good to get away." Worse thing: "the travel, left at 2 AM so that the kids woke up at sunrise." Talked with sister before the trip. Spent $750, did not use creditcard. During the fall, took two trips: Sanctuary Point and Sydney. Have family members in Sydney and friends in Hills District near Sydney. 6 to 8 weeks available for holiday time. No travel overseas during past year; no thoughts about overseas travel for next year.
Barbecues, going for a drink, parks, toy shopping, making love, playing with children, playing with a dog, poker machines.

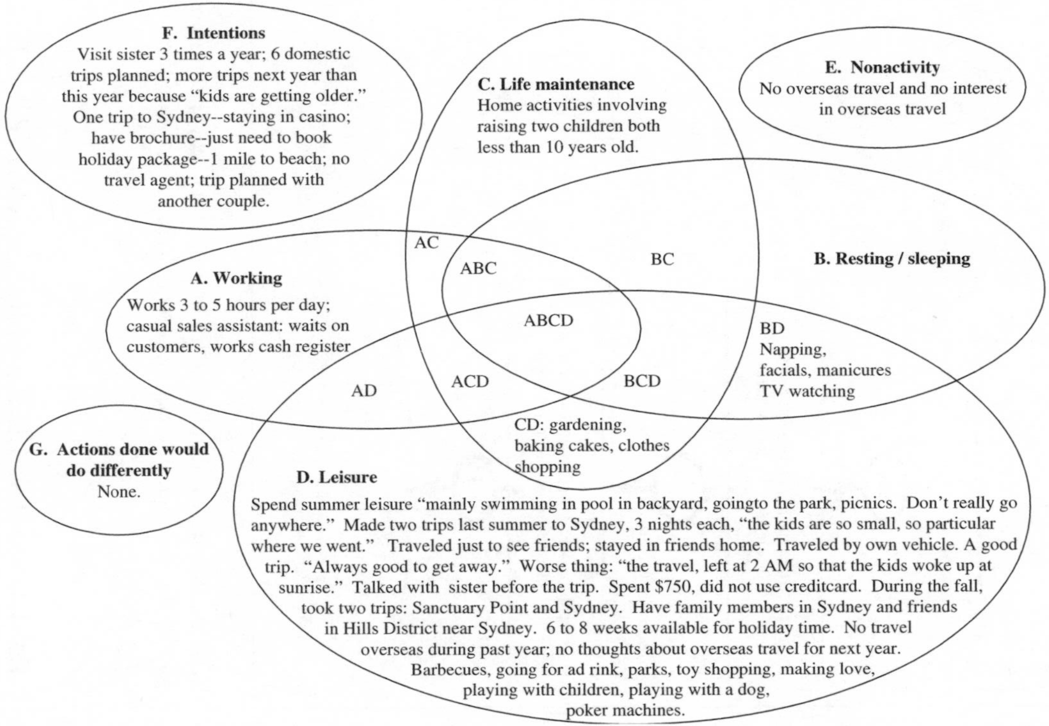

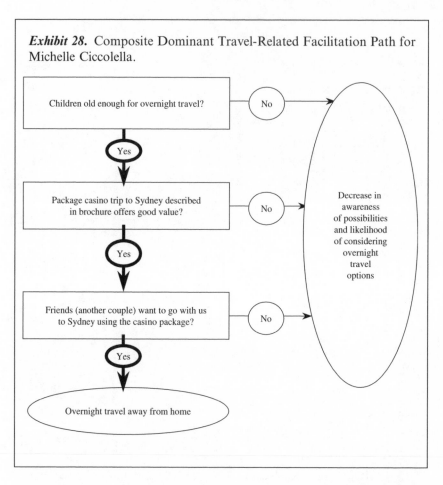

Exhibit 28. Composite Dominant Travel-Related Facilitation Path for Michelle Ciccolella.

offers, the failure to identify such families as a focal (i.e., target) customer segment and the lack of creating special deals to facilitate their travel would be mistakes.

DISCUSSION, LIMITATIONS, AND SUGGESTIONS FOR FUTURE RESEARCH

Exhibit 31 represents a composite generalized model of the facilitating and constraining factors described in one or more of the seven case studies.

Exhibit 29. Responses of Michelle Ciccolella to First Scenario and Ten Options.

Scenario 1. You have a good bit of money set aside for paying for one or two big purchases that you are thinking about making within the next few months. Here are some possibilities that you are thinking about or someone has mentioned to you.

Option:	Response:
• U: used car for work	I'd consider it.
• R: hotel, beach, South East Queensland	I'd consider it but not a strong possibility.
• K: new kitchen cabinets	I'd consider it but not pressing.
• B: renovating pink bathroom	Yeah, more likely.
• F: visiting with family members	Yep, an option [that I'd consider].
• S: buying shares of stock	Definitely!
• H: a house payment	Most definitely.
• D: used car for fun	No.
• W: wine tasting tour in South Australia	Would be nice.
• G: week in Adelaide	I'd consider it.

Final selection:
S. Shares hopefully [would] make me the most money.

Exhibit 31 illustrates the central conclusion of the study: lived experience theory is relevant and useful in explaining and describing the interactions of macro and micro facilitating and constraining factors affecting lifestyle, leisure, and travel behavior. For an individual each of the issues in Exhibit 31 may occur unconsciously, consciously, or with elements of both unconscious-automatic and conscious-strategic thinking (cf. Bargh, 2002; Wilson, 2002; Zaltman, 2003).

Note that the first issue (box 1) considers more than level of income related to leisure travel. The case studies of Andy Hill and Lynn Hale illustrate how a high-income household may appear cash strapped and a low-income household cash enabled depending on the interactions of macro- and microsystem factors in their lives.

For many individuals passing through the contingency steps leading to box 7 occurs automatically with little to no conscious thought or occurs in combination with conscious thoughts and tradeoffs that occur over seconds rather than minutes, hours, or days. The very limited relevancy and affect-referral responses of all the informants to each of the scenario options

Exhibit 30. Michelle Ciccolella's Responses to "Mad Money" Second Scenario.

Scenario 2[b]. You have set aside some "mad money" to pay for something you always wanted to have or do even if some people might say, "it was a frivolous thing to do". Here are some possibilities that you are thinking about or someone has mentioned to you.

Option:	**Response:**
• R: hotel, beach, South East Queensland	Yep. I'd consider it.
• W: wine tasting, South Australia	Love that!
• D: fun used car	Yep, definitely.
• G: week in Adelaide	Yes/no?? [Can't decide.]
• C: buy new clothes just for you	Most definitely in doubt. [Unlikely to consider.]
• P: go to France, tour Paris, wine region	Yes.
• Y: United States, visit friends, cities	Of course. Like that.
• J: Japan, the local culture	Not when I haven't seen other places.
• E: new, really great, furniture	Definitely would consider.
• Q: second thoughts, give or invest	Probably.
• M: own mad money option, describe here	Would make family debt free if a lot [of money].
• H: do things in Perth, Western Australia	Definitely; sister-in-law in Perth.
• I: Sydney, special events	Yes.
• B: Brisbane, some special events	Yes.
• N: Melbourne, special events	Yes, nice shopping in metro area.
• A: Alice Springs, Ayers Rock, tour	Consider it.
• S: Cairns, coastal Queensland and Islands	Definitely would; haven't been to Queensland.
• D: Darwin, 4-wheel driving, fishing, camping	No, not in others [consideration set].
• X: Canberra, educational/learning experience	Consider it.
• Z: Tasmania, Hobart, unspoiled beauty	Not first on my list.

Final selection:
M. Just would–family debt free. Help family to be free to do what they like to be happy.

Note: First Orientation to Stay Home but Children Getting Older (All over Seven-Years Old) and More Capable of Domestic Travel but Other Facilitating Factors Must Occur to Trigger Domestic Trip (e.g., Friends Going and Package Trip Available to Casino in Sydney); Sydney is 75 Miles North of Wollongong. Overseas Travel: No Experience, No Plans, No Substantial Interest in Overseas Destinations

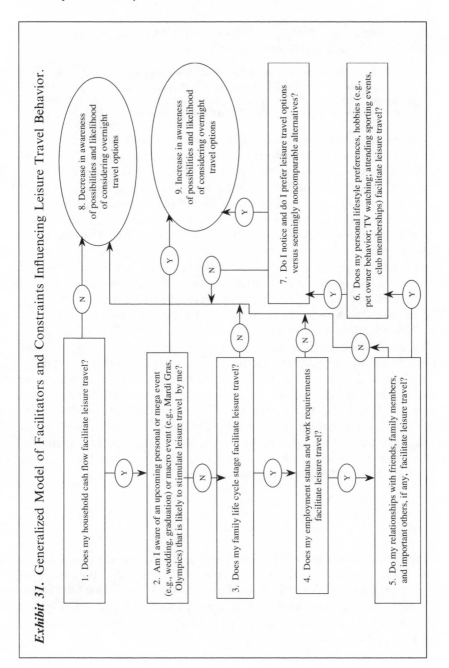

Exhibit 31. Generalized Model of Facilitators and Constraints Influencing Leisure Travel Behavior.

support and extend Tversky and Kahneman's discussion on the nature of thinking and making choices:

> People do not normally analyze daily events into exhaustive lists of possibilities or evaluate compound probabilities by aggregating elementary ones. Instead, they commonly use a limited number of heuristics, such as representativeness and availability. (Kahneman, Slovic, & Tversky, 1982; Tversky & Kahneman, 1984, p. 296)

Tversky and Kahneman's research focuses on how individuals make judgments about the probability of occurrence of events for which the probabilities are accurately known by the researcher. For personal choices in lived experiences and in evaluating scenarios from an informant's perspective, the concept relevancy to her life is both analogous and more applicable than the concept of representativeness – because relevancy covers not only the idea, "Yes, I've done that!" or but also, "Yes, I can see myself doing that," versus, "No, that's not [for] me." Affect-referral relates to availability (a mental process by the individual about her my past, present, or future life) of an event occurring – affect-referral (good versus bad for me) evaluations are likely to occur automatically with judgments regarding the personal availability of an event seen by the informant in her life.

Note that the path likely to occur with the greatest frequency (1-2-3-4-5-6-7 to 8 and 9) supports the main tenant of comparative analysis (e.g., Ragin, 1987) – multiple facilitating factors and constraining factors combine to result in a given event outcome. Such contingency path descriptions and explanations of behavior are particularly useful for building inductive theories of leisure and travel behavior. For testing deductive models of the influence of independent variables on respondents' intentions toward leisure activities, such modeling suggests the need for thorough examination of three-factor and more complex interaction effects – rather than focusing only on main and two-way interaction effects.

Limitations

This article focuses on building and probing theory from the perspective of case study research rather than generalizing findings to a population. A substantial number of replications of the case studies are needed to confirm or refute the reported descriptions and explanations before concluding that the described paths and outcomes are accurate among samples of informants or populations.

The accuracy and value of future research using long interviews are likely to be increased by incorporating second interviews with the same informants. These second interviews might be planned for a few weeks to one year after the first interviews. Data on whether or not leisure and travel plans became reality could be collected during these second interviews. The researcher's interpretations (i.e., etic observations) from the data collected from the informant from the first interview could be discussed with the same informant during the second interview and the informant's interpretations (i.e., emic observations) about the original findings could be collected – paradoxes in the data might be cleared up and additional insights gained. Also, conducting second interviews with the same informants recognizes the wisdom of Chris Rock's (an American comedian and philosopher) observation, "When you meet someone for the first time, you are not meeting that person; you are meeting the person's representative." Responses from a second interview are likely to uncover thoughts and knowledge usually held only unconsciously by informants – thoughts expressed only during the second interview due to unintended reflections from the first interview as well as due to the greater familiarity and trust of the informant felt toward the researcher (cf. Bargh, 2002; Woodside, 2004).

MARKETING STRATEGY IMPLICATIONS

Exhibit 32 considers marketing strategy implications designed to stimulate domestic leisure travel based on the seven general facilitating/constraining factors in Exhibit 31. Exhibit 32 implies a global strategy recommendation: implementing multiple strategies focusing on enhancing travel facilitators and reducing constraints is more likely to be effective than executing a single national image-advertising campaign.

Exhibit 32 summarizes several strategy implications that involve the cooperation across government marketing organizations (e.g., national, state, and provincial government units), NGOs, and sectors of the travel industry (e.g., airlines, coach firms, destination attractions, accommodation enterprises). While such strategies may be executed rather infrequently, examples of successfully implementing such cooperative marketing programs are available in the literature (e.g., see Brennan & Woodside, 1982).

Exhibit 32. Marketing and Positioning Theme Implications from Generalized Model.

Faciliator/Constraint Factor	Marketing and Positioning Theme Implecation
1. Does my household cash flow facilitate leisure travel?	1. Travel via credit card and debt is possible, legitimate, and worthwhile.
2. Aware of upcoming personal or mega event?	2. Seek/create mega events; reinforce need to attend mega and personal events.
3. Does my family life cycle stage facilitate leisure travel?	3. Create travel friendly environments and events for young children.
4. Does my employment status and work facilitate travel?	4. Create life-changing epiphany (e.g., graduations) themes.
5. Relationships- friends, family members facilitate travel?	5. Create relationship-bonding travel products and themes.
6. My personal lifestyle, hobbies, facilitate travel?	6. Nurture/sponsor regional and national lifestyle, hobby, meetings.
7. Do I notice and prefer leisure travel v. non comparable options?	7. Create/nurture frequent traveler programs and themes that a full rich life includes travel and destination experiences.

ACKNOWLEDGMENT

The authors are grateful for the funding grant provided by See Australia Ltd for conducting the empirical study that this article describes.

REFERENCES

Adaval, R., & Wyer, R. S. (1998). The role of narratives in consumer information processing. *Journal of Consumer Psychology, 7*(3), 207–245.

Bargh, J. A. (2002). Losing consciousness: Automatic influences on consumer judgment, behavior, and motivation. *Journal of Consumer Research, 29*, 280–285.

Beatty, J. E., & Torbert, W. R. (2003). The false duality of work and leisure. *Journal of Management Inquiry, 12*(3), 239–252.

Bergadaà, M. (1990). The role of time in the action of the consumer. *Journal of Consumer Research, 17*(4), 289–302.

Brennan, D. G., & Woodside, A. G (1982). Cooperative national advertising. *Journal of Travel Research, 20*(Spring), 30–34.

Bronfenbrenner, U. (1986). Recent advances in research on the ecology of human development. In: R. K. Silbereisen, K. Eyferth & G. Rudinger (Eds), *Development as action in context: Problem behavior and normal youth development* (pp. 287–309). New York: Springer.

Bronfenbrenner, U. (1992). Lived experience theory. In: R. Vasta (Ed.), *Six theories of child development: Revised formulations and current ideas* (pp. 187–249). London: Jessica Kingsley.

Corfman, K. P. (1991). Comparability and comparison levels used in choices among consumer products. *Journal of Marketing Research, 28*(3), 368–374.

Cotte, J., & Ratneshwar, S. (2001). Timstyle and leisure decisions. *Journal of Leisure Research, 33*(4), 396–409.

Cotte, J., Ratneshwar, S., & Mick, D. G. (2004). The times of their lives: Phenomenological and metaphysical characteristics of consumer timestyles. *Journal of Consumer Research, 31*(3), 333–345.

Feldman, L. P., & Hornik, J. (1981). The use of time: An integrated conceptual model. *Journal of Consumer Research, 7*(1), 407–419.

Floyd, M. F., Shinew, K. J., McGuire, M. A., & Noe, F. P. (1994). Race, class, and leisure activity preferences: Marginality and ethnicity revisited. *Journal of Leisure Research, 26*(2), 158–173.

Hall, E. T. (1983). *The dance of life.* New York: Anchor Press-Doubleday.

Hirschman, E. C. (1987). Theoretical perspectives of time use: Implications for consumer research. *Research in Consumer Behavior, 2*, 55–81.

Jackson, E. L. (1997). In the eye of the beholder: A comment on Samdahl and Jekubovich (1997), 'A critique of leisure constraints: Comparative analysis and understandings'. *Journal of Leisure Research, 29*(4), 458–468.

Johnson, M. (1984). Consumer choice strategies for comparing noncomparable alternatives. *Journal of Consumer Research, 16*(December), 300–309.

Johnson, M. (1988). Comparability and hierarchical processing in multialternative choice. *Journal of Consumer Research, 15*(December), 303–314.

Johnson, M. (1989). The differential processing of product category and noncomparable choice alternatives. *Journal of Consumer Research, 16*(December), 303–314.

Lewis, D., & Weigert, D. J. (1981). The structures and meanings of social time. *Social Forces, 60*(December), 432–457.

Kahneman, D., Slovic, P., & Tversky, A. (1982). *Judgment under uncertainty: Heuristics and biases.* Cambridge, UK: Cambridge University Press.

March, R., & Woodside, A. G. (2005). *Travellers' plans and behaviours.* London: CABI.

McGrath, J. E., & Kelly, J. R. (1986). *Time and human interaction: Toward a social psychology of time.* New York: Guilfor Press.

Phillip, S. F. (1998). Race and gender differences in adolescent peer group approval of leisure activities. *Journal of Leisure Research, 30*(2), 214–232.

Ragin, C. C. (1987). *The comparative method: Moving beyond qualitative and quantitative strategies.* Berkeley, CA: University of California Press.

Ransome, P. (1996). *The work paradigm.* Aldershot, UK: Avebury.

Raymore, L. (2002). Facilitators to leisure. *Journal of Leisure Research, 34*(1), 37–51.

Rhoads, C. (2002), Short work hours undercut Europe in economic drive, *Wall Street Journal, CCXL* (28), pp. A1, A6.

Schor, J. B. (1991). *The overworked American.* New York: Basic Books.

Scitovsky, T. (1992). *The joyless economy.* Oxford, UK: Oxford University Press.

Stanley, T. J., & Danko, W. D. (1996). *The millionaire next door*. New York: Pocket Books.

Stebbins, R. A. (1992). *Amateurs, professionals, and serious leisure*. Montreal: McGill-Queens University Press.

Stebbins, R. A. (1997). Serious leisure and well being. In: J. T. Haworth (Ed.), *Work, leisure, and well-being* (pp. 117–130). London: Routledge.

Tversky, A., & Kahneman, D. (1984). Extensional versus intuitive reasoning: The conjunction fallacy and probability judgment. *Psychological Review, 91*, 293–315.

Van Maanen, J. (1988). *Tales of the field*. Chicago: University of Chicago Press.

Weick, K. E. (1987). Organizational culture as a source of high reliability. *California Management Review, 29*(2), 112–127.

Weick, K. E. (1995). *Sensemaking in organizations*. Thousand Oaks, CA: Sage.

Wilson, T. D. (2002). *Strangers to ourselves: Discovering adaptive unconscious*. Cambridge, MA: Belknap Press.

Woodside, A. G. (2004). Advancing means-end chains by incorporating Heider's balance theory and Fournier's consumer-brand relationship typology. *Psychology & Marketing, 21*(4), 279–294.

Woodside, A. G. (2005). *Market-driven thinking*. Amsterdam: Elsevier.

Woodside, A. G., & Chebat, J. C. (1997). Updating Heider's balance theory in consumer behavior: A Jewish couple buys a German car and additional buying-consuming transformational stories. *Psychology & Marketing, 18*(5), 475–495.

Wright, P. (1975). Consumer choice strategies: Simplifying vs optimizing. *Journal of Marketing Research, 12*(1), 60–67.

Zaltman, G. (2003). *How consumers think*. Cambridge, MA: Harvard Business School Press.

Zerubavel, E. (1981). *Hidden rhythms: Schedules and calendars in social life*. Chicago: University of Chicago Press.

CHAPTER 3

PHOTO WEBSITE AND TV MINISERIES-INDUCED TOURISM: TWO MEGA-TRENDS IN TAIWAN

Yu-Shan Lin and Jun-Ying Huang

ABSTRACT

Two mega-trends are occurring in tourism in Taiwan. One is photo website-induced tourism and the other is TV miniseries-induced tourism. The paper discusses the two mega-trends in order. First, this work examines a 2003 Yahoo Anniversary Website named, "I left my heart in Aegean Sea," built by Justin, an engineer in Taiwan. Justin returned from the romantic Aegean Sea and placed 124 photographs he took onto a website to share with his friends. Unexpectedly, the website became a hit and the address was distributed via various chain e-mails. The site unintentionally helps to promote tourism to Greece, a destination relatively unknown to most Taiwanese. This study explores why Justin's website appeals to so many visitors, impressed them, and even draws them to plan travel to Greece and the Aegean. The effect of the website by analyzing messages left on the site. AIDA is used as the classification standard classifying whole messages. Then, the paper discusses the key success factors (KSFs) of this popular website. Finally, the paper provides suggestions and implications for the tourism industry and for nations seeking to promote tourism. The number of Taiwanese visiting Korea hit a record high in 2004, accounting for a 65% increase over the previous year and taking the first place in destination of departure nationals. Tourism data from 1999 to 2004 also indicates that the total number of tourists visiting Korea has grown

Advances in Culture, Tourism and Hospitality Research, Volume 1, 67–113
Copyright © 2007 by Elsevier Ltd.
ISSN: 1871-3173/doi:10.1016/S1871-3173(06)01003-2

steadily. Korean TV miniseries have likely contributed to an increase in tourists visiting Korea. The phenomenon is worth studying in depth.

INTRODUCTION

Traditionally in Taiwan, Greece is associated mainly with Greek mythology, Classical architecture, Athens, and the Olympic Games, but recently the country has become known as a place of beauty, romance, peacefulness, freedom, and endless blue and white. Taiwanese are increasingly interested in Greece and wish to travel there. The following interesting phenomena have been observed. A popular first prize in numerous lottery activities is now a trip to Greece or the Cycladic Islands. Many travel agencies are now providing various Greek itineraries, including various group package tours and foreign independent tours, and even specialized marriage and honeymoon itineraries (see Fig. 1). Five female graduate students of National Chiao Tung University coauthored a book entitled "Skip Classes for

Fig. 1. Travel Agencies Provide Various Greek Itineraries (*Source:* eztravel.com).

Greece" (see Fig. 2) describing their foreign independent tour experiences in Greece after coming back to Taiwan in February 2005. Chinese Television System released the TV series "Love of the Aegean Sea" in April 2004 (see Fig. 3). Lots of newly-opened stores are using Aegean Sea themes, including restaurants, coffee shops, motels, bed and breakfasts, and so on. Fig. 4 illustrates a coffee shop located on the north coast of Taiwan with a Greek décor. Moreover, Greek or Aegean style has become popular in many areas including architecture, decoration, painting, bedspreads, food, etc.

SKIP CLASSES FOR GREECE

Fig. 2. The Book "Skip Classes for Greece" (*Source:* books.com.tw).

Fig. 3. The TV Series "Love of the Aegean Sea" (*Source:* CTS website).

Fig. 4. A Coffee Shop Located on the North Coast of Taiwan (*Source:* home.kimo.com.tw/seawater0210/seawater10_play/2005083003.htm).

Furthermore, several wedding photography companies have promoted packages with names like "My Greek Wedding – Love in the Aegean Sea" that allow newlyweds to shoot wedding photographs at Taiwanese locations with a Greek or Aegean flavor (see Fig. 5). Some explanation must exist for this recent trend, and the answer appears to be a 2003 Yahoo Anniversary Website named "I left my heart in Aegean Sea" (see Fig. 6) (http://home.kimo.com.tw/yuchang_chen.tw/) since the above phenomena all followed the appearance of this website.

Justin, an engineer working for United Microelectronics Corp. (UMC) in Taiwan, returned from the Aegean Sea and put 124 photos chosen from the 1,400 pictures he took during his holiday on the website of Yahoo-Kimo in May 2003. Originally, Justin simply intended to share his photos with friends, and he put them on the website because they were too large to send by e-mail. On the first day, more than 6,000 visitors crowded into the

Fig. 5. The Package of Greek-Style Wedding Photographs Promoted by a Wedding Photography Company (*Source:* www.wed.com.tw/product/index.php?class = 277&sno = 16195190).

Fig. 6. The Website "I left my heart in Aegean Sea" (*Source:* home.kimo.com.tw/
yuchang_chen.tw/).

website. The abnormal traffic caused Yahoo-Kimo to close the website temporarily. Such big traffic visiting a non-profit website was highly unusual. After Yahoo-Kimo reactivated the website, visitor levels increased to tens of thousands daily. Perhaps, through a desire to share with other friends, many enthusiastic friends forwarded the beautiful website message by e-mail. For several weeks, 40–60 thousand visitors viewed the site daily. Over one million visitors visited the website during the first month, and nearly two million visited the site over a six-month period. Locus, a publishing company, took the opportunity to publish a photo book, 2004 desk calendar, and jigsaw featuring Justin's photographs. According to Zufryden (2000), website traffic is statistically significant in predicting the box office take of a new film, and thus the publisher's action made sense and good sales volumes were achieved.

RESEARCH MOTIVES AND OBJECTIVES

As standards of living improve, people are placing an increasing emphasis on leisure. People are increasingly actively seeking ways to relax and eliminate stress. Thus, travel has become a popular leisure activity. Numerous factors influence the destination choice, including advertising campaigns by destination countries, travel agency promotions, airline ticket discounting, movies or TV programs, word of mouth, personal preferences, and so on. Various nations and regions have made considerable efforts in tourism marketing and promotion. For example, Taiwan is pushing a "Doubling Tourist Arrivals Plan," which aims to double annual tourist numbers to two million and drive total passenger arrivals to over five million by 2008, and moreover 2004 has been designated as Taiwan Tourism Year; the Hong Kong Tourism Board has adopted the new slogan "Hong Kong – Live it! Love it!" as its global advertisement and has invited the famous actor, Jackie Chan, to be a travel ambassador promoting Hong Kong; the Thailand Tourism Division chose the slogan "Unseen Thailand" as a replacement for "Amazing Thailand" as its global marketing theme in 2003, and has been promoting some previously little known Thai scenic spots, such as the beautiful waterfall "Tee Lor Soo," the Grand Palace, etc. All such campaigns share a common goal of attracting more overseas tourists.

Due to the prevalence of network technology, the Internet has become the main channel for seeking and disseminating information. According to the statistics of the Taiwan Tourism Bureau (2005a) for 2004, 36% of visitors to Taiwan had seen official advertisements promoting Taiwan tourism on the Internet before choosing to visit Taiwan (a percentage that trailed only to those who had seen such advertisements in magazines or books), and 53% of visitors hoped to obtain information on Taiwanese tourism from the Internet in the future (the highest percentage for information source category). The survey demonstrates the growing importance of the Internet to travelers seeking information. The website created by Justin is undoubtedly extremely successful in introducing Greece and the Aegean Sea to many people within a short period of time. To explore why the website appealed to so many visitors, impressing them, and even leading them to plan a travel to Greece is useful. The website was highly effective in place marketing, but used a different approach to those generally prescribed by marketing theory. First, the website was not built by a government agency or tourism association. Furthermore, the website did not resemble word of mouth promotion because the subject was not the tourism place itself but rather a website. These distinctions merit further study.

The following section reviews the previous literature on photo website, photography, and tourism, Internet marketing on tourism, and the AIDA model. Subsequently, the messages on the website are analyzed. Finally, an integrated conclusion is presented. Therefore, this study has the following objectives:

1. Explore the substantial effect of the website "I left my heart in Aegean Sea".
2. Explore the key success factors (KSFs) of the popular Justin's website.

LITERATURE REVIEW

Photo Website

Online photo album or so-called photo sharing website has already been the popular hotspot on the Internet. Many people having more than one album is very common, and their intentions are sharing image works with friends, even a total stranger on the Internet.

Nowadays well-known photo websites are more than ten. Lin (2006) illustrated some of them as follows.

Flickr – The Most Suitable Photo Community for Bloggers
Flickr is absolutely the coolest and friendliest website among numerous photo sharing websites. Because of the mighty and flexible ability of photo management and various interactive mechanisms, Flickr becomes the most welcome online photo service provider in the blog world.

Flickr is built by a Canada company, Ludicorp. The original operation type is a group chatroom and offers a channel for internet friends exchanging their photos. Afterwards Flickr strengthens the function of photo management, especially the function of self-defined tag. Users can easily search for photos fitting in with specific keywords.

Flickr provides 20 MB upload flow per month for free accounts. If desiring to have complete functions, users must pay US$ 24.95 per year. Then, the upload flow can be raised to 2 GB and users can own unlimited storage space. Now, Flickr also offers added-value service, network image, which includes burning photos into DVD and printing photos on calendars or stamps.

FotoFlix – The Story-Telling Photo Album
Almost all photo websites support slide function, and play photos one by one automatically. However, most of them drift into conventional pattern

and lack of novelty. For users, this function just let them save strength to click the mouse. If you want to know what magical tricks online photo album can perform, FotoFlix provides the best demonstration.

The website parades itself as "Making your memories more memorable." That means the main selling point of FotoFlix is to let members produce multimedia albums, named "Flix." The website provides various album looks, and users can randomly arrange the order and time of photos' appearances, even add in favorite background music. Members can make a dynamic story-telling album. The album can be published at anywhere you imagine, including PhotoPage on FotoFlix, personal website, and blog.

Pixnet – Numerous Photos of Beauty
As to non-commercial online album, the best-known one in Taiwan is Wretch. In fact, Pixnet is also easy-to-use and free album website.

Pixnet and Wretch are the same; they are set up by students of National Chiao Tung University. Although not so popular as Wretch, Pixnet has more than one hundred thousand members.

Compared with other online album, Pixnet's interface is simpler and it makes users feel more comfortable. Pixnet also has more practical functions. It not only supports uploading ZIP files, but also provides the tool of tree contents for internet friends browsing photos more quickly. Pixnet also offers the function of leaving messages. Internet friends can leave messages to photos that he/she appreciates.

Besides, no matter what albums your friends use, such as Wretch, MSN Space, Taipeilink, or Flickr, you can add them into your good friends list on Pixnet. Although the album is free, its function is so complete.

Xuite – Integrated Services Provider
Blog, having strong community coherence, has already been fighting over on the Internet. In the past 2 years, websites of Sina, Microsoft, Yam successively offer Blog service. As the leader of Internet Service Provider (ISP) in Taiwan, China Telecom provides a service website named Xuite (pronouncing as "sweet") in August 2005. The website integrates several functions, blog, album, e-mail, and so on.

Strictly speaking, Xuite cannot be considered as free online album, and it is just a feedback of China Telecom toward its users. The significant characteristic of Xuite is its macro capacity (500 MB) and strong integrated function. You can use it directly only if you are China Telecom broadband users. Then, you do not need to transfer among various online albums and blog websites anymore.

Shutterfly – Totally Free No Matter How Many Photos You Put
The heavy burden of photo websites is the need of huge storage space.
Therefore, the free space, which photo websites provide, for the most part, is
quite limited (probably less than 50 MB). For consumers haggling over
every penny and unwilling to foot the bill for online space, it is worth to try
Shutterfly because of its unlimited free space.

The registration method of Shutterfly website is simple. Users use free
account and need not pay extra fees to enjoy complete album functions.
Everyone can have unlimited photo storage space and use whole functions
of online photo editing (such as removing red eye, framing photos, image
processing, print size alteration). Of course Shutterfly provides sharing
photos service, even users can establish "my collection" with personal address. Other internet friends can comment on photos inside, and also upload
photos in their personal computers or website accounts. It is a very popular
interpersonal communication way.

How Shutterfly run under providing free website space except advertisement revenue? The answer is image print service. Shutterfly targets on the
print market following image storage. It is not just usual photo prints, but
includes Print on Demand. Now, the website provides services for printing
cards, albums, calendars, T-shirts, mugs, magnets, mouse pads, and etc.
Every member can print his/her photos on various products through simple
customer order process. The business mode, which regards network photo
storage as basic service, is very popular because the users do not need to pay
for keeping network space every month and only need to pay when they
order products for themselves.

Compared with photo print online service, other derivative and fresh
products have better attraction. As to postcard, unit price is US$ 2.4 if order
amount is less than 9, but there is discount following increased order. If
having a lot of relatives and friends in the United States, you can print
personal postcard through Shutterfly to convey greetings. It is convenient
and caters to the newest trend.

Webshots – Make Desktop Become Dazzling Album
Which photo website has maximum users? According to the statistics provided by Nielsen NetRatings, users of Webshots, surpassing Yahoo and
America Online (AOL), are in the lead over a long period of time. Because
of the accomplishment, it attracts CNET to spend US$ 70 million for
acquisition. There are about 14 million visitors to Webshots every month at
that time. Now, photos on the website are nearly 330 millions, and this is
like a super large photo database.

Webshots was set up in 1995, and it is originally famous for providing high-definition desktop wallpaper and screen saver. After installing Webshots Desktop, the free desktop management tool, users can download mass professional photos as desktop wallpaper and set time for alternation. Users can also choose favorite photos as their screen savers. The simple and easily understanding operation method is very favorable. Since starting to add in photo sharing service in 1999, Webshots takes the first place of the biggest photo sharing websites in the United States for a long time.

The free account of Webshots has many limits. Users can only download five desktop wallpapers and track ten members' albums everyday. Besides, users need to brook interference of advertisements in the procedure. If desiring to enjoy integrated functions, you should pay US$ 29.88 each year. Then, you can keep the album space for 3000 photos, and download desktop wallpapers unlimitedly.

Photography and Tourism

Everyone surely has experienced taking photographs during a tour. Photographs provide indisputable evidence that the trip was made, that the program was carried out, and that fun was had (Sontag, 1977). Moreover, photographs help to record memories. Some scholars have studied photography in tourism. Chalfen (1979) investigated the theoretical relationships between photography and tourist types, particularly in terms of photographic behavior and photographic images. Chalfen provided no empirical evidence to support his argument that 'each tourist type can be characterized based on the photographs they take, which in turn "illustrate" alternative host–tourist relationships'. Cohen, Nir, and Almogor (1992) explored the interaction between strangers and the inhabitants of a local community, with a specific focus on stranger–local interactions in tourism photography. They focused their attention on the consequences of such interaction. Moreover, Markwell (1997) conducted an empirical study examining the spatial, temporal, and social dimensions of photography in a nature-based tour experience. Previous studies primarily focused on the impacts or roles of tourism photography, but few explored its promotional function. Photographic images of places and attractions help to form expectations regarding tours during the pre-travel stage (Markwell, 1997). Therefore, photographs of scenic spots are ubiquitous, for example in travel agency or tourism bureau websites, media advertisements, guidebooks, travel brochures, postcards, and so on. The case study described below attempts to identify the power of photographs.

Internet Marketing on Tourism

The Internet has proven effective for advertising, marketing, distributing goods, and providing information services (Hoffman & Novak, 1996). The information-intensive nature of the tourism industry suggests an important role for the Internet and Web technology in destination promotion and marketing (Doolin, Burgess, & Cooper, 2002). The Web has great potential for promoting regional tourism, and is relatively inexpensive compared with other promotion and advertising media (Standing & Vasudavan, 2000). An effective website can reach global audiences, being accessible 24 h a day from anywhere in the world. Notably, Hanna and Millar (1997) reported that following the initial welcome page, photographs of destinations are the most popular website content. Standing and Vasudavan (2000) believed that the major weakness of a website promoting the Western Cape area of South Africa was an excessive reliance on textual description and too few photographs. Their finding demonstrates the importance of website photographs in tourism marketing.

Although the web is itself a communication tool, a site needs the support of other media to reach a critical mass of visitors (Haas, 2002). Sites can be advertised online at other sites, be promoted free of charge via links, or traditional media can be used to promote the URL, including business cards, newspaper advertisements, letterheads, etc. (Standing & Vasudavan, 2000). Furthermore, building network traffic via tourism newsgroups, signature files, and electronic mails is another effective form of promotion (Sweeney, 2000). E-mail is obviously an excellent medium for marketing and recently has become very popular. E-mail is not only convenient but also can easily reach numerous targets. Of course lots of other media could also play the supportive roles, but these other media are not included in the present discussion.

AIDA Model

After defining the desired response, the communicator moves to developing an effective message. Ideally, the message should gain Attention, hold Interest, arouse Desire, and elicit Action (a model known as AIDA). In practice, few messages take the consumer all the way from awareness through purchase, but the AIDA framework suggests desirable qualities for any communication (Kotler, 2002).

METHOD

This study selects the case study approach. Data are drawn from the message board of Justin's website. The board used was an original one, and lasted from July 1 to November 2, 2003. Another new board was linked to the page of Locus (the publisher mentioned above). To avoid the interference effect, this work only examined the messages on the original board. These messages provide important clues regarding the influence of Justin's website. Visitors browsing the website left some 301 messages reflecting the initial impressions to the site. All of the messages are exhaustively analyzed and categorized. Substantially, the effects of the website are classified as motivating viewers to take action (making plans to visit), invoking desire (looking forward to visiting someday), stimulating an interest in Greece (intending to learn more about Greece, including its culture, history, architecture, cuisine, etc.), and creating an awareness of the website (creating personal feelings about the site). The classification is based on the AIDA model in the field of consumer behavior. Careful analysis of holistic messages confirms the substantial effect of the website. Thus, the mode is confirmed to be an effective marketing tool. Finally, implications for tourism practitioners are discussed.

RESULTS

All the messages are circumspectly analyzed, and the results are listed in Table 1. Messages dealing only with personal feelings or other matters and not related to visiting Greece are assigned to the "Attention" category. Meanwhile, messages demonstrating a slight interest in visiting Greece, for example indicating an increased interest in information on Greece, are classified as "Interest." Furthermore, messages expressing a clear intention to visit Greece someday are classified as "Desire." Finally, messages expressing a definite timetable for visiting Greece are categorized as "Action." Over 45% of the research objects exhibited aroused desire and elicited action, and announced precise plans to visit Greece right away or someday in the foreseeable future. The website had a considerable impact on browsers and indirectly promoted Greek tourism.

The messages were left by people not only from Taiwan, but also from other countries (10.3%), including the US, UK, Hong Kong, China, Malaysia, Singapore, Japan, and so on.

Table 1. Classified Messages – Attention, Interest, Desire, Action (AIDA).

Classified Messages	Frequency	Percentage	AIDA
Praise for works and be touched	67	22.3	Attention
Thank for sharing	18	6.0	
Recollect former Greek tour	14	4.6	
Share websites discussing Greece	1	0.3	
Question about the camera	3	1.0	
Make a comment out of personal feeling	14	4.6	
Others	17	5.7	
Subtotal	134	44.5	
Seem to be personally in the scene	20	6.7	Interest
Be interested in and like Greece	10	3.3	
Subtotal	30	10.0	
Buy books	47	15.6	Desire
Intend to have an independent tour and ask questions and details	5	1.7	
Dream of visiting	13	4.3	
Aspire to visit at once	53	17.6	
Subtotal	118	39.2	
Have visited or plan to visit recently	19	6.3	Action
Subtotal	19	6.3	
Total	301	100	

Some messages are excerpted below:

'You have clearly shown me the romance of Greece. I will visit Greece if I get the chance. Many thanks for your romantic memories Justin!' Alan Lu.

'Those pictures are gorgeous! You really have turned Greece into heaven. Because of this, I have decided to visit Santorini next month. You're a star!' Wai-Chi.

'Amazing! After browsing the website, I wish to visit Greece. I must share this great site with my friends.' Xiao-Mao.

'The Greek National Tourism Organization (GNTO) should make you an ambassador because my co-workers and friends are now all looking forward to seeing the legendary Aegean Sea with their own eyes.' Amber.

'Greece has long been a dream destination for many. Owing to some reasons, they are tardy for finding any information about going to Greece. After seeing your touching photos, lots of my friends are finally actively seeking information and planning to visit Greece....' Qing-Qing.

'...you really make us yearn for Greece. Recently I have heard so many people planning to visit Greece. The magic is so great.' Yao.

'...many friends around me are flying to Greece because of your photos....' Vicky.

'I heard who went to Greece this summer say that the Taiwanese she met in Greece all had browsed your website....' Ishtar.

DISCUSSION AND IMPLICATIONS

"I left my heart in Aegean Sea" is undoubtedly successful in terms of visitor numbers, publicity in other media, and so on. The KSFs of the website are discussed below.

The first factor seems to be related to the atmosphere in the time of Severe Acute Respiratory Syndrome (SARS). "I left my heart in Aegean Sea" was established in May 2003 when Taiwan was suffering from the SARS. Everyone was living in a state of fear. A website presenting touching photographs and fine music helped to bring calm, peace, courage, and hope, while dispelling browsers fears. Many browsers stated that they were greatly touched and even cried after viewing the photographs. Additionally, the fact that people were reluctant to travel by airplane, ship, train, and bus during the SARS crisis led to travel plans being put on hold. In this environment of real travel plans being more difficult to realize Justin's website catered to the unfulfilled desires of browsers to travel and dispelled their depression and fears.

The second factor seems to be the identity of the photographer attracting the attention of browsers. Many people became very curious about who had taken such amazing pictures, and they started to ask whether he was a professional photographer. People were extremely surprised to find that Justin was an engineer. The stereotype of an engineer is unsentimental, inflexible, and mechanical. To believe that such a romantic website had been created by an engineer was difficult for many people. Maybe there was a perceived paradox in the combination of a rational engineer taking such beautiful pictures of a romantic destination such as Greece. Besides, the website creator was simply an ordinary person, not a specialist. The fact that an ordinary engineer had gone to Greece as a backpacker and taken such beautiful photographs inspired others to do likewise and suddenly made Greece appear much nearer to Taiwan than previously.

The third factor seems to be the force of viral marketing. All marketing activities are ultimately viral in nature. Whether the virus can successfully diffuse depends on generating originality, creating topics, triggering browser resonance, and possessing deliverable value. Clearly, "I left my heart in Aegean Sea" behaved like a very strong virus. Stirred by the pictures they saw, most of browsers forwarded the URL address to their friends and associates. As such e-mails circulated, the website was introduced to millions of people and achieved an unexpectedly wide impact. Another key point was that the website was non-commercial. Generally, people are defensive toward e-mail marketing, but a message about a website shared voluntarily by people among their friends via e-mail channel is easily acceptable.

The fourth factor seems to contribute to individuals realization of their dreams. Kotler and Armstrong (2003) stated that Coca-Cola stands for "refreshment"; Marlboro stands for the "freedom of the open range"; Starbucks brands an urban "third space"; Pontiac represents "excitement." These brands place these meanings at the core of their products. Charley Revson of Revlon provided an excellent example, saying 'In the factory, we make cosmetics; in the store we sell hope.' These are what Levitt (1986) calls the "intangible properties" of the product. Consumers do not buy products for the products themselves. Similarly, browsers do not admire the website for the website itself. The intangible property of the website is a "dream." The website not only strikes the right chord but also touches the deepest human desires. People understand that their personal dream can be actualized through the website. Dreams thus are no longer merely dreams, but rather are realizable. As Justin said, 'Greece is not far; if you want to go you can. Dreams are also not far; if you take a first step they become nearer.'

The fifth factor seems to be the romantic atmosphere of the website. The website creator gave the site the romantic name "I left my heart in Aegean Sea." Moreover, he substituted a jumping red heart for the Chinese character of "heart" on the initial welcome page, and forced browsers to click this red heart to enter the next page. After entering, browsers found a series of beautiful sunrises, sunsets, blue skies, boundless oceans, beautiful cats, happy lovers, innocent children, magnificent buildings, and so on (see Figs. 7–12). The hearts of browsers resonated to these deep blue and white images. These vivid pictures and the accompanying gentle music created a

Fig. 7. Photos of the Website "I left my heart in Aegean Sea" (*Source:* home.kimo.com.tw/yuchang_chen.tw/).

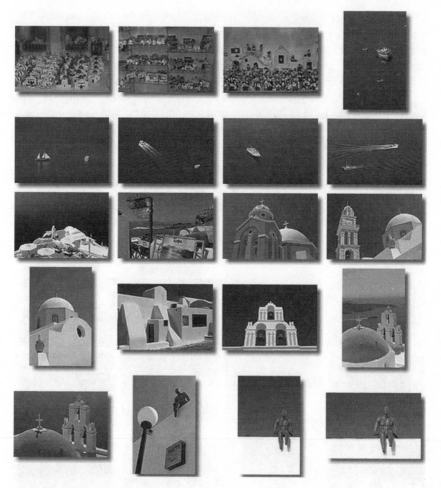

Fig. 8. Photos of the Website "I left my heart in Aegean Sea" (*Source:* home.kimo.com.tw/yuchang_chen.tw/).

very romantic feeling. Besides, the pronunciation of "Aegean Sea" in Mandarin closely resembles that of "love sea," a linguistic coincidence that invokes very favorable impressions about the area as a travel destination. All of these romantic elements add to the charm of the website.

The sixth factor seems to be simple website content. A common rule of thumb in advertising is to "keep it simple" (Roman, Mass, & Nisenholtz, 2003). "I left my heart in Aegean Sea" mainly consists of beautiful photos,

Fig. 9. Photos of the Website "I left my heart in Aegean Sea" (*Source:* home.kimo.com.tw/yuchang_chen.tw/).

carefully selected melodies, and brief statements. Because of no long-winded statements or irrelevant components, simply images and sounds, browsers can skim without any burden. Moreover, the original conception of the website was also very simple, being intended only for sharing memories with friends. Although not designed for advertising purposes, the website still helped to promote travel to Greece and the Aegean.

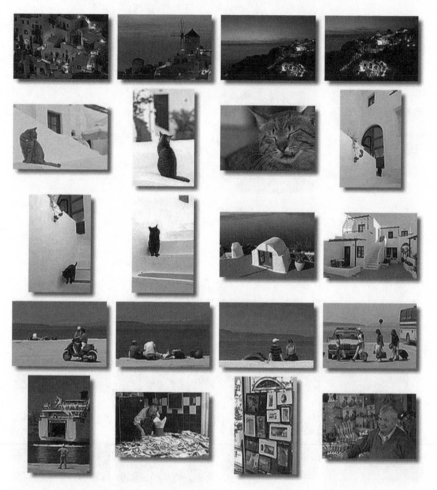

Fig. 10. Photos of the Website "I left my heart in Aegean Sea" (*Source:* home.kimo.com.tw/yuchang_chen.tw/).

A website originally intended to simply share photographs ended up un-intentionally promoting Greek tourism, and helps the GNTO access the Taiwanese market. Traditionally, nations use TV, magazines, Internet, direct mail, brochures, and leaflets to conduct advertising campaigns. Ad-ditionally, they may sign contracts with other nations for exchange visits, participate in travel shows, invite overseas journalists to visit, and so on. But the key question remains successfully firing up the enthusiasm of potential

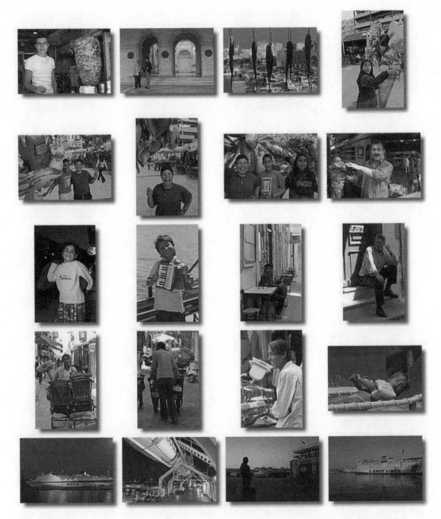

Fig. 11. Photos of the Website "I left my heart in Aegean Sea" (*Source:* home.kimo.com.tw/yuchang_chen.tw/).

tourists. "I left my heart in Aegean Sea" is undoubtedly a very successful case. Simply the touching photographs accompanied by soft music could touch quite a few people and even inspire them to action. The above case provides global countries and tourism promoters with a brand-new approach to promoting tourism. This new approach is totally different

Fig. 12. Photos of the Website "I left my heart in Aegean Sea" (*Source:* home.kimo.com.tw/yuchang_chen.tw/).

from traditional approaches, but has the potential for enormous impact. All marketing personnel should move beyond traditional methods and be much more original when seeking to attract international tourists. Using non-conventional, high-impact approaches can achieve an advantage in the competitive tourism market by bringing the promoted destinations closer to their target customers.

SECOND MEGA-TREND: TV MINISERIES-INDUCED TOURISM

Korean Wave Phenomenon

As quality of life has improved in developed countries, travel has become a widespread leisure activity. Travel destinations are affected by numerous factors, such as mass media advertisements, promotions by travel agencies and airlines, peer travel experiences, personal preference, etc. According to Taiwan Tourism Bureau data (see Table 2), 300,000 Taiwanese traveled to Korea in 2004. There was a 65% increase of the pervious year's total and the growth rate took the first place in destination of departure nationals. Additionally, the number of Taiwanese tourists traveling to Korea has increased over the last few years, especially a sudden increase in 2000. This study assumes, based on the success of Korean TV miniseries "Firework" (see Fig. 13) staged in Taiwan in 2000, that Korean TV miniseries play an important role in marketing South Korea to potential tourists. So far, more than 100 Korean TV miniseries have been broadcasted on several TV channels in Taiwan. In December 2005, nearly 20 miniseries have been broadcasted at the same time.

In the 1990s, Japanese TV miniseries caused a wave of Japan Hot across Asia. Japanese pop culture became the main stream in Taiwan. However, South Korea has made a considerable effort in developing its cultural industries in the past few years. Popular Korean TV miniseries have become vogue in Asian countries, forming a Korean wave. Korean TV miniseries

Table 2. Number of Taiwanese Arriving Korea in Past 6 Years.

Year	Number	Growth Rate (%)
1999	89,325	2.62
2000	108,831	21.84
2001	115,623	6.24
2002	120,208	3.97
2003	179,893	49.65
2004	298,325	65.83

Source: Taiwan Tourism Bureau, Ministry of Transportation and Communications (2005b).

Fig. 13.   Successful Korean TV Miniseries "Firework" (*Source:* cetv.com).

have already overtaken Japan miniseries in Taiwan, Hong Kong, Vietnam, and Singapore. Product placement in these miniseries has not only improved the exposure of Korean products, but it has strengthened South Korea's attractiveness as a tourist destination. The film locations for Korean TV miniseries have become the popular scenic spots. South Korea has also bought copyrights from TV station, and offers more than ten national TV stations in the Middle East, Eastern Europe, and Russia broadcasting miniseries such as "Hotelier," "Secret," "Four Sisters," "All in," etc. These shows will likely strengthen bilateral cultural exchange and enhance South Korea exposure in each country. Other South Korean products (automobiles, mobile phones, and 3C products) also become well known.

It seems that the hottest Korean wave attracts people to visit South Korea. The Korean wave has surged throughout not only Taiwan, but also the big Asia, such as Japan, China, Singapore, and Malaysia. The popularity of Korean TV miniseries seems successfully to promote South Korean tourism. This study first classifies Korean TV miniseries that induce tourism. Then, how South Korea executes place marketing to attract tourists and how Korean TV miniseries use product placement as a tool for promoting tourism is discussed.

Forms of TV Miniseries Tourism

Beeton (2005) classified film-induced tourism into several types, including on-location, commercial, mistaken identities, off-location, one-off events, and armchair travel. This study first discusses the types of tourism induced by Korean TV miniseries.

On-Location
The type includes film tourism as a primary travel motivator, film tourism as part of a holiday, film tourism pilgrimage, celebrity film tourism, and nostalgic film tourism.

The Gwangyeok-si area, located near the Incheon International Airport, now is famous after being shot in the miniseries "Full House." This area has become a popular tourist spot for fans of the miniseries. Locals have opened up Band B, restaurants, etc.

The house in "Full House" is an actual house made especially for the miniseries (see Fig. 14). The house cost approximately US$ 1 million and took two months to build. When visiting the "Full House" set, tourists can take pictures standing beside poster characters Rain and Hye-Kyo Song (see Fig. 15). For only US$ 500 tourists can stay overnight in the house. The furnishings inside the house are kept complete, but stage photos are added.

Off-Location
Off-location tourism includes studio tours and studio theme parks. Tourists can take tours of working film studios or visit a theme park built specifically for tourism.

Cine-I Studio, a theme park, was opened in Myeog-dong at the end of 2004. Fans can view studio sets of many notable Korean TV miniseries and movies, such as "Winter Sonata," "Joint Security Area," etc. Visitors can try on costumes and take photos as if they were actors or actresses.

The Korean Broadcasting System (KBS) Visitor's Hall is a mini museum exposing visitors the past, present, and future of South Korean

Fig. 14.   Full House is Famous for Miniseries "Full House" and Becomes a Popular Tourist Spot for Fans. (*Source:* tour2korea.com).

Fig. 15.   Big Poster in Front of "Full House" (*Source:* tour2korea.com).

broadcasting. In addition to the Music Observation section, News Anchor Experience section, Satellite and Compound Image section, and Entertainment section, the Hall includes the KBS Drama Awards section.

The Korea National Tourism Organization (KNTO) opened the Korean Entertainment Hall of Fame (see Fig. 16) in its headquarters in Seoul. The hall of fame is in a Tourist Information Center located on basement level one, easily accessible to fans and tourists. Many products relative to Korean

Fig. 16. Korean Entertainment Hall of Fame (*Source:* tour2korea.com).

Fig. 17. Dae Jang Geum Theme Park (*Source:* http://www.imbc.com/entertain/ mbcticket/mbcplay/2004/daejanggumtheme).

TV miniseries are for sale, and standing are posters available for taking photographs. Additionally, many video and audio exhibitions allow visitors to watch on-the-spot programs.

On-Location Theme Park
On-Location Theme Parks, not identified by Beeton, is a film location first and a theme park when filming stops. That is, it combines the two forms mentioned above. The prototype is the Dae Jang Geum Theme Park (see Fig. 17), which opened in December 2004.

"Jewel in the Palace" (see Fig. 18) garners a large audience in Taiwan, Hong Kong, and China. The Dae Jang Geum Theme Park, based on this

Fig. 18.   TV Miniseries "Jewel in the Palace" (*Source:* azntv.com).

miniseries, is open to tourists and fans and has become a very successful
tourism destination. The outdoor set has been restored to how it looked at
the time of filming and a theme park has been added that offers, in addition
to the existing facilities, a variety of events and programs for visitors to see,
enjoy, and experience. The Theme Park consists of 23 independent facilities
with detailed captions, including the King and Queen's residence, palace,
royal kitchen, guest house, government authority in charge of cooking, food
served in the palace, etc. Tourists can partake in many exciting events, such
as riding Korean palankeen, trying on traditional Korean costumes, throw-
ing arrows into a large jar, experiencing the flogging a criminal would have
received, playing archery games, etc. Furthermore, many exhibition rooms
exist where visitors can take a close look at royal Korean food and costumes. Visitors can also pose for photos with standing poster of characters
from the miniseries.

South Korea is famous for creating artificial scenic locations. Theme
parks and historical locations appear one by one based on Korean TV
miniseries. The historical play "Yi Sun-shin," produced by the KBS, is
developing its own scenic spot construction. The cultural village, called
Buan Movie Theme Park, will be completed by the end of 2005 and open in
the beginning of 2006 (see Fig. 19).

The Land Cultural Park, the filming location for the miniseries "Land,"
has been open and charging admission since August 2004 and has become
an extremely popular artificial scenic location in South Korea. Through

Fig. 19. The Location of "Yi Sun-shin" Becomes Buan Movie Theme Park, and There are Epitomes of Gyeongbokgung and Changdokgung in it. (*Source:* Min Sheng Daily).

these Korean TV miniseries and tourist attractions, foreigners can gain an improved understanding of Korean culture. This phenomenon enhances South Korea's exposure, and promotes tourism and cultural consumption.

Methods Used by Korean TV Miniseries to Create Attraction

In "Marketing Asian Places," Kotler (2001) noted that competition in the travel industry is like business, and a place needs to build its own image. A place's image can be influenced by original art, including movies, TV, greeting cards, music, and famous actors and musicians. A place's image can exist for several decades. A place without appeal can create a new attraction artificially. Although a place's climate, topography, or geographic location cannot be changed, it can create an attraction artificially to make itself more competitive. Kotler suggested ten approaches to create an attraction. This study discusses how Korean TV miniseries use these ways to create South Korea tourism attraction.

Natural Scenery
Natural scenery includes mountains and rivers, canyons, oceans, woods, etc. Some places have magnificent scenery or unusual sights and thereby possess innate advantages. The Himalayas in Nepal, the Great Barrier Reef in

Fig. 20. The Filming Location of "Winter Sonata" – Namisum (*Source:* tour2 korea.com).

Australia, and the rain forests of Borneo are just a few examples. "Winter Sonata," which has been shot at the beautiful Namisum (see Fig. 20) more than 30 times, has created a romantic atmosphere at Namisum.

History and Celebrity

Many Asian places market themselves via their connection with historical events or celebrities. Korean TV miniseries utilize history as subject matter. For example, "Jewel in the Palace" describes the striving history of a legendary girl who becomes a royal physician, "Business Ethic" depicts Shang-Wo Lin's struggle from poor to rich, and "Queen Myeong Seong" presents the lifetime of South Korea's most outstanding female politician in Korean modern history. "Queen Myeong Seong" is filmed in Gyeongbokgung, the first principal palace in ancient Korea and the greatest among the five ancient palaces in Seoul.

Shopping Mall

Every place can have commercial regions for buying foods, clothes, utensils, appliances, etc. "Guardian Angel" and "Romance" are filmed at the Dongdaemun Market, the largest wholesale and retail market in Korea. There are more than 20 comprehensive buildings, 30,000 specialty shops, and 50,000 manufacturers in the market.

Cultural Landscape

To increase value, many places invest in a destination's cultural capital. For instance, some small locations actively promote their cultural heritage, such as Sarawak on the island of Borneo and Tongyeong in South Korea.

Changdokgung, one filming location for "Jewel in the Palace," is a world heritage designated by the United Nations Educational, Scientific and Cultural Organization (UNESCO).

Amusement Place
Every place needs to offer recreation and amusement fields for its residents. Such areas typically have restaurants, pubs, cafes, clubs, discos, parks, community centers, zoos, playgrounds, etc. However, an increasing number of amusement parks have been built in recent years. Everland, the location of "My Love Patzzi," ranks worldwide as the eighth in drawing tourists. Lotte World, run by the chief actor in "Stairway to Heaven," is the largest indoor amusement park in the world. Walker Hill, Korea's largest casino famous for its luxurious casino and shows, is also the location of "Hotelier."

Playground
Sport stars can increase the attraction of a place, whereas teams can improve the profile of a city or country. The value of South Korea's football team is far beyond that typically associated with a victorious team, as fans all over the world comprise a vast potential market. An actor in "I Love Bear" plays the role of football coach who demonstrates football skills in the miniseries. In the miniseries "Lovers in Paris," the location of actors playing ice hockey is in the Mokdong Ice Rink; in the miniseries "All In," scenes of an actor receiving golf lessons – after returning from the United States – are shot at Jungmun Golf Course.

Festival
Numerous places host special activities. For example, after opening, the Dae Jang Geum Theme Park frequently presents traditional games and foods on holidays or special occasions. The park held a festival of traditional Korean foods, allowing tourists to taste traditional royal foods and experience folk cultures in celebration of the lunar new year.

Architecture, Memorial, and Sculpture
Another way is to build or restore local architecture, memorials, and sculptures. The Jeju Folk Village in South Korea, which preserves traditional architecture, is the place where Jang Geum learns medicine as a maidservant for the Jeju local government. There are large stage photos and descriptions of filming locations in the village to satisfy Jang Geum fans.

Museum
Museums typically collect historical heritages that are representative of national character. A place that lacks museums is like having a deficiency in festivals or sport teams. Museums can present the historical and cultural character of a place, and enhance its marketing potential. The filming location of an antique car that appears in "My Love Patzzi" is Samsung Transportation Museum, the earliest traffic museum in Korea.

Others
There are numerous other approaches for creating place attraction. For example, "the most of Asia" idea contains potential attraction. Generally, the combination of diversified attractions can enhance a place's attractiveness. Popular scenic locations can be linked with infrastructure, such as airports, TV stations, radio towers, etc. The Incheon International Airport, the gateway for most foreigners entering South Korea, is considered world class. Many Korean TV miniseries, such as "Save the Last Dance for Me," have been filmed there.

Korean TV miniseries take advantage of local buildings to create attraction to a place. In addition to turning locations and film studios into tourist destinations, KNTO opened the Korean Wave Cultural Center at the Incheon International Airport (see Fig. 21). The center is located at Gate 46, the primary gate for departing flights going to Southeast Asia, and features a large-screen TV airing some of South Korea's most popular TV miniseries ("Winter Sonata," "Autumn in My Heart," "Jewel in the Palace," etc.).

Fig. 21. Korean Wave Cultural Center is Located at Gate 46 of Incheon International Airport. (*Source:* tour2korea.com).

Fans can view these programs for free and take pictures alongside pictures of their favorite stars before departing. They can also shop for souvenirs from their favorite Korean miniseries.

Research Objectives

The objectives of the study are to investigate whether Korean TV miniseries play a primary role in promoting South Korean tourism, how the communication effect is, and how important the push and pull factors are for audiences to visit or wanting to visit South Korea. The possibility of product placement applying to South Korean scenic spots is discussed. By the way, Taiwanese dramas recently have also been exported to countries in Southeast Asia, South Korea, and China, and even penetrated the difficult Japanese market. In Japan, "Summer," a Taiwanese drama, is broadcast by SKY perfectTV and "Meteor Garden," another successful Taiwanese drama, is broadcast by Nippon Television Network (NTV). "Summer," the first Taiwanese star-based drama broadcast on Japan television, makes considerable use of the beautiful Peng-Hu's scenery. Although "Meteor Garden" relies heavily on star power to attract its audience, its filming locations in National Chung Cheng University have attracted numerous Thai tourists. Additionally, Japanese travel agencies have started offering tours featuring a "Meteor Garden" itinerary. The success of this show in attracting tourists to its locations is indicative of the power of media. Now, more and more Asian countries start to concern about the impact of TV series on tourism. This study aims to figure out the exact factors promoting Taiwanese to visit South Korea.

Literature Review

This literature review investigates the relationship between film and tourism, and relationship between push and pull factors and travel.

Relationship between Film and Tourism
Tooke and Baker (1996), who examined four UK case studies, investigated the relationship between television series and movies and the popularity of film locations as tourism destinations. They concluded that number of tourists visiting the four locations grew as a result of the movies and series. The main implication is that product placement, in this case a location, has

considerable value. Thus, taking steps to attract television film and movie companies to a location is a worthwhile means of exposing a location to potential tourists.

Riley, Baker, and Van Doren (1998) gathered data on 12 US locations to investigate whether movies affected tourism at these locations. The 12 locations were generated using four criteria: (1) the movie was a box office success; (2) the movie had an icon clearly associated with an accessible destination; (3) visitation data was accessible for analysis; and (4) the location collected visitation data prior to a movie's release. The authors believed that movies create exotic worlds that can be recreated by visiting filmed location(s). They collected and analyzed tourist data for 10 years prior to and 5 years after the release of each movie. Their principal finding was that the movies induced tourism. In most cases, a location's attraction is unique. Some locations have inherent physical properties that attract tourists, whereas others just happen to be the site where the theme or event occurred. These movies generated a 40–50% increase in tourism at these locations; this increase lasted at least 4 years.

Kim and Richardson (2003) developed a theoretical framework for the relationship between destination images and movies – as a form of popular culture. Their study employed an experimental design to assess a change in relation to a cognitive/affective image, familiarity, and interest in visiting of a location after viewing a movie featuring that location. Their experimental results indicated that the movie significantly affected audience's interest in visiting these locations. Their study provided empirical evidence that a popular motion picture significantly influence an audience's perception of a destination, and elucidated how a movie can promote tourism.

These studies all demonstrate that TV series or movies can induce tourism.

Relationship between Push and Pull Factors and Travel

Riley and Van Doren (1992) utilized a case study to determine whether a motion picture can attract US tourists to a location. In their opinion, motion pictures attract audiences to locations. In tourist motivation theory, pull factors attract tourists to specific destinations, whereas push factors make tourists have travel intentions. In their study, push factors only describe tourist-generating locations. The authors proposed that a location's attractiveness can have a considerable impact on viewers via film. For example, the movie "Crocodile Dundee" increased awareness of Australia's tourism attractions among potential travelers. Reasons for such attraction potential likely lie in motivation of escape, pilgrimage, and a quest for untainted environments. Such motivations are harnessed via storylines that offer vicarious contact over extended periods with the destination and its attraction features.

Oh, Uysal, and Weaver (1995), who evaluated the relationship between push and pull motivations for overseas travel for an Australian study sample of 1,030 respondents, utilized a canonical correlation approach. Canonical analysis generates four canonical variates; respondents were assigned to canonical variates to form four market segments (safety/comfort, culture/history, novelty/adventure, and luxury seekers). Study findings suggested that successfully matching push and pull items is a possible destination marketing strategy.

To market destinations effectively, it is first necessary to identify the motivation underlying an individual's will to travel and the destination attributes crucial to selecting overseas destinations. Simultaneous examination of push and pull motivations would be very effective for segmented markets, in designing promotional programs and packages, and in the decision-making process of destination development. If destination marketers have a clear understanding of why their products are in demand for each market segment group, they will be able to closely tailor their products to their customers' needs, and be able to select advertising and sales messages with enhanced accuracy to inform and persuade tourists to buy products (Holloway & Plant, 1988).

Baloglu and Uysal (1996) applied the canonical correlation approach that allows for simultaneous examination of push and pull motivations. They examined the relationship between these two motivation types for overseas pleasure travel for 1,212 German respondents. Analytical results provide significant insight into the segmentation of travelers, designing promotional plans and packages, and developing destination products.

Klenosky (2002) proposed a practical framework for examining the relationships between the pull attributes of a destination and the motivational forces important to individual travelers. These forces are the push factors that first influence one's decision to travel, and the means-end approach provides an useful alternative for examining the relationship between push and pull factors important in motivating travel behavior. Klenosky's study indicated that means-end approach can be applied in an empirical study of destination choice.

Kim, Lee, and Klenosky (2003) investigated the influence of push and pull factors on visitors to South Korean national parks. During the summer of 1999, 2,720 tourists visiting six National Parks in South Korea were surveyed to assess their reasons for visiting the parks (push factors) and evaluate how well the park performed on a select set of attributes (pull factors). Factor analysis identified four push factor domains (family togetherness and study, appreciating natural resources and health, escaping everyday routine, and adventure and building friendship) and three pull factor domains (key tourist resources, information and convenience of facilities, and accessibility and transportation) underlying respondent push and pull factor ratings. The most important push factors were "appreciating natural resources and health"; the relatively important pull factors were "accessibility and transportation" and "information and convenience of facilities." The authors, who also examined the relationship between push and pull factors, identified significant correlations among the two dimensions, obtaining findings similar to those obtained by Uysal and Jurowski (1994).

In summary, a push factor is the reason motivating tourism, whereas a pull factor is the reason why a destination is chosen. Both jointly comprise the principal elements underlying tourist behavior.

Methodology

In this study, an online questionnaire is designed to collect data. The survey period is one month, from July 1 to 30 in 2005. There are 390 answered questionnaires, but 333 valid ones after screening out 31 incomplete questionnaires and 26 ill-fitting research objectives. The questionnaire is composed of four parts:

The first part is utilized to screen the sample. The research subjects are asked the following questions: whether they watched a Korean TV miniseries in previous 6 months; how long on average they watch Korean TV miniseries per week; what Korean TV miniseries they like most; whether they have been to South Korea in past 5 years, and if their trip is motivated by the Korean TV miniseries they like most. These questions screen out the respondents who have not been to and would not want to visit South Korea.

The second part gauges the importance of pull factors. The research subjects are asked to answer in their opinion what makes South Korea an attractive tourist spot. There are in total 38 factors.

The third part gauges the importance of push factors. The research subjects are asked why they chose South Korea for tourism. There are 30 factors in total.

The final part obtains personal data, including gender, age, marital situation, education level, monthly income, and occupation.

Collected data are analyzed using SPSS software to process descriptive analysis and factor analysis.

Results

Table 3 presents a demographic profile in the study sample. In total, 270 respondents (81.1%) were female and 63 (18.9%) were male. Descriptive analysis of the respondents revealed that respondents were likely to be single

Table 3. Demographic Profiles of Samples (*N* = 333).

Variable	Percentage
Gender	
Male	18.9
Female	81.1
Age	
Under 18	6.9
18–35	67.9
36–50	22.8
Over 50	2.4
Marital status	
Single	66.7
Married	31.2
Divorced	1.2
Widowed	0.6
Other	0.3
Education	
Senior high/vocational school or under	41.1
College or university	53.2
Graduate school	5.7
Monthly income	
Under 20,000	35.1
20,000–39,999	40.8
40,000–59,999	17.1
60,000–79,999	6.0
80,000 and over	0.9
Occupation	
Civil servant	12.9
Company employee or businessman	30.3
Farmer/fisher	3.6
Student	43.2
Retirement	9.9
Hobo	0.0
Freeman	0.0
Other	0.0

(66.7%), and most had completed a college or university education (53.2%). Approximately 68% were 18–35 years of age, 40.8% had a monthly income of roughly $20,000–$39,999, and 43.2% were still in school.

The cross table of visiting South Korea, watching Korean TV miniseries, and visiting South Korea because of Korean TV miniseries is as follows (Table 4). Almost 80% frequently watching Korean TV miniseries (at least once per week) have visited or want to visit South Korea because of Korean TV miniseries. About 50% not frequently watching Korean TV miniseries have visited or want to visit South Korea as a result of Korean TV miniseries. Only about 20% not watching Korean TV miniseries during the past 6 months have visited or want to visit South Korea because of Korean TV miniseries.

Table 5 presents the important mean of push and pull factors. Safety is regarded as important item in both push and pull factors. For push factors, important items were experiencing a different lifestyle, entertainment and having fun, resting/relaxing, learning and increasing knowledge, appreciating beautiful scenes, having an enjoyable time with family, etc. For pull factors, in addition to convenience, cleanliness, budget, and tourism resources, which are generally considered important for travel location, Korean TV miniseries are the principal reason tourists are attracted to South Korea.

Tables 6 and 7 present the results of factor analysis. For push factors, seven factors are extracted – sports and social interaction, visiting dream and famous place, relaxation, adventure, experience and study, appreciating beautiful scenes and culture, safety and price promotion. For pull factors, nine factors are extracted – convenience, safety and cleanness, seaside and sports, culture, beautiful scenery and tourism resources, Korean TV miniseries, casinos and golf, nearness and cuisine, shopping, anaplasty, and quality hotels.

Discussion

Research results indicate that Korean TV miniseries are a key factor causing tourists to choose South Korea as their destination or want to visit South Korea. Tourism desires include watching the filming locations of Korean TV miniseries, reliving the moving plot, and fondness for actors and roles in the miniseries. Furthermore, the unique South Korean attractions communicated in the TV miniseries also garnered high scores, such as beautiful scenery, various tourism resources, etc. These are important decision-making

Table 4. Cross Table of Three Items – Visiting South Korea, Watching Korean TV Miniseries, and Visiting South Korea because of Korean TV Miniseries.

Whether Watching Korean TV Miniseries in Past 6 Months		Whether Visiting South Korea in Past 5 Years		Sum
		Yes	No, but want to	
Yes, frequently	Because of Korean TV miniseries	30	133	163
	%	14.6%	64.6%	79.1%
	Not because of Korean TV miniseries	16	27	43
	%	7.8%	13.1%	20.9%
	Sum	46	160	206
	%	22.3%	77.7%	100.0%
Yes, not frequently	Because of Korean TV miniseries	11	46	57
	%	9.6%	40.4%	50.0%
	Not because of Korean TV miniseries	18	39	57
	%	15.8%	34.2%	50.0%
	Sum	29	85	114
	%	25.4%	74.6%	100.0%
No	Because of Korean TV miniseries	1	2	3
	%	7.7%	15.4%	23.1%
	Not because of Korean TV miniseries	3	7	10
	%	23.1%	53.8%	76.9%
	Sum	4	9	13
	%	30.8%	69.2%	100.0%

Table 5.   Mean of Push and Pull Factors.

	Mean
Push factors	
Traveling to safe/secure places	4.37
Experiencing a different lifestyle	4.25
Being entertained and having fun	4.21
Resting/relaxing	4.20
Being free to act the way I feel	4.14
Learning new things, increasing knowledge	4.10
Releasing work pressures	4.05
Appreciating beautiful natural resources	4.02
Indulging in luxury	3.97
Having an enjoyable time with family	3.94
Pull factors	
Personal safety, even when traveling alone	4.62
Convenient facilities (e.g. restroom)	4.48
Standard of hygiene/cleanliness	4.44
Beautiful scenery	4.43
Budget traveling expenses	4.42
Well-organized tourist information system	4.42
Filming locations of Korean TV miniseries	4.37
Moving plots of Korean TV miniseries	4.23
Various tourism resources	4.23
Actors/roles of Korean TV miniseries	4.22

factors. The largest task in this research is to analyze the importance of push and pull factors relative to tourists visiting, or desiring to visit, South Korea.

After becoming caught in a financial storm, South Korea has recovered quickly and its economy has taken off in high gear. South Korean TV miniseries have captured the attention of many Asian viewers. Korean miniseries spare no expense in creating artificial scenery or filming at a variety of scenic locations. The mode makes these locations subsequently become tourist spots. Furthermore, South Korea acquires a considerable amount of foreign exchange and reaps economic benefit. This is, so to speak, very successful place marketing. Korean TV miniseries in Taiwan are not only idol series, but also historical plays, such as "Business Ethics," "The Legendary Doctor," "Queen Myeong Seong," and "Jewel in the Palace." Korean history and culture are successfully promoted while viewers watch these TV miniseries. From TV series to culture to tourism, this relationship is at play in many destinations throughout the world. South Korea has

Table 6. Factor Analysis of Push Factors.

Push Factor	Factor Loadings						
	1	2	3	4	5	6	7
Sports and social interaction							
Getting some exercise	0.767						
Watching sports events	0.782						
Enhancing health	0.670						
Visiting friends or relatives	0.682						
Visiting dream and famous place							
Fulfilling dream of visiting a place		0.658					
Visiting a destination which most people value and/or appreciate		0.703					
Relaxation							
Getting away from everyday life			0.830				
Releasing work pressures			0.876				
Resting/relaxing			0.801				
Adventure							
Being free to act the way I feel				0.690			
Being daring and adventuresome				0.742			
Experience and study							
Experiencing a different lifestyle					0.705		
Learning new things, increasing knowledge					0.660		
Being entertained and having fun					0.726		
Appreciating beautiful scenery and culture							
Appreciating historic/cultural resources						0.782	
Appreciating beautiful natural resources						0.814	
Safety and price promotion							

Table 6. (*Continued*)

Push Factor	Factor Loadings						
	1	2	3	4	5	6	7
Traveling to safe/secure places							0.683
Adventure of reduced air fares							0.669
Eigenvalue	9.793	2.274	1.815	1.677	1.526	1.305	1.116
Variance explained	32.644	7.580	6.051	5.589	5.087	4.350	3.721
Reliability coefficient	0.81	0.69	0.88	0.70	0.78	0.80	0.47

Table 7. Factor Analysis of Pull Factors.

Pull Factor	Factor Loadings								
	1	2	3	4	5	6	7	8	9
Convenience, safety and cleanness									
Standard of hygiene/cleanliness	0.759								
Personal safety, even when traveling alone	0.79								
Warm welcome for tourists	0.621								
Budget traveling expenses	0.637								
Well-organized tourist information system	0.703								
Convenient facilities (e.g. restroom)	0.801								
Seaside and sports									
Water sports		0.886							
Beaches for swimming/sunning		0.909							
Seaside		0.874							
Watching sports events		0.658							
Culture									
Opportunity to increase knowledge			0.669						
Museums/art galleries			0.676						
Show/live theater			0.674						
Local festivals			0.728						
Culture different from my own			0.744						
Historical/cultural attractions			0.753						
Beautiful scenery and tourism resources									
Beautiful scenery				0.735					
National parks/forests				0.781					
Interesting village				0.786					
Various tourism resources				0.719					

Table 7. (Continued)

Pull Factor	Factor Loadings								
	1	2	3	4	5	6	7	8	9
Exotic atmosphere				0.635					
Korean TV miniseries									
Filming locations of Korean TV miniseries					0.917				
Actors/roles of Korean TV miniseries					0.929				
Moving plots of Korean TV miniseries					0.881				
Casinos and Golf									
Golf						0.644			
Casinos						0.72			
Nearness and cuisine									
Easy accessibility							0.747		
Local cuisine							0.63		
Shopping									
Shopping								0.776	
Local crafts/handiwork								0.537	
Anaplasty and quality hotels									
First class hotels									0.549
Anaplasty									0.746
Eigenvalue	9.721	4.797	2.833	2.001	1.832	1.424	1.317	1.082	1.029
Variance explained	25.581	12.624	7.455	5.265	4.821	3.748	3.465	2.847	2.707
Reliability coefficient	0.87	0.92	0.86	0.86	0.90	0.62	0.49	0.66	0.46

made a considerable effort to create culture, and has become a new Asian tourism leader through Korean wave.

In promoting tourism, attracting global tourists to visit and changing intention into concrete action are the most important tasks. The Korean wave successfully attracts Asian tourists to visit South Korea. Korean TV miniseries have a substantial impact on tourist perception with respect to the importance of push and pull factors and contribute to their desire to visit South Korea. Therefore, global tourism authorities could apply the Korean model as a successful method of drawing tourists. Choosing some principal and representative tourist locations, cooperating with production companies shooting movies or TV miniseries, and utilizing a product placement approach can enhance the visibility of tourist locations in the international market. These methods can also educate foreigners about a country, improve their impression of a country, and induce their visiting motives. By utilizing the power of movies and television series, a country can create tourist attractions and market itself to viewers worldwide, thereby promoting the development of tourism-related industries.

CONCLUSION

Movie-induced tourism is too numerous to enumerate, and the latest example is "the Da Vinci Code." The blockbuster has spawned a series of tours to locations mentioned in the movie. Besides movie, photo website and TV miniseries also become new inducements to tour. As elaboration of the study, Justin's photo website greatly promotes Greek tourism, and South Korean TV miniseries extremely generates South Korea tourism. The two mega-trends are not only sweeping across Taiwan, but influencing lots of people in various countries because of Internet without boundary and TV miniseries broadcasting in several countries at the same time. Therefore, the two mega-trends of promoting tourism are worth particular concern. Marketing personnel should put them to good use and then achieving remarkable success is expectable.

ACKNOWLEDGMENT

The authors would like to thank the National Science Council of the Republic of China, Taiwan for financially supporting this research under Contract No. NSC 93-2416-H-214-002-.

REFERENCES

Baloglu, S., & Uysal, M. (1996). Market segments of push and pull motivations: A canonical correlation approach. *International Journal of Contemporary Hospitality Management,* *8*(3), 32.

Beeton, S. (2005). *Film-induced tourism.* Clevedon: Channel View Publications.

Chalfen, R. M. (1979). Photography's role in tourism: Some unexplored relationships. *Annals of Tourism Research, 6*(4), 435–447.

Cohen, E., Nir, Y., & Almogor, U. (1992). Stranger–local interaction in photography. *Annals of Tourism Research, 19*(2), 213–233.

Doolin, B., Burgess, L., & Cooper, J. (2002). Evaluating the use of the web for tourism marketing: A case study from New Zealand. *Tourism Management, 23*(5), 557–561.

Haas, R. (2002). The Austrian country market: A European case study on marketing regional products and services in a cyber mall. *Journal of Business Research, 55,* 637–646.

Hanna, J. R. P., & Millar, R. J. (1997). Promoting tourism on the Internet. *Tourism Management, 18*(7), 469–470.

Hoffman, D. L., & Novak, T. P. (1996). Marketing in hypermedia computer-mediated environments: Conceptual foundations. *Journal of Marketing, 60*(3), 50–68.

Holloway, J. C., & Plant, R. V. (1988). *Marketing for tourism.* London: Pitman Publishing.

Kim, H., & Richardson, S. (2003). Motion picture impacts on destination images. *Annals of Tourism Research, 30*(1), 216–237.

Kim, S., Lee, C., & Klenosky, D. (2003). The influence of push and pull factors at Korean national parks. *Tourism Management, 24,* 169–180.

Klenosky, D. (2002). The "pull" of tourism destinations: A means-end investigation. *Journal of Travel Research, 40*(4), 385–395.

Kotler, P. (2002). *Marketing management* (11th ed.). New Jersey: Prentice Hall.

Kotler, P., & Armstrong, G. (2003). *Principles of marketing* (10th ed.). New Jersey: Prentice Hall.

Kotler, P., Hamlin, M. A., Rein, I., & Haider, D. H. (2001). *Marketing Asian places: Attracting investment, industry and tourism to cities, states and nations.* New York: Wiley.

Levitt, T. (1986). *The marketing imagination.* New York: The Free Press.

Lin, X. Z. (2006). Start network new life from six photo websites. *Business Next,* January

Markwell, K. (1997). Dimensions of photography in a nature-based tour. *Annals of Tourism Research, 24*(1), 131–155.

Oh, H., Uysal, M., & Weaver, P. (1995). Product bundles and market segments based on travel motivations: A canonical correlation approach. *International Journal of Hospitality Management, 14*(2), 123–137.

Riley, R., Baker, D., & Van Doren, C. (1998). Movies induced tourism. *Annals of Tourism Research, 25*(4), 919–935.

Riley, R., & Van Doren, C. (1992). Movies as tourism promotion: A "pull" factor in a "push" location. *Tourism Management, 13,* 267–274.

Roman, K., Mass, J., & Nisenholtz, M. (2003). *How to advertise* (3rd ed.). New York: Thomas Dunne Books.

Sontag, S. (1977). *On photography.* New York: Farrar, Strauss and Giroux.

Standing, C., & Vasudavan, T. (2000). The marketing of regional tourism via the Internet: Lessons from Australian and South African sites. *Marketing Intelligence & Planning,* *18*(1), 45–48.

Sweeney, S. (2000). *Internet marketing for your tourism business: Proven techniques for promoting tourist-based businesses over the Internet.* Gulf Breeze: Maximum Press.

Tooke, N., & Baker, M. (1996). Seeing is believing: The effect of film on visitor numbers in screened locations. *Tourism Management, 17,* 87–94.

Tourism Bureau, Ministry of Transportation and Communications, Republic of China. (2005a). 2004 Inbound passengers' consumption and tendency survey. Retrieved 1 March, from http://202.39.225.136/indexc.asp.

Tourism Bureau, Ministry of Transportation and Communications, Republic of China. (2005b). Yearbook of tourism statistics on executive information system. Retrieved 29 August, from http://202.39.225.136/indexc.asp.

Uysal, M., & Jurowski, C. (1994). Testing the push and pull factors. *Annals of Tourism Research, 21*(4), 844–846.

Zufryden, F. (2000). New film website promotion and box-office performance. *Journal of Advertising Research, 40*(1/2), 55–64.

CHAPTER 4

MAKING THE MEMORY COME ALIVE AND ACTIVE: USING ORAL HISTORY IN TOURISM AND LEISURE RESEARCH

J. M. Trapp-Fallon and Joseph Boughey

ABSTRACT

The paper discusses oral history interview analysis (OHIA) and the out-comes of oral history research, what Frisch (1990) describes as making the memory come alive and active. OHIA is a process of interdisciplinary reflection that revitalizes many of the debates about 'common-sense interpretation' (Lummis, 1987, p. 113). This article addresses different examples of the ways that the recorded interview /spoken word is used in research. Thomson and Perks are in no doubt that the OHIA influences 'theory, method and politics' of qualitative research. The present article aims to raise awareness of the issues and also to offer suggestions for good practice in tourism and leisure research.

INTRODUCTION

Oral history is a subfield of ethnographic research. For oral history data collection, the researcher enters natural contexts and allows the speaker to

Advances in Culture, Tourism and Hospitality Research, Volume 1, 115–129
Copyright © 2007 by Elsevier Ltd.
All rights of reproduction in any form reserved
ISSN: 1871-3173/doi:10.1016/S1871-3173(06)01004-4

present their view of the world for the record (Thomson & Perks, 1983). This offers rich qualitative information for the researcher as it reflects both life history and personal experience. However, unlike other ethnographic research methods, this not only offers the possibility of direct quotation of the inter- viewee's words in the transcript but also records their speech. This paper con- siders evidence from oral history interviews with people who were influential in, and involved with, the retention and restoration of historic tourist assets.

Scientific research advocates method replication. Social science research recognizes that replication may not be realistic and duplication in human situations is unlikely. Oral historians can research the background of their topic, ensure meanings are clear, allow the development of the topic, pos- sibly revealing new information, and offer those interested the opportunity to hear their interviews, thus allowing the process to be interpreted each time it is heard. While Veal (1997, p. 141) asserts that it 'is better to read the results of the research than to read about the methodology per se,' it is a sharing of information about the method that brings validity to the study and affords others an interpretation for their context and time (Carr, 1964 cited in Aitchison, Macleod, & Shaw, 2000, p. 96). This paper considers both results and methodology, exposing problems of interpretation of meanings in oral and other recorded sources.

One such problem might be that when hearing the recording, the role of the interviewer and the partnership in the dialogue is made explicit (Portelli, 1981). The recordings usually require some form of written documentation and a number of examples can be found. Fraser wrote accompanying notes to written transcripts and called himself a 'midwife to other's history' (Fraser, 1973, p. 7), while Stewart developed a fictional narrative to bring coherence to her findings (Stewart, 1993). Wright (2001) believes he writes an 'analytical prose that moves in and out of history' and in so doing reveals much about twentieth century culture and the way that people make sense of the world (Wright, 2001, p. 487). Lacey is fully aware of 'the selection and processing by the privileged recorder' (Aitchison et al., 2000, p. 96) believing historians to produce a 'beguiling narrative' (Lacey, 2003, p. xviii) for public consumption.

The analysis of the spoken word can be augmented by another voice, music or visuals, which include adaptation and additional material. Augmentation 'enables historians to intervene directly in the generation of historical evi- dence relating to the recent past' and to gain validity from additional sources. Oral history can be informative and precise (Lummis, 1987, p. 11) and in- volves an iterative process involving an evolving and ongoing process of understanding on the researcher's behalf (Veal, 1997, p. 140) in which ideas can be 'refined and revised' (Veal, 1997, p. 131). Weinberg (2002) expresses his dissatisfaction with the criticisms of qualitative research, feeling that all research must be thought-provoking and available for discussion and challenge. He believes that researchers must consider what are the most appropriate methods and subjects for their study and justify their reasoning, scrutinizing all sources to achieve greater validity and credibility.

To attempt oral history interview analysis and develop research outcomes, some understanding is required about the nature of oral history research, its particular features and suitable applications. Texts about methodologies in tourism and leisure research may discuss interviews (e.g., Veal, 1997), but this may not constitute 'oral history' as such, rather a survey of current opinions in depth. Hammersley and Atkinson (1995) acknowledge the importance of interview data for life-history work, while Finn, Elliott-White, and Walton (2000) suggest that life history and memory work can be developed in tourism and leisure research. Neither emphasize the term 'oral history,' but this is not peculiar to tourism and leisure research and many further recent examples can be found (Schutt, 1996; Saunders, Lewis, & Thornhill, 2003; Fisher, 2004). Consequently, since oral history seems to lie in the domain of local libraries and museums, tourism and leisure researchers may not have considered its possible applications. The potential of oral history has been discussed elsewhere (Trapp-Fallon, 2003), and this paper further contends that oral history has much to offer, with 'personal testimony gaining recognition as a valuable element of contemporary historical interpretation' (Cambrook, 2004, p. 3).

This paper seeks to demonstrate that oral history work can contribute to exploratory, descriptive and explanatory studies. The paper discusses particular features of the oral history process as a recursive approach and explains that its application to the discovery of perspectives may offer new insights, as well as identifying patterns and relationships between variables. Many oral history research reports are from practitioners originating from various academic disciplines who recognize its importance. Jost Krippendorf advocates a holistic, integrated and all-embracing inter-disciplinary approach to tourism research (see Vanhove, 2003). Oral history also surpasses this by highlighting the need for researchers to make their work both transparent and accessible as a resource for others to use.

ORAL HISTORY, TOURISM AND LEISURE

Some practical examples of oral history work were developed from conversations recorded by one of the authors (JB) in Northern England, covering three areas of investigation carried out for the National Waterways Sound Recording Project of the (then) Boat Museum at Ellesmere Port. The first is the restoration of navigation on the Ashton and Peak Forest Canals between 1965 and 1974, over which participants from varied perspectives were studied. The second is the founding and founders of the Boat Museum itself, between 1972 and the 1980s.The third is the history of leisure boating on the Shropshire Union Canal, combining oral work with scattered written sources (Boughey, 2005).

Ladkin (1999) criticizes oral history approaches as weak and biased, preferring to develop a combined qualitative and quantitative approach for a work history analysis of UK hotel managers. Finn et al. (2000) point out that no research exists using life histories identified in tourism and hospitality research, and the nearest is perhaps Gmelch's (2003) study of Caribbean workers. He edited his interviews into narratives of their working lives in order to gain 'an insider's view of the work of tourism and its impact on individuals'. His aim was to fill the void identified by Crick (1989) and Stronza (2001), namely the lack of the local voice in the literature on tourism (Gmelch, 2003, p. x). Twenty narratives are divided into four sections that reflect different workplaces and settings in Caribbean tourism – airport, hotel, beach and attractions. Each introduces the setting, with the interviews edited to fit the context. The author explains that he made the transcripts 'topically coherent and interesting for readers' (Gmelch, 2003, p. 38). While this transparency could generate criticism, Gmelch's interviewees checked the narratives in agreement to his editing of their words. This indicates the ability of interviews to illustrate voices and perspectives that might otherwise be silenced or silent, and consequently lost – a consistent theme in work in oral history.

Fricke and Ahearn's (2002) work on hip-hop music features an introduction by a member of the music community and then lists all their interviewees as 'The Players'. The transcriptions of interviews are presented alongside personal observations, posters and photographs. The text follows the chronology of the decade covered in the book and divides easily into colourful sections which each include materials from the time. This recent oral history work combines the visual with the written word to evoke time, place and image, and thus has an advantage in presentation over work like Fraser's (1973), who wrote when publishing with these resources was not available. JB's work provided a somewhat primitive example, in which he recorded the comments by one participant while they watched a propaganda film about the campaign to restore the Ashton Canal.

APPROACHES TO ORAL HISTORY

Technological developments have had considerable impact on oral history research, since the advent of tape recordings in the 1940s. Portable equipment has made oral history recording much easier and less intrusive, with high sound quality enabling results to be broadcast and included in museum displays. More recent developments include the availability of voices online, with some archives enabling researchers to hear original sound recordings as well as view transcripts. One example of this achievement is The National Sound Archive and its collections, including 6,000 interviews for the Millenium Memory Bank, which include transcriptions, interview details and recordings.

Like other forms of ethnography, oral history 'places most importance on the person's own interpretations and explanations of their behaviour' and has the 'lives of ordinary people at its centre' (McNeill, 1990, pp. 86–87). While Small (1999, p. 31) suggests that by 'merely speaking the memory' without writing much detail can be lost, oral historians listen in an attempt to understand the past and to record voices so that others can also later hear and make their own interpretations. This view tends to privilege the spoken word, assuming that the spoken word is closest to true meaning. This 'phonocentrism' lays at the heart of the work of Saussure, 'who saw speech as coming first over the written word, hearing word and concept going together, the voice collapsed into the thought processes' (Crotty, 1998, p. 207). By hearing someone speak, the listener may feel nearer to the original thought and, "when we hear speech we attribute to it a 'presence' which we take to be lacking in writing" (Selden, Widdowson, & Brooker, 1996, pp. 171–172). However, writing includes elements of self-reflection and review that can be lacking in spoken accounts. JB interviewed a former boatman about Chester in the 1920s and 1930s whose unstructured spoken accounts proved very hard to follow, but whose memories proved accurate and insightful when queries were raised in a subsequent lengthy written correspondence.

Tourism and leisure research may benefit widely from the understanding of attitudes and opinions, such as those from memories of holidays, that may also shape present-day perceptions (Finn et al., 2000, p. 77). The perspectives of those working in tourism and leisure, as well as consumers, can be explored, including the involvement of enthusiasts and volunteers. The latter can provide insights into the historical evolution of enthusiasm, its legacies and influence, and thus appreciate the origins of perspectives. Lengthy discussions of a subject may enable an interviewer to open up an intimate and personal world, focusing on the meanings attached to people, events and places. This provides greater depth and richness than factual data, helping to identify and assess emotions, values, attitudes (Clark et al., 1999) and sometimes to appreciate the impact of social change.

While identification and sampling of a population might be important (Finn et al., 2000), for oral history work this can rarely be achieved, as many encounters are opportunistic (Thompson's (1992) early work for *The Edwardians* provides an exception). Themes and categories can nevertheless be derived from the individuals that may have a wider significance within the larger population. Examples of this have been gained from JB's interviews with early pleasure boaters on British lowland canals. Here, boaters' experiences of exploration were linked to their involvements in campaigns for retention that often led to much personal inconvenience and boat damage. This appeared to be linked both to the politics of waterways revival (for tourism as well as transport use) and to a certain resistance to particular modernist lifestyles (underlying, perhaps, at least some of the later concern for 'heritage'), although many variations in feelings and approaches were developed. The subjective experience thus discovered has resonances in Samuel and Thompson's view of oral history:

> As soon as we recognize the value of the subjective in individual testimonies, we challenge the accepted categories of history. We introduce the emotionality, the fears and fantasies carried by the metaphors of memory, which historians have been so anxious to write out of their formal accounts. And at the same time the individuality of each life story ceases to be an awkward impediment to generalization, and becomes instead a vital document of the construction of consciousness, emphasizing both the variety of experience in any social group, and also how each individual story draws upon a common culture … . (Samuel & Thompson, 1990, p. 2)

Oral history can thus link an individual account to broader forces, without invalidating individual experiences or rendering those experiences entirely idiosyncratic.

Thompson (1988) stresses the limitation of the written sources upon which many historians rely, and many areas of tourism and leisure have been relatively undocumented, both over factual detail and over motives and meanings. Thus, JB interviewed the sons of two early 1930s operators of self-drive hire boats and a trip boat (their fathers had died in 1956 and 1964). It emerged that these began operations both as a minor business speculation and as a means of supporting their own leisure boating and a coach trip business. While the precise meanings of these small-scale operations to their founders were unclear, their sons were able to explain some details about boats and operations and to suggest motives.

Research texts may suggest the use of in-depth interviews when there are few informants available and also as a preliminary to further quantitative or qualitative research. Many oral history questions involve data and observations that can be obtained far more fruitfully than by a simple questionnaire. Expectations about the length, purpose and conduct of an interview may need to be clearly established, with agreement and understanding over its objectives. This emphasizes the relative degree of control held, in what can be a relationship of uncertain power. Taking an oral history approach therefore allows the process to be open and reflexive, acknowledging that the interview may develop in an unforeseen way, revealing previously unexpected information, social and interpersonal connections and meanings. Oral history may involve multiple interviews over many hours, with much time for interim reflection by interviewer and interviewees.

Interviewers often develop long conversations with their respondents, with risks that they may lead responses, suggest answers and invite agreement or disagreement. If a friendly conversational atmosphere cannot be developed without influencing the interviewee's responses, a recorded dialogue may need to be consciously pursued. An example of the latter lay in interviews with two longstanding campaigners for waterways revival, a subject over which JB had already published strong views (Boughey, 1998). The recordings thus involved long and sometimes heated conversations in which one campaigner, in particular, argued about many of JB's published explanations of events and personalities; this enabled clarification of this respondent's perspectives and subsequent reflections.

By encouraging conversation, an oral history interview may be informal and non-directive, with no predetermined list of questions. If the interviewee has the opportunity to speak freely about events, behaviour and beliefs, he or she may be able to continue speaking without interruption. Unanticipated lines of enquiry or explanation may emerge, with a delicate balance between some direction of the conversation and the need for the interviewee to tell their own story, whether this is a personal life history or is representative of others. This introduces questions of ownership, of memories and recorded history, that may invoke resistance to some elements of disclosure; this sense of ownership may be linked to feelings about museums, or revived, restored or retained waterways or railways. Indeed, in such cases, an interview may partly centre around attempts to claim credit, to stress the importance of past involvement and past roles and to contest present-day meanings. As with interviews conducted in the public domain – police, media or employment – oral history interviews can often become an exercise in persuasion.

The reflexivity of the process has advantages for research, as by exploring the ways of expressing ideas and words used, more meaning may be revealed. The interviewee has opportunities to express their own thoughts and perspectives, often over areas that have never or rarely been the subject of reflection, and this may foster fruitful discussions that provides rich data for research and ideas that may provoke further research. If oral history interviews are conducted carefully, with questions and their purpose made clear, the flexible and responsive interaction allows meanings to be clarified, while topics can be covered from a variety of angles (Saunders et al., 2003, p. 253).

Some people are more likely to agree to be interviewed than to complete a questionnaire (Saunders et al., 2003), while interviewees whose background is in management often prefer feedback and some assurances as to how their observations might be used. Credibility is usually enhanced if themes are identified and discussed before the interview, and the ability of both the interviewee and interviewer to prepare with prior research, whether documentary investigation or reflective recollection, enhances the validity of the discussion. Saunders et al. (2003) testify to the preparation allowing for triangulation – the checking of spoken data against alternative sources. JB's interviews with retired waterways engineers indicated this concern for cross-checking, of amplifying records that could be partly verified from documentary sources, and the engineers' wish both for publication and for the use of their accounts without distortion. JB's published accounts of inland waterways in the 1960s supplied unexpected observations. The engineers agreed with much of his interpretation, and thus his credibility as a researcher, but volunteered that the account had over-stressed the role of two named individuals whose involvement, they felt, had been insignificant.

Research and Interpretations

Oral history and a flexible inductive approach cannot aim to achieve the replication of research findings. The rationale for the research should be fully recorded so that other researchers can understand the processes and be enabled to reuse, and perhaps reinterpret the data collected. Research may not be repeatable because it is specific to a time and a place and the recognition that many topics are complex and dynamic. Any attempt to ensure that the research could be repeated might indeed undermine the whole process and fail to recognize the role of the researcher in the process. The nature of the researcher, their individual biases and interaction with the interviewee, should also be acknowledged; different researchers might yield very different outcomes. This might generate distrust and the need to approach a previously quoted source with a different stated agenda and aims.

Oral historians need to listen carefully to the recorded words and to consider any inferences, as well as to follow up any possible lines of enquiry generated during the interview. By their very nature interviews are inductive, presenting opportunities to interpret information, to achieve greater understanding and possibly to formulate explanation and theory. To help this process Veal suggests that the initial terms of reference and conceptual framework will help to sort and evaluate the information gathered in relation 'to the questions posed and the concepts identified' (Veal, 1997, p. 135).

While much of oral history study concerns the processes involved, other needs can also be evoked and perhaps met by encouraging participants to speak. Walle (2003) discusses the strategic use of oral history, using oral history/folklore to encourage a wider level of participation in an event and gather useful first-hand information about fish and fishing in Pennsylvania. His success in achieving his aims suggests a considerable fit between what he describes as the vernacular and the seriousness in cultural events (Walle, 2003, p. 81). This corresponds, in part, to JB's researches into the origins and perspectives behind the founding and early development of the Boat Museum at Ellesmere Port. This drew on a community, not of people local to Ellesmere Port, but of those interested in preserving artefacts and elements of inland waterways transport. These participants themselves drew upon memories and investigations of people associated with boats and traffics. In one sense the continuation of the Museum, despite commercial pressures, represents an attempt to reproduce and transmit elements of a culture whose participants have largely disappeared. Oral history provides one way of linking with, and preserving memories and lineages of, that lost culture. This can stretch to the sense of authenticity, that those who witnessed an earlier period have themselves witnessed those who have recorded them. Investigations here aimed to discern the values of people who sought through the Museum to reflect the lives of boatpeople, alongside surviving examples of their craft, so that the interpretation of the Museum itself and the authenticity of its displays could be assessed.

Ladkin (1999, p. 38) has suggested some positive attributes of life histories, which can be related to the results of oral history interviews. It is suggested that the past as recalled aids understanding of the present; thus, JF's work in South Wales revealed the reasons for some disillusionment with campaigning groups which was not documented in the literature. In particular, the interpretation of historic environments on display for tourism (or a background to it) reflects past values and views of those environments, and their transmission through conservation and display. In both authors' investigations of restoration campaigns, the social networks of those involved were revealed by interviews, along with ways in which these had been modified over the years. The views of those involved in voluntary work suggested why there was a lack of commitment towards restoration among young people today; one reason for non-participation could be the very attitudes disclosed in the interviews. This could be contrasted with the interviews with people who were youthful when the Ashton campaign was under way, and their motives then and in retrospect. These issues relate both to the past and provide indications of the future.

Some Limitations

The view that the interview process will result in a purer truth than other sources may be countered by problems related to the interview process itself, its recording and interpretation.

As outlined above, in a sense, an oral history interview is very like a job interview or giving evidence in court – and it can prove to be a selective exercise in persuasion. Interviewees may avoid the truth, may invent when their lack of knowledge is exposed by the interview process, and may be more positive than researchers believe them to be in reality.

Sensitivity may well become an issue in the conduct of the interview, and the interviewee may choose not to reveal or discuss a topic. Sometimes this sensitivity concerns matters that were secret, such as doubt about whether a waterway could have been retained, or private yet significant details about individuals; one of the latter resulted in the interviewee insisting upon a 50-year embargo on his comments. In other cases, employment had involved confidentiality, and to breach this after retirement, as with the waterways engineers, could affect friendships with those still in post or fellow retirees. Selectivity thus produces a limited perspective and often one that is partial. Memories may also spark painful elements in reminiscence, and the processes involved in the evoking of memories – of approaching recall though today's meaning and narrative – may render those memories factually suspect. Indeed, 'memories' may reproduce myths, as in what is believed rather than what can be verified (Thompson, 1988). A part mythology in the inland waterways revival was a belief in the omnipotence of certain charismatic individuals, and interviews revealed that these views sometimes persist.

The time-consuming elements of the interview may well limit the respondents' care in their answers. JB's work suggested that interviewees sought to end the conversation just as the most interesting points were being raised, as the early part of conversations were partly involved in establishing credentials and gaining confidence. At all times the researcher was the guest, and one solution was to arrange a further session.

While interviewers' preparation and readiness for the interview helps overcome bias, this may clash with the need to preserve an open mind, and may seem to disadvantage the researcher. A well-informed interviewer has credibility and a basis for assessing the accuracy of the information offered, but this may prove daunting to an interviewee from a different background, who may perceive a challenge to the validity of their memories and judgements. However, sometimes a lack of background may make it hard to follow what the interviewee is saying, and to probe deeper with useful questions. The sheer quantity of background documentary research should be stressed; the oral history route is rarely the cheapest in time or financial resources.

The process of transcription presents many problems for practical applications of oral history work. The lack of verbatim transcription highlights the need to hear the voice and reminds us that the recording itself is the primary document. This may be illustrated by a transcription from the Museum of Welsh Life, Cardiff (one typical of South Wales archives):

> She used to ride the shire horses bare back when they brought goods from bakery and mineral water well on their property. Did bakery and mineral water and soft drinks rounds. Old floats built in Pontypridd by father-in-law. Before buses, people walked or caught trains. Canals used for trips as well as cargo. Mr Morris aged 73 also included. Barges carried clay from Cornwall for Nantgarw China Works and steel for Dowlais. Mrs Morris' father started engineering and bus making company after World War 1. Called Imperial Motor Company, biggest in South Wales. Had 13 six wheelers. Name changed in 1936/7 when Red and White Company took over and father became a director. Buses had to clock in about every five miles.

This transcript features many limitations. It is unclear, for instance, whether 'floats' were special canal craft or road vehicles, or whether 'trips' on the canal were regular passenger carrying or special excursions. The ratio of transcribing time to recorded time is always high, and this may well be the reason why the above transcription is so short. Transcription may include careful editing (although this will have to be sensitive) to improve presentation and flow, and may also involve checking and amplification by the interviewee (Frisch, 1990). Some transcripts can, however, be used to analyse the results of interviews in a more methodical and complete manner than is possible with notes.

Perks and Thomson (1998) believe that the problem at the heart of oral history is the transition between the individual account and the social interpretation. The interviewer must attempt to distinguish between the 'authentic' voice, and the one that the interviewee believes to be the one that wants to be heard (Hammersley & Atkinson, 1995). The audio recording does not provide a perfect and comprehensive record (Hammersley & Atkinson, 1995, p. 187). Non-verbal behaviour is not captured and audio recordings do not remove the need for observation and field notes.

Results and Strengths

Oral history provides a significant element in research into the history of tourism and leisure, which is often poorly documented. Thus, while there were scattered fragments towards a history of early pleasure boating on the Shropshire Union Canal, it was oral history interviews, many of which were opportunistic, that provided many critical details (Boughey, 2005). Especially where there was voluntary input, or detailed political campaigning, written sources may provide only a limited, albeit crucial element. Thus, the Ashton Canal restoration was the subject of Ministry of Transport files, which reveal just how precarious was the future of many of Britain's inland waterways in the 1960s, and the very poor case for the Ashton Canal in this context (Boughey, 1998). However, interviews were able to reveal how the principal waterways engineer involved in the restoration was initially extremely sceptical, became supportive of the restoration, organized the engineering work involved, and damaged his own health in the process. However, confidentiality prevented many of his observations being formally recorded.

The Ashton investigations also revealed the multi-layered nature of the restoration campaign. Varied perspectives emerged, from the official engineers who took formal responsibility, to the youthful enthusiasts who organized working parties, and the 'suits' (all now deceased) who used their local contacts to develop local authority support for the restoration. Finally, one former local councilor, who was extensively recorded, had dealt with all sides and acted as intermediary. The grain of these interactions could not be captured through written sources. However, the best oral histories are often rooted in extensive documentary research. In the Ashton Canals case, the extensive records of the restoration society (Peak Forest Canal Society), including committee minutes, had been deposited and were perused and analysed at considerable length before interviews were conducted.

Investigations that are based solely on interviews may succeed in recording impressions, but may fail to capture some of the history involved, especially the broader context of historical detail.

The Ashton study indicates the relevance of oral history to contemporary research into tourism and leisure practices. Many practices in tourism and leisure rely on voluntary or community involvement. The multiple interpretations of community involvement, which the Ashton case illustrated, must be stressed. Any assumption that there is a single direction and purpose to in voluntary involvement, or that such involvement is always conflict-free, are dashed by studies of actual involvement, especially when oral history interviews enable discussions after a safe period of time has elapsed. Similar comments apply to the development of museums and their attempts to ensure a measure of authenticity in what they seek to explain. JB's study of the founders of the Boat Museum in the 1970s indicates some variations in the apparent consensus in the 1970s, and a considerable difference between any consensus and the later commercially oriented visitor attraction that it has become. The oral history work has helped to set in context the values of the founders, and has enabled these to be examined and either evoked or challenged. Again, the origins of conflicts between present-day stakeholders in the Boat Museum, some voluntary, some representing 'communities' of sorts, can be discerned and stressed through oral history study.

This view leads to a final role for oral history, in the potential restoration of historical validation to those people who helped to make history (Thompson, 1988). The ownership of oral history could help to develop a degree of confidence in, and ownership of, their own history. One possible consequence could be renewed confidence in their own involvement in present and future developments in leisure provision. Oral history could provide one spur in movements that seek to defeat the passivity of consumerism and to take back the production and control of tourist and leisure assets – whether or not these are assets which themselves reflect history, like museums and historic canals. This might lead to co-option, to partnership, or a transfer of control and ownership – in effect, creating a new history for future historians to consider.

CONCLUSION

By discussing some practical problems and potentialities involved, oral history work informs tourism and leisure researchers. If a deeper understanding is sought of why events in tourism and leisure occurred, how decisions were made and how events unfolded, then the inductive approach offered by oral histories can be very appropriate. By choosing to use oral history methods, the researcher has the opportunity to gain exciting and rounded evidence, but this evidence may be challenging and cannot stand alone (Lummis, 1987). Oral historians in tourism and leisure should follow Elton's (1974) advice and consider that they are dealing with reality. The study of tourism and leisure can be enhanced by oral history research, not just to explain the past but to illuminate some aspects of the future.

REFERENCES

Aitchison, C., Macleod, N. E., & Shaw, S. J. (2000). *Leisure and tourism landscapes social and cultural geographies*. London: Routledge.

Boughey, J. (1998). *Charles Hadfield: Canal man and more*. Stroud: Sutton Publishing.

Boughey, J. (2005). Early pleasure boating on the Shropshire Union Canal. *Waterways Journal*, 7, 53–71.

Cambrook, F. (2004). News Page, Future Meetings. *Oral History*, *32*(spring), 3.

Carr, E. H. (1964). *What is history?* Penguin: Harmondsworth.

Clark, M., Riley, M., Wilkie, E., & Wood, R. C. (1999). *Researching and writing dissertations in hospitality and tourism*. Oxford: Thebalden Press.

Crick, M. (1989). Representations of international tourism in the social sciences; sun, sex, sights, savings and servility. *Annual Review of Anthropology*, *18*, 307–344.

Crotty, M. (1998). *The foundations of social research: Meaning and perspective in the research process*. London: Sage.

Elton, G. R. (1974). *The practice of history 5th impression*. Glasgow: Collins.

Finn, M., Elliott-White, M., & Walton, M. (2000). *Tourism and leisure research methods data collection, analysis and interpretation*. Harlow, Essex: Pearson Education.

Fisher, C. (2004). *Researching and writing a dissertation for business students*. Harlow, Essex: FT Prentice-Hall.

Fraser, R. (1973). *The pueblo: A mountain village on the Costa del Sol*. London: Allen Lane.

Fricke, J., & Ahearn, C. (2002). *Yes,yes,y'all. Oral history of hip-hop's first decade*. Cambridge, USA: Da Capo Books.

Frisch, M. (1990). *Shared authority: Essays on the craft and meaning of oral and public history*. New York: State University Press.

Gmelch, G. (2003). *Behind the smile: The working lives of Caribbean tourism*. Bloomington and Indianapolis: Indiana University Press.

Hammersley, M., & Atkinson, P. (1995). *Ethnography principles and practice* (2nd ed.). London: Routledge.

Lacey (2003). *Great tales from English history cheddar man to the peasant's revolt*. London: Little Brown.

Ladkin, A. (1999). Life and work history analysis: The value of this research method for hospitality and tourism. *Tourism Management*, *20*, 37–45.

Lummis, T. (1987). *Listening to history: The authenticity of oral evidence*. London: Hutchinson.

McNeill, P. (1990). *Research methods* (2nd ed.). London: Routledge.

Perks, R., & Thomson, A. (Eds) (1998). *The oral history reader*. London: Routledge.

Portelli, A. (1981). The peculiarities of oral history. *History Workshop Journal, 12*, 96–107.

Samuel, R., & Thompson, P. (Eds) (1990). *The myths we live by*. London: Routledge.

Saunders, M., Lewis, P., & Thornhill, A. (2003). *Research methods for business students* (3rd ed.). Harlow, Essex: Pearson Education.

Schutt, R. K. (1996). *Investigating the social world: The process and practice of research*. California: Pine Forge Press.

Selden, R., Widdowson, P., & Brooker, P. (1996). *A readers guide to contemporary literary theory*. Herts: Harvester Wheatsheaf.

Small, J. (1999). Memory-work: A method for researching women's tourist experiences. *Tourism Management, 20*, 25–35.

Stewart, S. (1993). *Ramlin Rose: The boatwoman's story*. Oxford: Oxford University Press.

Stronza, A. (2001). Anthropology of tourism: Forging new ground for eco-tourism and other alternatives. *Annual Review of Anthropology, 30*, 261–283.

Thompson, P. (1988). *The voice of the past: Oral history* (2nd ed.). Oxford: Oxford University Press.

Thompson, P. (1992). *The Edwardians: The remaking of British society* (2nd ed.). London: Routledge.

Thomson, P., & Perks, R. (1983). *Telling it how it was: A guide to recording oral history*. London: BBC Education.

Trapp- Fallon, J. (2003). Searching for rich narratives of tourism and leisure experience: How oral history could provide an answer. *Tourism and Hospitality Research: The Surrey Quarterly Review, 4*(4), 297–306.

Vanhove, N. (2003). Obituary of Jost Krippendorf. *Tourism and Hospitality Research: The Surrey Quarterly Review, 4*(4), 381–382.

Veal, A. J. (1997). *Research methods for leisure and tourism a practical guide* (2nd ed.). London: Pearson.

Walle, A. H. (2003). Building a diverse attendance at cultural festivals: Embracing oral history/ folklore in strategic ways. *Event management, 8*, 73–82.

Weinberg, D. (Ed.) (2002). *Qualitative research methods*. Oxford: Blackwell.

Wright, P. (2001). The last days of London. In: I. Borden, J. Kerr, J. Rendell & A. Pivaro (Eds), *The unknown city contesting architecture and social space* (Chapter 29). Cambridge, MA: Massachusetts Institute of Technology.

CHAPTER 5

ACCEPTED STANDARDS UNDERMINING THE VALIDITY OF TOURISM RESEARCH ☆

Sara Dolnicar

ABSTRACT

This paper draws attention to accepted measurement and research method standards in empirical research on tourism. Some standards stand out because they are superior to alternative approaches. However, many have emerged because the measurements and methods used in prior work were assumed to be optimal (or at least valid) for solving particular problems. Unfortunately this assumption is inaccurate. Yet, the reviewing process favors the use of such standards (often without demanding evidence) over the introduction of novel approaches, even if these are justified.

This paper focuses on three accepted standards in empirical tourism research which have the potential to undermine the validity of findings: the uncritical use of ordinal multi-category answer formats, the derivation of cross-cultural comparisons that do not consider cultural response biases resulting from response styles, and the standard step-wise procedure used in data-driven market segmentation. This paper describes the potential dangers of these standard approaches and makes recommendations for researchers to consider before choosing to adopt any of the above approaches.

☆ This research was supported by the Australian Research Council (through grants DP0557257 and LX0559628).

Advances in Culture, Tourism and Hospitality Research, Volume 1, 131–181
ISSN: 1871-3173/doi:10.1016/S1871-3173(06)01005-6

1. INTRODUCTION

Much research accepts the approaches and techniques used and published in the past as established, valid procedures. The practice of citing several authors of prior studies (the more the better) who use a certain approach or technique, instead of explaining the reason for choosing this procedure and justifying why it is the best solution for the problem is a dominating logic in the research community. This insight is not new. Thomas Kuhn (1970, p. 6) refers to this phenomenon as the 'tradition-bound activity of normal science' and defines 'scientific revolutions' as 'tradition-shattering complements' that move science forward.

The practice of uncritically following other authors' approaches (or in a seemingly uncritical manner) is prevalent in tourism research. Although not uncommon in other area of research, it is nevertheless undesirable, and has several effects that contradict the fundamental principles of scientific research, by (1) tolerating the uncritical use of approaches and techniques; (2) not providing incentives to introduce new approaches and techniques; and (3) discouraging the use of new approaches. Authors who introduce new approaches must justify their deviation from the norm in the most rigorous fashion, whereas uncritical acceptance of the current standard does not require extensive explanation in the reviewing process.

In the increasingly competitive research market, a new researcher who needs to build their CV and rationally analyzes how the acceptance rate of their publications can be maximized is likely to conclude that (1) they can spend significantly less effort to conduct a study if they follow the established standards in a field of research because no justification will be required for the choice of method, measurement technique, or data analytic approach; and (2) using the established standard is much safer because the risk of rejection will be significantly lower. In sum, uncritically following the approaches taken by authors in the past, and reviewers' willingness to accept citations (rather than justifications) as reasons for adopting a particular approach lead to stagnation, rather than development and innovation of a field of research – in this case empirical tourism research.

This paper describes three common aspects of empirical tourism research that lead to the development of emerging standards: the uncritical use of ordinal multi-category answer formats in data collection, cross-cultural comparisons ignoring response style bias, and the use of a particular stepwise procedure in data-driven market segmentation. For each of these three aspects: (1) a review of the discussion in the broader scientific community is presented; (2) hypotheses are formulated about the precise nature of the respective accepted standard within tourism research; (3) empirical evidence is provided to support or reject these hypotheses; (4) potential dangers resulting from the uncritical use of outlined standard approaches are discussed; and (5) a series of questions or aspects is provided, which may be helpful to empirical tourism researchers in deciding whether or not to adopt these standard approaches in their future studies.

2. ANSWER FORMATS

In empirical social sciences where the responses of subjects to the researcher's questions form the basis of theoretical (or practical) insight, the *question* is the scientist's measurement instrument. Where an atmospheric chemist uses a thermometer or a barometer, the social scientist uses a question. An atmospheric chemist would never consider using an uncalibrated or untested thermometer or barometer to measure temperature or air pressure. The same should be true for an empirical social scientist. The question asked is the main measurement instrument, and it has to be carefully chosen or developed to ensure that it reliably measures what it is supposed to measure.

How to best ask questions to get valid results is therefore an issue of interdisciplinary interest, and is of fundamental importance to any research field in which the collection of primary data are required to investigate a research question. The importance of question formulation has been acknowledged by social scientists in many areas since the early 19th century. Consequently, a vast body of literature exists in psychology, sociology, psychometrics, and marketing, which investigates the effects of various aspects of questionnaire design on the validity of results. Some researchers go as far as to question whether survey responses can at all be viewed as valid measurements. Feldman and Lynch (1988, p.431), for instance, "show how observed correlations among beliefs, attitudes, intentions and behaviours may be affected by the process of measurements." The underlying argument is that respondents frequently do not have cognitions, which are easily accessible to answer a question. Instead, they compute or create them in response to questions. Such a computation process is strongly influenced by the order, context and wording of the question in the survey. Earlier responses will have an influence on how later questions will be answered. Feldman and Lynch's study demonstrates clearly that the validity of measurement in the social sciences is by no means a given. Instead a significant amount of effort in pre-analysis of questions for specific populations is needed to minimize the self-validation and other detrimental effects on the validity of survey findings.

The present study, however, focuses on only one area of questionnaire design: alternative response formats. The typical aim of prior studies into the effects of alternative response formats has been to determine which response format is optimal, where optimality is defined differently, depending on the study. The terms 'answer format' and 'response format' are used interchangeably here, and are understood to mean the format in which respondents are requested to answer questions. A large number of different answer formats have been proposed in the past; most of them can, however, be classified as nominal, binary ordinal, or metric in nature. An example of each of those response formats is provided in Fig. 1.

Within each of the four broad categories several different response formats exist, and these differ in subtle but very important ways. For example, a binary scale can force people either to commit to answering either 'yes' or 'no' (full binary scale). Alternatively, respondents might be asked only to tick the 'yes' box if they agree with a statement (affirmative binary scale). An example of an affirmative binary scale case is the question, 'Which of the following European cities do you perceive as expensive?', followed by a list of European cities, where respondents are asked to tick all cities they intend to visit. This is the typical format (referred to also as pick-any data) that is widely used in brand image measurement, where respondents are asked to tick how they perceive several brands (or destinations) with regard to several attributes. The full binary scale allows the researcher to interpret a 'yes' answer as meaning that a respondent perceives Paris as expensive, and a 'no'

NOMINAL   Which is your country of residence?
                                ☐   Austria
                                ☐   USA
                                ☐   Australia
BINARY   Do you think Paris is expensive?
                                ☐   Yes
                                ☐   No
ORDINAL   Did you perceive public transportation in Paris as
                                ☐   Very reliable
                                ☐   Reliable
                                ☐   Unreliable
                                ☐   Very unreliable
METRIC   How many days will you spend in Paris during this trip?........

Fig. 1. Examples of Answer Formats.

answer as meaning the respondent does not perceive Paris as expensive. Another option, 'I have never heard of Paris,' could be added to ensure that no irrelevant judgments are recorded. In the case of the binary affirmative scale, the 'yes' option can be interpreted as meaning that the respondent perceives Paris as expensive. However, if the respondent does not tick 'yes,' it is unclear what they are expressing. No answer could mean 'I have never heard of Paris,' a state which could again be included as an answer option in order to exclude irrelevant answers. But it could also capture people who do not want to make a choice, are tired at the end of a long questionnaire or cannot be bothered thinking about another question.

Both alternatives are useful in different contexts. In the brand image measurement context the binary affirmative scale is typically used, presumably because it is not essential to know precisely what the respondent's perception is, if it is not 'Paris is expensive.' For other research questions, however, it is essential that the respondent commits to one response. A recent study into alternative water sources (Dolnicar & Schäfer, 2006) is a good example. One aim of this study was to assess the level of knowledge the Australian population had about recycled water and desalinated water. Given the relatively low level of knowledge, pre-tests using the affirmative binary answer format showed that respondents who were unsure about whether, for example, recycled water was purified sewage, simply did not respond. The result was a data set that contained very few responses that answered the research questions regarding the population's knowledge level about these water sources, or which aspects the population was well- or ill-informed about and therefore required information campaigns.

The selection of the kind of response formats, such as affirmative binary versus full binary, can lead to major variations in results, among other factors. Even within one response format option, the wording of the question can lead to dramatic variations in results. For example, different responses can be elicited from a question worded, 'Do you think Paris is expensive?' compared to 'Do you think Paris is very expensive?'.

This example illustrates two important effects. First, small modifications in response format can have major impacts on the data obtained, and consequently on the results. These effects may make it impossible to answer the very research question they were developed to investigate, as illustrated by the alternative water sources study. Second, there is no single best option for all problems. Each research question requires the social scientist to investigate alternative answer formats, evaluate their advantages and disadvantages and choose the most valid measurement instrument for the problem and the sample under study.

The above example was based on questions requiring binary answers, arguably the simplest possible response format. The complexity of potential response format side-effects increases further when a multi-category ordinal response is required from respondents.

The methodological dangers of both ordinal and binary scales have been extensively discussed by Scharf (1991), and Kampen and Swyngedouw (2000). Kampen and Swyngedouw (2000) classify most of the ordinal variables used in tourism research, such as items capturing agreement levels with statements or satisfaction levels with service components, as 'unstandardized discrete variables with ordered categories,' and state that this is the most undesirable of all ordinal options. As opposed to categories of income or age, there is no underlying objective measure that is simply divided using known threshold values.

On the contrary, different scale points (for example, 'slightly agree' or 'quite satisfied') are likely to mean different things to different respondents, which makes interpretation extremely difficult. Also, equidistance is not assured. The distances between scale points are likely to be unequal, and could be perceived as different by different respondents. The results will not necessarily be invalid, but they could be. If ordinal data are used, it is safer to use data analytic methods that have been developed for this scale level. For example, computing a mean value on a five-point ordinal response format does not produce valuable insights, because the result cannot be interpreted unambiguously – what exactly does an average of 3.7 mean, if 3 is 'moderately satisfied' and 4 is 'very satisfied?' The widely spread treatment of data resulting from multi-category ordinal response formats as being interval-level data are very common. The typical justification is that Likert scale data can be assumed to be interval scaled. This was certainly not intended by Likert (1932), who claimed metric properties only for the summated scale, not the single items.

Billiet and McClendon (2000), McClendon (1991), and Watson (1992) draw attention to another problem inherent in Likert scales: the susceptibility to acquiescence or yea-saying bias, or, more generally, response styles. This aspect will be discussed in detail in the section on cross-cultural response styles.

A further difficulty is that multi-category ordinal scales lead to different responses independent of the number of answer categories offered to the respondents. The decision whether to use three, five, seven, or nine points in the answer format affects the results. The effect of the choice of answer format is clearly a methodological artifact, and should not be interpreted as content.

The quality of ordinal scales strongly depends on the rigor of operationalization of the construct under study, the extent to which the validity of the chosen response format for the research question has been studied, and the calibration to mean the same to all respondents. If the construct is not well defined, and leaves a lot of space for interpretational differences, ordinal scales are not a very precise measurement instrument, and results remain ambiguous. The main dangers are that ordinal answer formats typically used in tourism research: (1) are not operationalized well (what does it mean to a hotel manager that a tourist slightly agrees that having a swimming pool is important? Should the hotel manager build the pool?); (2) do not offer answer options that mean the same thing to all respondents ('moderately satisfied' does not mean the same thing to all hotel guests); (3) capture both individual and cross-cultural response styles to a higher extent than alternative answer formats, as will be discussed in detail later; (4) do not have equal intervals between answer options (the difference between 'very satisfied' and 'moderately satisfied' is not necessarily the same as the difference between 'very dissatisfied' and 'moderately dissatisfied'); and (5) typically have not been tested for validity for the research problem at hand.

Despite the above insecurities involved in using multi-category ordinal scales, such response formats (particularly specific answer formats within that group, such as the Likert scale (Likert, 1932)) have become the 'industry standard' in empirical tourism research as well as other fields, such as marketing.

While (to the author's knowledge) theoretical comparisons of the difficulties and insecurities related to each of the alternative answer formats are rare (some have been discussed above), a large number of empirical studies have been conducted in the past comparing binary with ordinal response formats. The aim of these studies was to determine which of the two generally is the better response format in the social sciences. Although, as previously mentioned, the author does not hold to the notion that a generally better scale can be found, the findings of these studies are briefly reviewed below, with different streams of prior work using different criteria for 'better' or 'optimal.'

Several authors define optimality as 'reliability' and compare results from different scales according to how reliable they are. Interestingly, the majority of this type of work concludes that the number of response options given to respondents does not influence reliability (Bendig, 1954; Peabody, 1962; Komorita, 1963; Komorita & Graham, 1965; Matell & Jacoby, 1971; Jacoby & Matell, 1971; Remington, Tyrer, Newson-Smith, & Cicchetti, 1979; Preston & Colman, 2000). More recently, Rungie et al. (2005) demonstrate reliability issues in the context of brand image measurement using affirmative binary scales, and hypothesize that ordinal multi-category measurement would lead to similar levels of unreliability. However, several studies conclude that an association between reliability and response options exists (Symonds, 1924; Nunnally, 1967; Oaster, 1989; Finn, 1972; Ramsay, 1973).

A similar variety of conclusions emerge when validity is used as a criterion of optimality of an answer format. Jacoby and Matell (1971), Chang (1994), and Preston and Colman (2000) conclude that response options and validity of findings are not related. Contrarily, the results obtained by Loken, Pirie, Virnig, Hinkle, and Salmon (1987), and Hancock and Klockars (1991) indicate that a larger number of options (for example, using a seven-point scale instead of a five-point scale) increases validity.

A third stream of research into the effects of response options uses factor analysis results to compare whether different scale formats result in different interpretations, thus using structural equivalence as the criterion for the quality of a response format. Martin, Fruchter, and Mathis (1974), Percy (1976), Green and Rao (1970), and Dolnicar, Grün, and Leisch (2004) chose this research approach. Green and Rao conclude that at least six answer options should be included, whereas Martin et al., Percy, and Dolnicar et al. found no significant differences in the factor results.

Finally, a few authors have investigated the perspective of consumer friendliness of surveys. Jones (1968) and Preston and Colman (2000) conclude that respondents prefer to have more options, and also found that this reduced perceived speed. Dolnicar (2003) and Dolnicar et al. (2004) conclude that ordinal scales are perceived as significantly more difficult to answer and take significantly more time to complete.

As illustrated, prior studies comparing response formats lead to quite different conclusions: a frequency count of recommendations across response option studies would lead the scientific community to believe that seven-point scales are the optimal choice (Cox, 1980). The popularity of such multi-category ordinal response formats in the social sciences has been noted by Peterson (1997), Van der Eijk (2001), and Dolnicar (2002). This supports the notion that response format decisions are not able to be generalized: depending on the research questions, the construct under study, and the nature of the sample, different response formats will be appropriate or inappropriate, will produce very valid, moderately valid, or invalid results. However, the acceptance of an emerged standard is potentially a very dangerous decision that can – in the worst case – lead to invalid results or the inability to even answer the research question.

2.1. Are we 'following the recommendation of...' in Our Choice of Answer Formats?

Often we cannot assess whether an author has uncritically chosen a particular scale, or whether they have invested considerable time and effort in their decision. Typically, information allowing us to make this judgment is not available in manuscripts. We cannot therefore empirically evaluate the extent to which emerged standards are accepted uncritically, or compare the proportion of studies that are based on a thorough analysis of the response format before fieldwork is conducted. Consequently, testing the level of validity of conclusions drawn in published empirical tourism research. If in doubt, we should assume that the authors have thoroughly evaluated their response format. The empirical illustration here cannot aim to state the proportion of uncritical use of response formats or the proportion of findings with questionable validity. It can, however, analyze the proportion of studies that are prone to the abovementioned problems due to the use of accepted standards without explanation and discuss their potential dangers, or look at how these potential dangers have been addressed. The inability to test for critical use and validity of findings thus limits the empirical investigation to the following three hypotheses derived from the insights from prior research as reviewed above:

H1.1. Empirical tourism researchers predominantly (in more than 80 percent of studies) use multi-category ordinal scales.

H1.2. The majority of empirical tourism researchers (more than 50 percent) do not provide reasons for their choice in the manuscript.

H1.3. The majority of empirical tourism researchers (more than 50 percent) do not point out the dangers or insecurities associated with their choice in the manuscript.

H1.4. The majority of empirical tourism researchers (more than 50 percent) use data analytic techniques, which are not suitable for the response format used.

The method selected to investigate the research aims of this study is a literature review of academic tourism research published in 2005 in three of the main journals that publish empirical social sciences[1] research: the *Journal of Travel Research, Annals of Tourism Research*, and *Tourism Management*. All articles published in 2005 were screened and classified as being either empirical or non-empirical in nature. In order to be classified as empirical for the purpose of this review, disaggregate data had to form the basis of the investigation, and the subjects under study had to be tourists.

Sixty-five studies published in the three outlets in 2005 were classified as empirical and included in the review. Each study was reviewed in detail and coded with seven variables relevant to hypotheses H1.1 to H1.4: (1) the answer format used, following the classification illustrated in Fig. 1; (2) the specific answer format, such as 'Likert scale,' if mentioned; (3) whether someone else's work was cited to justify the use of the used response format; (4) whether an explanation was provided as to why the chosen response format was deemed the best choice for the research question at hand; (5) whether the dangers associated with this response format were discussed; (6) which method was used to analyze the data; and (7) whether raw data or a summated scale value was used for data analysis.

Coding was undertaken separately for each of the constructs investigated in each of the published studies, and descriptive statistics were computed to test hypotheses H1 to H4.

The results are provided in Table 1. Citations of prior work were used in 17 percent of the studies, which at first appears to indicate that researchers may not be following emerged standards at all with regard to answer formats. However, only five percent of the authors provided an explanation of why they chose the answer format. An even lower proportion (three percent) discussed potential dangers of the answer formats used.

With respect to which answer formats were actually used, the high proportion of studies using multi-category ordinal scales assumed in hypothesis H1.1 was actually surpassed, with 88 percent of all studies using ordinal scales (either ordinal only or in combination with other scales). Only two studies explicitly stated the nature of the scale as being nominal, binary, ordinal, or metric. Mostly the authors showed scale but did not discuss its mathematical properties and implications.

The main methods of data analysis were factor analysis (either alone or in combination with other analytic techniques more than half of all empirical studies used this technique), descriptive statistics, analysis of variance, and logistic regression. Factor analysis and analysis of variance require metric data levels. More than half of the empirical studies undertaken in tourism research do not use methods appropriate for the answer format in the instrument.

This leads to the following findings with respect to H1.1 to H1.4. Hypothesis H1.1 cannot be rejected because the vast majority of empirical tourism studies uses a multi-category ordinal answer format, either as the sole measurement instrument or in combination with other answer formats.

Table 1. Answer Formats Used in Empirical Tourism Research.

Component of Standard Research Approach	Alternatives	Frequency	Percent
Answer format used	Nominal only	5	8
	Binary only	1	2
	Ordinal only	49	75
	Metric only	0	0
	More than one of the above	9	14
Specific answer format	Likert scale	43	66
	Semantic differential	3	5
Cited prior work to justify use of response format	Yes	11	17
	No	54	83
Explanation provided	Yes	3	5
	No	62	95
Dangers discussed	Yes	2	3
	No	63	97
Method of data analysis	Factor analysis	13	20
	Factor analysis combined with other analyses	23	35
	Descriptive statistics	9	14
	Logistic regression	4	6
	Cluster analysis	2	3
	Discrete choice modeling	2	3

Hypothesis H1.2 cannot be rejected either, because no explanation for the use of the response format was provided in 95 percent of the studies reviewed. Dangers associated with response styles are only discussed in three percent of all studies. Consequently, H1.3 cannot be rejected. Finally, in more than half of the studies analytic techniques are used, which require higher than ordinal data level, indicating that a significant proportion of research applies analytic techniques unsuitable for the data properties.

The fact that hypotheses H1.1 to H1.4 could not be rejected indicates that empirical tourism research as a field is very prone to confounding the result component of a finding with the measurement artifact component, resulting from the use of response formats that often appear not to have been validated and calibrated for the particular research problem at hand.

2.2. A Few Things to Consider When Choosing a Response Format

This section cannot provide the magic solution to all research problems: the single best response format. Instead it aims to list several aspects that empirical tourism researchers may want to consider when choosing their response format. Each aspect is discussed independently. The selection of the optimal response format, however, requires us to account for all the following points in an integrated manner:

1. Is the speed of completing the questionnaire critical? Decreasing the time required to complete a survey can be necessary for at least one of the two reasons: (a) longer questionnaires are more expensive, because respondents are paid more to compensate for their time in self-administering the survey, or the expenses for interviewer time increase; and (b) longer questionnaires are known to lead to a reduction in data quality (Johnson, Lehmann, & Horne, 1990). Typically, high quality data are the primary aim of an empirical social scientist. If questionnaire length is a concern, the use of binary response formats is recommended, because the time saved is about 30 percent, with aggregated results showing very little deviation from ordinal scales (Dolnicar, 2003; Dolnicar et al., 2004).

2. Is the increased detail available by using ordinal multi-category scales required to answer the research question? Multi-category ordinal response formats enable frequency counts of all options, which the binary answer format cannot provide. The crucial question is: is this additional detail required? The best way to answer this question is to determine what the research question is, and in which way the data will be analyzed. If it is essential to know what proportion of respondents are 'moderately satisfied,' and if frequently counts will be computed to assess this proportion, a multi-category ordinal or metric response format is needed. If analyses will be based on means or analytic techniques that use the mean value as a basis, a binary answer format may be sufficient because it has been demonstrated in the past that at the aggregate level the mean derived from a binary scale essentially leads to the same interpretation as the typically (incorrectly) computed mean across a limited number of ordinal multi-category scale points (Dolnicar, 2003; Dolnicar et al., 2004).

3. Can it be reasonably assumed that all respondents will perceive the ordinal response options in the same way? For example, will 'very satisfied' mean the same thing to all respondents? If this can be reasonably assumed, the multi-category ordinal response format is a suitable choice. If not, then the seemingly higher level of precision is contaminated to an extent that it is questionable whether the responses can be interpreted beyond positive versus negative (and thus binary) statements.

4. Can it reasonably be assumed that the distances between the ordinal multi-category answer alternatives are perceived as the same? For

example, will the difference between 'satisfied' and 'very satisfied' be perceived as identical to the difference between 'dissatisfied' and 'very dissatisfied?' One could argue that this is not the case; that instead, the jump to 'very dissatisfied' is significantly larger from 'dissatisfied' than the distance between the two positive scale points. If equidistance can be shown in presets or can be reasonably assumed, the multi-category ordinal scale is suitable. Otherwise, choosing an ordinal multi-category format has the consequence that data-analytic techniques assuming metric data have to be eliminated from the portfolio of applicable methods for such data, because computation of distance is meaningless – even misleading. In such cases a metric response format could be considered if a high level of detail is required in the response, or a binary format if this is not the case.

5. Further decisions that need to be made based on the construct under study if multi-category ordinal response formats are chosen include (a) whether the response format should be unipolar (for example, from 'not expensive' to 'very expensive') or bipolar (from 'very cheap' to 'very expensive'); (b) how many scale points should be used; (c) whether all response alternatives should be verbalized, or only the endpoints; and (d) how will the response alternatives or endpoints should be verbalized (as 'very expensive' or 'strongly agree').

6. Will the sample include respondents from different cultural backgrounds? If so, binary response formats may be the preferable solution if there is not sufficient time to undertake rigorous testing of various levels of equivalence before the fieldwork. Binary formats were recommended in this context by Cronbach (1950), in order to reduce cross-cultural response bias. This aspect will be discussed in more detail in the next section.

3. CROSS-CULTURAL RESPONSE STYLES

Much empirical tourism research will be confronted with individuals from different cultural backgrounds. The more global that tourism becomes, the smaller the proportion of demand-oriented studies that can use samples of respondents from only one country or cultural background. Empirical research in tourism often aims to reveal differences between cultural groups or tourists from different countries of origin.

The need to compare respondents from different countries or cultural backgrounds exposes the discipline to several potential result contaminants: culturally biased response norms can cause different scale usages independent of the information passed on by completing a questionnaire; questions can be interpreted differently; and the underlying constructs measured might not be identical. Therefore, the most concerning potential mistake resulting from cross-cultural response styles is that differences in group means can become uninterpretable (Chun, Campbell, & Yoo, 1974), although typically the comparison of means across countries or cultures constitutes the central analysis in cross-cultural comparisons.

The tourism research literature has not broadly discussed the potential dangers of interpreting empirical data derived from surveys conducted in different languages in different places (with the exception of Kozak, Bigne, & Andreu, 2003, in the context of satisfaction research, and Dolnicar & Grün, in press). However, psychologists, sociologists, and market researchers have investigated cross-cultural issues in empirical research extensively. The following overview is based on the review by Dolnicar and Grün (in press).

The number of potential pitfalls is huge, as Sekaran (1983) discusses in detail. The central problem is equivalence. However, equivalence has to be ensured at several different levels. Sekaran categorizes them into the following areas: functional equivalence, equivalence of instruments (vocabulary equivalence, idiomatic equivalence, grammatical, and syntactical equivalence), conceptual equivalence, transferability of concepts, data collection, sampling, scaling, data analysis, and measurement equivalence. Functional equivalence means that the behavior to be measured should be naturally occurring. Conceptual equivalence refers to the requirement that the object of study should have the same meaning in all cultures included in the study. The criterion of transferability looks at whether concepts can be transferred to different cultures. Vocabulary, idiomatic, grammatical, and syntactical equivalence are part of the equivalence of instruments, and relate to the translation process of survey instruments, the use of idioms that may not be directly translatable to another language, and the grammatical form of the questions (which is particularly important when long or complex text components need to be translated). Data collection could cause bias if there are different methods of data collection in different countries. Sampling can cause bias if the samples of different countries are not all representative of the local population or directly matched. Scaling equivalence requires that the response format used should elicit responses in the same way from all groups of respondents. Measurement bias could result from different cultural sensitivities to topics studied. Data analysis could distort findings if data from different cultural groups are analyzed in different ways.

Kozak et al. (2003) provide a similar review specifically for the context of cross-cultural satisfaction research in tourism, and they distinguish between functional, conceptual, instrument, and measurement equivalence.

Measurement bias is the area most critical to the majority of cross-cultural studies conducted in empirical tourism research. For example, a survey of visitors to Austria is not confronted with the typical problems listed above, and sampling is based on representatives of each country or cultural subgroup who visit Austria. Representativity of the home country's population, or matching of individuals across countries of origin, is consequently not a relevant criterion. Rather, the representativity of each country or cultural group for the visiting pattern to Austria is of importance. Measurement equivalence, however, is relevant in all contexts and for all constructs measured in typical empirical tourism research.

Smith and Reynolds (2002) further break down the aspect of measurement bias, and differentiate between *response sets* and *response styles*. Response sets describe differences in responses that are due to how respondents from different cultures would like to be perceived. In contrast, response styles are used for differences in responses that are systematically related to the response format. Smith and Reynolds conclude that 'Failure ... to detect differences in cross-national response bias will ... affect data comparability, may invalidate the research results and could therefore lead to incorrect inferences about attitudes and behaviors across national groups' (2002, p. 450).

This section focuses on the discussion and investigation of emerged standards in the area of cross-cultural response styles. Several empirical studies have been conducted that aim to detect cross-cultural response styles. Chun et al. (1974) tested differences in extreme response styles between US and Korean students, and concluded that a significant difference exists, and that US students were more prone to demonstrate an extreme response style. Bachman and O'Malley (1984) investigated differences between colored and Caucasian high school seniors in responding to Likert questionnaire items, and found that colored students were more likely to use extreme response options. Hui and Triandis (1989) concluded from their study that Hispanic respondents use extreme scores more often than non-Hispanic respondents, and this is supported by the Marin, Gamba and Marin (1992) study. Watkins and Cheung (1995) found differences in response styles between survey participants across countries, and also detected that the variation is higher among women. Clarke III (2000) found that Hispanics and colored respondents exhibited higher levels of extreme response styles than the other groups, and that the French used more extreme responses than Australians. Van Herk, Poortinga, and Verhallen

(2004) identified response style biases in countries within the EU, with respondents from the Mediterranean showing higher levels of both extreme and acquiescence response styles than respondents from northwestern Europe.

These findings indicate that cross-cultural response styles do exist, and that they represent a major threat to empirical tourism research based on data collected from respondents from different countries or cultural backgrounds.

3.1. Are we 'following the recommendation of …' in Conducting Cross-cultural Comparisons? An Empirical Investigation

Based on the review of prior work and the nature of empirical tourism research, the following hypotheses are formulated regarding the accepted standards with regard to cross-cultural response bias, and the extent to which cross-cultural empirical tourism research findings are endangered by response styles:

H2.1. The majority of empirical tourism studies (more than 50 percent) are based on multicultural samples (that is, samples including respondents from more than one cultural group or country).

H2.2. The majority of empirical tourism studies using multicultural samples (more than 50 percent) draw comparisons between respondents from countries and/or cultural backgrounds.

H2.3. The majority of empirical tourism studies using multicultural samples (more than 50 percent) use the multi-category ordinal response format.

H2.4. The majority of empirical tourism studies using multicultural samples (more than 50 percent) do not mention potential problems resulting from cross-cultural response styles.

H2.5. The majority of empirical tourism studies using multicultural samples (more than 50 percent) do not assess the extent of cross-cultural response style contamination.

H2.6. The majority of empirical tourism studies using contaminated multicultural samples (more than 50 percent) do not correct for cross-cultural response style contamination.

The same review procedure as outlined in Section 2.1 was used. Answers to the following questions were coded into a data set:

(1) Did the sample include respondents from different countries or cultural backgrounds? For all studies for which this was the case, additional data were coded.
(2) Was a comparison across countries or cultural backgrounds undertaken?
(3) Which response format was used?
(4) Was any aspect related to problems with cross-cultural studies mentioned?
(5) Was the extent of the contamination assessed?
(6) Was data corrected for the contamination?

The frequency counts for these variables are included in Table 2.

At least one-third of articles published in 2005 used samples that included respondents from more than one country of origin or cultural background. Given that the sample is not described sufficiently in many studies, this proportion could be as high as half of all studies. Of those studies that use multicultural data, 36 percent actually draw cross-cultural conclusions. Hypotheses H2.1 and H2.2 therefore must be rejected. The proportion of studies endangered by cross-cultural response styles among all empirical studies published in 2005 is not more than 50 percent, based on 2005

Table 2.   Approaches in Empirical Cross-Cultural Tourism Research.

Component of Standard Research Approach	Alternatives	Frequency	Percent
Multicultural data set used among all	Yes	10	34
empirical studies	No	0	0
	Not clear	10	15
Comparison of countries/cultural	Yes	8	36
backgrounds	No	14	64
Answer format used	Nominal	2	9
	Binary	0	0
	Ordinal	19	86
	Metric	1	5
Potential problems mentioned	Yes	2	9
	No	20	91
Extent of contamination assessed	Yes	2	9
	No	20	91
Corrected for contamination	Yes	2	0
	No	20	91

publications between 34 and 49 percent of studies include multicultural samples.

Hypothesis H2.3 cannot be rejected, because 86 percent of respondents used the multi-category ordinal answer format. Hypotheses H2.4 to H2.6 cannot be rejected either, because the vast majority (91 percent) of empirical studies based on multicultural data do not discuss the dangers associated with this approach, do not assess the danger of response styles, and do not correct for response style contamination.

3.2. A Few Things to Consider Regarding Cross-cultural Response Styles

Essentially there are three ways to avoid problems with cross-cultural response styles: (1) not to conduct them (which admittedly is not much help for those who do); (2) to choose a response format that is less susceptible to cross-cultural response styles; and (3) to assess the existence/extent of the response bias and correct for it.

With respect to the second recommendation (to use response formats less susceptible to response styles), there has been little empirical research undertaken to determine which response formats would be suitable. Clarke III (2000, 2001) found that lower numbers of response options in multi-category ordinal scales lead to more extreme answers. This is not surprising, given that the number of options is lower. However, neither study identified differences between cultural groups with respect to this shift toward extreme answer options. This means that a certain kind of response style (extreme response style) is more prominent the fewer the scale point. However, it does not seem to be the case that different cultures shift to extreme answers more or less frequently. Cronbach (1950, p. 21) recommended the use of binary format instead of multi-category ordinal scales, as well as the following recommendation: 'Since response sets are a nuisance, test designers should avoid forms of items which response sets infest.' Given the unambiguous findings reported above regarding the way that multi-category ordinal scales are highly prone to cross-cultural response styles, binary answer formats should be seriously considered as an alternative if ordinal or metric level data are not essential. Lower-level, high-quality data may be preferable to higher-level, contaminated data.

Regarding option 3 (to assess the existence/extent of the response bias and correct for it), several authors have made suggestions how cross-cultural response styles can be corrected for (Cheung & Rensvold, 2000; Byrne & Campbell, 1999; Greenleaf, 1992a, 1992b; Van de Vijver & Poortinga, 2002;

Welkenhuysen-Gybels, Billiet, & Cambre, 2003). Their recommendations range from very simple approaches, for example, investigating if systematic response patterns can be detected for the same cultural group; to modeling approaches that try to extract the extreme response and acquiescence bias from the actual information content and then correct the data accordingly. These approaches have one thing in common: they assume to know the extent to which data are contaminated and then be able to correct for this contamination. This assumption has the disadvantage that exactly which type of contamination occurs, and its extent, are unlikely to be evident. The decision to make a particular correction, therefore, carries the danger of transforming the data incorrectly, and by doing so, introducing new contaminations.

Dolnicar and Grün (in press) took a different approach, which takes precisely this danger into consideration. They recommended identifying the subset of all correction methods that are theoretically appropriate for a particular data set at hand, correcting the data using all correction techniques and then computing the results for the uncorrected and all corrected data sets. Where no deviations in findings occur, a firm conclusion about cross-cultural differences can be drawn. If, however, the findings differ independently of the correction method used, conclusions must be drawn with care, and should draw the reader's attention to the possibility that response styles may be causing detected differences (or no differences) between respondents from different cultures or countries.

While this article has focused on response style effects in cross-cultural comparisons, the equivalence dimensions discussed in literature review should be considered and discussed in any study that involves cross-cultural comparisons.

4. MARKET SEGMENTATION

It is now widely accepted among tourism researchers that tourists are not one homogeneous group of people who seek the same benefits from a destination, have the same expectations, undertake the same vacation activities, and perceive the same vacation components as attractive. Tourists are highly heterogeneous. In the optimal case, the tourism industry should therefore cater for individuals and their specific vacation needs. While this approach may be feasible in online interfaces (for example, by supporting individual people in their destination choice), it is not feasible to modify the entire marketing mix of a tourism business or destination to suit individual needs. The next best option to individual customization is the identification or definition of groups of similar tourists: market segments.

Because of its benefits, the concept of market segmentation has been embraced both by the tourism industry and tourism researchers. The aim of market segmentation studies is to identify, construct, or define market segments, and profile their characteristics in sufficient detail to make them an actionable target market for tourism industry. Every market could be segmented in myriad different ways, and each of these possible segmentations of the market is not equally attractive. Ideal segments would contain tourists with similar tourism needs and behaviors, and similar socio-demographic profiles. They are targets who are profitable, who could be easily reached with marketing communication messages, who match the strengths of the tourism destination or business, and whose needs are not catered for by major competitors. Such ideal segments would be highly attractive from the tourism industry point of view, because they would have the most potential for profit increase through more targeted marketing activities, with a higher effect on market demand within the targeted segment.

Consequently, it is the tourism researcher's aim to explore markets, and suggest market segments to the tourism industry that are as ideal as possible. The researcher must choose between large numbers of possible segmentation solutions; a decision, which is better made based on the structure of the data, rather than on the subjective opinion of the tourism researcher or manager. The segmentation research approach, which aims to investigate data structure systematically, therefore represents the key to successful data-driven market segmentation. Failing to explore the market (data) in such a way as to identify or construct ideal segments can lead to an irreversible competitive disadvantage for the tourism business or destination that uses the segmentation as their basis for marketing action. Consequently, it is crucial to ensure that the research approach to market segmentation is rigorous and avoids potential misinterpretations.

This burden of responsibility is different for different kinds of segmentation studies. In the case of a priori (Mazanec, 2000) or *commonsense* segmentation (Dolnicar, 2004) and extensions thereof (concepts 1, 3, 4, and 5, according to the classification of segmentation studies proposed by Dolnicar, 2004) the crucial decision is the selection of the segmentation criteria. For example, a destination might choose to target young tourists using age as the commonsense criterion. On closer evaluation, however, it might be that using the stage in the family lifecycle would have been a better choice, because the destination's strength lies in providing optimal services to young families, rather than young singles or groups of young tourists. In the case of post-hoc (Myers & Tauber, 1977), a posteriori (Mazanec, 2000) or *data-driven* segmentation (Dolnicar, 2004) and extensions thereof (segmentation concepts 2, 4, 5, and 6), this burden of responsibility rests on the research approach of the data-driven segmentation study undertaken. Because the process of data-driven segmentation consists of numerous components, most of them requiring the researcher's decision, it is more difficult to avoid potential misinterpretations or suboptimal procedural decisions than is so for a priori segmentation studies.

In addition to grouping segmentation studies in a priori (commonsense) and data-driven (a posteriori, post-hoc) studies, data-driven studies can be further classified as either *response-based* or *step-wise*. The step-wise procedure aims to group respondents according to certain variables in the first step, and describing them in the second. Typical descriptors, or background variables, are variables relevant to marketing, for example, the media behavior of segments, their purchasing frequency, and the amount of money spent on holidays per year. In the step-wise procedure the grouping is based purely on the variables selected, for example, travel motives. The background variables do not interfere with the determination of the segments. Response-based segmentation uses one or more variables, which are relevant from a marketing perspective as the dependent variable in the segmentation process, thus confounding, for example, the travel motive segments with their media behavior. The segments are consequently not pure travel motivation segments.

This section discusses step-wise, data-driven procedures because they dominate the area of segmentation studies in tourism research. All stages (discussed in detail below) are depicted in Fig. 2.

The **study design** stage is mentioned in Fig. 2 because many segmentation studies have design requirements different from other studies. Segmentation studies aim to identify all market segments in the market. Sometimes small niche markets are of particular interest because they may provide a distinct competitive advantage. It is therefore not necessarily desirable for a segmentation study to include a representative sample of respondents. If identification of segments is the primary aim, the sample must be as heterogeneous as possible – it should include the widest variety of respondents in sufficient number to enable the cluster algorithm to identify niches.

At the **data collection** stage, variables must be carefully developed before being included in a questionnaire. It is not good practice either to include all items that seem interesting without pre-testing or theoretical justification, or to include as many redundant items as possible to achieve a high alpha value (Cronbach, 1951), if this happens at the expense of the conceptualization of

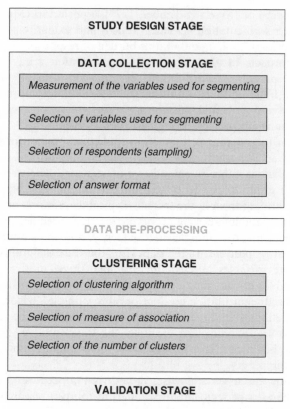

Fig. 2. Outline of Stages of a Step-wise, Data-Driven Market Segmentation Study.

the construct of interest or respondent fatigue, while not providing any information of additional value. Evidence demonstrates the negative effect of only one or two variables that are unrelated to the segmentation (Milligan, 1980, 1996), which leads to the strong advice both from methodological researchers (for example, Milligan) and marketing scientists (Punj & Stewart, 1983) to exercise extreme care in selecting variables.

The approach typically used for scale development in tourism research follows Churchill's early recommendations (Churchill, 1979). Since then, Churchill (1998, p. 30) himself, while pleased with the improvement of **measurement** in the area of marketing, expressed criticism about the way in which his paradigm was frequently misinterpreted: 'The bad news is that measurement seems to almost have become a rote process, with the

Paradigm article serving as backdrop for the drill, thereby supposedly lending legitimacy to what seems to be at times thoughtless, rather than thoughtful, efforts.'

Two (groups of) authors have recently proposed alternatives to Churchill's ruling paradigm of scale development. As Finn and Kayande (2005, p. 12) expressed in a review of the Churchill scale development procedure: 'Step-by-step applications overemphasize validation numbers at the expense of conceptual rigor. Numbers [are] often misleading due to misidentification of relevant objects of measurement.' Recommendations for improvement of the present scale development paradigm have been proposed by Rossiter (2002), who criticizes the lack of conceptualization and questions the need for multi-items in particular instances; and Finn and Kayande (1997), who criticize the limitation of the scaling of characteristics of individuals, although typically, researchers are not interested in single individuals, because, for example, psychological measurements are.

Given that the data set is the most fundamental basis for good market segmentation, careless selection of items to be included in the questionnaire can critically affect the quality of results. Whenever a tourism researcher conducts a segmentation study, data collection should be planned as an integral part of the study, to ensure that all important pieces of information are obtained without burdening respondents with unnecessary items. If a segmentation researcher is, however, confronted with a secondary data set in which redundant items are included, the direct inclusion of such items into the segmentation process should be critically questioned.

In sum, the dangers of uncritically following measurement paradigms when the segmentation base is collected include: (1) the construct that is of central interest could be badly conceptualized; (2) respondents could be confronted with large numbers of questions that are highly redundant, which is likely to lead to lower data quality due to respondent fatigue; (3) items that are not redundant and thus measure a different dimension of a construct (and might well be the most important items for identifying niche markets) may be eliminated because they reduce the values of reliability measures; and (4) by including many redundant items, the segmentation researcher has only shifted the variable selection problem from the pre-survey to the pre-segmentation phase. The process by which the items were derived has to be described in detail to clarify that the construct of interest is best captured by the selected variables, and that the variables can be expected to differentiate between segments.

If the construct that was measured for the purpose of segmenting is used for segmentation, the next step (the **selection of variables** to be used in the segmentation process) is unnecessary. However, segmentation studies are sometimes conducted based on data that was collected for an entirely different reason. The biggest danger with respect to the choice of variables to be included in the segmentation process in this case is the uncritical inclusion of as many variables as possible, in the hope that some structure will emerge (Aldenderfer & Blashfield, 1984; Everitt, 1979). Or, as Milligan (1996, p. 348) puts it: 'Far too many analyses have been conducted by including every variable available ... Most researchers do not appreciate the fact that a variable should be included only if a strong justification exists that that variable helps to define the underlying clustering.'

The question of how many respondents are required to group them, based on a certain number of variables, cannot be answered easily. **Sample** size requirements essentially depend on two factors: the methodological approach chosen to analyze the data (parametric approaches require minimum sample sizes, whereas non-parametric explorative analyses do not), and the structure of the data (if the data set is very well structured, only a few variables may be needed to group individuals correctly; if, however, the data set is not at all well structured, a lot of information from many respondents is required to determine the best grouping). While the choice of method is under the researcher's control, the data structure is not.

The only recommendation that has been published (to the author's knowledge) has been Formann's (1984), in the context of latent class analysis (a parametric procedure). He states that a sample of at least 2^k is needed to segment the respondents based on k variables; preferably $5*2^k$ should be available. The number 2 indicates that Formann assumes that a binary answer format will be used. If an ordinal format is used, the number 2 has to be exchanged by the number of ordinal scale categories chosen. Imagine, for example, a block of 20 travel motives, which respondents are asked either to agree or disagree (binary scale) with. If these 20 items are to be used as a segmentation base using a parametric procedure, the required sample size is 1,048,576 respondents. If 15 items are used, 'only' 32,768 respondents are needed, and with 10 items, 1,024 completed surveys are sufficient to segment the market, based on the travel motives.

The next stage, the **selection of answer format**, will not be discussed in detail in this section because it has been dealt with in detail in the section on answer formats. However, it is worth noting here that all cluster algorithms used to segment markets are based on distance computations, as illustrated in Fig. 3, in which depicts a very simple case of three respondents and three variables. Respondents answered on a binary scale. If the match of answers is used as a measure of similarity, respondent 1 and respondent 2 reach a

	Want to rest	Want excitement	Want security
Respondent 1	0	1	0
Respondent 2	0	1	1
Respondent 3	1	0	0

Fig. 3. Data Set Example.

value of 2, because they both want excitement during their holiday and both do not want to rest. Respondent 3 achieves a value of 1 with respondent 1, because neither cares about security, and a value of 0 with respondent 2. In this case (using the proposed distance measure and a hierarchical algorithm), respondents 1 and 2 would be assigned to one market segment. If the absolute Euclidean distance were used, the distance between respondent 1 and 2 would be$|(0-0)+(1-1)+(0-1)| = 1$. For respondents 1 and 3 it would amount to 2, and for respondents 2 and 3 it would be 3; again indicating that respondents 1 and 2 are the least dissimilar.

Given that similarity or dissimilarity of response vectors is used in the cluster step, the choice of distance measure is very important, especially regarding its suitability for the answer format selected. As noted in the section on answer formats, the use of multi-category ordinal scales is most complicated, because equidistance cannot be assumed, and therefore, the most common distance measure, Euclidean distance, is not an appropriate choice.

In Fig. 2 the box representing **pre-processing** of data are depicted in light grey in order to indicate that (while it appears that pre-processing of data has developed to become an accepted standard in empirical tourism research) pre-processing is not an essential component of the step-wise, data-driven segmentation process. Aldenderfer and Blashfield (1984) discuss the issue of data pre-processing through standardization and other forms of transformations, extensively. They review several studies, which came to different conclusions in respect to the effect of data standardization on results. In sum, the dangers of pre-processing are that: (1) the relations of variables to each other could be changed; (2) differences between segments could be reduced; and (3) segments identified are done so in a space different from originally postulated (Ketchen & Shook, 1996).

The most frequently used method of pre-processing in market segmentation is factor analysis. While factor analysis can help eliminate variables that measure the same construct, and by doing so prevent one construct being weighted higher in the segmentation solution, the danger associated with this procedure is that differences between segments that are not clearly separated from each other cannot be detected as easily (Aldenderfer & Blashfield, 1984). However, Aldenderfer and Blashfield found no evidence of negative impact if the data contained well-separated segments.

Arabie and Hubert (1994) take a clearer position on the use of factor analysis in the context of clustering. They state that '"tandem" clustering is an outmoded and statistically insupportable practice,' because data are transformed, thus the nature of the data is changed before segments are searched for. This is supported by Milligan (1996), who, based on experimental findings that clusters in variable space are not well represented by clusters in component space, states that the researcher has to address in which space the segments are postulated to exist.

In tourism research, the typical reason stated for using factor analysis is the need to reduce the number of variables. This argument poses two questions:

(1) Why was the number of items not reduced in the variable measurement stage to retain a reasonable number of relevant, non-redundant questions that are expected to discriminate between segments?
(2) If the researcher did not have any influence on the data collection, and is faced with a data set with too many variables, why is factor analysis preferred over simpler ways of variable selection, which avoid data transformation?

The most illustrative argument against the uncritical use of factor-cluster analysis in tourism research is provided by Sheppard (1996). He explains the paradox that homogeneity has to be assumed for factor analysis, whereas heterogeneity is explored by cluster analysis. He also demonstrates in an empirical example that the results derived from factor-cluster analysis, cluster-factor analysis, and cluster analysis based on raw data lead to totally different conclusions. In his example, the factor-cluster approach led to results different from cluster analysis on its own, and effectively failed to identify the true segment structure in the data. Furthermore, he demonstrated how the exclusion of items based on low loadings with factors can undermine the aim of the entire segmentation study, if the low loading item actually represents a relevant discriminating variable between segments. When 'accurate and detailed' segmentation results are the aim of the study (the case for most tourism segmentation studies), Sheppard recommends clustering of raw data directly. Sheppard's study shows that assumption (5), discussed in the section on the standard research approach, is not appropriate, because factor-cluster analysis not only leads to different, but inferior, results if the aim is the identification of market segments.

In sum, there are number of problems associated with the practice of using factor analysis in the pre-processing stage of a segmentation study to reduce variables: (1) the data are transformed and segments are identified based on the transformed space not the original information respondents gave, which leads to different results; (2) with a typical explained variance of between 50 and 60 percent, up to half of the information that was collected from respondents is discarded before segments are identified or constructed; (3) eliminating variables that do not load highly on factors with an eigen-value of more than 1 means that potentially the most important pieces of information for the identification of niche segments are discarded, thus making it impossible ever to identify such groups; and (4) interpretations of segments based on the original variables are not possible – segments can only be interpreted with respect to their factor score values.

The broad term used to subsume all algorithms used in step-wise, data-driven market segmentation is cluster analysis. This term describes a large number of algorithms for grouping observations based on similarity or dis-similarity.

Extensive Monte Carlo simulations have shown that most algorithms can identify the correct segmentation solution if the data are highly structured (Buchta, Dimitriadou, Dolnicar, & Leisch Weingessel, 1997). However, if this is not the case, the algorithm chosen does not act as a neutral tool in the segmentation exercise; rather, it creates a segmentation solution. Also, each algorithm has different tendencies regarding which kind of segments it creates. Or, as Aldenderfer and Blashfield (1984, p. 16) put it: 'Although the strategy of clustering may be structure-seeking, its operation is one that is structure-imposing.'

This has two consequences for the researcher aiming to segment a market: (1) it is important to know whether the data used as a segmentation base is well structured; and (2) the solution is likely to depend on the algorithm chosen, which makes the selection of an appropriate segmentation algorithm a crucial step in the process.

The limitations of algorithms and the ways they influence the nature of the solution are well known for most algorithms. For example, hierarchical procedures are not suitable for very large data sets because the hierarchical clustering algorithm requires the computation of all pair-wise distances at each stage of grouping, as in the example above with three respondents. Within the group of hierarchical procedures single linkage procedures create chain formations in the final segmentation solution (Everitt, 1993);

self-organizing neural networks not only partition the data, but also render a topological map of the segmentation solution that indicates the neighborhood relations of segments to one another (Kohonen, 1997; Martinetz & Schulten, 1994); fuzzy clustering approaches relax the assumption of exclusiveness (for example, Everitt, 1993); and ensemble methods use the principle of systematic repetition to arrive at more stable solutions (for example, Leisch, 1998, 1999; Dolnicar & Leisch, 2000, 2003). These are just a few of the distinct properties that different techniques have.

One example of an ensemble technique is bagged clustering, which has only recently been introduced into tourism research (Dolnicar & Leisch, 2003). Its major advantage is that it investigates the structure of the data while simultaneously producing a segmentation solution. Comparative studies (Dolnicar & Leisch, 2004) have found bagged clustering to produce more stable and therefore more reliable segmentation solutions.

One component of the segmentation algorithm is the **measure of association** used, as mentioned above. The measure of association chosen must be suitable for the answer format, which means that it must be able to deal with binary, ordinal, or metric-level data. Euclidean distance, the most widely used measure, is suitable for binary data and metric data to determine a particular kind of distance. It is not suitable for ordinal data unless it has been shown that the distances between the categories are perceived as equidistant by all respondents.

Arguably, the most critical decision in the process of step-wise, data-driven segmentation is the decision of **how many clusters** to choose, a problem that remains unsolved since the wider adoption of clustering techniques (Thorndike, 1953). Similar to the decision about which algorithm to use, this decision depends on the nature of the data being analyzed. If the data is very highly structured in terms of density structure (that is, clear market segments exist), every algorithm can recommend the correct number of clusters (Buchta et al., 1997). If, however, the data are not highly structured (which, based on the author's experience, is the typical case in the social sciences), deciding on the number of clusters is very difficult. Many different approaches and indexes have been proposed in the past (for comparative studies see Milligan, 1981; Milligan & Cooper, 1985; Dimitriadou, Dolnicar & Weingessel, 2002; Mazanec & Strasser, 2000).

The issue of **validity** of market segmentation solutions cannot be discussed independently of the aim of the segmentation exercise, and the aim is not independent of the available data. The aim of detecting natural clusters that exist in the data (Aldenderfer & Blashfield, 1984) is only suitable if the data are highly structured and actually contains natural density clusters. This can be assessed by investigating the stability of solutions if computed repeatedly for the same number of clusters. If the stability results indicate that natural segments do not exist in the data – which is the implicit assumption made by Mazanec, Grabler, Maier and Wöber (1997) and Wedel and Kamakura (1998) – the aim of the market segmentation exercise is to identify the most managerially useful segments. The most common case in market segmentation is to construct artificial groupings, even though this aim is counterintuitive. Such solutions are valuable because the segments constructed are more homogeneous groups of individuals, which can be targeted with customized messages. The degree of managerial usefulness can be evaluated by inspecting the segment profiles and assessing the match with organizational strengths – or by assessing stability and choosing the most stable solution. Stability is a major issue in data-driven market segmentation as compared to the a priori approach (Myers & Tauber, 1977).

While stability is one condition of validity, if naturally occurring segments are the focus, another aspect of validity is independent of whether natural groups are identified or whether artificial groups are constructed. Segments should be distinctly different from one another. Given that the clustering algorithm produces a solution where segments are distinctly different with respect to the variables used in the segmentation process (the segmentation base), testing for significance of difference in the segmentation base is not a legitimate test for distinctness. However, additional information that is available about the respondents can be used to test whether segments are distinctly different. Depending on the number and data scale of the additional variables, and the number of segments, different approaches can be used to assess the distinctness of the segments. Options include discriminant analysis, analysis of variance, χ^2 tests, and binary logistic regression.

4.1. Are we 'following the recommendation of ...' in Market Segmentation? An Empirical Investigation

The following hypotheses were formulated regarding emerged standards for step-wise, data-driven market segmentation in empirical tourism research.

H3.1. In the majority of segmentation studies (more than 50 percent) data are not specifically collected for the purpose of segmentation.

H3.2. In the majority of segmentation studies (more than 50 percent) no explanation is provided for the measurement of variables.

H3.3. In the majority of segmentation studies (more than 50 percent) no explanation is provided for the selection of variables.

H3.4. In the majority of segmentation studies (more than 50 percent) the sampling strategy is not developed in view of the segmentation study.

H3.5. In the majority of segmentation studies (more than 50 percent) the segmentation base is of multi-category ordinal nature.

H3.6. In the majority of segmentation studies (more than 50 percent) data are pre-processed using factor analysis.

H3.7. In the majority of segmentation studies that pre-process data (more than 50 percent) no explanation for pre-processing is provided.

H3.8. In the majority of segmentation studies (more than 50 percent) the measure of association used is not stated.

H3.9. In the majority of segmentation studies (more than 50 percent) data structure is not investigated.

H3.10. In the majority of segmentation studies (more than 50 percent) the choice of the number of clusters is based – at the most – on one run per number of clusters.

H3.11. In the majority of segmentation studies (more than 50 percent) the segmentation solution is not validated.

Of the 65 empirical tourism studies reviewed in 2005, only eight were segmentation studies. Table 3 includes the frequency counts of relevance to test the above hypotheses.

The information contained in the reviewed articles is insufficient to allow testing of H3.1. The classification of whether data were collected in view of the segmentation has proven to be very subjective, and the two coders involved instead chose to report this hypothesis as not testable. Both H3.2 and H3.3 cannot be rejected because 75 percent of studied articles do not contain an explanation for the measurement of variables, or explain why the variables used as segmentation base were chosen.

Hypothesis H3.4 generated a situation similar to that faced with H3.1: the articles in which the study was reported do not clearly indicate whether the sampling strategy took into account the fact that the study aim was segmentation.

Hypothesis H3.5 cannot be rejected, because 88 percent of studies use multi-category ordinal answer formats. Hypothesis H3.6 cannot be rejected,

Table 3. Approaches in Data-Driven Market Segmentation of Tourists.

Component of Standard Research approach	Alternatives	Frequency	Percent
Explanation for measurement of variables provided	Yes	2	25
	No	6	75
Explanation for selection of variables provided	Yes	2	25
	No	6	75
Answer format	Ordinal	7	88
	More than one	1	13
Pre-processing	No	2	25
	Yes – factor analysis	5	63
	Yes – other	1	13
Explanation for pre-processing if pre-processed	Yes	6	100
Explanation for selection of clustering algorithm	Yes	0	0
	No	6	75
	Cited another author	2	25
Measure of association stated	Yes	0	0
	No	8	100
Data structure investigated	Yes	0	0
	No	8	100
Number of clusters selection	Based on 1 run per number of clusters	8	100
	Based on data structure investigation	0	0
Validation	Yes	7	
	No	1	

because 63 percent of studies use factor analysis before segmenting respondents. Hypothesis H3.7 should be rejected, because all of the studies that pre-process data explain why they do so. Unfortunately, the explanation is typically that the number of items has to be reduced. As mentioned above, this problem should have been addressed earlier in the study, and not at the analytic stage, where elimination of items comes at a high price with regard to information loss.

Hypotheses H3.8 and H3.9 cannot be rejected, because no study mentioned the measure of association or investigated data structure before grouping the individuals. Strongly associated with the fact that structure is not investigated before segmenting is the fact that all segmentation studies decided on the number of clusters by using only one computation of each number of clusters in the appropriate range. This indicates that it is likely that many of the findings will have a strong random component driving the results. Hypothesis H3.10 therefore cannot be rejected. Fifty percent of all segmentation studies used the k-means clustering algorithm, and 25 percent used Ward's clustering.

Hypothesis H.11 cannot be supported. Seven out of eight studies did validate the segmentation solution, although the predominant method is the use of χ^2 tests and analysis of variance, which are not corrected for multiple testing (six studies).

While recent studies provide sufficient empirical evidence to validate the claim that the standard research approach in data-driven market segmentation is still prevalent in tourism, several, more general conclusions can also be drawn:

(1) There is a lack of conceptual transparency of segmentation studies generally (do clusters actually exist in the data, or does the solution merely represent one of the many possible groupings?).
(2) The explorative and structure-imposing nature of segmentation studies (one computation with one algorithm of a cluster analytic procedure is assumed to deliver the true results) is generally not acknowledged.
(3) The dangers of some of the emerged standards in components of this standard research procedure are not discussed, thus leading to potential misinterpretations of results.

In sum, the review of recently published segmentation studies indicates that the standard approach hypotheses above do exist. Also, there is a clear pattern of repeating designs that have been published before without explaining why this design is suitable or preferable for the research problem at hand.

Prior reviews in the field support these findings. For example, Frochot and Morrison (2000) review 14 data-driven benefit segmentation studies, and their findings support some of the standard components this paper covers (although they explicitly state that they do not perceive that a common standard has emerged).

(1) Items in surveys are generally not pre-tested (which leads the chosen segmentation base to include large numbers of possibly redundant items).
(2) Data are typically of ordinal format, and use five- or seven-scale points.
(3) Nine out of 14 studies used the so-called factor-cluster approach, mostly Varimax, and rotated the factor solution.

Baumann (2000) reviews 243 segmentation studies from literature prior to 2000 in the broader area of business studies. Dolnicar (2002) analyzes the tourism-focus subset. According to these reviews, two-thirds of market segmentation studies in tourism use some kind of ordinal data scale, about one-fifth uses binary data, and metric data are virtually not used at all for the variables selected as segmentation bases. The majority of studies factor analyze data sets (43 percent) and use factor scores as segmentation base instead of the original data. Only 38 percent do not pre-process data at all, and about six percent standardize the data.

With respect to the clustering algorithms chosen, 40 percent use *k*-means clustering, and another 40 percent use Ward's clustering. The reports do not include reasons and procedures for selecting a particular number of segments in one-third of the studies, more than two-thirds use heuristics and/or a subjective judgment to make this decision, which results in one-third selecting three clusters and another third choosing a four-cluster solution. Approximately half of the studies examine some form of validity, in which 15 percent used discriminant analysis, nine percent compared results with external variables, and two percent investigated the match with theories or prior findings. Furthermore, 80 percent of the studies do not mention which similarity measure is used to group respondents, or that the number of variables used is typically not harmonized with the available sample size. Samples sizes (ranging from 46 to 7,996, with a median value of 461) and number of variables in the segmentation base (ranging between 3 and 56) are uncorrelated.

Tourism researchers strongly adhere to the standard research approach in step-wise, data-driven market segmentation, and empirical tourism research follows this emerging standard procedure much more consistently than other disciplines, for example, marketing. Therefore, the question regarding the origin of this standard approach arises. An attempt to find the roots of the standard procedure can take two approaches: (1) review the pioneering publications in data-driven market segmentation in tourism published in the early 1980s; and (2) study in detail articles that are frequently cited as justification for the use of the standard approach.

The pioneering publications review leads to the conclusion that many of the standard components have indeed been used by authors who originally introduced step-wise, data-driven market segmentation into tourism research, and were consequently setting the benchmark for future work. However, many of these pioneering studies did not provide detailed reasoning or a methodological discussion of the problems associated with this particular approach. For example, Calantone, Schewe, and Allen (1980) use 20 important attributes from 1,498 respondents, using a six-point response scale. These attributes were first factor analyzed, and then cluster analyzed. The authors referenced Haley (1968) as the methodological source for their work, who represents the original source for benefit segmentation. Haley does not recommend the use of factor analysis for pre-processing in his paper. He mentions that Q-sort factor analysis could be applied as a grouping algorithm, not as a pre-processing tool, but does not discuss many other methodological issues of data-driven segmentation.

Goodrich (1980) segmented 230 respondents based on 11 benefit attributes, which were collected using a seven-point answer format. He pre-processed the 11 benefits using factor analysis, and cluster analyzed the factor scores. He did not provide an explanation or reference for adopting this procedure. Crask (1981) clustered tourists based on factor scores (explaining 57 percent of the variance of the original ordinal data). The stated aim was to determine underlying dimensions based on the 15 variables included in the questionnaire, which measured the importance tourists assigned to certain vacation attributes. He did not provide an explanation of how the 15 motivational variables were derived or why they might be expected to capture the construct adequately. The author did not cite any methodological/statistical source supporting the chosen procedure. Mazanec (1984) used raw data to segment tourists based on benefits. The author used a binary data format, provided a detailed explanation why binary data were deemed preferential to ordinal data and did not compute factor analysis before clustering the data.

The second approach taken to investigate the roots of the standard data-driven segmentation research approach in tourism leads to similar conclusions. At least one author of a data-driven segmentation study in tourism cited the articles discussed below as a justification of the method-ology used. Park, Yang, Lee, Jang and Stokowski (2002, p. 58) provide a typical example: 'The factor-cluster combination for segmentation used in this study is a basic type of segmentation methodology (Dimanche, Havitz, & Howard, 1993) and is widely used in tourism.' However, Dimanche et al. (1993) do not postulate the use of the factor-cluster approach uncritically. They segment tourists based on a particular construct (involvement), for which a scale had been developed and which has repeatedly been shown to have a specific underlying factor structure. The reason for using factor anal-ysis before clustering is consequently not because it has any methodological advantages or to follow an established procedure, but because it is a natural result of the structure of the construct as it was found to be more easily measurable. Typically this is not the case in data-driven segmentation studies in tourism, however. Dimanche et al. provide justifications for each step of their analysis, including the choice of the clustering algorithm, which is atypical of most segmentation studies conducted in the last decade. They cite Aldenderfer and Blashfield (1984) and Smith (1989) as sources for using factor-cluster analysis. They also cite Smith (1989) as the source of classifying market segmentation in tourism into a priori and factor-cluster, rather than proposing this classification themselves, as indicated in the above citation. Tracing further by following the references used by Dimanche et al. (1993) requires the study of Aldenderfer and Blashfield (1984) and Smith (1989), with the former representing a general social sciences handbook on cluster analysis and the latter a tourism-specific analysis handbook.

Aldenderfer and Blashfield do not recommend factor-cluster analysis as a suitable tool for pre-processing. They mention factor analysis as an alternative to cluster analysis for the purpose of developing numerical taxonomies, as do Sokal and Sneath (1963). They refer, however, to Q-sort factor analysis, which is based on the correlation matrix of units (respondents), rather than characteristics (variables, questions), a procedure that (to the author's knowledge) so far has not been applied in tourism. It also does not appear to be particularly suited for data analytic situations in which large numbers of respondents answer only a few questions, as opposed to uses in biology, where a few specimens are classified on the basis of a large number of characteristics. Aldenderfer and Blashfield explicitly point out that there is controversy about whether one should pre-process data at all before clustering.

Smith, however, postulates the existence of two segmentation approaches in tourism research: a priori segmentation and factor-cluster segmentation. Factor-cluster segmentation is a term that appears to have been coined by empirical tourism researchers, because it does not occur in other disciplines. This classification is misleading, because it does not mention the vast number of other existing ways to segment respondents in an a posteriori or data-driven manner, and which has been described in detail by numerous experts in cluster analysis and numerical taxonomy (Sokal & Sneath, 1963; Aldenderfer & Blashfield, 1984; Everitt, 1993). Also, Smith's discussion of market segmentation analysis fails to cite a single publication of methodological nature to support the claims made and the methods proposed. The only two references on data-driven segmentation are empirical examples of segmentation studies using the factor-cluster approach, one of which is an internal working paper, the other a study conducted by the author himself.

Frochot and Morrison (2000, p. 32) conclude from their review of benefit segmentation studies that 'it would appear that the combination of factor and cluster analysis seems to be superior due to its effectiveness in reducing sometimes large number of benefit statements to a smaller set of more un- understandable factors or components.' Interestingly, their conclusion con- tradicts their statement on page 31, that items that might help to discriminate between segments should not be eliminated. This is what factor analysis typically does: it integrates variables into factors, in which case highly discriminating variables for a particular segment may only carry a low loading value. Or, such variables may simply be dropped due to low loadings on a factor (Nunnally, 1967, recommends a value of 0.3/0.4 for loadings to factors as a criterion for retentions of variables), or because such items may well form their own factor with low explained variance that is likely to be dropped following the most commonly used Kaiser criterion, which recommends the inclusion of all factors with an eigenvalue above 1 (Stevens, 2002).

Cha, McLeary, and Uysal (1995) also choose the factor-cluster approach, using six factor scores that explain only 50 percent of the original 30 motivational items (this is 50 percent of the information collected from respondents). They do not discuss the consequences of eliminating half of the information contained in the raw data, or the homogeneity assumption of factor analysis, which is in contradiction with the heterogeneity assumption of segmentation. Their argument for factor analyzing raw data are to identify underlying motivational factors, but do not provide a methodological jus- tification for this approach, nor an explanation why such a large number of motivational items (30) were originally included in the questionnaire.

Shoemaker (1994) also conducts factor analysis, but appears to use the resulting factor scores in a more critical manner. The starting points of his analysis were 39 items. Factor analysis resulted in 12 factors. Shoemaker used those 12 factor scores, but included seven additional items that were not well represented by the factor analysis. This is a sensitive approach – in line with the recommendation by Frochot and Morrison (2000) – which makes use of factor analysis to reduce the dimensionality of the problem. However, given that factor analysis assumes homogeneity and recommends eliminations of variables that are not well represented by the factor solution (but might be essential to identify market segments), he includes additional variables of relevance. Interestingly, this informed use of factor analysis as a pre-processing tool in market segmentation is not used by the authors citing Shoemaker as a reference for factor-cluster analysis.

Sheppard (1996) is a particularly interesting case. His study is cited in- correctly on numerous occasions. Authors of segmentation studies refer to his study to justify the use of factor-cluster segmentation, although

Sheppard points out the inconsistency of this approach and states clearly (p. 57) that 'Cluster analysis on raw item scores, as opposed to factor scores, may produce more accurate or detailed segmentation as it preserves a greater degree of the original data.' Conducting factor analysis is appropriate, according to Sheppard, if a generalizable instrument is being developed, an instrument for the entire population, assuming homogeneity, not heterogeneity.

In sum, the standard research procedure for exploratory data-driven market segmentation as it is used in tourism research has developed within the field. Market segmentation studies in other disciplines do not reflect the high level of adherence to these standards, and methodological and statistical publications of general nature express reservations with regard to many of the components of the standard research approach outlined above.

4.2. A Few Things to Consider When Segmenting Markets

First, data-driven segmentation is by definition an exploratory process. If it were a confirmatory process, the definition of an expected segment structure would have to be postulated based on theory, and it would have to be established whether the empirical data significantly deviates from this postulated structure. While this approach can be taken, it does not seem to be the main aim of tourism researchers, whose primary interest is the exploration and description of market information in view of deriving potentially useful segments. Furthermore, typical data-driven methodology does not provide for this option. Even model-based segmentation methods, such as finite mixture models (Wedel & Kamakura, 1998) or latent-class analyses, do not define the structure of postulated segments ex ante. They propose models, which typically differ in the number of segments, but do not hypothesize a certain nature of segments. Consequently, it is the responsibility of the researcher not to draw to strong conclusions about the results.

The exploration of data leads to the conclusion that one particular segmentation solution should be chosen. However, this is not necessarily the better, or only, solution. Aldenderfer and Blashfield (1984, p. 14) put it in the context of cluster analysis: 'it is important to recognize the fundamental simplicity of these methods. In doing so, the user is far less likely to make the mistake of reifying the cluster solution.'

Second, the empirical data available to tourism researchers typically does not contain true clusters. Sometimes it does not contain any clear data structure at all. However, any kind of cluster analysis searches for structure. If there is no structure, cluster analysis will impose structure, for example, when clustering 1,000 respondents based on only two variables answered on a 100-point scale. Taking this example further, the answers of the 1,000 respondents to the two questions are not correlated, and each respondent uses a different point on the 100-point scale to answer the questions. This would lead to a two-dimensional plot of the data, where respondents are essentially evenly spread across the two-dimensional plane. In this case, clusters do not exist. Yet if we use k-means clustering, we will obtain clusters that will tend to be spherical in nature and of roughly equal size. Whereas, if we use single-linkage hierarchical clustering, we are likely to find chain-like clusters.

Evaluating the actual structure in the data is important. Consider whether the segmentation aim is true clustering (when density clusters actually do exist in the data), stable clustering (if there is data structure, but not of the density cluster type), or constructive clustering (if no structure exists in the data, as illustrated in the above example). Dolnicar and Leisch (2001) illustrate these options with artificial data of different structures, and provide recommendations of how to assess data structure, which is essentially based on replications of computations, to determine compliance between independently derived solutions. Constructive clustering is a perfectly legitimate approach, because managerially, it might still be better to focus on a more homogeneous part of the market, even if no true segments exist. Clarity about the nature of the segmentation study undertaken is important because it has major implications on the kind of conclusions that can be drawn, and it provides conceptual transparency to the reader and user of such a study.

With respect to the stages outlined in Fig. 2, it is important to consider the following aspects when developing and conducting a step-wise, data-driven segmentation study.

With respect to the measurement of variables for segmentation, the contributions by Churchill (1998), Finn and Kayande (1997), Rossiter (2002), and Finn and Kayande (2005) give an excellent overview of the current discussion on scale development in the social sciences. The guiding principle all these authors emphasize is that scale development is not a process that can be undertaken by following a step-by-step recipe. Clear specifications about what the construct to be measured is and what it is not are essential; item generation should be based on as many different sources as possible in order to assure that no relevant components of the construct are omitted; validity of measures should be assessed carefully; and typical measures of scale quality should be used to point to possible problems with the scale, rather than to take radical measures, possibly at the expense of the ability of the scale to capture the actual construct. For example, Churchill (1998) mentions five ways in which the coefficient alpha can easily be increased while reducing the validity of the scale. Finn and Kayande (2005, p. 13) put it like this: 'researchers need to think more carefully about the nature of ... constructs, to work much harder up front to generate and select items for their scales, and to design answer categories.'

In terms of answer categories, a choice of three out of four **answer formats** are available in the context of segmentation studies: binary, ordinal, and metric, which have different advantages and disadvantages. For binary and metric data format, which can be obtained by asking respondents to respond with 'yes' or 'no' (binary) or by asking them for a percentage evaluation or to make a cross at a point on a line that best represents their response (metric), clear measures of distance exist. This is of particular importance for segmentation that is based on distance computations. Metric data (if a continuous underlying construct can reasonably be assumed) allows the use of all data analytic methods, and thus does not impose certain statistical techniques on the researcher. Binary data enables respondents to complete surveys significantly faster (about 30 percent) than ordinal or metric surveys, which reduces fatigue and non-response effects, thus improving data quality. Mazanec (1984, p. 18) states explicitly that he views it as 'preferable to economize on scale levels rather than on the number of benefit items.' Furthermore, 'Measurement of benefits is easiest for the respondent if he is asked only to evaluate a benefit item as being important or not important.' The main disadvantage of these answer format alternatives is that respondents are not very familiar with them, and that they may not reflect the nature of the underlying construct. For example, while constructs such as behavioral intentions appear highly suited for a binary scale, attitudes may require more options to allow respondents to express their views. Suitability of the scale for the construct under study should be assessed in the pre-testing phase of the questionnaire.

Thus the recommendation is to thoroughly investigate what kind of information is actually needed. Researchers should consider making more use of either binary or metric formats. By doing so, they would benefit from avoiding the dangers associated with ordinal scales discussed above.

If ordinal scales emerge as the most suitable answer format for a particular construct, one alternative to avoid measurement problems is to use the summated scale across items if there are multiple underling dimensions, which is the procedure Likert (1932) originally proposed for the scale named after him. By using summated scores, normal distribution can be assumed when analyzing the data. So, if a construct has several dimensions that are measured by subscales, the summated values over the subscales could safely be used as the segmentation base.

The main recommendation with respect to the answer format chosen by the researcher, however, is to use data analytic techniques that are suitable for the nature of the data available. For many statistical techniques that are typically used, rank-based alternative procedures exist and should be used to avoid making wrong assumptions about the data.

Regarding the **sample** of respondents, segmentation researchers must ensure that the number of variables used as segmentation base is not too high, given the number of respondents available and the fact that it is rarely known a priori how well the data are structured. Formann's (1984) recommendation for binary data sets of at least 2^k respondents provides a good guideline for the minimum requirements, where 'k' stands for the number of variables if parametric procedures are used. If non-parametric procedures are used to explore segmentation solutions, no such rule exists. Sample size requirements increase with decreasing data structure. The appropriateness of the number of variables given a certain sample size can consequently only be assessed when data structure analysis is undertaken. Formann's rule is still a useful guideline to evaluate reasonable sample sizes for certain numbers of variables.

For segmentation purposes – the aim of which is identification or construction of market segments – the sample does not necessarily have to be representative, unless it is important to be able to state the proportion of each segment within total population. It is, however, essential to have the full range of respondents with respect to the construct under study represented in the data. If small niche segments are expected, it may even be recommendable to try to over-sample these respondents to ensure that they can be detected if they do differ from other segments in the hypothesized way.

If the number of items is too large for the available sample size and variables have to be **selected** before clustering, it is advisable to pre-analyze the data (using simple frequency counts or factor analysis) and exclude variables based on the findings, rather than transforming the space, as is the case with using factor scores resulting from factor analysis. For example, Gitelson and Kerstetter (1990) state that if more than 90 percent do not rate a benefit, it should be excluded. While this might be a very general rule that risks excluding a highly discriminating variable, as stated in Frochot and Morrison (2000), a combination of such a frequency criterion with factor analysis results might be preferable. If items have low agreement or disagreement levels and load highly on a factor that includes many other items, it is likely that little information will be lost by excluding it from cluster analysis. Of course, it would be preferable not to include such items with little additional information value in the questionnaire in the first place. But if the researcher is faced with a data set of this nature, the suggested procedure would be preferable to reduce the number of items, as opposed to factor analyzing and using the factor scores for cluster analysis.

If factor analysis is the preferred method of pre-processing, a procedure that accounts for heterogeneity in the data should be adopted, such as mixtures of factor analyzers, which is discussed in McLachlan and Peel (2000).

However, generally the raw, untransformed data that was collected from respondents should be used for segmentation purposes, because any form of pre-processing leads to a transformation of the segmentation space in which the segments were not postulated originally and relations between variables are changed.

Some transformations may be needed if variables are not the same in nature. For example, if the annual income in dollars is one variable and agreement or disagreement with the statement that 'the natural environment of the destination is important' are both included in the segmentation base, variables would need to be standardized, because the variables with the higher range of values would otherwise have more weight in the grouping process. But this frequently does not appear to be the case, because most tourism researchers use one block of questions to measure the same construct for their analysis (for example, all motivation items, all vacation activities undertaken, or all benefits sought from their vacation). Such items are typically questioned about using the same answer options, making transformation unnecessary.

Another case where transformations may be needed occurs when response styles exist in the data and contaminate the information contained. For example, respondents from certain cultural backgrounds may tend to use extreme values, while others may prefer the middle of the scale. Such contamination may have to be eliminated by transforming the raw data.

If the number of variables is too high and variables need to be eliminated, it is preferable to eliminate them and use the raw data of the remaining items for segmentation analysis, rather than using transformations such as factor scores.

The **clustering algorithm** and underlying **measure of association** should be chosen, while taking into consideration the nature of the data and the known properties of different clustering algorithms.

Although there is still no single optimal solution for determining the best **number of clusters**, two generic approaches can be recommended: (1) clustering can be repeated numerous times with varying numbers of clusters, and the number that renders the most stable results can be chosen; or (2) multiple solutions can be computed and selection is undertaken interactively with management.

After the segmentation solution has been determined it should be **validated**. First, the reliability can be assessed by testing the stability of the solution. If the same grouping emerges when computed numerous times, the segmentation solution is reliable if different solutions emerge from each computation. Second, the distinctness of the derived solution can be assessed by testing whether the segments are significantly different with respect to information that was not used in the original segmentation process. For example, benefit segments of tourists would be seen as externally valid if, for example, their expenditure patterns for different vacation activities differ significantly as well. If segments differ in benefits and no other characteristics, the validity and usefulness of the segments should be questioned.

5. CONCLUSIONS

This paper aimed to highlight how several standards have emerged in empirical tourism research that have the potential to undermine the validity of results. Three aspects of empirical tourism research were selected because they are frequently studied, and researchers appear to strongly adhere to emerged standards.

The review of empirical studies published in 2005 in the top three tourism journals led to the conclusions that: (1) multi-category ordinal scales dominate survey research in tourism despite the numerous disadvantages of this answer format and the availability of alternatives; (2) a large number of studies are based on multicultural data sets and ignore the danger of response style effects, potentially distorting their findings; and (3) a standard procedure for step-wise, data-driven segmentation has developed in the field of tourism (and even given a special name: factor-cluster analysis), the major danger of which is the elimination of about half of the information contained in the original data set through factor analysis before segments are identified or constructed.

Further aims of the article were to: (1) increase empirical tourism researchers' awareness that emerged standards are not necessarily the optimal solution; (2) encourage empirical tourism researchers to reflect more critically on their choice of measurement instruments and techniques of data analysis; (3) encourage empirical tourism researchers to dedicate a few sentences in their manuscript that explain why they have chosen a particular approach, so that an 'explain why' culture will slowly replace the current 'cite why' one; (4) encourage reviewers to request explanations and in so doing motivate researchers to engage in (2) and (3); and (5) strengthen and enhance the field of empirical tourism research so that it becomes more open to new approaches which can be shown to outperform emerged standards.

The three areas that this paper covered are almost certainly not the only ones in which standards emerge in tourism research. Rather, the selected areas reflect topics of interest to the author. To help the field move forward, experts in other fields should provide similar reviews on topics they are intimately familiar with and share their insights with the wider tourism research community, and the top tourism journals should be open to publishing such manuscripts.

NOTE

1. According to the Oxford English Dictionary the social sciences encompass 'The scientific study of the structure and functions of society; any discipline that attempts to study human society, either as a whole or in part, in a systematic way.'

ACKNOWLEDGMENT

This research was supported by the Australian Research Council (through grants DP0557769, DP0557257 and LX0559628). The author thanks Katrina Matus for her help as a research assistant for this study and Friedrich Leisch, Bettina Grün, and John Rossiter for their feedback on various components of the study.

REFERENCES

Aldenderfer, M. S., & Blashfield, R. K. (1984). *Cluster analysis*. Beverly Hills: Sage Publications.
Arabie, P., & Hubert, L. (1994). Cluster analysis in marketing research. In: R. Bagozzi (Ed.), *Advanced methods of marketing research* (pp. 160–189). Cambridge: Blackwell.
Bachman, J. G., & O'Malley, P. M. (1984). Yea-saying, nay-saying, and going to extremes: Black-white differences in response styles. *Public Opinion Quarterly, 48*(2), 491–509.
Baumann, R. (2000). *Marktsegmentierung in den Sozial- und Wirtschaftswissenschaften: eine Metaanalyse der Zielsetzungen und Zugänge*. Diploma thesis, Vienna University of Economics and Management Science, Vienna.

Bendig, A. W. (1954). Reliability and the number of rating scale categories. *Journal of Applied Psychology, 38*(1), 38–40.

Billiet, J. B., & McClendon, M. J. (2000). Modeling acquiescence in measurement models for two balanced sets of items. *Structural Equation Modeling: A Multidisciplinary Journal, 7*(4), 608–628.

Byrne, B. M., & Campbell, T. L. (1999). Cross-cultural comparisons and the presumption of equivalent measurement and theoretical structure – A look beneath the surface. *Journal of Cross-Cultural Psychology, 30*(5), 555–574.

Buchta, C., Dimitriadou, E., Dolničar, S., Leisch, F., & Weingessel, A. (1997). *A comparison of several cluster algorithms on artificial binary data scenarios from travel market segmentation.* Working Paper # 7, SFB Adaptive Information Systems and Modelling in Economics and Management Science, Vienna.

Calantone, R., Schewe, C., & Allen, C. T. (1980). Targeting specific advertising messages at tourist segments. In: D. E. Hawkins, E. L. Shafer, & J. M. Rovels (Eds), *Tourism marketing and management* (pp. 133–147). Washington, D.C.: George Washington University.

Cha, S., McLeary, K. W., & Uzsal, M. (1995). Travel motivations of Japanese overseas travelers: A factor-cluster segmentation approach. *Journal of Travel Research, 34*(1), 33–39.

Chang, L. (1994). A psychometric evaluation of four-point and six-point Likert-type scales in relation to reliability and validity. *Applied Psychological Measurement, 18*, 205–215.

Cheung, G. W., & Rensvold, R. B. (2000). Assessing extreme and acquiescence response sets in cross-cultural research using structural equation modeling. *Journal of Cross-Cultural Psychology, 31*(2), 187–212.

Chun, K. T., Campbell, J. B., & Yoo, J. H. (1974). Extreme response style in cross-cultural research – Reminder. *Journal of Cross-Cultural Psychology, 5*(4), 465–480.

Churchill, G. A. (1979). A paradigm for developing better measures of marketing constructs. *Journal of Marketing Research, 16*, 64–73.

Churchill, G. A. (1998). Measurement in marketing: Time to refocus? In: J. D. Hess & K. B. Monroe (Eds), *Proceedings of the 14th Paul D. converse symposium* (pp. 25–41). Chicago: American Marketing Association.

Clarke III, I. (2000). Extreme response style in cross cultural research: An empirical investigation. *Journal of Social Behaviour and Personality, 15*(1), 137–152.

Clarke III, I. (2001). Extreme response style in cross-cultural research. *International Marketing Review, 18*(3), 301–324.

Cox, E. P. (1980). The optimal number of response alternatives for a scale: A review. *Journal of Marketing Research, 17*(4), 407–422.

Crask, M. (1981). Segmenting the vacationer market: Identifying the vacation preferences, demographics, and magazine readership of each group. *Journal of Travel Research, 20*, 20–34.

Cronbach, L. (1950). Further evidence on response sets and test design. *Educational and Psychological Measurement, 10*, 3–31.

Cronbach, L. J. (1951). Coefficient alpha and the internal structure of tests. *Psychometrika, 16*, 297–334.

Dimanche, F., Havitz, M. E., & Howard, D. R. (1993). Consumer involvement profiles as a tourism segmentation tool. *Journal of Travel and Tourism Marketing, 1*(4), 33–52.

Dimitriadou, E., Dolnicar, S., & Weingessel, A. (2002). An examination of indexes for determining the number of clusters in binary data sets. *Psychometrika, 67*(1), 137–160.

Dolnicar, S. (2002). Review of data-driven market segmentation in tourism. *Journal of Travel and Tourism Marketing, 12*(1), 1–22.

Dolnicar, S. (2003). Simplifying three-way questionnaires – Do the advantages of binary answer categories compensate for the loss of information? *ANZMAC CD Proceedings,* Adelaide.

Dolnicar, S. (2004). Beyond 'Commonsense Segmentation' – A systematics of segmentation approaches in tourism. *Journal of Travel Research, 42*(3), 244–250.

Dolnicar, S., & Grün, B. (in press). Cross-cultural differences in survey response patterns. *International Marketing Review.*

Dolnicar, S., & Grün, B. (in press). Culture-specific response style effects. *International Journal of Culture, Tourism and Hospitality Research.*

Dolnicar, S., & Leisch, F. (2000). Behavioral market segmentation using the bagged clustering approach based on binary guest survey data: Exploring and visualizing unobserved heterogeneity. *Tourism Analysis, 5*(2–4), 163–170.

Dolnicar, S., & Leisch, F. (2001). Knowing what you get – A conceptual clustering framework for increased transparency of market segmentation studies. Presented at the Marketing Science 2001 (Abstract Proceedings available).

Dolnicar, S., & Leisch, F. (2003). Winter tourist segments in Austria – Identifying stable vacation styles for target marketing action. *Journal of Travel Research, 41*(3), 281–293 (Charles Goeldner Article of Excellence Award).

Dolnicar, S., & Leisch, F. (2004). Segmenting markets by bagged clustering. *Australasian Marketing Journal, 12*(1), 51–65.

Dolnicar, S., Grün, B., & Leisch, F. (2004). Time efficient brand image measurement – Is binary format sufficient to gain the market insight required? *CD Proceedings of the 33rd EMAC conference.*

Dolnicar, S., & Schäfer, A. I. (2006). Public perception of desalinated versus recycled water in Australia. *Proceedings of the AWWA Desalination Symposium 2006.*

Everitt, B. S. (1979). Unresolved problems in cluster analysis. *Biometrica, 35*, 169–181.

Everitt, B. S. (1993). *Cluster analysis.* New York: Halsted Press.

Feldman, J. M., & Lynch,, J. G., Jr. (1988). Self-generated validity and other effects of measurement on belief, attitude, intention and behaviour. *Journal of Applied Psychology, 73*(3), 421–435.

Finn, A., & Kayande, U. (1997). Reliability assessment and optimization of marketing measurement. *Journal of Marketing Research, 34*(2), 262–276.

Finn, A., & Kayande, U. (2005). How fine is C-OAR-SE? A generalizability theory perspective on Rossiter's procedure. *International Journal of Research in Marketing, 22*, 11–21.

Finn, R. H. (1972). Effects of some variations in rating scale characteristics on the means and reliabilities of ratings. *Educational and Psychological Measurement, 32*(2), 255–265.

Formann, A. K. (1984). *Die Latent-Class-Analyse: Einführung in die Theorie und Anwendung.* Weinheim: Beltz.

Frochot, I., & Morrison, A. M. (2000). Benefit segmentation: A review of its application to travel and tourism research. *Journal of Travel and Tourism Marketing, 9*(4), 21–45.

Gitelson, R. J., & Kerstetter, D. L. (1990). The relationship between sociodemographic variables, benefits sought and subsequent vacation behavior: A case study. *Journal of Travel Research, 28*, 24–29.

Goodrich, J. (1980). Benefit segmentation of US international travelers: An empirical study with American Express. In: D. E. Hawkins, E. L. Shafer, & J. M. Rovels (Eds), *Tourism marketing and management* (pp. 133–147). Washington, D.C.: George Washington University.

Green, P. E., & Rao, V. R. (1970). Rating scales and information recovery – How many scales and response categories to use? *Journal of Marketing, 34*(July), 33–39.

Greenleaf, E. A. (1992a). Improving rating scale measures by detecting and correcting bias components in some response styles. *Journal of Marketing Research, 29*(May), 176–188.

Greenleaf, E. A. (1992b). Measuring extreme response style. *Public Opinion Quarterly, 56*(3), 328–351.

Haley, R. J. (1968). Benefit segmentation: A decision–oriented research tool. *Journal of Marketing, 32*, 30–35.

Hancock, G. R., & Klockars, A. J. (1991). The effect of scale manipulations on validity: Targeting frequency rating scales for anticipated performance levels. *Applied Ergonomics, 22*(3), 147–154.

Hui, C. H., & Triandis, H. C. (1989). Effects of culture and response format on extreme response style. *Journal of Cross-Cultural Psychology, 20*(3), 296–309.

Jacoby, J., & Matell, M. S. (1971). Three-point Likert scales are good enough. *Journal of Marketing Research, 8*, 495–500.

Johnson, M. D., Lehmann, D. R., & Horne, D. R. (1990). The effects of fatigue on judgments of interproduct similarity. *International Journal of Research in Marketing, 7*(1), 35–43.

Jones, R. R. (1968). Differences in response consistency and subjects' preferences for three personality inventory response formats, *Proceedings of the 76th annual convention of the American psychological association*, (pp. 247–248).

Kampen, J., & Swyngedouw, M. (2000). The multi-category controversy revisited. *Quality & Quantity, 34*(1), 87–102.

Ketchen, D. J., Jr., & Shook, C. L. (1996). The application of cluster analysis in strategic management research: An analysis and critique. *Strategic Management Journal, 17*, 441–458.

Kohonen, T. (1997). *Self-Organizing Maps* (2nd Ed.). Berlin: Springer.

Komorita, S. S. (1963). Attitude content, intensity, and the neutral point on a Likert scale. *Journal of Social Psychology, 61*, 327–334.

Komorita, S. S., & Graham, W. K. (1965). Number of scale points and the reliability of scales. *Educational and Psychological Measurement, 25*(4), 987–995.

Kozak, M., Bigne, E., & Andreu, L. (2003). Limitations of cross-cultural customer satisfaction research and recommending alternative methods. *Journal of Quality Assurance in Hospitality and Tourism, 4*(3–4), 37–59.

Kuhn, T. S. (1970). *The structure of scientific revolution* ((2nd ed.)). Chicago: University of Chicago Press.

Leisch, F. (1998). *Ensemble methods for neural clustering and classification*. Doctoral thesis, Institut für Statistik, Wahrscheinlichkeitstheorie und Versicherungsmathematik, Technische Universität Wien, Austria.

Leisch, F. (1999). *Bagged Clustering*. Working Paper # 51, SFB Adaptive Information Systems and Modeling in Economics and Management Science. http://www.wu-wien.ac.at/am

Likert, R. (1932). A technique for the measurement of attitudes. *Archives of Psychology, 140*, 44–53.

Loken, B., Pirie, P., Virnig, K. A., Hinkle, R. L., & Salmon, C. T. (1987). The use of 0–10 scales in telephone surveys. *Journal of the Market Research Society, 29*(3), 353–362.

Marin, G., Gamba, R. J., & Marin, B. V. (1992). Extreme response style and acquiescence among Hispanics – The role of acculturation and education. *Journal of Cross-Cultural Psychology, 23*(4), 498–509.

Martin, W. S., Fruchter, B., & Mathis, W. J. (1974). An investigation of the effect of the number of scale intervals on principal components factor analysis. *Educational and Psychological Measurement, 34*, 537–545.

Martinetz, T., & Schulten, K. (1994). Topology representing networks. *Neural Networks, 7*(5), 507–522.

Matell, M. S., & Jacoby, J. (1971). Is there an optimal number of alternatives for Likert scale items? Study I: Reliability and validity. *Educational and Psychological Measurement, 31*, 657–674.

Mazanec, J. (2000). Market segmentation. In: J. Jafari (Ed.), *Encyclopedia of tourism.* London: Routledge.

Mazanec, J. A. (1984). How to detect travel market segments: A clustering approach. *Journal of travel research, 23*(1), 17–21.

McClendon, M. J. (1991). Acquiescence and recency response-order effects in interview surveys. *Sociological Methods and Research, 20*, 60–103.

Mazanec, J., Grabler, K., Maier, G., & Wöber, K. (1997). *International city tourism: Analysis and strategy.* London: Pinter/Cassell. http://tourism.wu-wien.ac.at/cgi-bin/ift.pl?aktuell/literatur.htm#ICT

Mazanec, J., & Strasser, H. (2000). *A nonparametric approach to perceptions-based market segmentation: Foundations.* Vienna: Springer. http://tourism.wu-wien.ac.at/cgi-bin/ift.pl?aktuell/springer.html

McLachlan, G., & Peel, D. (2000). *Finite mixture models.* New York: Wiley.

Milligan, G. W. (1980). An examination of the effect of six types of error perturbation on fifteen clustering algorithms. *Psychometrika, 45*, 325–342.

Milligan, G. W. (1981). A monte carlo study of thirty internal criterion measures for cluster analysis. *Psychometrika, 46*(2), 187–199.

Milligan, G. W. (1996). Clustering validation: Results and implications for applied analyses. In: P. Arabie & L. J. Hubert (Eds), *Clustering and classification.* River Edge: World Scientific Publication.

Milligan, G. W., & Cooper, M. C. (1985). An examination of procedures for determining the number of clusters in a data set. *Psychometrika, 46*(2), 187–199.

Myers, J. H., & Tauber, E. (1977). *Market structure analysis.* American Marketing Association: Chicago.

Nunnally, J. C. (1967). *Psychometric theory* (1st ed.). New York: McGraw-Hill.

Oaster, T. R. F. (1989). Number of alternatives per choice point and stability of Likert-type scales. *Perceptual and Motor Skills, 68*, 549–550.

Park, M., Yang, X., Lee, B., Jang, H.-C., & Stokowski, P. A. (2002). Segmenting casino gamblers by involvement profiles: A colorado example. *Tourism Management, 23*(1), 55–65.

Peabody, D. (1962). Two components in bipolar scales: Direction and extremeness. *Psychological Review, 69*(2), 65–73.

Percy, L. (1976). An argument in support of ordinary factor analysis of dichotomous variables.' In *Advances in Consumer Research* Vol. III.

Preston, C. C., & Colman, A. M. (2000). Optimal number of response categories in rating scales: Reliability, validity, discriminating power, and respondent preferences. *Acta Psychologica, 104*, 1–15.

178 SARA DOLNICAR

Punj, G., & Stewart, D. W. (1983). Cluster analysis in marketing research: Review and suggestions for application. *Journal of Marketing Research, 20*, 134–148.

Ramsay, J. O. (1973). The effect of number of categories in rating scales on precision of estimation of scale values. *Psychometrika, 37*, 513–532.

Remington, M., Tyrer, P. J., Newson-Smith, J., & Cicchetti, D. V. (1979). Comparative reliability of categorical and analogue rating scales in the assessment of psychiatric symptomatology. *Psychological Medicine, 9*, 765–770.

Rossiter, J. R. (2002). The C-OAR-SE procedure for scale development in marketing. *International Journal of Research in Marketing, 19*, 305–335.

Rungie, C., Laurent, G., Dall'Olmo Riley, F., Morrison, D. G., & Roy, T. (2005). Measuring and modelling the (limited) reliability of free choice attitude questions. *International Journal of Research in Marketing, 22*(3), 309–318.

Scharf, A. (1991). *Konkurrierende Produkte aus Konsumentensicht.* Frankfurt: Verlag Harri Deutsch.

Sekaran, U. (1983). Methodological and theoretical issues and advancements on cross-cultural research. *Journal of International Business Studies, 14*(2), 61–73.

Sheppard, A. G. (1996). The sequence of factor analysis and cluster analysis: Differences in segmentation and dimensionality through the use of raw and factor scores. *Tourism Analysis, 1*, 49–57.

Shoemaker, S. (1994). Segmentation of the US travel market according to benefits realized. *Journal of Travel Research, 32*(3), 8–21.

Smith, S. L. J. (1989). *Tourism analysis: A handbook.* Harlow, England: Longman.

Smith, A. M., & Reynolds, N. L. (2002). Measuring cross-cultural service quality: A framework for assessment. *International Marketing Review, 19*(4–5), 450–481.

Sokal, R. R., & Sneath, P. H. A. (1963). *Principles of numerical taxonomy.* San Franscisco: Freeman.

Stevens, J. (2002). *Applied multivariate statistics for the social sciences* (4 ed.). Mahwah, New Jersey: Lawrence Erlbaum Associates.

Symonds, P. M. (1924). On the loss of reliability in ratings due to coarseness of the scale. *Journal of Experimental Psychology, 7*, 456–461.

Thorndike, R. L. (1953). Who belongs in the family? *Psychometrika, 18*(4), 267–276.

van de Vijver, F. J. R., & Poortinga, Y. H. (2002). Structural equivalence in multilevel research. *Journal of Cross-Cultural Psychology, 33*(2), 141–156.

Van der Eijk, C. (2001). Measuring agreement in ordered rating scales. *Quality and Quantity, 35*(3), 325–341.

van Herk, H., Poortinga, Y. H., & Verhallen, T. M. M. (2004). Response styles in rating scales – Evidence of method bias in data from six EU countries. *Journal of Cross-Cultural Psychology, 35*(3), 346–360.

Watkins, D., & Cheung, S. (1995). Culture, gender and response bias. *Journal of Cross-Cultural Psychology, 26*(5), 490–504.

Watson, D. (1992). Correcting for acquiescent response bias in the absence of a balanced scale: An application to class consciousness. *Sociological Methods and Research, 21*(1), 52–88.

Wedel, M., & Kamakura, W. (1998). *Market segmentation – conceptual and methodological foundations.* Boston: Kluwer Academic Publishers.

Welkenhuysen-Gybels, J., Billiet, J., & Cambre, B. (2003). Adjustment for acquiescence in the assessment of the construct equivalence of Likert-type score items. *Journal of Cross-Cultural Psychology, 34*(6), 702–722.

APPENDIX 1: REVIEWED LITERATURE

Alexandros, A., & Jaffry, S. (2005). Stated preferences for two cretan heritage attractions. *Annals of Tourism Research, 32*(4), 985.

Andereck, K. L., Valentine, K. M., et al. (2005). Residents' perceptions of community tourism impacts. *Annals of Tourism Research, 32*(4), 1056.

Apostolakis, A., & Jaffry, S. (2005). A choice modeling application for greek heritage attractions. *Journal of Travel Research, 43*(3), 309–318.

Ballantyne, R., Carr, N., et al. (2005). Between the flags: 'An assessment of domestic and international university students' knowledge of beach safety in australia. *Tourism Management, 26*(4), 617.

Baloglu, S., & Love, C. (2005). Association meeting planners' perceptions and intentions for five major US convention cities: The structured and unstructured images. *Tourism Management, 26*(5), 743.

Beldona, S. (2005). Cohort analysis of online travel information search behavior: 1995–2000. *Journal of Travel Research, 44*(2), 135–142.

Bigne, J. E., Andreu, L., et al. (2005). The theme park experience: An analysis of pleasure, arousal and satisfaction. *Tourism Management, 26*(6), 833.

Bigne, J. E., Andreu, L., et al. (2005). Quality market orientation: Tourist agencies' perceived effects. *Annals of Tourism Research, 32*(4), 1022.

Blain, C., Levy, S. E., et al. (2005). Destination branding: Insights and practices from destination management organizations. *Journal of Travel Research, 43*(4), 328–338.

Bloom, J. Z. (2005). Market segmentation: A neural network application. *Annals of Tourism Research, 32*(1), 93.

Bonn, M. A., Joseph, S. M., et al. (2005). International versus domestic visitors: An examination of destination image perceptions. *Journal of Travel Research, 43*(3), 294–301.

Brown, G., & Getz, D. (2005). Linking wine preferences to the choice of wine tourism destinations. *Journal of Travel Research, 43*(3), 266–276.

Carr, N. (2005). Poverty, debt, and conspicuous consumption: University students tourism experiences. *Tourism Management, 26*(5), 797.

Chen, H. M., & Tseng, C. H. (2005). The performance of marketing alliances between the tourism industry and credit card issuing banks in Taiwan. *Tourism Management, 26*(1), 15.

Chhabra, D. (2005). Defining authenticity and its determinants: Toward an authenticity flow model. *Journal of Travel Research, 44*(1), 64–73.

Choi, H. S. C., & Sirakaya, E. (2005). Measuring residents' attitude toward sustainable tourism: Development of sustainable tourism attitude scale. *Journal of Travel Research, 43*(4), 380–394.

Cole, S. T. (2005). Comparing mail and web-based survey distribution methods: Results of surveys to leisure travel retailers. *Journal of Travel Research, 43*(4), 422–430.

Connell, J. (2005). Toddlers, tourism and tobermory: Destination marketing issues and television-induced tourism. *Tourism Management, 26*(5), 763.

Daruwalla, P., & Darcy, S. (2005). Personal and societal attitudes to disability. *Annals of Tourism Research, 32*(3), 549.

Duman, T., & Mattila, A. S. (2005). The role of affective factors on perceived cruise vacation value. *Tourism Management, 26*(3), 311.

Enright, M. J., & Newton, J. (2005). Determinants of tourism destination competitiveness in Asia Pacific: Comprehensiveness and universality. *Journal of Travel Research, 43*(4), 339–350.

Espino-Rodriguez, T. F., & Padron-Robaina, V. (2005). A resource-based view of outsourcing and its implications for organizational performance in the hotel sector. *Tourism Management, 26*(5), 707.

Fleischer, A., & Tchetchik, A. (2005). Does rural tourism benefit from agriculture? *Tourism Management, 26*(4), 493.

Frochot, I. (2005). A benefit segmentation of tourists in rural areas: A Scottish perspective. *Tourism Management, 26*(3), 335.

Haley, A. J., Snaith, T., et al. (2005). The social impacts of tourism: A case study of Bath, UK. *Annals of Tourism Research, 32*(3), 647.

Hall, C. M. (2005). Biosecurity and wine tourism. *Tourism Management, 26*(6), 931.

Hou, J. S., Lin, C. H., et al. (2005). Antecedents of attachment to a cultural tourism destination: The case of Hakka and non-Hakka Taiwanese visitors to Pei-Pu, Taiwan. *Journal of Travel Research, 44*(2), 221–233.

Hwang, S. N., Lee, C., et al. (2005). The relationship among tourists': Involvement, place attachment and interpretation satisfaction in Taiwan's national parks. *Tourism Management, 26*(2), 143.

Johnson, C., & Vanetti, M. (2005). Locational strategies of international hotel chains. *Annals of Tourism Research, 32*(4), 1077.

Jones, S. (2005). Community-based ecotourism: The significance of social capital. *Annals of Tourism Research, 32*(2), 303.

Kang, I., Jeon, S., et al. (2005). Investigating structural relations affecting the effectiveness of service management. *Tourism Management, 26*(3), 301.

Kang, S. K., & Hsu, C. H. C. (2005). Dyadic consensus on family vacation destination selection. *Tourism Management, 26*(4), 571.

Kim, D. Y., Hwang, Y. H., et al. (2005). Modeling tourism advertising effectiveness. *Journal of Travel Research, 44*(1), 42–49.

Kim, H., & Kim, W. G. (2005). The relationship between brand equity and firms': Performance in luxury hotels and chain restaurants. *Tourism Management, 26*(4), 549.

Kim, S. S., Chun, H., et al. (2005). Positioning analysis of overseas golf tour destinations by Korean golf tourists. *Tourism Management, 26*(6), 905.

Kim, S. S., & Morrsion, A. M. (2005). Change of images of South Korea among foreign tourists after the 2002 FIFA World Cup. *Tourism Management, 26*(2), 233.

Kim, S. S., & Petrick, J. F. (2005). Residents': Perceptions on impacts of the FIFA 2002 World Cup: The case of Seoul as a host city. *Tourism Management, 26*(1), 25.

Kim, S. S., & Prideaux, B. (2005). Marketing implications arising from a comparative study of international pleasure tourist motivations and other travel-related characteristics of visitors to Korea. *Tourism Management, 26*(3), 347.

Kwan, A. V. C., & McCartney, G. (2005). Mapping resident perceptions of gaming impact. *Journal of Travel Research, 44*(2), 177–187.

Lawton, L. J. (2005). Resident perceptions of tourist attractions on the gold coast of Australia. *Journal of Travel Research, 44*(2), 188–200.

Lee, C. K., Lee, Y. K., et al. (2005). Korea's destination image formed by the 2002 World Cup. *Annals of Tourism Research, 32*(4), 839.

Lee, C. K., & Taylor, T. (2005). Critical reflections on the economic impact assessment of a mega-event: The case of 2002 FIFA World Cup. *Tourism Management, 26*(4), 595.

Litvin, S. W. (2005). Streetscape improvements in an historic tourist city: A second visit to king street, Charleston, South Carolina. *Tourism Management, 26*(3), 421.

Mohsin, A. (2005). Tourist attitudes and destination marketing – The case of Australia's northern territory and Malaysia. *Tourism Management, 26*(5), 723.

Needham, M. D., & Rollins, R. B. (2005). Interest group standards for recreation and tourism impacts at Ski areas in the summer. *Tourism Management, 26*(1), 1.

O'Leary, S., & Deegan, J. (2005). Ireland's image as a tourism destination in France: Attribute importance and performance. *Journal of Travel Research, 43*(3), 247–256.

Okumus, F., Altinay, M., et al. (2005). The impact of Turkey's economic crisis of february 2001 on the tourism industry in northern Cyprus. *Tourism Management, 26*(1), 95.

Okumus, F., & Karamustafa, K. (2005). Impact of an economic crisis: Evidence from Turkey. *Annals of Tourism Research, 32*(4), 942.

Page, S. J., Bentley, T., et al. (2005). Tourist safety in New Zealand and Scotland. *Annals of Tourism Research, 32*(1), 150.

Page, S. J., Bentley, T. A., et al. (2005). Scoping the nature and extent of adventure tourism operations in Scotland: How safe are they? *Tourism Management, 26*(3), 381.

Pearce, P. L., & Lee, U. I. (2005). Developing the travel career approach to tourist motivation. *Journal of Travel Research, 43*(3), 226–237.

Perez, E. A., & Nadal, J. R. (2005). Host community perceptions a cluster analysis. *Annals of Tourism Research, 32*(4), 925.

Petrick, J. F. (2005). Segmenting cruise passengers with price sensitivity. *Tourism Management, 26*(5), 753.

Petrzelka, P., Krannich, R. S., et al. (2005). Rural tourism and gendered nuances. *Annals of Tourism Research, 32*(4), 1121.

Plummer, R., Telfer, D., et al. (2005). Beer tourism in Canada along the Waterloo-Wellington ale trail. *Tourism Management, 26*(3), 447.

Pyo, S. (2005). Knowledge map for tourist destinations – Needs and implications. *Tourism Management, 26*(4), 583.

Qu, R., Ennew, C., et al. (2005). The impact of regulation and ownership structure on market orientation in the tourism industry in China. *Tourism Management, 26*(6), 939.

Reichel, A., & Haber, S. (2005). A three-sector comparison of the business performance of small tourism enterprises: An exploratory study. *Tourism Management, 26*(5), 681.

Reisinger, Y., & Mavondo, F. (2005). Travel anxiety and intentions to travel internationally: Implications of travel risk perception. *Journal of Travel Research, 43*(3), 212–225.

Sarigollu, E., & Huang, R. (2005). Benefits segmentation of visitors to Latin America. *Journal of Travel Research, 43*(3), 277–293.

Sheehan, L. R., & Ritchie, J. R. B. (2005). Destination stakeholders exploring identity and salience. *Annals of Tourism Research, 32*(3), 711.

Sirakaya, E., Delen, D., et al. (2005). Forecasting gaming referenda. *Annals of Tourism Research, 32*(1), 127.

Suh, Y. K., & McAvoy, L. (2005). Preferences and trip expenditures – A conjoint analysis of visitors to Seoul, Korea. *Tourism Management, 26*(3), 325.

Tsai, H. T., Huang, L., et al. (2005). Emerging E-commerce development model for Taiwanese travel agencies. *Tourism Management, 26*(5), 787.

Yoon, Y., & Uysal, M. (2005). An examination of the effects of motivation and satisfaction on destination loyalty: A structural model. *Tourism Management, 26*(1), 45.

CHAPTER 6

GENDER IN BACKPACKING AND ADVENTURE TOURISM

Jenny Cave and Chris Ryan

ABSTRACT

This paper reports both quantitative and qualitative findings derived from a sample of 494 backpackers in New Zealand. The objectives of the paper include (a) examining gender differences in perceptions of the backpacking experience and (b) illustrating how mixed research methods aid in deriving richer understandings of a social phenomenon. While predispositions emerge from genders, wherein males are more oriented towards hard-core adventure activities and less reflection and females tend to more reflection as to the nature of the activity and self-image, intra-gender differences are important. The 'truths' of the experiences are complex, individualistic and need to be contextualised among issues of flux, orthodoxy, commodification, image generation and possibly a sense of curiosity about self and place.

INTRODUCTION

Substantial academic literatures exists in both tourism and leisure studies showing that gender is a distinguishing feature in outdoor activities. Indeed, throughout the 1970s to 1980s, a consistent theme for analysis was the number and nature of factors that inhibited female participation in sport,

Advances in Culture, Tourism and Hospitality Research, Volume 1, 183–213
Copyright © 2007 by Elsevier Ltd.
ISSN: 1871-3173/doi:10.1016/S1871-3173(06)01006-8

outdoor activities, and albeit to a lesser degree, adventure tourism. However, in the last part of the twentieth century, previous minority life-style trends became more dominant, among which were the changing career choices of females and the emergence of not only delayed marriage and child birth, but also the increasing perception of the status of single lifestyles as being socially acceptable. Additionally, high divorce rates meant an emergence of older females adopting more adventurous lifestyles, while within marriage it might also be contended that females had different expectations to those of the past and were more willing to travel in the company of other females and not simply as a spouse (see for a review of these issues, Ryan & Trauer, 2005). Within the backpacking market sector, significant changes were also occurring with increasing commercialisation of the product. From the supply perspective, providers of backpacker accommodation found their clientele began to include significant numbers of older people and those using the accommodation during periods of normal paid holiday leave from work. The previously dominant market of those taking extended travel patterns of several months became diluted by these new groups, who none-theless were appreciative of the culture of the traditional market, which is, in part, an important ingredient of the appeal for the use of backpacking accommodation. The product thus changed, as smaller rooms with en suite facilities began to appear.

Parallel to this there was also increasing amounts of evidence that back-packers travelled to, saw and participated in the same things that were the domain of supposedly more 'mainstream' tourists (Ryan & Mohsin, 2001). Adventure tourism also was becoming more commodified (Cloke & Perkins, 1998, 2002). Commentators noted the role of media and industry in generating images that were consumed as a part of self-identity and self-expression, and indeed argued that in adventure tourism, tourists sought not the unfamiliar but an acquisition of an activity and lifestyle made familiar through the media and which appealed to them (Trauer and Ryan, 2005; Cater, 2005).

PURPOSE AND METHOD OF THE STUDY

This paper reports research findings that explore gender differences among visitors using backpacker accommodation in New Zealand with some refer-ence to the concept of *curiositas*. The paper considers the following themes: expectations and changing lifestyles available to females, the commodification of adventure, the way backpackers participate in adventure tourism and the ways in which gender impacts upon adventure experience evaluation.

The paper includes the following structure: (a) a brief discussion of the use of quantitative and qualitative research methods; (b) a description of gender differences with reference to adventure holidaying; (c) details of the questionnaire construction and reliability with reference to the statistical component of the research; (d) a short description of the sample; (e) results derived from the quantitative component of the study; (e) a description of the means of analysing qualitative data; (f) results of the qualitative analysis; and (g) discussion of results.

Mixed Methods Research

Both quantitative and qualitative data collected from the sample permits a comparison of findings. The survey includes open-ended questions asking, "Thinking of any cultural and adventure activity undertaken, which was special to you: (a) Describe this activity? (b) What made it special? and (c) In what ways was it special?" These questions complement the items used to derive quantitative data. The intention of using these questions is to encourage respondents to tell the researchers about the complexities of their remembered experience. By asking the same questions to a large number of people and then splitting the sample into male and female respondents, the study sought to uncover the presence or absence of the common underlying dimensions of understanding by each gender. The personal construct theory argues that humans communicate by the means of shared understanding and despite the variability of humankind and the influence of preconceptions, family members and friends, or media images, the underlying dimensions of understanding are thought to be comparatively few as well as being time, place and activity specific. Consequently, the repetition of common ideas emerges when a topic is discussed in interviews, especially, if a common question structure is used (Kelly, 1955; Allport, 1955, 1961).

The open-ended question format seeks rich qualitative data from respondents. Holidays, in particular adventure experiences, are known to be influenced by the factors, such as leisure motivation (Beard & Ragheb, 1983), the degree of arousal and challenge (Csikszentmihalyi, 1975), an experience (or not) of 'flow' (Csikszentmihalyi, 1990), levels of competence and mastery (Ryan, 1997) and the degree of involvement in the activity (Havitz & Dimanche, 1990). Consequently, such heightened responses might be expressed in emotive rather than formal language. Qualitative data reports the 'voice of the source', capturing how people interpret the complexity of their world and aiding understanding of events from the perspective of the participants (Cavana, Delahaya, & Sekaran, 2001). If, as literature informs us, genders experience adventure and travel differently, and a 'special' adventure experience is described that reflects events that are unusual, out of the ordinary, distinctive or in any other way 'not ordinary', then such differences should be reflected in the data. Such data complement statistical data and might be said to enrich the totality of findings.

LITERATURE REVIEW

Miller (1986) argued that women had been denied power in many aspects of their lives except within the context of caring institutions. Henderson and Allen (1991, p. 101) noted that through care 'women have been allowed limited access to power over others' but continued to analyse the thesis that senses of responsibility could be an inhibiting factor in engaging certain types of leisure activities. These factors helped to define the social structures of what constituted female leisure, particularly within family frameworks. Harrington (1991, p. 125) provided empirical evidence to support this hypothesis in a study of 270 female faculty members and concluded:

> While the mainstream literature in leisure studies often assumes that leisure is residual time after a man's hours on the job, the same cannot be assumed for women. While men may stay longer at work to finish a job, women are more likely to take work home because they have to be there to take care of the children, make dinner and do the housework. Responsibilities for caring for others in the home ... is also a partial explanation for why a women's leisure is likely to centred in the home.

The analysis does not wholly depend upon gender, but is reflective of the gender roles within a specific life stage. However, the analyses of the 1970s and early 1980s suggested that the social norms of family expectations extended beyond those women who were married with children. In part, the literature of this period was informed by the studies of gender differences in play. For example, Millar (1974) and Connor and Serbin (1977) noted differences in boys and girls in the type of play in which they engaged, and a thesis was that these patterns carried into later life and into more formal leisure activities. Indeed, Grant (1984) observed that in the early days of female hockey, the emphasis lay more on participation than competition, even to the extent that in initial tournaments organised by the International Federation of Women's Hockey Association, tournaments were structured to avoid the emergence of an overall winner.

With reference to adventure holidaying and travel, Little (2002) note that the imagery and history of such activities are male dominated. Little and Wilson (2005) cite Clarke (1988, p. 78) as saying, "for centuries the oceanic voyage and the journey to the interior were wholly, solely and exclusively men's business". They argue one consequence is that while increasingly women undertake these pursuits, the traditional imagery is masculine. Hence, a question arises as to what extent females shape their own self-perception with reference to those images. For the current authors what is important is not only the evidence presented by Little and Wilson of a personalisation of 'the adventure' and a reluctance for self-description as an 'adventurer' by females, but also the re-construction of the nature of the adventure experience as discussed by Cloke and Perkins (1998, 2002). It is here suggested that the conclusions reached by Little and Wilson can be applied to the participants of both genders who engage in these types of activities, that both accept dominant models in the construction of self to arrive at often similar notions of self-empowerment and that the intra-gender difference might be as important as inter-gender difference.

Research in the mid-1980s questions the view that gender is a sole and sufficient explanatory determinant of holiday experiences. For example, Hirschman (1984) distinguishes between the sex and gender roles with reference to measures of flow, although many of these types of studies referred to more general leisure pursuits than solely holidaying. Davidson (1996, p. 91) notes "the dearth of literature that explores holiday experiences of women or seeks to determine whether, how or why women's holiday experiences are different from mens' ". However, sufficient evidence exists, as Ryan (2002) reviews, to suggest that gender was not wholly a sole determinant of holiday experience and that for both men and women the presence of children and life stage were significant factors in the holiday choice as to both type of holiday and destination. However, within the parenting role, mothers certainly sought more relaxation than male counterparts and structured relaxation differently from males (see, for example, various discussions by Cantwell & Sanik, 1993; Davidson, 1996; Deem, 1996; Massey, 1994; Madrigal, Havitz, & Howard, 1992; Ryan, 1995; Wearing & Wearing, 2005).

With specific reference to adventure tourism, there has been a growing literature of female perceptions of such tourism (e.g., Culp, 1998; Galpin, 1987; Little, 2000, 2002; McIntyre, Burden, & Kiewa, 1993). This literature illustrates themes that are applicable to both genders, and these include adventure as being a new experience, stepping into the unknown, stepping from beyond the 'comfort zone', leaning about personal capacities in emotional, social and cognitive terms. Work by Cater (2005) and Ferguson and Todd (2005), for example, offer similar analyses regardless of gender. It can be suggested that there is a growing homogeneity between genders in their wish to collect the experiences offered by the commercial adventure tourism industry, particular in Australasia. A number of commentators also suggest that the nature of adventure tourism has changed significantly in the last decade with a wider range of activities emerging that offer thrill, adrenalin-rising activities but with comparatively little inherent risk. Bungy jumping is, perhaps, the example *par excellence* of this type, while the New Zealand operators offer combinations of 'big thrills', such as jet boating, helicopter trips and bungy jumping in which it might be said that two of the three involve the 'adventurer' in a passive spectator role. In white-water rafting where danger does exist, for the most part the participant is a passenger, albeit active when commanded by the guide. Ewert and Jamieson (2003) offer an analysis of the adventure tourism products located on a matrix formed by the dimensions of independent participant or a member of a structured group on the one hand, and highly controlled or high un-certainty on the other. Trauer (2006) offers a similar analysis based upon the degrees of hard vs. soft adventure and the nature of participant situational and continuing involvement.

It appears that there are at least two patterns of related change occurring. On the one hand, there are changing social demographics of female lifestyle. Ryan (2001) notes the significant growth in women's only travel, as does Trollope (1998). Females are perceiving and selecting from more lifestyles than simply that of the 'carer' role. On the other hand, adventure tourism has evolved to offer a range of product that permits 'dabbling', a collection of adrenalin experiences open to those with comparatively little skill (Ewert & Jamieson, 2003; Trauer & Ryan, 2005; Trauer, 2006). Thus, there are those seeking new forms of self-identification in the roles that they wish to adopt in contemporary society, and a product that creates desirable images of achievement and surmounting challenge. This latter product of adventure tourism also offers signs and symbols of that achievement through the pur-chase of souvenir videos, t-shirts, videos and other forms of clothing that 'sign' one as a member of a desired social group (Ferguson & Todd, 2005; Cater, 2005). These signs convey meanings to both adherents and non-adherents, although as Ferguson and Todd (2005) note, there may well be subtleties and nuances of meanings within sub-sets of adherents (for exam-ple, the wearing of a Hackett bungy jumping t-shirt would be considered 'naff' by a hard adventure core in Queenstown). The acquisition of signage and ability to purchase are independent of gender and dependent upon the

perceived desirability of the experience (and thus personality of the pur-
chaser and the ability to overcome constraints upon purchase; see
McGuiggan, 2002). Some evidence that the purchase of adventure activities is independent of gender is provided by an analysis of New Zealand's
International Visitor Survey's raw data made available to the authors by the
Ministry of Tourism and A. C. Neilsen in 2005. Conducting chi-square tests
between gender and nominated highlights of their New Zealand experience
with reference to adventure type products found no significant statistical
difference between males and females.

Past research shows that a key market segment associated with the
adventure sector is that of the users of backpacker accommodation. Ryan,
Trauer, Cave, Sharma, and Sharma (2003) analysed the nature of adventure
experiences among a sample of backpackers in New Zealand and found
many itemised commercial adventure products such as sky diving and scuba
diving among their memorable highlights. Similarly, Richards and Wilson
(2004) cite backpackers as the highest type of patrons of adrenalin products
in their sample.

It is a characteristic of an analysis of the post-modern world that the
de-differentiation of categories is formed in a modern period. It can be
argued that tourism provides many such examples. History and fantasy
merge with technology to produce new structures of entertainments as at
theme parks. Perceptions and illusions of risk differ from more objective
assessments of danger in adventure tourism. Place and time become spatially
and temporally displaced from the original, as, for example, Amsterdam is
visited at Huis Ten Bosch in Sasebo, Japan, or icons of New York and Paris
are viewed in Las Vegas. Places once known for heavy industry become
playful places within which people work. Within these tropes of flux and
change, not only are new opportunities emerging, but also anxieties as previously dominant structures loose power. Outside of tourism, the new
meanings of family emerge with approval of the civil unions that reinforce
notions of the reciprocal responsibilities between peoples previously thought
marginal. Male and female roles become differently socially structured.
Concerns over masculinity have been both academically analysed and been
part of popular culture (e.g., see Ticknell & Chambers, 2002 analysis of *The
Adventures of Priscilla, Queen of the Desert* and *The Real Monty*). Within
such flux exists an épistème of *curiositas* which:

> urges the traveller to self-confidently explore the limits between that which is known or
> familiar to us and to engage willingly with the 'Unknown', seeking out challenges that
> call into question accepted worldviews (Sobecki, 2002, p. 342).

Curiositas, a term derived from the medieval Latin, does not merely mirror the modern word 'curiosity' but also contains notions of anxiety, care, refinement, elaboration and curious enquiry. It was seen as a potential threat to orthodoxy, and therefore received with suspicion and hostility by the Church (Zacher, 1976). This term may have currency in adventure tourism, which, at one level may be a carefully constructed thrill within the structured parameters of management, but at another is the construction of psychological challenge defining the statements and image of self-adopted by both genders. It may be perceived as a contested ground where females adopt the male images as their own and redefine their own competences and orthodoxies by enacting thrill seeker roles, which increasingly become predicated upon participation and where gender ceases to be important. One is a bungy jumper first in self-definition, and gender may be second.

QUESTIONNAIRE CONSTRUCTION

The results and research reported here is one of a series of studies being undertaken both co-operatively and independently in New Zealand, Australia and Scotland. This study concentrates upon New Zealand and continues the work reported by Ryan et al. (2003). As noted above, the study contained both quantitative and qualitative data. The questions had to take into account the issues raised by the above literature review and permit a gender-based comparison of experiences that reflected possible differences in motive, flow, socialisation and perceptions. The study was also informed by a past work with backpackers and adventure holiday makers; in particular, those associated with researchers from Australasia, where a large number of similar items have been used in the questionnaires constructed for the past research (e.g., Ryan et al., 2003). Two justifications have been generally offered for the selection of items. The first relates to the nature of activities thought to appeal to backpackers and which are known to be patronised by them. These include adventure sports, such as white-water rafting and bungy jumping, cultural activities such as visiting locations of Maori or Aboriginal culture and social activities such as the importance of socialising and making new friends. Additionally, these scales have often, albeit not always, included contrary activities for a number of reasons, including the testing of the degree to which a sample might simply be using a response set. For example, such items include 'visiting casinos' and 'visiting city parks' that are not commonly attractive to backpackers and adventure tourists.

The second justification has been the selection of activities congruent with the four dimensions of the leisure motivation scale (Beard & Ragheb, 1983). To recap, these are social, intellectual, competency acquisition and escape/relaxation needs. Therefore, items such as 'socialising' and 'making new friends' fit with the social dimension, 'visiting museums' and 'places of indigenous people's culture' equate with intellectual needs and many of the adventure needs might be said to represent various forms of escape, fantasy fulfilment or ego enhancement needs. The results from these studies have not, however, always replicated the four dimensions of the leisure motivation scale when using factor analysis, but this is to be expected for a number of reasons. For example, a simple listing of activities and place attributes are not wholly congruent with the leisure motivation scale because, with reference to the backpacker and adventure tourism market segments, challenge and skill/competence acquisition can easily overlap with escape needs. It is, thus, quite possible for individual items to load on more than one factor, while more than four factors are not uncommon with, for example, specific factors loading on a specific indigenous people's factor, while other cultural activities form a separate factor.

The questionnaire comprised five main sections, namely (a) an importance scale relating to the selected attributes and activities found within New Zealand, (b) a satisfaction scale using the same items, (c) a section on desired accommodation attributes, (d) an assessment of satisfactions with accommodation and (e) responses to open-ended questions. A final section sought data on socio-demographics. Reliability of the data was checked for each of the scales using split-half correlations and alpha coefficients. For the importance scale, the split-half correlations (using various approaches such as Guttman and Spearman–Brown) were approximately 0.78, while alphas were about 0.83. For the satisfaction scale, the alphas were about 0.82, while the split-half tests were 0.83. Similar values were found with reference to the accommodation scales (importance items – alphas and correlations of 0.70; satisfaction items – alphas and correlations of about 0.80). Consequently, the data appears to possess the attributes of consistency of response. Finally, the level of sampling adequacy was checked by the use of the Kaiser–Myer–Olkin statistic, and was found to be about 0.84, which is normally deemed sufficient to permit further statistical analysis.

This paper reports data derived from the first two and last sections.

THE SAMPLE

Respondents were approached in the Hamilton bus station and backpackers' accommodation in Hamilton and Raglan, Waikato, New Zealand, in the summer of 2004. While attempts were made to adhere to random sampling methods, on several occasions the numbers present in the hostel were small and under those circumstances, all respondents were asked to respond to the self-completion questionnaire. Consequently, the sample is of a convenience nature, but is thought to be the representative of those using accommodation during the period of the survey.

The sample, therefore, comprised 494 respondents whose gender and ages are shown in Table 1. It is notable that about 20 percent of the sample is over the age of 31 years and this is consistent with other samples that indicate that backpacker accommodation is no longer the sole preserve of those under the age of 25 years. Of the sample, 23.6 percent were married. The sample was international in nature, with 30 percent coming from New Zealand, 18 percent from China, 10 percent from the USA and Canada, 7 percent from Australia, 6.4 percent from the UK and Ireland and 5.7 percent from Japan. The presence of Chinese respondents is explicable by reference to the large numbers now studying in New Zealand (Ryan & Xie, 2003), and the location of the study area as being close to three New Zealand universities, two large polytechnics and a large number of private sources of education in Auckland that cater for this group.

Table 1.   Sample Characteristics.

Age Groups	Male	Female	Total
Under 18 (years)	14	21	35
19–24	99	137	236
25–30	70	53	123
31–40	20	26	46
41–50	12	10	22
51–60	7	13	20
Over 60	3	9	12
Total	225	269	494

ANALYSIS OF QUANTITATIVE DATA

Table 2 lists the mean scores of importance attributed to a range of activities available in New Zealand. It shows that the most important activities were those of doing new activities with friends and socialising, hereby reinforcing the findings of Loker-Murphy (1996) with reference to the importance of social interaction. The adventure activities for which New Zealand is famous are rated highly by the total sample, while at the other extreme farm visits, cycling, horse riding and visiting casinos are less well-rated.

With reference to gender, gender for the most part is not a distinguishing variable with reference to assessment of the importance of these variables.

Table 2. Mean Scores for Importance of Attributes/Activities (7-Point Scale, where 7 is the Maximum Score).

	N	Mean	Standard Deviation
To do new activities with friends	436	5.539	1.5759
To just spend time socializing	446	5.484	1.5718
To visit national parks	422	4.915	1.7182
To go white-water rafting	374	4.818	1.8260
To go canoeing/kayaking (rivers)	389	4.771	1.8323
To visit sites of Maori culture	412	4.762	1.9006
To go whale watching	383	4.742	1.8443
To go tramping	386	4.741	1.8291
To go shopping	448	4.690	1.9374
To go jet boating	379	4.689	1.8795
To go sea kayaking	372	4.597	1.8888
To go bungy jumping	369	4.520	2.1303
To take scenic boat cruises	389	4.506	1.7255
To visit museums and historical sites	417	4.506	1.7515
To go on bush walks	418	4.486	1.8637
To visit city parks and gardens	439	4.358	1.7141
To go wine tasting	375	4.277	1.9411
To take city tours	403	4.243	1.9006
To buy other souvenirs	395	4.218	1.8886
To go mountain biking	346	4.136	1.8978
To buy Maori arts and crafts	374	4.120	2.0118
To watch others bungy jump	382	4.079	1.9466
To visit farms	388	4.028	2.0146
To go horse riding	365	3.975	1.9950
To go cycling	345	3.846	1.8900
To visit casinos	360	3.722	2.0442

Table 3.   Influence of Gender on Activities and Attributes as a
Distinguishing Variable.

Attribute/Activity	Males	Females	t-Test	Probability
To go wine tasting	4.0	4.5	−2.50	0.013
To just spend time socialising	5.3	5.6	−2.09	0.037
To visit sites of Maori culture	4.5	5.0	−2.71	0.007
To go shopping	4.0	5.2	−6.65	0.000

Statistically significant differences exist only in four categories, which are shown in Table 3.

Thus far, the data implies that gender is relatively unimportant in terms of the importance attributed to adventure and other tourism products. But how are these activities evaluated by respondents? Again, using a t-test to compare the mean scores across the items by the variable gender revealed that there was little significant difference, with only the items 'shopping', 'horse riding' and 'socialisation' revealing any difference at values of $p < 0.05$. Females scored higher in all of these three items.

However, an issue is whether there are dimensional differences between the two sexes, and hence the data were divided into two samples, males and females. A factor analysis using principal component analysis with varimax rotation was then run on both sub-samples, having first used the Kaiser–Meyer–Olkin test of sampling adequacy on each sub-sample (the values were in excess of 0.82). The approach revealed that similarities and differences exist between the two genders and Table 4 summarises the findings.

The separate factor analyses for the assessment of importance of New Zealand's attributes by each gender tend to replicate each other. In both instances, the factor that explains most of the variance is associated with the thrill-seeking adventure products that are heavily promoted in backpackers' accommodation. The second and third factors also reinforce many of the stereotypes of New Zealand adventure and heritage products, and thus it appears that possibly both genders are responding to advertising signage that indicates importance of the product. A symbiosis exists whereby tourists are informed these products are important, they attribute importance to them, but they are possibly important because they appeal to the nature of this audience – that is, of backpackers. The interesting comparison, however, lies in the factor analysis of the evaluation scale, where most of the variance for males continues to be explained by the adventure products. However, the analysis for females indicates more underlying dimensions,

Table 4. Summary of Factor Analysis for Males and Females by Scales.

Factor	Males (Satisfaction Factors)	Females (Satisfaction Factors)	Males (Importance Factors)	Females (Importance Factors)
1	Core adventure products Go white-water rafting Go bungy jumping Go mountain biking Go jet boating Go canoeing Go sea kayaking Go horse riding Go cycling Take a scenic boat cruise Eigenvalue 8.42 % of variance 32.40	Man-made heritage Buy Maori arts and crafts Buy souvenirs Visit museums Visit sites of Maori culture Take city tours Eigenvalue 7.84 % of variance 30.14	Core adventure products Go white-water rafting Go mountain biking Go bungy jumping Go jet boating Go canoeing Go sea kayaking Go horse riding Go cycling Take a scenic boat cruise Eigenvalue 10.15 % of variance 39.02	Core adventure products Go water rafting Go sea kayaking Go bungy jumping Go canoeing Go jet boating Go mountain biking Go whale watching Go cycling Go horse riding Eigenvalue 8.78 % of variance 33.76
2	Man-made heritage Visit sites of Maori culture Buy Maori arts and crafts Buy souvenirs Visit museums Go whale watching Eigenvalue 2.10 % of variance 8.08	Adventure products Go sea kayaking Go canoeing Go white-water rafting Go whale watching Go mountain biking Eigenvalue 2.37 % of variance 9.11	Natural heritage Go bush walking Go tramping Visit national parks Visit city gardens and parks Visit museums Eigenvalue 2.13 % of variance 8.18	Man-made heritage Buy Maori arts and crafts Buy souvenirs Visit museums Take city tours Visit farms Take a scenic boat cruise Eigenvalue 2.58 % of variance 9.94
3	City-based activity Take city tours Take wine tours Go shopping Casino going Visit farms Visit city gardens and parks Eigenvalue 1.86 % of variance 7.16	Natural heritage Go bush walking Visit national parks Go tramping Eigenvalue 1.52 % of variance 5.84	Social heritage Buy souvenirs Buy Maori arts and crafts Visit sites of Maori culture Go whale watching Eigenvalue 1.85 % of variance 7.10	Natural heritage Go bush walking Visit national parks Go tramping Visit city gardens and parks Eigenvalue 1.93 % of variance 7.41

Table 4. (Continued)

Factor	Males (Satisfaction Factors)	Females (Satisfaction Factors)	Males (Importance Factors)	Females (Importance Factors)
4	Natural heritage Go bush walking Visit national parks Go tramping Eigenvalue 1.48 % of variance 5.68	City gardens Visit city gardens and parks Eigenvalue 1.29 % of variance 4.98	Urban activities Casino going Take wine tours Take city tours Go shopping Visit farms Eigenvalue 1.28 % of variance 4.92	Socialise Socialising Go shopping New activities with friends Eigenvalue 1.37 % of variance 5.28
5	Socialise Socialising New activities with friends Eigenvalue 1.28 % of variance 4.93	Adventure products 2 Go bungy jumping Go jet boating Go cycling Eigenvalue 1.26 % of variance 4.83	Socialising New activities with friends Eigenvalue 1.12 % of variance 4.31	Casino going Take wine tours Eigenvalue 1.18 % of variance 4.56
6		Casino going Take wine tours Eigenvalue 1.08 % of variance 4.16		
7		Socialising Go shopping New activities with friends Eigenvalue 1.02 % of variance 3.94		
8		Go horse riding Visit farms Eigenvalue 1.01 % of variance 3.47		

and the factor accounting for most variance is now that relating to some of the man-made/cultural heritage products, while adventure products are divided with the first adventure products incorporating products that might be said to more closely involve natural settings, while the adrenalin products of bungy jumping and jet boating are separated into another category.

The statistical evidence points to gender differences in evaluating the consumption experience, even though both genders attribute similar degrees of importance to the product. Not surprisingly, a cluster analysis based on the whole sample found that over 40 percent of males falling into the clusters characterised by high scores on white-water rafting and bungy jumping compared to 32 percent of females. The sample was also divided into two by gender and a cluster analysis undertaken of each group separately. The males divided into almost four equal cluster groups with one emphasising socialising alone, another socialising and water-based activity sports, and the remaining two being characterised by the patterns of high or low scores across all items. The female sample was less evenly balanced with 42 percent of the sample falling into one group tending to high scores across adventure, cultural and social activities and another of 21 percent emphasing socially based activities. The data support of notion that intra- as well as inter-gender differences exist, but there is some evidence that behind the consumption of these products, there are predispositions to different gender evaluations. To better assess these possible gender-based predispositions, respondents were asked to identify a special activity, describe the identity, indicate what made it special for them and to say in ways it was special.

THE ANALYSIS OF QUALITATIVE DATA

Typically, content analysis is used to identify the patterns of qualitative data (Patton, 1990), using constant comparative analysis to separate the themes (Glaser & Strauss, 1967) It is important to note that in the qualitative analysis 'the human-is-instrument' for both, the collection and analysis of data. This gives rise to a paradox whereby the researcher has to be acutely 'tuned-in' to the experiences and meaning systems of others, and yet at the same time, be aware of how one's own biases and preconceptions may influence the analysis and interpretation (Cavana et al., 2001). Content analysis can be achieved by using manual decision support systems, or alternatively through a statistical analysis of key word or phrase occurrences (Krippendorf, 1980). Some statistical techniques for building models of personal constructs are those based on the neural network theory (Lippman,

1992) and connectionist modelling (Allport, 1955; Kelly, 1955). Artificial neural network (ANN) software derived from such work seeks to emulate human processes of meaning creation, and thus is useful to the researcher in replicating response complexity and creating models of how humans make sense of the world. Inputs to the model are the sequencing and placing of words used by the respondents within a text, while the outputs are the spaces occupied by those words after two intervening analytical processes. The first analytical process is a manipulation of the text by the researcher, while the second is the allocation of weights in an unsupervised feed-forward architecture. Feed-forward refers to a uni-directional flow and information processing in which each node can only receive information from a node prior to it in the system (NeuralWare, 1993). The networks produced are very dense, even with simply a small number of inputs and outputs, and the model can incorporate non-linear relationships. Multiple iterations of the second analytic process can be done to allowing the researcher to unpack the initial dense output into separate themes, and to test the validity of their distinctness. The activation capabilities of software such as NVIVO, TextSmart or CATPAC, among others enables clear demonstration of the relationships between layers of those constructs, and thus to build a model of the concepts shared by a respondent group. Such analytical approaches, described by Duda and Hart (1973) have been adopted by tourism researchers to forecast visitor flows and hotel occupancy (Law, 2001; Pattie & Snyder, 1996; Tsaur, Chiu, & Huang, 2002), but has not until recently been used to assess more psychological dimensions such as perceptions of place or cultural perceptions (Ryan, 2000; Ryan & Cave, 2002, 2004). Some of the advantages of such analytic tools are their capacity to sustain credibility, reduce uncertainty and enhance the reliability issues associated with the manual qualitative techniques. Yet, by defining structural relationships within the respondents' frame of understanding 'real experience', they can add complexity to the empirical models which might otherwise be bound by assumptions about the dataset, for example, that the sample must be normally distributed, possess homogeneity, and that the variables are truly independent and not subject to multicollinearity. The software used in this paper is TextSmart (SPSS, 1997).

The analytical processes are as noted: the first is manipulation of the text by the researcher. To commence, the researcher 'cleans' the raw data to minimise irregularities within the dataset. This is done using text formatting tools such as spell check and edit. Initially, the survey data are converted to rich text, formatted so that each successive question can be distinguished by the software, cleaned to ensure that spelling is correct, terminology consistent and irrelevant, redundant and missing data codes are removed. The process of cleaning actually benefits the research by immersing the analyst in the detailed content of responses.

The second analytic process allocates weights in an unsupervised feed-forward architecture. In TextSmart, this stage is commenced by importing the 'cleaned' data along with alias and excluded term lists into the software, which are cross-edited using Boolean tools, to create a common terminology both within and between the datasets and questions within the survey. Next, the researcher can choose whether to automatically generate or manually construct the categories (primary themes) and charts. A 'brushing' tool allows the researcher to verify and interrogate the data on-screen. Specific words and phrases can be cross-checked concurrently in the windows that show: edited datasets, alias lists, exclusion lists, suggested categories and category plots. Additional tools are 'word frequency' and 'category frequency' charts of survey responses and category composition. The linkages between terms are mapped in category plots. Inspection of the proximity to or distance from matching coloured blocks shows the relationships within the responses.

The researcher proceeds to identify the patterns in the data aided in his/her decision-making by the documentation capacity of the software, and by the on-screen visualisation tools. The number of 'edits', or sessions undertaken depends upon the complexity of the topic; the semantic differentials used by respondents; the range of meaning ascribed to words used; the cultural diversity within the sample; the level of familiarity that the researcher has with the topic; the intuitive and conceptual abilities of the researcher; and a practical consideration-time available. On average, the researchers have found that a minimum of four edits is necessary per question (with rare exceptions), in sessions that last no less than 5 h at one time. Thus, this analysis has taken a minimum of 80 h to complete, excluding the initial data cleaning.

The initial 'edit session' seeks to ensure consistency of meanings across linkages – thus, in this instance, the word 'cave' was associated with 'glow worms' and with various adventure activities and thus needed to be separated. The next typically removes 'noise' such as definite and indefinite articles. While important to human speech, in the textual output, such grammatical terms create clustered terms, which deflect the co-occurrence of the key ideas. Subsequent edits concentrate on refining the lists of aliases (words or short phrases which have common meaning) and exclusions (words or phrases which are not cogent to the topic). Categories are usually generated in each session and assigned descriptors or primary theme names by the researcher. Matching colour blocks may intersect (c.f. Venn diagrams) or be located some distance apart. Underlying constructs become more evident with each successive edit. The category plot plus the category list and word frequency outputs, together describe the relationships between ideas and themes across the respondent population.

RESULTS OF QUALITATIVE ANALYSIS

To assist the reader to understand this complex array of output, and to overcome the difficulty of replicating the colour output on which TextSmart relies, the authors have developed two graphic methods to summarise the data. In the interests of brevity, the results derived for the first question, a description of the special activity, are presented more fully than the results for subsequent questions. The summaries are presented as a theme summary chart and a personal construct diagram (see Table 5 and Fig. 1). The theme summary chart combines information from the category plot (text and colour block), the category chart (text and numbers) and the word frequency chart (text and numbers). It complements the visual output of the category

Table 5.   Theme Summary Chart – Female Describe, Edit 4: 10/70.

Category (Primary Level)	Secondary and Tertiary Level Themes	Colour Plot (# Associated)
Awesome	Interesting, very. **Awe**. Skydiving, activity, adventure. Great, good, **watch**, urban, bush. **Beautiful**	Magenta (86)
Unfamiliar	**Maori**, Tikanga Maori, material culture, performance. Heritage, people, hot springs. **On my own, personal challenge**. See, remote. Auckland, exciting	Mustard (57)
Conflicting emotions	**Opportunity**, fear, **could not achieve**. Feel, cool, whale watching. Travel, Fiordland, special	Royal blue (44)
Unfamiliar	Also. Rotorua. **Marae**. Gardens. **Swim with dolphins**, river	Orange (41)
Never before	Snow, walking, kayaking, sea. Enjoyment, scenic. Experience, **nature**	Green (41)
With others	**Friends**. Under the stars, camping. Beaches, mountains	Pink (36)
Awesome	Really, enjoyed. **National parks. Lakes**. Stayed	Brown (35)
Conflicting emotions	Fun, **bungy jumping**. Taupo	Aqua (32)
With others	**Guides**. Caving. **Relatives**, horse riding, glow-worm caves, Hamilton, shopping	Pale blue (30)
Never before	**Adrenalin**. Wine trails, Queenstown, jet boat, white-water rafting, never done before	Dark green (30)

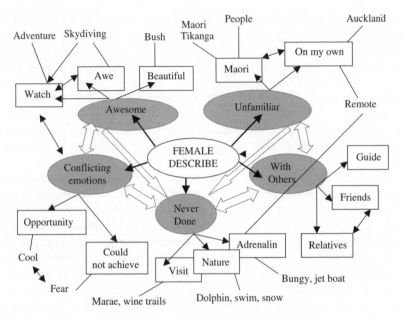

Fig. 1. Personal Constructs – Female Describe.

plots. A category (primary theme) is identified in the left column; secondary and tertiary-level themes of which the category is composed are listed in the central column. The right column gives a numeric count of the co-occurrence of terms in each category, identified by original colour to indicate the strength of association of terms; i.e., theme hierarchy. A category name (primary-level theme name) is a word chosen by the researcher to, where possible reflect the respondent terminology and to relate to other concepts in the theme group. A secondary-level theme is indicated by bold type. That 'personal challenge' is a secondary theme, is corroborated by the evidence from the frequency chart, alias list and its appearance in a central location during earlier edit sessions. Tertiary-level themes from each category are also shown in this column, for example, 'skydiving, activity, adventure'.

The personal construct diagram attempts to outline the mental constructs of the respondents in terms of theme relationships. Primary themes are indicated by the grey-coloured ovals, and secondary themes by the outlined boxes. Tertiary themes are not so boxed. Theme centrality and position within the output layers is determined by the comparison of successive edits as well as by the frequency of occurrence.

The analysis will first detail the responses of females and then those of males.

Describing the adventure females

In the case of this question, Appendix A reproduces the category plot output from the fourth edit session in which a frame of analysis of 10 categories and 70 terms was used. The resultant category plot shows the physical proximity of the primary and secondary themes. These are explicated by the theme summary chart, Table 5.

Secondary themes for 'awesome' (magenta blocks) are 'sense of awe, watch, beautiful' and these also are associated with 'skydiving, adventure, urban, bush, interesting, very, great, good, and activity', implying that while in the main women took part in extreme adventure activities, on other hand the theme 'unfamiliar' (mustard blocks) is associated with 'Maori, and personal challenge'. Further inspection of Table 5 hints at encounters with Maori culture. The secondary theme 'Maori' is associated with 'Tikanga Maori, material culture, performance, heritage, people, as well as hot springs and gardens'. Rotorua, as a centre of Maori tourism, is located quite closely to these terms. The 'personal challenge' secondary theme links not only to other cultures, but also to exciting urban environments and to remote natural places such as 'swim with dolphins, and river'. Closer reading of the respondent's words indicates that for females, being alone in an unfamiliar culture or remote place is both a threat and a pleasure. However, for 'conflicting emotions' (indicated by a royal blue block) paradoxes and contradictions emerge. Secondary themes here are 'opportunity' and 'could not achieve' indicating a paradoxical degree of hesitation in the face of activities which they felt perhaps should be undertaken, and the contradiction of travel into unknown perceptually remote environments. But these are explicated to some degree by the associated expressions of 'bungy jump, fun and Taupo' as well as 'fear, feel, cool, whale watching (open sea), travel, Fiordland and special.' If read alongside the other primary theme 'unfamiliar' which located 'urban, Auckland and exciting' together they hint at facing fears which might be more easily overcome in urban environments.

The primary theme, with others is linked to friends, relatives as well as to guides. Friends link with under the stars, camping, beaches and mountains, whereas 'relatives' (parents, lover, siblings) is a term that is more closely related to horse riding, glow-worm caves, Hamilton and shopping. Guides link with caving. This suggests softer-styled adventure undertaken with family members and more adventurous activity undertaken with peers. The final primary theme 'never before' is associated with nature, marae, adrenalin and swim with dolphins. The secondary theme, 'nature' maps to snow, walking, kayaking, sea, enjoyment and scenic experience, and adrenalin is linked logically, to Queenstown, jet boat, white-water rafting, never done and wine trails.

These results indicate that the range of cultural and adventure activities engaged in by females in this sample is very wide. A strong emphasis emerges for 'soft' adventure activities such as horse riding, visiting gardens, whale watching, as well as those that can be called 'hard' adventure – bungy jumping, white-water rafting and kayaking, etc. The association of adventure and nature is very clear. 'sleeping under the stars' is mentioned many times as an element of 'personal challenge' and associated with camping, national parks and Taupo. However, this phrase was one of the prompt questions, so biased results may be emerging here.

Several geographic locations are mentioned, which may be artefacts of where the survey was done (Waikato, New Zealand) but may also indicate the associations of destinations with adventure that had not been noted prior to this survey. Queenstown typically is well known and marketed as the adventure capital of New Zealand and here is mentioned alongside jet boats, white-water rafting, bungy jumping and adrenalin. Fiordland relates with mountainous rainforest travel, special, cool and whale watching. Taupo is associated with national parks, nature, camping under stars, beaches, mountain and also bungy jumping. Rotorua relates with cultural experiences, marae visits, museum, performance, Tikanga Maori, Maori material culture, heritage, hot springs and people. Auckland is called exciting, like and cool.

Personal and group relationships are evidently important. 'Friends' relates with camping, sleeping under the stars, beaches and mountains and Auckland. 'Relatives' is featured along with glow-worm caves and horse riding. Guided experiences are mentioned as well, associated with the cultural experiences of Rotorua and soft adventure experiences.

Relationships between concepts are sketched in Fig. 1, the personal construct diagram. Inspection of this diagram shows the complexity of the personal constructs. Theme hierarchies imply a linearity which is complicated somewhat by themes, which are related to ideas, in other categories. The primary theme of conflicting emotions co-exists strongly with never before, as does with others (indicated by bi-directional arrows). Awesome co-exists with conflicting emotions. Interestingly, the primary theme never before relates with all other primary themes – which imply its power as a driver for the 'special' nature of activities for women. At the secondary theme level, conflicting emotions relates to awesome; unfamiliar links to with others. At the tertiary level, cool and fear are interchangeable; as are friends and relatives, watch and awe. Personal challenge links to Maori, Auckland and remote.

Tertiary themes such as opportunity, cool, fear, but could not achieve reveal a degree of paradox that may relate to theory of flow as outlined by Csikszentmihalyi (1975, 1990), wherein challenge, emotional response and physical capacity intersect. Similarly, flow may also be seen in the emotionally charged language of the category 'unfamiliar', associated with 'alone', 'on my own/personal challenge' is featured in association with 'remote places', 'snow', 'walking', 'kayaking', 'under the stars' and in unfamiliar urban environments such as Auckland and Rotorua, where Maori culture and heritage are encountered. 'unfamiliar' is linked to encounters in specific environments – 'urban' as well as with 'Maori culture' and 'remote nature'. Interestingly, 'awesome' is linked in the category plot to 'pleasure, hard adventure, plus beauty', as well as 'watch' – indicating both active and passive participation.

The importance of personal relationships is evident in the association of 'never before' with being 'alone', which is also listed with 'unfamiliar' and 'with others' (friends, relatives). Note, that the use of the word 'friend' is somewhat euphemistic, since it in the raw data it appears as boyfriend, lover, acquaintance, school friend, family friend and peer group, etc.

Finally, a nodal element in the female description appears to be the primary theme 'never before'. Its position in the diagram and other data suggest that this element is influenced by all other primary themes, the directionality of which is indicated in Fig. 2 by pale grey arrows.

Males

The frame of analysis used for the 'male describe question' produced in this paper is three edit sessions, using 10 categories based on 70 terms. The results describe two primary themes for special adventure and cultural activities, being 'with others' and 'not before'. The significance of mates, old friends and girlfriends, as well as special one-time events like proposing to one's future wife, or the birth of a first grandchild is mentioned frequently. 'Nature' is emphasised as a primary theme, as is 'real adventure', and 'open skies', and 'sheer pleasure'. Appendix B indicates the TextSmart output for males.

The theme chart (Table 6), combines information from the TextSmart outputs; category plot and the category and word frequency charts and reveals five key themes. In order of priority, these are 'sheer pleasure', 'with

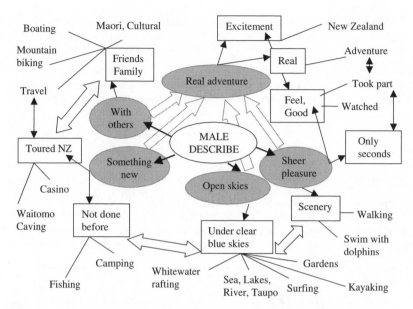

Fig. 2. Personal Constructs – Male Describe.

others', 'real adventure', 'not before', 'open skies' and 'speed'. The primary theme 'sheer pleasure' (magenta) maps to secondary themes indicated by bold type of 'feel good', but also to two other items lower in the chart of only seconds (speed and brevity of experience (pale pink)) and also scenery (aqua blue). High-energy adventure activities such as bungy jumping, sky-diving and the slightly more passive 'swimming with dolphins' are associated with the sheer pleasure primary theme. Interestingly, watched appears with this concept, as do hedonistic terms such as 'feel, good, fun, awesome and beautiful.' The next most important item is 'with others.' 'Others' for males means mates, friends and girlfriend as well as spouse, or partner. 'Relatives' are mentioned, but with less frequency. Implying that participation in adventure activities for males occurs more with a small circle of intimates, than with a large organised group. The real adventure theme relates with the secondary themes of excitement and real. Males believe that adventure activities must possess the attributes of authenticity (of experience and of New Zealand's environment) as well as being interesting, enjoyable. The primary theme something new relates with secondary themes of not done before and toured New Zealand. These cluster respectively with fishing, camping, amazing and Auckland, casino, places, Waitomo and

Table 6. Theme Summary Chart – Male Describe Edit 3: 10/70.

Category (Primary Level)	Secondary and Tertiary Level Themes	Colour Plot (# Associated)
Sheer pleasure	Bungy jumping, watched, **feel good**, fun	Magenta (50)
With others	**Family**, **friends**, cruise, mountain biking, boating. Cultural, Maori, visit, historical	Mustard (30)
Open skies	Waikato, kayaking, sea, river	Royal blue (29)
Real adventure	Interesting, activity. **Excitement**, enjoyable. **Real. Adventure**	Orange (27)
Something new	**Not done before**, fishing, camping. Amazing. Auckland, casino, **toured**, **NZ**, places. Waitomo, caving	Green (23)
Open skies	**Under clear blue skies**. Gardens. Surfing, white-water rafting	Pale pink (20)
Sheer pleasure	Skydiving. Lakes, Taupo, **only seconds**	Brown (20)
Sheer pleasure	Trip, awesome, swim with dolphins, **scenery**. Walking, beautiful	Aqua blue (15)

caving. Finally, the 'open skies' theme links numerically with gardens, surfing, white-water rafting and visually in the category plot with hot-air balloons, climbing, hot pools, camping, high, ground and river.

DISCUSSION

The discussion here refers not only to the above analysis, but also to some points that emerged from the analysis of other data not reported above where supporting evidence emerged. Two issues are discussed (a) Do the two analytical methods produce congruent findings? and (b) What are the implications of these findings for gender difference?

   Initially, comparing mean scores by means of *t*-tests showed little difference between genders, but separately undertaking the factor analysis for males and females generated variations. It was found that the males' scores were heavily discriminated by the scores on core adventure products with socialising being a factor that accounted for least variance. There is arguably congruence between Fig. 2 and Table 4 with males emphasising core adventure, activity and doing things for the first time. Table 4 is of interest, in that while females attribute importance to core adventure products, the main discriminatory factor is based upon man-made heritage. It is also notable that the females' factor analysis for satisfaction generates more dimensions than in the case of males. Fig. 2 indicates that males are centred more clearly on activity, while females in both Table 4 and Fig. 1 tend to more dispersed patterns of explanation, in that it is the sense of doing things for the first time as much as the activity itself which is important emotionally. Perhaps, it may be thought problematic to wholly compare results derived from the two methodologies, but it is contended that (a) the two sets of results are not wholly contradictory and (b) the open-ended responses add both complexity and richness to the analysis.

What then are the implications of the findings? Comparisons between male and female responses highlight commonalities and differences. One contrast is that the sense of conflicting emotions and non-achievement that appeared often for females does not generally emerge for the males, who appear supremely confident and somewhat hedonistic. Being alone is hardly mentioned by males, implying possibly a less reflective approach to activities. From the perspective of males, the data appear to provide evidence that males are more largely motivated by the achievement-oriented goals and the values of 'mastery, assertiveness and self-efficacy' and support the findings of Reisinger and Mavondo (2002) derived from a different quantitative methodology.

Does this have implication for curiositas? Baudrillard (1998, pp. 80–81) suggests that consumption as a social factor is based more upon the systems of organisation than upon enjoyment or pleasure. It is noted that "The circulation, purchase, sale, appropriation of differentiated goods and signs/objects today constitute our language, our code, the code by which the entire society *communicates* and converses." Thus, he goes onto observe a revival of *universal curiosity* where everything has to be tried, "... driven by a vague sense of unease – it is the 'fun morality' or the imperative to enjoy oneself, to exploit to the full one's potential for thrills, pleasures or gratifications". (Baudrillard, 1998, p. 81). Males appear to 'buy into' this consumptive pattern. Alternatively, Bakhtin (1993, p. 2) argues for 'once occurent event(s) of being' that, according to Shotter and Billig (1998, p. 14) are periods within which "in this brief and fleeting moments, that we not only express ourselves and 'show' each other the nature of our own unique 'inner' lives, but we also shape our living relations both to each other and to our surroundings". It is tempting to succumb to the argument (and indeed possibly the cliché) that females portray evidence of this emotion and are more likely to exhibit *curiositas* as initially defined.

The truth appears much more complex and fluid. Baudrillard's rejection of concepts of 'inner being' and the sacralisation of the (increasingly commodified?) body arguably represents one alternative and Bahktin's ascription of the importance to carnival as the expressions of self and rejection of systems another, and the experiences of backpackers and their experience of adventure fill this continuum providing evidence for both perspectives. While gender predispositions exist, they remain but predispositions sufficiently fluid to inhibit prediction of attitudes and nature of experience based on gender alone. However, as Cater (2005) and Ferguson and Todd (2005) have argued, the role of imagery and willingness to adopt images as the partial statements of self possess importance in any analysis of backpackers, and it is tempting to conclude that psychological predisposition, interpretation of social structure and life stage are as important as gender.

REFERENCES

Allport, G. (1955). *Becoming: Basic considerations for a psychology of personality*. New Haven: Yale University Press.

Allport, G. (1961). *Pattern and growth in personality*. New York: Holt, Rinehart and Winston.

Bakhtin, M. M. (1993). In: M. Holquist (Ed.), *Towards a philosophy of the act*. Austin, TX: University of Texas Press. (Trans. and notes by V. Lianpov).

Baudrillard, J. (1998). In: C. Turner (Trans.), *The consumer society: Myths and structures*. London: Sage.

Beard, J., & Ragheb, M. G. (1983). Measuring leisure motivation. *Journal of Leisure Research, 15*(3), 219–228.

Cantwell, M. L., & Sanik, M. M. (1993). Leisure before and after parenthood. *Social Indicators Research, 30*, 139–147.

Cater, C. (2005). Looking the part: The relationship between adventure tourism and the outdoor fashion industry. In: C. Ryan, S. J. Page & M. Aicken (Eds), *Taking tourism to the limits* (pp. 183–206). Oxford: Pergamon.

Cavana, R., Delahaye, B., & Sekaran, U. (2001). *Applied business research: Qualitative and quantitive methods*. Milton, Queensland: Wiley.

Clarke, I. F. (1998). Wandering women: To the uttermost ends of the earth. *Tourism Management, 9*(2), 171–175.

Cloke, P., & Perkins, H. C. (1998). Cracking the canyon with the awesome foursome: Representations of adventure tourism in New Zealand. *Environment and Planning D: Society and Space, 16*(2), 185–218.

Cloke, P., & Perkins, H. C. (2002). Commodification and adventure in New Zealand tourism. *Current Issues in Tourism, 5*(6), 521–549.

Connor, J. M., & Serbin, L. A. (1977). Behaviorally based masculine and feminine activity preference scales for preschoolers: Correlates with other classroom behaviors and cognitive tests. *Child Development, 48*, 1411–1416.

Csikszentmihalyi, M. (1975). *Beyond boredom and anxiety*. San Francisco, CA: Jossey-Bass.

Csikszentmihalyi, M. (1990). *Flow – the psychology of optimal experience*. New York: Harper & Row.

Culp, R. (1998). Adolescent girls and outdoor recreation: A case study examining constraints and effective programming. *Journal of Leisure Research, 30*(3), 356–379.

Davidson, P. (1996). The holiday and work experiences of women with young children. *Leisure Studies, 15*(2), 89–103.

Deem, R. (1996). Women, the city and holidays. *Leisure Studies, 15*(2), 105–119.

Duda, R. O., & Hart, P. E. (1973). *Pattern classification and scene analysis.* New York: Wiley.

Ewert, A., & Jamieson, L. (2003). Current status and future directions in the adventure tourism industry. In: J. Wilks & S. J. Page (Eds), *Managing tourist health and safety in the new millennium*, (pp. 67–83). Oxford, UK: Pergamon Press.

Ferguson, S., & Todd, S. (2005). Acquiring status through the consumption of adventure tourism. In: C. Ryan, S. J. Page & M. Aicken (Eds), *Taking tourism to the limits* (pp. 185–192). Oxford: Pergamon.

Galpin, T. (1987). *Is it really a man's world? Male and female outdoor adventure leaders rate their competency.* U.S. Department of Education, pp. 3–14.

Glaser, B. G., & Strauss, A. L. (1967). *The discovery of grounded theory.* Chicago: Aldine.

Grant, C. H. B. (1984). The gender gap in sport: From Olympic to intercollegiate level. *The Institute for Sport and Social Analysis: Arena Review, 8*, 31–47.

Harrington, M. A. (1991). Time after work: Constraints on the leisure of working women. *Loisir et Société, 14*(1), 115–133.

Havitz, M., & Dimanche, F. (1990). Propositions for testing the involvement construct in recreation tourism contexts. *Leisure Sciences, 12*, 179–195.

Henderson, K. A., & Allen, K. R. (1991). The ethic of care: Leisure possibilities and constraints for women. *Loisir et Société, 14*(1), 97–114.

Hirschman, E. C. (1984). Leisure motives and sex roles. *Journal of Leisure Research, 16*(3), 209–223.

Kelly, G. A. (1955). *The psychology of personal constructs.* New York: Norton.

Krippendorf, K. (1980). *Content analysis: An introduction to its methodology.* Beverly Hills, CA: Sage.

Law, R. (2001). The impact of the Asian financial crisis on Japanese demand for travel to Hong Kong: A study of various forecasting techniques. *Journal of Travel and Tourism Marketing, 10*(2/3), 47–65.

Lippman, R. P. (1992). An introduction to computing with neural nets. In: C. Lau (Ed.), *Neural networks: Theoretical foundations and analysis* (pp. 5–23). New York: Institute of Electrical and Electronic Engineers (IEEE) Press.

Little, D. E. (2000). Negotiating adventure recreation: How women can access satisfying adventure experiences throughout their lives. *Society and Leisure, 23*(1), 171–195.

Little, D. E. (2002). How do women construct adventure recreation in their lives? Why we need to re-engage with the essence of adventure experience. *Journal of Adventure Education and Outdoor Learning, 2*(1), 55–69.

Little, D. E., & Wilson, E. (2005). Adventure and the gender gap: Acknowledging diversity of experience. *Society and Leisure, 28*(1), 185–208.

Loker-Murphy, L. (1996). Backpackers in Australia: A motivation-based segmentation study. *Journal of Travel and Tourism Marketing, 5*(4), 23–46.

Madrigal, R., Havitz, M. E., & Howard, D. R. (1992). Married couples' involvement with family vacations. *Leisure Sciences, 14*, 287–301.

Massey, D. (1994). *Space place and gender.* Oxford: Polity Press.

McGuiggan, R. L. (2002). A model of vacation choice: An integration of personality and vacation choice with leisure constraints theory. In: G. I. Crouch, R. R. Perdue, H. J. P. Timmermans, M. Uysal (Eds), *Consumer psychology of tourism, hospitality and leisure,* (Vol. 3, pp. 169–180). Wallingford: CABI.

McIntyre, N., Burden, J., & Kiewa, J. (1993). Women's involvement in adventure activities. Paper presented at the 5th World Wilderness Congress, September 1993, Tromso.

Millar, S. (1974). *The psychology of play.* New York, NY: Jason Aronson.

Miller, J. B. (1986). *Toward a new psychology of women* (2nd ed.). Boston: Beacon Press.

NeuralWare. (1993). *Reference guide: Software reference for professional II/plus and neural-works explorer.* Pittsburgh, PA: NeuralWare.

Pattie, C. D., & Snyder, J. (1996). Using a neural network to forecast visitor behaviour. *Annals of Tourism Research, 23*(1), 151–164.

Patton, M. (1990). *Qualitative evaluation and research methods.* Newbury Park, CA: Sage.

Reisinger, Y., & Mavondo, F. (2002). Exploring the relationships among psychographic factors in the female and male youth travel market. *Tourism Review International, 8*(2), 69–84.

Richards, G., & Wilson, J. (2004). The global nomad: Motivations and behaviour of independent travellers worldwide. In: G. Richards & J. Wilson (Eds), *The global nomad: Backpacker travel in theory and practice* (pp. 14–42). Clevedon: Channel View Publications and Atlas.

Ryan, C. (1995). Beaches and life-stage marketing. In: M. Conlin & T.G. Baum (Eds), *Island tourism* (pp. 79–93). Chichester: Wiley.

Ryan, C. (1997). Rafting in the Rangitikei, New Zealand – an example of adventure holidays. In: D. Getz & S. J. Page (Eds), *The business of rural tourism – international perspectives* (pp. 162–190). London: International Thomson Business Press.

Ryan, C. (2000). Tourists' experiences, phenomenographic analysis, post-positivism and neural network software. *International Journal of Tourism Research (formerly Progress in Tourism and Hospitality Research), 2*(2), 119–131.

Ryan, C. (2002). Motives, behaviours, body and mind. In: C. Ryan (Ed.). *The tourist experience – a new introduction* (pp. 27–57). London. Continuum.

Ryan, C., & Cave, J. B. J. (2002). *Tourism Auckland: Report on perceptions of domestic and international visitors to Auckland report prepared for Tourism Auckland.* Tourism Management Department, Waikato Management School.

Ryan, C., & Cave, J. B. J. (2004, February). Letting the visitor speak: An analysis of destination image through the use of neural network software and powerpoint presentation. Paper presented at the creating tourism knowledge: Cauthe 2004, Brisbane, Australia.

Ryan, C., & Mohsin, A. (2001). Backpackers: Attitudes to the 'outback'. *Journal of Travel and Tourism Marketing, 10*(1), 69–92.

Ryan, C., & Trauer, B. (2005). Ageing populations – trends and the emergence of the nomad tourist. In: W. Theobald (Ed.), *Global tourism* (3rd ed., pp. 510–528). Oxford: Butterworth Heinemann.

Ryan, C., Trauer, B., Cave, J., Sharma, A., & Sharma, S. (2003). Backpackers – what is the peak experience?. *Tourism Recreation Research, 28*(3), 93–96.

Ryan, C., & Xie, J. (2003). Chinese students – a New Zealand tourism niche?. *International Journal of Tourism Sciences, 3*(1), 95–120.

Shotter, J., & Billig, M. (1998). A Bakhtinian psychology: From out of the heads of individuals and into the diagouges between them. In: M. M. Bell & M. Gardiner (Eds), *Bakhtin and the human sciences* (pp. 13–29). London: Sage.

Sobecki, S. (2002). Mandeville's thought of the limit: The discourse of similarity and difference in the travels of Sir John Mandeville. *The Review of English Studies, 53*(211), 329–343.

SPSS. (1997). *TextSmart 1.0. Users Guide*. Chicago: SPSS Inc.

Ticknell, E., & Chambers, D. (2002). Performing the crisis: Fathering, gender and representation in two 1990s films. *Journal of Popular Film and Television, 29*(4), 146–155.

Trauer, B. (2006). Conceptualising special interest tourism – frameworks for analysis. *Tourism Management, 27*(2).

Trauer, B., & Ryan, C. (2005). Adventure tourism and sport – an introduction. In: *Taking tourism to the limits* (pp. 177–184). Oxford: Pergamon.

Trollope, J. (1998). Women travelling alone. *Sunday Times* (travel supplement), October.

Tsaur, S.-H., Chiu, Y. C., & Huang, C. (2002). Determinants of guest loyalty to international tourist hotels – a neural network approach. *Tourism Management, 23*(4), 397–405.

Wearing, B., & Wearing, S. (2005). Refocusing the tourist experience; the flâneur and the choraster. *Leisure Studies, 15*, 229–243.

Zacher, C. K. (1976). *Curiosity and pilgrimage: The literature of discovery in fourteenth-century England*. Baltimore, MA: The John Hopkins University Press.

APPENDIX A. CATEGORY PLOT – FEMALE: DESCRIBE, EDIT 4: 10 CATEGORIES/70 TERMS

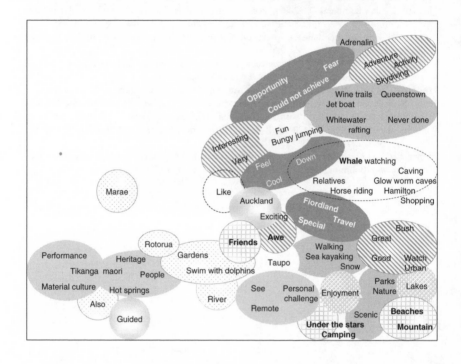

APPENDIX B. CATEGORY PLOT – MALE: DESCRIBE, EDIT 3: 10 CATEGORIES/70 TERMS

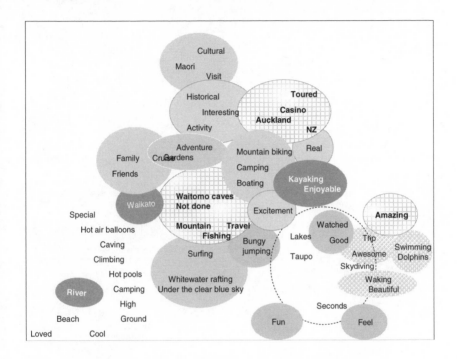

CHAPTER 7

SPATIALLY DIFFERENTIATED UTILITY FUNCTIONS FOR URBAN GREENSPACE: A TEST BASED ON CONJOINT CHOICE EXPERIMENTS

Aloys Borgers, Harry Timmermans and
Peter van der Waerden

ABSTRACT

This chapter argues that consumer preferences are formed as a result of continued interaction with the environment. Preferences are a function of reinforcement learning and consumer experiences. If this assumption is accurate, conjoint choice and preference models, which typically assume spatial invariant preference functions, might produce invalid or even misleading results. We therefore formulate two models that explicitly allow testing whether preference functions are influenced by location. The context of the choice of urban parks in the Eindhoven region, The Netherlands, illustrates the approach. Results support the assumption that preference for urban park attributes differ by location of the respondents.

Advances in Culture, Tourism and Hospitality Research, Volume 1, 215–226
Copyright © 2007 by Elsevier Ltd.
ISSN: 1871-3173/doi:10.1016/S1871-3173(06)01007-X

INTRODUCTION

The research community on consumer psychology of leisure behaviour has developed a multitude of theories, measurement approaches and models to better understand consumer valuation of leisure alternatives. Theories and models such as Fishbein and Ajzen's attitude theory (Ajzen & Fishbein, 1977) and Luce's choice theory (Luce, 1959) typically assume that attitudes, motivations (Noe & Uysal, 1997) and utilities are either idiosyncratic or vary by socio-economic group. Applications based on these and related theories (Field, 2000; McGuire, O'Leary, & Dottavio, 1989; Payne, Mowen, & Orsega-Smith, 2002; Tinsley, Tinsley, & Croskeys, 2002) focus on the outcomes of a particular measurement instrument (multi-item scales; experimental designs) and do not in their very approach take learning into consideration. Implicitly, these approaches assume that consumers have reached some type of equilibrium.

However, preferences and utilities for leisure alternatives are formed and continuously adapted by the interaction and cumulative experiences of individuals with their environment. Individuals experience their environment, judge such experiences, learn and in doing so form preferences. In addition, preferences can be formed on the basis of social interaction, other means of communication and mental simulation. If this reasoning is accepted, it follows that preferences may not only vary according to socio-demographic attributes, but also by location.

This paper addresses consumer utility for urban green space. First, it empirically tests, using conjoint choice experiments administered in the Eindhoven region, The Netherlands, whether evidence of spatially diverging utilities for urban greenspace can be found, If such differences exist, it is not readily evident which effect will be dominant. On the one hand, one might argue that individuals living in central parts of the city have a lower utility for greenspace, compared to individuals living on the edge of town because their decision to reside in central city areas may suggest that they attach lower importance to urban greenspace. An alternative hypothesis however may be that the relative lack of greenspace in their immediate area increases their utility for urban greenspace. In more general terms, the utility derived from greenspace attributes may differ between central and suburban locations.

The paper reports the results of a project, based on conjoint experiments, which aimed at measuring consumer utilities for urban greenspace. The alternative hypotheses will be tested using conjoint choice experiment data of a sample of 111 respondents. The paper is organised as follows. First, we will develop two alternative models. One model incorporates a single spatial effect, which is supposed to scale the utility function dependent on location. The second model is a generalization and assumes that differences may occur for every attribute included in the utility function. Second, the data used to estimate the model is described next. This is followed by a discussion of the estimation and the results. Finally, we will draw some conclusions and discuss some limitations of the study.

THE MODEL

Generic Specification

Assume a spatial object j can be described in terms of a set of attributes $\{X_{jk}\}$, $k = 1, 2, \ldots K; j = 1, 2, \ldots, J$. Let subscript i represent an individual. Consistent with traditional conjoint models, assume that individuals derive some utility U_{ij} from the attribute profile describing object j. Thus, $U_{ij} = f(\{X_{jk}\})$. Now, unlike traditional conjoint models, assume an individual lives in a certain spatial environment s, and that each environment influences individual utilities. Let ϕ_s denote this effect.

Consistent with conjoint analysis, assume that we observe the responses of individuals living in s to attribute profile or spatial object j. Let R_{ij}^s denote this response. We assume that this response can be decomposed into a true preference or utility and a self-selection effect. That is:

$$R_{ij}^s = U_{ij} + \phi_s + \varepsilon_{ij} \tag{1}$$

Then, following conventional discrete choice theory, the probability of choosing an alternative is equal to:

$$p_{ij}^s = \frac{\exp(R_{ij}^s)}{\sum_{j' \in J} \exp(R_{ij'}^s)} \tag{2}$$

Or,

$$p_{ij}^s = \frac{\exp(U_{ij} + \phi_s)}{\sum_{j' \in J} \exp(U_{ij'} + \phi_s)} \tag{3}$$

Note that these effects can only be estimated relative to the utility of a base alternative. If ϕ_s is relatively high, we will observe a higher average response value in s, given a space-invariant utility derived from the attribute values. This might be interpreted that the concerned individuals have lower expectations. The expectations of the people experiencing this latent effect will be lower, and hence the estimated utility and choice probabilities will be higher. Vice versa, if ϕ_s is lower, expectations increase and the utility response to the same attribute profiles will be lower.

Attribute-specific Function

The generic model assumes that individuals living in a particular area have some latent probability of different expectations about choice alternatives. This assumed effect was captured in terms of a single parameter. However, it may also be that such effects are attribute-specific. This would imply that expectations due to self-selection are attribute-specific. The resulting specification can be written as:

$$p_{ij}^s = \frac{\exp \sum_k (\beta_k + \phi_{sk}) X_{jk}}{\sum_{j' \in J} \exp \sum_k (\beta_k + \phi_{sk}) X_{j'k}} \tag{4}$$

The interpretation of this model is similar to the general model, except that expectations are now defined for each attribute separately as opposed to a single general effect. Thus, this model allows for the possibility that the utility of certain attributes are invariant to spatial location, whereas other variables are sensitive to space and may reflect self-selection. These effects are represented in terms of deviations from the overall (average) attribute-effect. Again, all parameters are estimated relative to the utility of a base alternative.

DATA

Sample

Respondents were recruited from the City of Eindhoven, located in the South of the Netherlands. The sampling frame consisted of two parts. First, the City of Eindhoven sampled at random street addresses from their database. People were asked whether they would be willing to participate. A total of 750 respondents were recruited this way. The email addresses of these people were obtained. Secondly, members of a panel, organised by the City of Eindhoven, were invited to participate. An additional 778 respondents were recruited this way. Thus, in total, 1628 people were invited to participate in the study through the Internet. Some of these live in the City of Eindhoven, while others live in the suburbs. Potential participants were given the link to the web site where they could complete the experiment. In total, 111 respondents completed the experiment, representing a response rate of 7.3%, which is a typically response rate for this mode of administration without incentives, pre-screening and reminders.

The majority of the respondents were male (59.5%). In terms of age, the majority of the respondents were between 25 and 54 years of age, 15.3 percent were older than 55. The majority of the respondents had no children. There is evidence of sampling bias, which seems rather typical for Internet questionnaires. Females are underrepresented in the sample. The elderly and the young people are also underrepresented. As for household composition, 2 person households without children are overrepresented. The analyses reported in this paper relate to the sample. If the results are used to say something about the Eindhoven population at large, the data should be weighted accordingly.

Selection of Attributes and Attribute Levels

The selection of attributes in conjoint choice experiments is always a trade-off between relevance, reliability and respondent burden (Louviere, Hensher, & Swait, 2000). A larger number of attributes implies that, in principle at least, conclusions can be drawn with regard to a larger number of policies or design options, increasing the relevance of the study. Moreover, the number of attributes should also suffice to provide a valid representation of the choice alternatives of interest. Urban parks can only be characterized realistically with a relatively large number of attributes. On the other hand, respondent burden will also increase with an increasing number of attributes, albeit perhaps not linearly. In turn, higher respondent burden may jeopardize the reliability of the responses.

Keeping these conflicting considerations in mind, in the present study, a total of 22 attributes were selected. Table 1 lists the chosen attributes. First, the distance between the place of residence and the urban park was varied in the experiment. It is believed that distance to the park will influence the probability that a park will be chosen to conduct a particular activity. Secondly, consistent with most types of choice models, the type/size of park was selected as an influential attribute. The third attribute selected was the type of green. In addition, a set of attributes was chosen to represent the kind of activities that can be conducted in the park and the presence or absence of particular facilities. Finally, accessibility, safety, maintenance and the presence of other people were varied in the experiment.

Table 1. Selected attributes and their levels.

Attribute	Attribute levels
Distance to the urban park	400 m
	800 m
	1600 m
	3200 m
Type and size of the urban park	Local park, 1/2 ha
	Neighbourhood park, 8 ha
	District park, 20 ha
	City park, 250 ha
Type of green (mainly)	Grass and flowers
	Trees and bushes
Accessibility by public transport	Yes/No
Presence of water	Yes/No
Possibility to sport/play	Yes/No
Possibility to walk the dog	Yes/No
Possibility to walk	Yes/No
Possibility to enjoy relaxation	Yes/No
Possibility to enjoy a wonderful view	Yes/No
Possibility to organize something	Yes/No
Visited by many people at the same time	Yes/No
Is safe	Yes/No
High maintenance	Yes/No
Cleanliness	Yes/No
High ecological value	Yes/No
Availability of benches with tables	Yes/No
Availability of café, place to eat something, kiosk	Yes/No
Availability of a playground for children	Yes/No
Availability of toilets	Yes/No
Availability of lighting	Yes/No
Availability of dustbins	Yes/No

In addition to the number of attributes, a decision needs to be made about the number of levels for each attribute. For categorical attributes, the number of attributes is often given by definition or by the design options. The researcher has more of a choice for the numerical attributes. Some combinations of attribute levels result in relatively large numbers of profiles, which might increase costs and respondent demand. In the present study, therefore, the number of attribute levels for an attribute was chosen to be equal to either 2 or 4. More specifically, two attributes had four levels, while all other attributes were dichotomous. Table 1 lists the attribute levels used in the experiment.

Experimental Design

We selected two attributes with four levels each, and twenty attributes with two levels each. Hence, the full factorial design involves $4^2 2^{20} = 16.777.216$ profiles. From these, an orthogonal fraction, consisting of 128 profiles was selected. These 128 profiles were combined at random to create 128 choice sets, ensuring that the same profile did not appear twice in the same choice set. Next, these 128 choice set were divided at random into blocks of 8 choice sets. Respondents were shown a randomly selected block of 8 choice sets. This design strategy allows the estimation of a linear additive utility function and the multinomial logit model.

Experimental Task

Choice sets consisted of two hypothetical urban parks, plus a base alternative, defined as any other park. Usually respondents are requested to choose from each choice set the alternative they like best. In the present study, however, respondents were asked to allocate 10 trips among these two hypothetical parks and the base alternative. This allows them to take into account the different reasons they might have for visiting the parks.

ESTIMATION RESULTS

The responses to the experimental design were aggregated into choice frequencies and the second model described in the previous section was estimated using these choice frequencies. Effect coding was used to represent the attribute levels, which means that the estimated coefficients for the attribute levels capture departures in utility between the corresponding attribute levels and the average utility. Effect coding was also used to differentiate between respondents living in Eindhoven $(+1)$ and those living in the suburbs (-1).

Because the base alternative was defined as another park, we could not estimate the model with a single spatial effect only. Therefore, we will only report the results of the more specific model. The goodness of fit of the model was equal to 0.07. First, however, we will discuss the estimated part-worth utilities for the complete sample. Table 2 reports the estimated part-worth utilities and the derived relative importance of the attributes. The results demonstrate that, on average, distance to the urban park is the

Table 2. Part-worth utilities and relative importance of attributes for general model.

Attribute	Attribute levels	Utility	t-value	Relative Importance
Base		0.1799	7.559	
Distance to urban park	400 m	0.3486	11.884	0.73
	800 m	0.1095	3.979	
	1600 m	-0.0726	-2.616	
	3200 m	(-0.3855)		
Type and size of urban park	Local park, 1/2 ha	-0.3189	-10.385	0.61
	Neighbourhood park, 8 ha	-0.1150	-3.808	
	District park, 20 ha	0.1416	4.784	
	City park, 250 ha	(0.2923)		
Type of green (mainly)	Grass and flowers	-0.0856	-5.121	0.17
	Trees and bushes	(0.0856)		
Accessibility by public transport	Yes/No	-0.0616	-3.799	0.12
Presence of water	Yes/No	0.0253	1.592	0.05
Possibility to sport/play	Yes/No	0.0363	2.184	0.07
Possibility to walk the dog	Yes/No	0.0783	4.811	0.16
Possibility to walk	Yes/No	0.1427	8.615	0.29
Possibility to enjoy relaxation	Yes/No	-0.0053	-0.319	0.01
Possibility to enjoy a wonderful view	Yes/No	0.0705	4.396	0.14
Possibility to organize something	Yes/No	0.0562	3.253	0.11
Visited by many people at the same time	Yes/No	-0.0075	-0.435	0.02
Is safe	Yes/No	0.0277	1.618	0.06
High maintenance	Yes/No	-0.0239	-1.462	0.05
Cleanliness	Yes/No	0.0180	1.115	0.04
High ecological value	Yes/No	-0.0086	-0.520	0.02
Availability of benches with tables	Yes/No	-0.0003	-0.017	0.00
Availability of café, place to eat, kiosk	Yes/No	0.0899	5.492	0.18
Availability of a playground for children	Yes/No	0.0098	0.593	0.02
Availability of toilets	Yes/No	0.0200	1.277	0.04
Availability of lighting	Yes/No	0.0148	0.937	0.03
Availability of dustbins	Yes/No	0.0026	0.152	0.01

most influential attribute, followed by size/type of park. The part-worth utilities for distance indicate that utility decreases at a decreasing rate with increasing distance. As expected, on average, the part-worth utilities for size/type of park increase with increasing size. All estimated parameters for those two attributes are significant at the conventional 5 percent probability level.

Next in importance are respectively possibilities to walk, availability of café, place to eat, kiosk, type of green, possibility to walk the dog, possibility to enjoy a wonderful view, accessibility by public transport, possibility to organize something, and possibility to sport/play. All estimated parameters are significant at the conventional level. Moreover, all signs are in anticipated direction, except for accessibility by public transport. Upon reflection, the negative sign might reflect the fact that public transport in the city is rarely used for visits to parks, and only by particular segments of the population.

All remaining attributes are not significant at the 5 percent probability level. This implies that either these attributes are considered not very important or that diverging preferences cancel out at the aggregate level within the sample. Within this group of attributes, safety, presence of water and maintenance are slightly more important. The availability of many facilities is deemed not very important, although the sign of maintenance is negative. The least important attributes are ecological value of the park, presence of benches with tables, availability of playgrounds for children and availability of dustbins.

Having discussed the aggregate utility function, we can now discuss the results of the formulated spatial-effects model. The goodness-of-fit of this model measured in terms of Rho-square is 0.08. However, our specific interest is in the utility differences. Is there evidence of any difference in utility between people living in Central Eindhoven and those living elsewhere in the region? The results are provided in Table 3.

Table 3 shows that some spatial effect parameters are significant at the conventional 5 percent probability level. Respondent living in Eindhoven attach a significantly lower utility to the possibility of walking the dog, to accessibility by public transport and to the availability of playgrounds for children. These results suggest that the possibilities for walking the dog and playgrounds are less important for people living in the city. Accessibility to public transport is also less relevant for people living in the central area of the city.

Table 3 also demonstrates that the effect of a wonderful view is higher for people living in the city, which suggests compensation. Also, the distance

Table 3. Parameter estimates for the model with spatial effects parameters.

Attribute	Attribute levels	Average		Spatial effect	
		Coeff.	t-value	Coeff.	t-value
Base		0.1733	7.238		
Distance to urban park	400 m	0.3571	10.949	-0.0316	-0.969
	800 m	0.0771	2.449	0.0911	2.892
	1600 m	-0.0865	-2.830	0.0236	0.773
Type and size of urban park	Local park, 1/2 ha	-2.2978	-8.715	-0.0284	-0.830
	Neighbourhood park, 8 ha	-0.0600	-1.792	-0.1258	-3.756
	District park, 20 ha	0.1078	3.175	0.0545	1.604
Type of green (mainly)	Grass and flowers	-0.0869	-4.584	0.0026	0.135
Accessibility by public transport	Yes/No	-0.0256	-1.352	-0.0737	-3.890
Presence of water	Yes/No	0.0170	0.938	0.0108	0.595
Possibility to sport/play	Yes/No	0.0286	1.536	0.0101	0.541
Possibility to walk the dog	Yes/No	0.1122	6.091	-0.0792	-4.303
Possibility to walk	Yes/No	0.1363	7.200	0.0180	0.950
Possibility to enjoy relaxation	Yes/No	-0.0076	-0.401	0.0062	0.327
Possibility to enjoy a wonderful view	Yes/No	0.0572	3.181	0.0385	2.142
Possibility to organize something	Yes/No	0.0447	2.277	0.0147	0.749
Visited by many people at the same time	Yes/No	0.0093	0.476	-0.0270	-1.380
Is safe	Yes/No	0.0427	2.229	-0.0309	-1.613
High maintenance	Yes/No	-0.0130	-0.708	-0.0043	-0.232
Cleanliness	Yes/No	0.0171	0.958	0.0025	0.138
High ecological value	Yes/No	-0.0198	-1.068	0.0324	1.750
Availability of benches with tables	Yes/No	0.0064	0.325	-0.123	-0.626
Availability of café, place to eat, kiosk	Yes/No	0.1052	5.680	-0.0308	-1.662
Availability of a playground for children	Yes/No	0.0426	2.265	-0.0557	-2.964
Availability of toilets	Yes/No	0.0261	1.470	-0.0099	-0.557
Availability of lighting	Yes/No	0.0138	0.777	0.0077	0.435
Availability of dustbins	Yes/No	0.0054	0.286	-0.0062	-0.331

decay effect as measured by the distance to urban park attribute is steeper for people living in the city. Table 3 also evidences that the range of utility for the type and size of park is larger for the people living in the city.

None of the spatial effects for the other attributes are significant at the 5 percent probability level for the given sample size. Nevertheless, a patterns in the signs of the attributes emerges: people outside the city of Eindhoven derive a lower utility to attributes that express an intense use of urban parks, and a higher importance for most facilities. They may reflect their lifestyles, away from the urban scene, more directed to nature or at least suburban environments with more natural elements.

CONCLUSIONS AND DISCUSSION

This study assumes that individual's utility for spatial choice alternatives may vary as a function of the location of individuals. We assume that individuals' expectations are formed as a function of their experiences, and that these experiences may differ depending on where they live. Two models of spatially diversified utility functions based on conjoint experiments were formulated, one assuming that the spatial effect occurred at the overall level of the choice alternatives, the other, more detailed, model allowing for differences in utilities at the attribute level.

The second model was tested in the context of consumer choice of urban parks in the Eindhoven region, The Netherlands. The findings of the model estimation supported the premise underlying this study. Evidence of spatially dependent utility functions was found. Estimated parameters suggest that the utility people derive from park attributes reflect their daily way of life. In addition, there is evidence of compensation: some attributes that are less or not available in the direct living environment are appreciated more.

If these findings can be replicated in other study areas, the proposed model specification and approach is a potentially valuable way of testing alternative hypotheses about spatially induced preference functions. Such additional research is required because the present study has a number of limitations.

Unfortunately, the sample size was rather small. Sample size in itself is not necessarily a problem as long as the sample is representative in terms of the dependent variable (responses to experimentally varied attributes of urban parks) of the analysis. Under such circumstances, a small sample size only means that the standard errors are large, implying that some of the estimated parameters will not be significant. In the present study, however, because an Internet survey was used, there is also evidence of differential non-response as a function of socio-demographics. If these socio-demographics are systematically related to preferences, a biased result will be obtained. In future research, such sample bias should be avoided, perhaps by applying mixed sampling methods.

We also cannot rule out the alternative hypothesis that some of the utility differences that we found are caused by differences in particular socio-demographics between people living in Eindhoven and in the suburbs. Ideally, one would simultaneously estimate the effects of socio-demographics, but given the small sample size that was not a feasible option in the present case. Descriptive analyses did indicate however that the distributions of many socio-demographic variables, such as gender, were not statistically significantly different between the locations. Other variables such as household composition however were. A further test therefore is quite important as we have found in previous studies for instance that utilities differ between men and women and albeit to a lesser degree between households of different composition.

Overall then, although some comments can be made, it is best to view the empirical part of this study as an illustration of the approach. Although the results seem plausible, a larger and more representative sample, which allows additional analysis, is required.

REFERENCES

Ajzen, I., & Fishbein, M. (1977). Attitude-Behavior relations: A theoretical analysis and review of empirical research. *Psychological Bulletin, 84*(5), 888–918.

Field, D. R. (2000). Social groups and parks: Leisure behavior in time and space. *Journal of Leisure Research, 32*(1), 27–31.

Louviere, J. J., Hensher, D. A., & Swait, J. D. (2000). *Stated choice methods: Analysis and application.* UK: Cambridge University Press.

Luce, R. D. (1959). *Individual choice behaviour.* New York: Wiley.

McGuire, F. A., O'Leary, J. T., & Dottavio, F. D. (1989). The importance of selected facilities, programs and services to older visitors to National Parks. *Journal of Park and Recreation Administration, 7*(3), 1–8.

Noe, F. P., & Uysal, M. (1997). Evaluation of outdoor recreational settings: A problem of measuring user satisfaction. *Journal of Retailing and Consumer Services, 4*(4), 223–230.

Payne, L. L., Mowen, A. J., & Orsega-Smith, E. (2002). An examination of park preferences and behaviors among urban residents: The role of residential location, race and age. *Leisure Sciences, 24*(2), 181–198.

Tinsley, H. E. A., Tinsley, D. J., & Croskeys, C. E. (2002). Park usage, social milieu, and psychosocial benefits of park use reported by older urban park users from four ethnic groups. *Leisure Sciences, 24*(2), 199–218.

CHAPTER 8

ADVANCING THEORY ON CONSUMER PLANS, ACTIONS, AND HOW MARKETING INFORMATION AFFECTS BOTH

Roger March and Arch G. Woodside

ABSTRACT

Consumers plans are not always what they eventually do; conversely, what consumers do, they do not always intend. The same axiom holds true for consumption behavior. Consumers often first form intentions to purchase goods or services, or to consume experiences. Then they actuate these intentions, not actuate them – or consume something unplanned for. An unplanned behavior may be the result of either an unpremeditated and spontaneous action (impulse purchase) or a previous intention that has been postponed or forgotten. Research in mostly retail settings confirms the remarkable prevalence of unplanned purchases, which account for one-half or more of total purchases (Kollat & Willett, 1968; Point-of-Purchase Institute, 1995, cited by Wood, 1998, Socio-economic status, delay of gratification, and impulse buying. Journal of Economic Psychology, 19, 295–320.). This paper explores the nexus between planned and actual behavior by examining the influences upon intentions and actual behavior, whether they are planned, unplanned or in fact, not done at all. We offer fresh theoretical insights into the consumer decisions in the field of leisure behavior and provide strategic insights into how marketing strategists can

Advances in Culture, Tourism and Hospitality Research, Volume 1, 227–256
Copyright © 2007 by Elsevier Ltd.
ISSN: 1871-3173/doi:10.1016/S1871-3173(06)01008-1

*segment their market more efficiently and communicate information more
effectively to their intended customers.*

This paper explores consumer plans and actions from three perspectives.
First, the influence of product information on both planned and realized
consumption behavior is considered by grouping respondents into users and
non-users of product information and investigating possible differences in
consumption patterns.

Second, changes that occur between planned and realized behavior are
examined in the context of customer characteristics, such as product experience, income, and geographical origin. These two areas of inquiry represent
the major managerial applications of this article.

Third, the article probes theory by applying Mintzberg's (1978) model of
planned and unplanned organizational strategy to consumer strategies for
the purchases of products and services (see Fig. 1). Heretofore, Mintzberg's
(1978) model is untested in the consumer behavior academic literature. The
model has two advantages for consumer behavior researchers: it offers a
new technique for matching intentions to actual behavior, and, by extension, enables the identification of products whose actual consumption levels
have failed to match the intended consumption levels. Most importantly, it
offers a rich interpretation of how people behave.

The illustrated area of application (tourism behavior) is not the dominant
FMCGs (fast moving consumer goods) focus found in the literature on
planned and actual buyer behavior. Previous research into the intentions
and consumption has overwhelmingly focused on planned behavior, or
intentions, and specifically with two aims: to improve the use of intention

Fig. 1. Types of Strategies.

measurement to improve the predictive power of future behavior and to influence purchase behavior. Though a multitude of factors and situations interfere or constrain an individual's ability to act upon his or her intentions (e.g., Belk, 1974, 1975; Filiatrault & Ritchie, 1988), intention is still an important construct found to be related to actual behavior.

While an increasing number of scholars have developed an interest in impulse buying since the 1980s (Gardner & Rook, 1988; Rook & Fisher, 1995; Dittmar, Beattie, & Friese, 1996; Beatty & Ferrell, 1998; Weun, Jones, & Beatty, 1998; Agee & Martin, 2001), the characteristics and antecedents of unplanned behavior in the broader sense remain unexplored and unknown. Indeed, some scholars neglect to mention the subject altogether. East (1997), for example, in his book on consumer behavior, makes no mention of the concept, although he briefly outlines compulsive shopping, a variation of the term. Table 1 summarizes the empirical research undertaken into unplanned and impulse purchase behavior.

The complexity of the "unplanned" concept may be one of the reasons for this lack of interest. Behavior can be unplanned yet done, either in the form of impulse buying (e.g., purchase of a chocolate bar at the supermarket check-out counter) or (for the want of a better term) unplanned purchases (when knowledge of and interaction with the task environment and time pressure combine to force a decision that otherwise would have been foregone, see Bettman, 1979). To complicate matters more, not all impulse buying may be totally unplanned. Rook and Hoch (1985) found that some people *"plan* on being impulsive" (my emphasis) as a shopping strategy (p. 25). Cobb and Hoyer (1986) draw an interesting distinction between impulse planners and partial planners. While both cohorts appear to be impulse purchasers because they delay brand decisions until entering the consumption environment, impulse planners act almost entirely in a spontaneous manner, while partial planners exhibited careful in-site purchase behavior and were price sensitive.

Unplanned behavior may also be unplanned and not done, as conceptualized in the Mintzberg matrix. Three scenarios are possible: the product may have been considered and rejected; it may have not been considered and rejected; or it may have not entered the consumer's awareness set. Reflecting on Weick's approach to intention-behavior dichotomy, Bettman, Luce, and Payne (1998) highlight a growing belief among consumer decision researchers that preferences for options of any complexity or novelty are often constructed and not simply revealed in making a decision. They cite the analogy used by Gregory, Lichenstein, and Slovic (1993) whereby consumer preference formation is "more like architecture, building some defensible set

Table 1.   Summary of Empirical Research on Unplanned and Impulse Purchasing.

Investigator(s)	Percentage of Unplanned Purchases	Research Setting	Tested for Influence of		Identified Precursor Variables of Unplanned or Impulse Behavior
			Product Information	Demographics	
Clover (1950)	60–15	19 store types	No	No	
West (1951)	44/27/42	Grocery, drug, variety	No	No	Unplanned purchases differed across product category
Cox (1964)	n.a.	Supermarket	No	No	Shelf space
Kelly (1965)	n.a.	Supermarket	No	No	Display location
Kollat and Willett (1968)	50.5	Supermarket	No	Income/ education/ occupation	Unplanned purchases increased with money spent and size of shopping list
Williams and Dardis (1972)	33/37/31	Speciality/ department/ variety	No	Income/gender	Low level of brand awareness indicates propensity for unplanned purchases
Prasad (1975)	39.3/62.4	Department/ discount stores	No	Income/ education	The greater the transaction size, the more likely are unplanned purchases
Bellenger et al.(1978)	38.7	Supermarket	No	Age/race/ gender	Age and race were significant for certain product lines
McGoldrick (1982)	7	Pharmacies	No	No	In-store displays
Cobb and Hoyer (1986)	12	Supermarket	No	Age/sex/ household size	Gender (males more likely to make unplanned purchases)
Rook and Fisher (1995)	n.a.	CD retail store purchases	No	No	Normative evaluations influence subsequent impulse buying behavior
Dittmar et al.(1996)	n.a.	Survey of shopping habits	No	Yes	Attitudes to shops and gender were key variables

Table 1. (*Continued*)

Investigator(s)	Percentage of Unplanned Purchases	Research Setting	Tested for Influence of		Identified Precursor Variables of Unplanned or Impulse Behavior
			Product Information	Demographics	
Beatty and Ferrell (1998)	n.a.	Recall of recent shopping trip	No	No	Time in store; enjoyment of shopping; 'impulse buying tendency'
Bayley and Nancarrow (1998)	n.a.	Survey of product items	No	No	Socio-psychological models developed to explain impulse purchase behavior
Weun et al.(1998)	n.a.	Develop and test an instrument to predict impulse purchases	No	No	Antecedents of impulse behavior were not investigated
Agee and Martin (2001)	n.a.	Purchasing from infomercials	Yes	Yes	Exposure to advertising increases likelihood of purchase; only demographic to influence purchase was age children

n.a. = not applicable.

of values, rather than archaeology, uncovering values that are already there" (p. 181). Little wonder therefore that Rook and Garnder (1993) concluded that impulse buying is still in a relatively immature state, especially compared to other areas of consumer research such as attitude research (Beatty & Ferrell, 1998).

As Table 1 indicates, previous research into the nature of planned, unplanned and actual consumption has happened mainly in the supermarket setting. Key findings are summarized below:

- Despite the large number of items that customers usually intend buying in supermarkets, Peterson (1987) found that just 30 percent of shoppers made shopping lists (cited by Shapiro and Krishnan, 1999, p. 170).
- The incidence of unplanned purchases rises with the size of the shopping bill and the numbers of items purchased (Kollat & Willett, 1968; Prasad, 1975).

- Since supermarkets often require a high degree of searching and scanning for desired items, the likelihood of the customer being distracted and engaging in unplanned purchase behavior is increased. Most of this scanning is done completely subconsciously by the peripheral vision, which sifts out those items that are worthy of closer scrutiny (Bruce & Green, 1991).

BUILDING FROM THE WORK OF MINTZBERG

Mintzberg (1978) proposes a model to illustrate the relationship between planned behavior and behavioral outcomes (see Fig. 1). Mintzberg explored planning and outcomes as they related to organizations in pursuit of strategic goals. Though he never subsequently attempted to empirically verify his parsimonious model, Mintzberg's conceptual contribution is useful if untested. He was the first to illustrate the variety of outcomes – planned and unplanned – that arise from intended and unintended actions. Mintzberg identifies three main types of strategies: *deliberate* strategies that are planned and enacted and *emergent* strategies that occur even though they were not intended (both of these he termed 'realized' strategies), and *unrealized* strategies that are planned but not enacted. Of these, Mintzberg suggests that deliberate strategies are the most commonly examined in the management planning literature (Mintzberg, 1994). His third case, *emergent* strategy, where a realized 'pattern' was not intended, has been of less interest to researchers and practitioners. "Deliberate" strategies will be hereinafter called "realized." We believe that the term better embodies the twin notions of both planning *and* completion. According to The Australian Oxford Dictionary (p. 349), "deliberate" is defined as "intentional," a term which focuses more on the cognitive decision to act and less on the process that culminates in the act being carried out. "Realized" more appropriately emphasizes an end result rather than "deliberate" which, notwithstanding Mintzberg's own views, focuses more on the initial act rather than the culmination of behavioral actions.

We now add a fourth behavioral category, termed "unplanned/not done" behavior, it refers to, as the name suggests, outcomes that are neither planned nor done; these four possible outcomes are illustrated in Fig. 2. The importance of this fourth outcome lies in the implications it has for organizations when their marketing communications elicit such non-response from consumers. The need for management to identify and understand

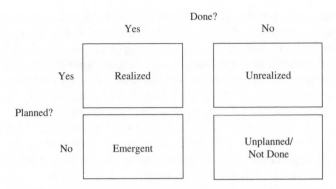

Fig. 2. The Planned and Done Strategy Grid: Realized, Emergent, Unrealized, and Unplanned/Not Done Strategies.

behavior that are both unplanned and not realized is, arguably, as important as that for purchases that are planned and carried out. Put another way, the customer that organizations does not have may be its most important. But even this hitherto ignored outcome of "unplanned/not done" has a further dimension: consumers may have considered the product but rejected it, or they may have not considered it and therefore rejected it. Clearly, a firm's understanding of its existing and potential customers would be enhanced by insights into the factors underlying rejection of its product at the planning and the actual consumption stage.

Consider Mintzberg's three strategies in the consumer context. Deliberate strategies are self-explanatory and need little comment. Everyday we decide upon and then enact a range of consumption behavior: from buying a morning coffee to filling the tank with petrol on the way home from work. Similarly, unrealized strategies are not uncommon. We plan to go shopping at lunchtime only for an urgent job at work to intervene and cause postponement of the action. Or a decision to buy a new Sony stereo system is changed after finding information about a less expensive and seemingly equally good system from Panasonic. (For the present purposes, it does not matter whether the unrealized action relates to a product category or brand.) Emergent strategies, which occur when unplanned behavior is enacted, most commonly take the form of impulse purchasing in consumer shopping situations. As was discussed earlier, no empirical research has been undertaken beyond this research setting.

To summarize therefore, Mintzberg's work offers both conceptual and managerial insights for the marketing discipline. In terms of theoretical development, his typology can be applied to individual consumer behavior as well as to its original context, organizational behavior. Just as he extended the conceptualization of strategy in the management domain, marketers can generate deeper insights into consumer planning and implementation of consumption intentions by teasing out the influences that explain the shifts that occur between the expression of intention and the performance of the consumption behavior (cf. Howard & Sheth, 1969; Engel, Blackwell, & Miniard, 1993; Peter & Olson, 1999). Logic suggests that it is conceivable for individuals not to succeed in pursuing the strategies they intended. Equally, it is probable that individuals end up pursuing strategies they never envisaged. What it adds is the notion that an intention is a preliminary stage of a process that may or may not culminate in a consumption behavior.

Managerially, the model provides marketing strategists a strategic tool that facilitates a richer understanding of reasons for a product's lack of appeal in the marketplace. The Mintzberg grid can be used to classify products of an organization's product mix by comparing the amount of intended consumption of each product with the amount that was actually consumed; then generating an arithmetic measure for each product to represent that difference; and finally using that measure to allocate each product to one of the four consumption behavioral outcomes. The differences between intentions and actual consumption behavior require greater attention for several reasons. First, there is a need to more accurately identify and quantify the intervening and unforeseen factors that divert intentions away from the eventual behavioral outcomes. Lilien, Kotler, and Moorthy (1992), in a review of marketing models, argue that there is a lack of exploration into the mechanisms that underlie the link between intentions and behavior. More recently, Shapiro and Krishnan (1999) argue that memory represents an intervening variable between intention formation and behavior, and not only one antecedent of intentions.

Second, given differences in intention-behavior link between durables and low-involvement products (Kalwani & Silk, 1982), the typical consumer behavior model may not capture the dynamics of consumption behavior in, for example, a services context (cf. Hawkins & Hoch, 1992). Morwitz (1997a), for example, has shown that the intention-behavior relationship will differ across product types.

Third, Morwitz (1997b) urges further research into factors that moderate the relationship between intention and behavior in consumption environments that entail a sequence of transactions or a bundle of products. Fourth, limiting research to prepurchase settings (as often occurs) can understate the amount and influence of the information that customers have at their disposal at the time of actual purchase (Bloch, Sherrell, & Ridgway, 1986). Fifth, an increasingly prominent theme in recent behavioral decision research is that preferences are-rather than retrieved from memory and real experience-often constructed when consumers need to choose one alternative from a set of alternative products, services or courses of action (Kardes 1994, Bettman et al., 1998). Sixth, there is a need to improve our understanding of the influence of information on consumer behavior (Bettman & Park, 1980). Prior information is obviously very useful in narrowing the scope of the choice task early in the decision process by allowing the consumer to focus on certain brands and attributes. Lastly, unforeseen situational opportunities and constraints arise which are extremely difficult to predict (Belk, 1975).

PLANNED, UNPLANNED AND REALIZED BEHAVIOR IN LEISURE AND TOURISM

Since the focus for this paper is consumption (and non-consumption) undertaken by tourists in a tourism destination, we turn to the tourism and leisure literature for further theoretical or empirical insights. Unfortunately, work carried out in these academic domains reveal a similar scarcity in identifying the influences upon either unplanned or planned behavior. In an exhaustive review of research in leisure and tourism, Ritchie (1994) laments the lack of attention paid to the context of decision-making in consumer behavior, while Otto and Ritchie (1996) highlight the challenge of examining consumer behavior in the tourism setting.

Young and Kent (1985) examine planned and actual behavior related to leisure campers, and found that intentions were slightly more influenced by the respondents' motivations than by the composition of the social group they were travelling with. Crotts and Reid (1993) found that most visitors to Alachuca County in Florida had decided upon recreational activities prior to arrival. Those travellers who made 'activity decisions' after arrival were typically long-haul, international visitors. In Tsang's (1993) survey of information search and travel planning behavior of international visitors to New Zealand, over 40 percent of respondents indicated they pre-planned no vacation activities (cited by Hyde, 2000). Only a minority of visitors had pre-planned their length of stay in each sub-destination within New Zealand.

Jeng (1997) asked respondents to imagine a 2–4 day domestic vacation trip, and consider what elements they might plan before departure. He identified a set of core sub-decisions made *before* departure, including date of trip, primary destination, location of overnight stay, and travel route. He went on to identify a set of secondary sub-decisions, made before departure but considered to be flexible, including choice of attractions and activities. This subset made way for a third set of *en route* decisions, including where to dine, where to shop, and where to stop and rest. The one important caveat in this study was that dependents were asked to consider a short domestic trip, not an overseas one. Stewart and Vogt (1999) adopt a case-based decision theory to understand how consumers plan for, and actuate, vacation travel. This approach assumes that consumers deal with uncertainty by basing their judgments of the current situation (or alternatives) on similar cases they have encountered previously; in other words, on past experience. The tourist plans for a series of activities and experiences for a future trip, but while he/she is on-site, a cycle of actuation-failure-revision-actuation occurs. Intuitively, this scenario approximates the complex process by which many of us decide upon plans, and then alter, abandon or implement the said plans.

Perdue (1986) touched upon the subject in a modest investigation that sought to empirically verify the proposition that unplanned yet realized behavior yielded higher spending than unplanned and unrealized behavior. He found that consumers who purchase a product that they had not planned for are likely to express satisfaction with the product as a means of justifying the purchase to themselves and other members of their travelling party.

Ajzen and Driver (1992) used leisure activities as the research setting for testing the theory of planned behavior. They found that the theory was useful in predicting influences upon intentions and actual behavior from intentions. The research had the limitation of being confined to college students and only five leisure activities were studied. Existing models of decision behavior such as TPB have been developed for tangible products, rather than intangible services such as tourism products. The tourism product is an experiential product with emotional undertones whose decision process differs vastly from the rational, problem-solving scenario applied to many tangible products. Mayo and Jarvis (1990) argue that "travel is a special form of consumption behavior involving an intangible, hetero-geneous purchase of an experiential product" (cited in Gilbert, 1991, p. 98). As a consequence, existing models omit important realities of tourist be-havior. To cite Um and Crompton (1990, p. 437):

> It should be noted that perceptions of alternative destinations' physical attributes in the awareness set ... are susceptible to change during the period of active solicitation of information stimulated by an intention to select a travel destination.

Finally, several writers argue that the benefits *realized* from a consumption experience may be more useful to understand than the benefits that consumers say they intend to seek (Dann, 1981; Pearce & Caltabiano, 1983; Woodside & Jacobs, 1985; Shoemaker, 1994). Research that investigates the process by which intentions are actualized into actual behavior and eluci- dates the influences that result in unplanned as well as planned behavior has a valuable contribution to make to the marketing discipline. Vacation space (or any leisure environment), by its very nature, encourages the consumer to engage in spontaneous consumption behavior. The decision task environ- ment in the tourist consumption system is complex and the decision process that tourists initiate can be highly arbitrary (Zajonc, 1982). Society's norms embodying rational behavior are weakened, to be replaced by stimulus seeking behavior; and the imperatives on fiscal rectitude fewer. So irrational is much of tourist behavior that some scholars portray it as 'play' (Berlyne, 1960, cited by Godbey & Graefe, 1991; Buck, 1978; Graburn, 1977) while others have conceptualized it as novelty seeking (Cohen, 1972; Plog, 1974; Crompton, 1979; Dann, 1981) and sought empirical testing of the concept (see, for example, Snepenger, 1987; Yiannakis & Gibson, 1992; Mo, Howard, & Havitz, 1993; Basala & Klenosky, 2001). Parr (1989) sums it up: " ... some [travelers] had little idea of what they wanted to see and do ... Some people enjoyed the element of the unknown ... they felt they were on an adventure, full of surprises and spontaneity." In short, impul- siveness is OK when you are having fun. This premeditated 'irrational' dimension of the tourist/leisure experience contrasts starkly with the super- market or shopping mall environment investigated by Rook and Fisher (1995) where consumers are more likely to experience, monitor and evaluate buying impulses. While the prevalence of unplanned behavior, regardless of dimension, may be greater in these environments, the usefulness and strategic importance of better understanding the nature of unplanned con- sumption activities in tourist and leisure environments is without question.

This paper focuses on: (1) the differences between planned and realized discretionary tourism behavior, (2) the influence of product information on planned and realized tourism behavior, and (3) the influence of customer characteristics on planned and realized tourism behavior.

RELATIONSHIP BETWEEN PLANNED AND REALIZED CONSUMPTION BEHAVIOR

Investigating the discrepancies between planned and realized consumption activities is the core research focus here. Six consumption behavior common to the tourism and leisure experience are used as dependent variables: spending (planned budget versus actual money spent), length of stay in the destination (planned number of days versus actual days stayed), attractions (planned to visit and actually visited), destinations (planned to visit and actually visited), accommodations (planned to use and actually used), and activities (planned to do and actually done). A starting point for our investigation is whether consumers will, overall, consume or spend more or less than they plan. An obvious enough question perhaps, but few studies have sought an answer. In a pioneering study, Kollat and Willett (1968) conclude, "there is a strong tendency for actual expenditure to approximate spending intentions" (p. 29) and that shoppers are "more likely to spend less than they anticipated than they are to spend more than planned" (p. 30). They surmise, "that measured purchase intentions should correspond more closely to actual purchase intentions when the customers' time and effort are minimized" (p. 29). Taken at face value, this early finding is puzzling. How could consumers engage in unplanned purchases and adhere to their intended budget – unless they abandon some planned purchases? In the absence of evidence that people abandon significant amounts of purchases to compensate for their unplanned purchase behavior, it would seem likely that spending intentions are exceeded, to varying degrees, by actual expenditures. Indeed, the work of Abratt and Goodey (1990) confirms this logic. In their study of supermarket shopping behavior, 41 percent of respondents reported that they had spent more than their expressed spending intention, which suggests, "the proposition that consumers tend to spend more than they planned may hold" (p. 119).

Pertinent to this research setting is the vacation planning study of Hyde (2000). Hyde's work was the only longitudinal study examining the differences between travellers' plans and their eventual behavior. He reported several interesting findings related to the present investigation: (a) respondents had fewer than seven specific planned elements in their planning and that almost half were sub-destinations (and this despite that travellers' vacations had a mean of 33 elements), (b) few attractions or activities had been planned, and (c) a minority of travel parties had a pre-planned travel route. He found that of the vacation elements that travellers had specifically planned, a large proportion – a mean of 73 percent – were actioned. (It should be noted that a limitation of his work was the small qualitative sample of 20 travel parties; all respondents were first-time visitors, none of who were visiting friends or relatives.) On the basis of preceding discussion, the following proposition is now formally stated:

P_1. Realized consumption behavior is greater than planned for most specific services relating to a purchased service system.

Numerous studies in the marketing field examine the relationship between planned purchases and actual purchase behavior (Young, DeSarbo, & Morwitz, 1998; Warshaw, 1980; Manski, 1990). While the observed relationships are generally positive, the strength of the relationship has differed from study to study, depending on the contingencies inherent in the research setting. Three contingencies critical in tourist behavior and consumption plans are product experience, motivation, and in the tourist consumption system, composition of the travel party.

Past experience affects consumers' plans (Fazio & Zanna, 1981; Morwitz & Schmittlein, 1992). Product experience is critical when studying the dynamic choice processes of consumers new to a market (Heilman, Bowman, & Wright, 2000). Experience teaches people how to plan and that the actual behavior of consumers with product experience will more closely approximate their plans their consumers with no or little product knowledge (Stewart & Vogt, 1999). Routine and habitual buyer behavior allows for purposive and intelligent behavior without deliberation (Katona, 1975). Visitors who vacation at the same place regularly are likely to engage in little pre-arrival planning, relying instead on their accumulated knowledge and experience from previous visits (Fodness & Murray, 1999).

Underlying motivations have a significant influence on the traveller's behavior (Morrison, 1996). Travellers visiting friends or relatives (VFR) are more likely to rely on the advice of their hosts, less likely to use product information and therefore more likely to deviate between planned and eventual behavior (Gitelson & Crompton, 1983). Leisure travellers, on the other hand, are more likely to engage in pre-arrival planning by obtaining information, particularly if they are first-time visitors. Novelty seekers, operationalize in this study as seekers of new culture, tend to seek more information, undertake more activities but also engage in more unplanned activities (Gitelson & Crompton, 1983), in contrast to visitors seeking familiarity in the destination, whose behavior are more likely to approximate their eventual behavior.

In the general marketing environment, the social setting (presence or absence of others) that characterizes the consumption of a product or service influences both planned and actual behavior, as it does other consumer behavior (Stayman & Deshplande, 1989). Fisher (2001) found that greater collaboration led to higher decision quality and smaller deviations between consumers' planned and actual expenditures. In leisure settings, the behavior of travellers is heavily influenced by the composition of the travelling party (McIntosh & Goeldner, 1990). Leisure travel is a product that is jointly consumed, and leisure travel activities reflect the influence of – direct and indirect – of all those travelling together (Chadwick, 1987). This phenomenon is particularly noticeable when children are present (or absent). It is safe to assume that travelling with children in a tourist destination requires greater planning and forethought than is required by couples or tourists travelling alone. Therefore, groups with children are likely to plan their trip itinerary prior to, rather than after, arrival in the destination (Fodness & Murray, 1999). Also, large travel parties comprising friends require greater coordination in order to meet differential needs than will couples or individuals travelling alone.

In the context of contingencies, the following proposition is now formally stated based on the foregoing discussion:

P_2. The level of matching between planned and realized actions varies as a function of contingency factors: composition of travel party, product experience, and motivations. (a) For composition of travel party, the fewer the number of members, the more likely will planned behavior match actual behavior. (b) For product experience, the greater the experience the more likely will planned behavior match actual behavior. (c) For motivation, the planned behavior of novelty seeking individuals will be less likely to match their actual behavior, while the planned behavior of familiarity seeking individuals will be more likely to match their actual behavior.

The third proposition related to this section examines the relationship between shifts in planned and realized behavior according to increases in the time spent in the consumption system. While research into time pressure effects has a long and deep history in both economics (Stigler, 1961) and psychology (Hendrick, Mills, & Kiesler, 1968; Wright, 1974; Bishop & Witt, 1970), consumer researchers arrived late to the topic (Feldman & Hornik, 1981; Hornik, 1982; Nichols, 1983; Iyer, 1989; Gross, 1994; Leclerc, Schmitt, & Dube, 1994). Howard and Sheth, (1969) include time pressure as an exogenous variable in their classic, *The Theory of Buyer Behavior* and they commented that little was known about it. Writing in the marketing literature, Jacoby, Speller and Berning (1976) provide an excellent synthesis of work in the field, but felt compelled to sub-title their paper, "An interdisciplinary overview," due to the "scant attention" (p. 320) the topic had received in the marketing field. Payne, Bettman, and Johnson (1987) (cited by Iyer, 1989) allude to, but did not examine, the time variable in a conference paper. Time has been shown to constrain unplanned purchases (Iyer, 1989) while time availability was linked to search activity in a retail setting (Beatty & Smith, 1987). Iyer (1989) found that time pressure, and the lack thereof, reduced unplanned purchases. In the tourism literature, determinants of planning time have been investigated (Zalatan, 1996), but the interaction between time in the consumption system and consumption behavior has not. In this study, time is operationalized as length of stay and categorized as a contingency influence.

All other things being equal, we may assume that the longer the length of stay, the greater is the likelihood that individuals will engage in unplanned behavior. In one study, Beatty and Ferrell (1998) treat time available as an external exogenous variable (along with budget available). In this study however, since our main focus is to identify the characteristics of individuals engaged in planned, unplanned, and actual consumption, time is defined as length of stay in the destination and treated as a dependent variable.

Kollat and Willett's (1968) research suggests that unplanned purchases were more likely to occur on a large shopping (grocery) trip than on a small one to buy just a few items. (This finding was confirmed years later by Inman & Winer, 1998.) Prasad (1975) found that the level of unplanned purchases increased with the size of the shopper's total transaction. Beatty and Ferrell (1998) found that time available, an exogenous variable, was particularly influential in the length of time devoted to browsing and purchasing. On the basis of preceding discussion, the following proposition is formally stated:

P₃. Increases in length of stay in a destination region for planned and realized behavior related to increases in the number of destination-area consumption activities, although the increase in the number of activities by length of stay is greater for realized rather than planned behavior.

The ability of individuals to anticipate outcomes is related to the availability of information, as well as to the individual's cognitive abilities. If information is available in the consumption environment, *ceteris paribus*, the more accurately individuals should be able to anticipate their future outcomes; conversely, the absence of information heightens uncertainty and makes decision making more difficult and the outcomes less predictable. While marketing communications are widely assumed to have a positive impact on consumption behavior, the extent of the influence has long been debated. The supply of tourist information, typically in the form of a visitor information guide (VIG), is a critical element of the communication strategy of tourism marketing organizations. The VIG is important for three reasons: first, since a leisure trip is a high risk purchase, involving the use of discretionary dollars, a VIG serves to reassure the consumer that his/her decision is the correct one; second, since the intangibility of the tourism product means that the consumer is heavily reliant on information, whether it be printed, word-of-mouth, or electronic; and third, since the majority of holiday makers visiting a particular place are likely to be first-time visitors, information about the destination is essential (Wicks & Schuett, 1991).

Despite this importance, little research has been undertaken in the tourism field to substantiate the widespread belief that visitors who use printed information will, all other things being equal, consume more than those visitors who do not. Ritchie (1994, p. 10) laments, "[W]e are still far from a clear understanding of the effectiveness of the various forms of advertising and promotion which are used so extensively by tourism marketers." For example, though the investigation of trip-planning behavior was a main research objective of the authors' research into travel preferences of the U.S. outbound travel market, Rao, Thomas, and Javalgi (1992) did not ask respondents the degree to which different information sources influenced their trip decisions. Fesenmaier, Vogt, and Stewart (1993) examine the influence of information on future travel plans (defined as trip purpose, travel route, and information search strategies), and although the impact of information upon the actual behavior was neglected, general support was found for their propositions. In a related study, Fodness and Murray (1999) identify a strong correlation between the number of information sources accessed and the length of stay, and the number of information sources accessed and overall spending. Little wonder, therefore, that in his study of VIGs produced by regional tourism bodies (RTBs) in the United Kingdom. Alford (1998) concludes that though the guides "represent a major slice of the RTB marketing budget, [the RTBs] have little means of gauging the effectiveness of this publication, other than receiving general feedback from suppliers, distributors, and information gathered through surveys" (p. 67). Co-authors of one of the most recent studies of tourist information search and usage drew the conclusion that "[a]dditional research on tourist information search is needed in many areas" (Fodness & Murray, 1999, p. 229).

Destination marketing organizations need to better understand the extent to which printed information influences consumer choices and consumption outcomes. As studies have shown, the more activities and opportunities an individual is aware of at the intended destination, the greater is the individual's likely level of consumption (Chadwick, 1987; McIntosh & Goeldner, 1990; Moutinho, 1988). In addition, Etzel and Wahlers (1985) report a positive relationship between increasing levels of information search and increasing travel expenditures. One of the core propositions is that product information significantly increases the level of consumption behavior undertaken by consumers, relative to those individuals who do not receive product information. When this assumption is applied to the proposition generated earlier, that realized behavior exceeds planned behavior, we can postulate that the consumers who have received versus have not received the VIG and who have completed their visit to the destination report higher consumption behavior.

On the basis of foregoing discussion, the following propositions are offered:

P_4. Consumers with product information are more likely to both plan and engage in more tourist consumption behavior than those without product information (see Fig. 3, Panel A).

P_5. Consumers use product information more while in the consumption site than prior to entering the consumption site (see Fig. 3, Panel B).

P_6. Consumers who use product information plan and report higher consumption behavior (such as spending and length of stay) than consumers who do not use product information (see Fig. 3, Panel C).

Studies have shown that experience of the destination plays a significant role in various aspects of travel planning and activities, including information use (Etzel & Wahlers, 1985), time spent planning (Zalatan, 1996), and destination attractiveness (Hu & Ritchie, 1993).

While conventional wisdom suggests that consumers with little or no product experience are likely to require and seek more information than experienced consumers, Bettman and Park (1980) have argued that consumers with little prior knowledge will engage in less information search if the nature of the search task appears overwhelming. Individuals in the exit survey who received the VIG are likely to record the highest number of (realized) activities, while their counterparts in the entry survey who did not receive the VIG will register the smallest number of (planned) activities.

The foregoing discussion results in the following proposition:

P_7. Within a given time period (period the consumer is in the tourism destination), first-time consumers planning and actually doing the trip use product information more than experienced consumers (see Fig. 3, Panel D).

Famous destinations and major tourist attractions benefit, by definition, from high brand awareness. Iconic attractions are 'pull factors', or motivators that influence tourists to visit. Information plays a minor role in prompting purchase or visit. For visitors to Prince Edward Island, the home of *Anne of Green Gables*, Charlottetown, is the island province's major (and probably only) icon. Conversely, unknown destinations require information

Tourist Activities   **% using product information**

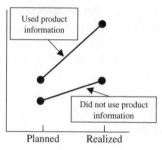

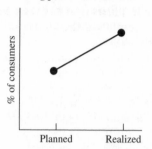

Panel A: Propositioned Differences   **Panel B**: Propositioned Differences
between Planned and Realized   between Planned and Realized
Consumption Behavior   Use of Information

Spending   **Use of VIG by experience**

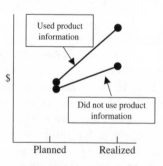

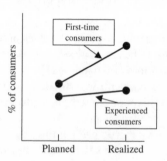

Panel C: Propositioned   **Panel D**: Propositioned
Differences between Planned and   Differences between Planned and
Realized Spending According to   Realized Use of Information
Use of Information   According to Product Experience

Fig. 3. Impact of Product Information On Planned and Realized Consumption
Behavior (Panels A–E).

to generate visitation. For that reason, consumers exposed to product information are more likely to visit unknown places than consumers not exposed to such information.

H₈. The more unknown an attraction is, the greater the influence of
product information about that attraction on planning and actual
consumption of the experience.

This examination informs our understanding of how customer characteristics shape both planned and unplanned consumption behavior. One of the main shortcomings in research on unplanned consumption has been the inadequate consideration of consumer characteristics. As Table 1 reveals, only five empirical studies on the subject of planned and unplanned behavior incorporate demographics or other consumer characteristics. Cobb and Hoyer (1986) felt sufficiently concerned about the neglect of research into customer characteristics associated with unplanned and impulse purchasing that they labelled it a "shortcoming" (p. 389). From a strategic marketing viewpoint, understanding the characteristics of target segments is fundamental in creating an effective communication mix.

The relationship between distance travelled and behavior is especially pertinent in the tourism context. There are a number of perspectives. First, the distance travelled to a consumption site has been used as a surrogate for risk in previous marketing studies, namely, Newman and Stein's (1971) study of information seeking behavior related to new cars and household durables, and the tourism-related study by Fesenmaier and Johnson (1989) into involvement in the vacation planning process. These investigations suggest that individuals travelling long distances will plan more due to higher perceived risk associated with the distance involved. Schul and Crompton (1983) confirmed as such: "information search [is] likely to be greater for major (that is long-distance travel) rather than minor (short-distance) investments" (p. 25). Greater planning may suggest that eventual behavior will more likely match intended behavior. On the other hand, the very fact that long distances are required are likely to compel consumers to purchase low-risk package tours, rather than attempt to make their own travel arrangements.

P9. The greater the distance that consumers travel to engage in destination-specific consumption activities, the greater the difference in expenditures between planned and realized activities.

The influence of experience on planned and actual behavior is a fascinating area of our study. Research shows that intention formation is affected by past experience (Fazio & Zanna, 1981; Morwitz & Schmittlein, 1992). Product experience is critical when studying the dynamic choice processes of consumers new to a market (Heilman et al., 2000). Since experience teaches people how to plan, the consumption actions of experienced consumers will more closely approximate their plans than consumers with little or no product knowledge (Stewart & Vogt, 1999). Routine and habitual buyer behavior allows for purposive and intelligent behavior without deliberation (Katona, 1975). Experienced consumers should be better able to assess the risks associated with engaging in particular behavior and to understand the factors that will influence the decision less than experienced consumers. For example, how long it takes to drive to particular destinations on an island, which route offers the best scenery, which attractions are worth spending time and money on, and what accommodation is of value-for-money, are all questions more readily answered by the experienced rather than the inexperienced visitor. Consequently, proposition H10 states that experienced consumers differ from inexperienced consumers in two ways: they plan fewer consumption activities and the difference between planned and realized consumption activities will be less for experienced consumers than for inexperienced consumers.

Product experience in this study relates to the number of times a respondent has visited Prince Edward Island. Consumers with previous experience should have more accurate predictions of whether or not they will engage in particular future behavior than consumers with little or no experience. Again, experienced consumers should be better able to assess the risks associated with engaging in particular behavior and to understand the factors that will influence the decision than less experienced consumers. For example, how long it takes to drive to particular destinations on the island, which route offers the best scenery, which attractions are worth spending time and money on, and what accommodation is of value-for-money are all questions more readily answered by the experienced rather than the inexperienced tourist.

Experienced shoppers in a supermarket environment, for instance, were found to repeat the same choice as the previous consumption experience and to have well-articulated preferences when they are familiar with the preference object (Bettman et al., 1998). Morwitz and Schmittlein (1992) found that past usage of a durable good moderated the accuracy of future purchase intentions. Among individuals who stated an intention to purchase a personal computer (PC) in the following six months, 48 percent of those with experience of a PC fulfilled their intentions, while only 29 percent with no experience fulfilled their intentions. Similarly, Vernplanken, Aarts, and van Kippenberg (1997) report that respondents who frequently performed a certain behavior (a particular mode of transport) searched for less information about which travel mode to use and were more likely to focus on information about the habitual choice than alternative choices, compared to those who less frequently performed the behavior. Past behavior therefore acts as an internal source of information. And as consumers' experience with a product increases, consideration sets are likely to be increasingly stable over time (Klenosky & Rethans 1988; Mitra 1995). This would suggest that first-time customers would display less consistency that will, in return, be reflected in greater discrepancies between planned and actual behavior. Aarts, Vernplanken, and van Knippenberg (1998) argue that habitual behavior becomes capable of being automatically activated by features of the situation and context in which the behavior occurs.

Much of the consumer research in this area has dealt with product brands rather than product categories. Brand loyalty and awareness become, therefore, critical issues for the researcher to understand. But what of product categories that lack powerful brands – or in situations when the powerful brands are simply not available? If we consider the variety of typical leisure consumption activities in a destination such as Prince Edward Island, few involve products with which travellers register any brand recognition whatsoever. There are no international hotel chains such as Hilton and Sheraton and no famous natural or man-made attractions such as Canadian Rockies or Disneyland, and no famous restaurants. The only study adopting this perspective found that preference reversals are less prevalent for familiar product categories (Coupey, Irwin, & Payne, 1996). Given the large amount of consumption occurring in product categories in which brands are not important, this finding needs to be verified.

As discussed earlier, the influences upon unplanned purchasing that have been identified include characteristics of the shopping party (Kollat & Willett, 1968), personality traits (Raju, 1980), and proclivity to visit stores (Granbois, 1968). Neither Kollat and Willett (1968) and Prasad (1975) found that socio-economic characteristics were a significant explanatory factor in shoppers performing unplanned buying behavior. Supporting the argument that inexperience and information seeking behavior are positively related is the finding by Bloch et al. (1986) who, in investigating consumer search procedures for clothing and personal computers, found that heavy searchers were heavy spenders within the product class. Higher spending was associated with higher product awareness and frequent contact with information providers and retailers. (They also identified two types of searchers: ongoing/ hedonistic searchers and prepurchase searchers. Hedonistic searchers enjoyed the activity of seeking out information, perhaps even more than any actual consumption experience.)

Within the tourism literature, customer experience is commonly defined as whether the visitor is a first-time or repeat traveller. Similar to other consumption systems, it is assumed that first-time visitors to a destination have little product knowledge and will likely therefore spend more than their experienced counterparts. Woodside, Trappey, and MacDonald (1997), for instance, support findings in other fields that experienced consumers undertake fewer consumption activities than inexperienced ones. Etzel and Wahlers (1985) sought to identify the characteristics of people who request travel information and those who do not. Several interesting findings emerged: first, information seekers tend to spend more than consumers who do not seek out information; second, the greater the frequency in product consumption, the less likely consumers would seek information; and third, experienced travellers were more likely to request information. However, a major weakness in the study was the assumption that request for information equated with information used and, ultimately, actual behavior.

The influence of experience upon consumption behavior in the travel context is well documented. Studies show product experience of the destination plays a significant role in various aspects of travel planning and activities, including information use (Etzel & Wahlers, 1985); time spent planning (Zalatan, 1996); risk perception (Roehl & Fesenmaier, 1992); site choice (McFarlane, et al., 1996); destination attractiveness (Hu & Ritchie, 1993); and satisfaction with a destination (Mazursky, 1989a, 1989b).

P_{10}. Experienced consumers are less likely to engage in unplanned activities compared to inexperienced consumers.

Attitudes toward planning differ between individuals. For some individuals, the planning of holidays, including the collection of vast amounts of information, is an integral part of the whole experience; for others, a holiday is a spontaneous experience, in which pre-determined activities and time allocations are an anathema; and there are many individuals who fit somewhere in between. Greater planning of a holiday would, arguably, reflect greater involvement and commitment in the destination, which would then be reflected in higher expenditures. Vacation behavior has been shown to differ according to specific socio-demographic variables (Gitelson & Keresetter, 1990). Morwitz and Schmittlein (1992) suggest that economic factors such as wealth will increase the likelihood of intentions matching actual behavior. On the other hand, individuals with greater discretionary income would presumably be capable of engaging in a greater degree of unplanned, impulsive consumption.

P_{11}. The higher the income level and therefore the greater ability to undertake consumption behavior, the greater the likelihood of unplanned consumption activity.

Early research in the tourism and leisure field flagged the association between social context and the individual's decision process. Burch (1969) was one of the earliest to discuss the importance of the social group in relation to recreation and tourist behavior. His personal community proposition suggested that such behavior is seldom an isolated individual decision. Christensen and Yoesting (1973) confirmed his thesis, and argued that the choice and use of recreational facilities are related to the social context in which the individual is located.

Leisure travel is a product that often is jointly consumed, and tourist activities reflect the influence (both direct and indirect) of all those travelling together (Chadwick, 1987). The behavior of tourists is heavily influenced by the composition of the travelling party (McIntosh & Goeldner, 1990). Travel party size can influence behavior in several ways. First, a group of travel companions, whether extended family, friends or colleagues, require more time for planning and a stronger need for information than do couples or singles (Fesenmaier & Lieber, 1988, cited in Stewart & Vogt, 1999). Conversely, independent travellers are more likely to engage in unplanned behavior. According to Hyde (2000), "the [independent] tourist avoids vacation planning because flexibility of action and experiencing the unknown are key amongst the hedonic experiences they seeking" (p. 188). Second, groups comprising children require greater planning efforts to coordinate schedules and differential needs than groups without children (Fodness & Murray, 1999). Third, Fisher (2001) found that collaboration led to higher decision quality and smaller deviations between consumers' planned and actual expenditures. Fourth, a respondent travelling alone has more flexibility in changing plans than a respondent travelling with children or with a group of friends. Morwitz (1997) posits that the intent-behavior relationship for *durable products* might actually be weaker when the approval of more than one person is required than products involving a single decision maker. Fifth, preferences for travel experiences can differ according to the travel party composition (Basala & Klenosky, 2001). Here the role of the family members is highly influential (Moutinho, 1988; Dimanche & Havitz, 1994).

P_{12}. The smaller the travel party size, the less the difference between planned and realized behavior.

SUMMARY

This paper examines the influences on consumers' planned and unplanned strategies in the purchases of products and services in a tourist consumption system. The rationale underlying proposed theory relates to the need to better understand some of the determinants of consumption behavior, particularly when they differ significantly from planned behavior. Two critical determinants are product information and demographics such as income, age, and geographical location.

The application of the Mintzberg strategy matrix offers a useful conceptual tool for future examinations of divergences between planned, unplanned, and actual behavior. Managerially, this paper highlights the importance of product information as a means of positively influencing consumer demand for products and services.

Theory related to planned and unplanned behavior was examined. Beginning with empirical and conceptual research in the field of social psychology, the discussion then summarized the contributions made in the marketing and

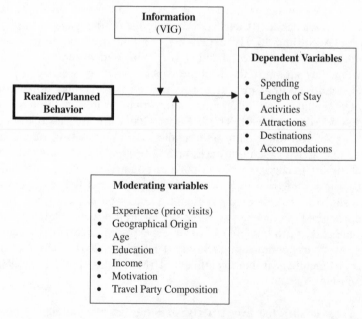

Fig. 4.   Modeling the Hypothesized Relationships.

tourism fields in the area of intentions and behavior. Fig. 4 summarizes the marketing-related empirical research carried out in the topic area.

REFERENCES

Aarts, H., Vernplanken, B., & van Knippenberg, A. (1998). Predicting behavior from actions in the past: Repeated decision making or a matter of habit. *Journal of Applied Social Psychology, 28,* 1355–1374.

Abratt, R., & Goodey, S. D. (1990). Unplanned buying and in-store stimuli in supermarkets. *Managerial and Decision Economics, 11,* 11–121.

Agee, T., & Martin, B. A. S. (2001). Planned or impulse purchases? How to create effective infomercials. *Journal of Advertising Research, 41,* 35–42.

Ajzen, I., & Driver, B. L. (1992). Application of the theory of planned behavior to leisure choice. *Journal of Leisure Research, 24*(3), 207–224.

Alford, P. (1998). Positioning the destination product – Can regional tourist boards learn from private sector practice? *Journal of Travel & Tourism Marketing, 7,* 53–68.

Basala, S. L., & Klenosky, D. B. (2001). Travel-style preferences for visiting a novel destination: A conjoint investigation across the novelty-familiarity continuum. *Journal of Travel Research,* (November), 172–182.

Bayley, G., & Nancarrow, C. (1998). Impulse purchasing: A qualitative exploration of the phenomenon. *Qualitative Market Research: An International Journal, 1,* 99–114.

Beatty, S. E., & Ferrell, M. E. (1998). Impulse buying: Modeling its precursors. *Journal of Retailing, 74,* 169–191.

Beatty, S. E., & Smith, S. M. (1987). External search effort: An investigation across several product categories. *Journal of Consumer Research, 14,* 83–95.

Belk, R. W. (1974). An exploratory assessment of situational effects in buyer behavior. *Journal of Marketing Research, 11,* 156–163.

Belk, R. W. (1975). Situational variables and consumer behavior. *Journal of Consumer Research, 2,* 157–163.

Bellenger, D. N., Robertson, D. H., & Hirschman, E. C. (1978). Impulse buying varies by product. *Journal of Advertising Research, 18,* 15–18.

Berlyne, D. E. (1960). *Conflict, arousal and curiosity.* New York: McGraw hill.

Bettman, J. R. (1979). Memory factors in consumer choice: A review. *Journal of Marketing, 43,* 37–53.

Bettman, J. R., Luce, M. F., & Payne, J. W. (1998). Constructive consumer choice processes. *Journal of Consumer Marketing, 25,* 187–217.

Bettman, J. R., & Park, C. W. (1980). Effects of prior knowledge and experience and phase of the choice process on consumer decision processes: A protocol analysis. *Journal of Consumer Research, 7,* 234–248.

Bishop, D. W., & Witt, P. A. (1970). Sources of behavioral variance during leisure time. *Journal of Personality and Social Psychology, 16,* 352–360.

Bloch, P. H., Sherrell, D. L., & Ridgway, N. M. (1986). Consumer search: An extended framework. *Journal of Consumer Research, 13,* 119–126.

Bruce, V., & Green, P. R. (1991). *Visual perception.* London: Lawrence Erlbaum Associates.

Buck, R. C. (1978). From work to play: Some observations on a popular nostalgic theme. *Journal of American Culture, 1*(3), 543–553.

Burch, W. R. (1969). The social circles of leisure: Competing explanations. *Journal of Leisure Research, 1*, 125–147.

Chadwick, R. A. (1987). Concepts, definitions, and measures used in travel and tourism research. In: J. R. B. Ritchie & C. R. Goeldner (Eds), *Travel, tourism and hospitality research*. New York: John Wiley.

Christensen, J. E., & Yoesting, D. R. (1973). Social and attitudinal variants in high and low use of outdoor recreational facilities. *Journal of Leisure Research, 5*, 6–15.

Clover, V. T. (1950). Relative importance of impulse buying in retail stores. *Journal of Marketing, 62*(Winter), 67–81.

Cobb, C. J., & Hoyer, W. D. (1986). Planned versus impulse purchase behavior. *Journal of Retailing, 62*, 384–409.

Cohen, E. (1972). Towards a sociology of international research. *Social Research, 39*, 164–182.

Coupey, E., Irwin, J. R., & Payne, J. W. (1996). *Product category familiarity and preference evaluation*. Working Paper, Stern School of Business. New York University, New York.

Cox, K. (1964). The responsiveness of food sales to shelf space changes in supermarkets. *Journal of Marketing Research, 1*, 63–67.

Crompton, J. (1979). Motivations for pleasure vacation. *Journal of Leisure Research, 6*, 408–424.

Crotts, J. C., & Reid, L. J. (1993). Segmenting the visitor market by the timing of their activity decisions. *Visions in Leisure and Business, 12*, 4–7.

Dann, G. M. S. (1981). Tourist motivation: An appraisal. *Annals of Tourism Research, 8*, 187–219.

Dimanche, F., & Havitz, M. E. (1994). Consumer behavior and tourism: Review and extension of four study areas. *Economic Psychology of Travel and Tourism, 3*, 37–57.

Dittmar, H., Beattie, J., & Friese, S. (1996). Gender identity and material symbols: Objects and decision considerations in impulse purchases. *Journal of Economic Psychology, 15*, 391–511.

East, R. (1997). *Consumer behavior: Advances and applications in marketing*. London: Prentice-Hall.

Engel, J. F., Blackwell, R. D., & Miniard, R. W. (1993). *Consumer behavior* (7th ed.). New York: Dryden Press.

Etzel, M. J., & Wahlers, R. G. (1985). The use of requested promotional material by pleasure travelers. *Journal of Travel Research, 12*, 2–61.

Fazio, R. H., & Zanna, M. P. (1981). Direct experience and attitude behavior consistency. *Advances in Experimental Social Psychology, 14*, 161–202.

Feldman, L. P., & Hornik, J. (1981). The use of time: An integrated conceptual model. *Journal of Consumer Research, 7*, 407–419.

Fesenmaier, D. R., & Johnson, B. (1989). Involvement-based segmentation. *Journal of Tourism Research, 28*, 293–300.

Fesenmaier, D. R., & Lieber, S. R. (1988). Destination diversification as an indicator of activity compatibility: An exploratory analysis. *Leisure Studies, 10*, 167–168.

Fesenmaier, D. R., Vogt, C. A., & Stewart, W. P. (1993). Investigating the influence of welcome center information on travel behavior. *Journal of Travel Research, 34*, 47–52.

Filiatrault, P., & Ritchie, J. R. B. (1988). The impact of situational factors on the evaluation of hospitality services. *Journal of Travel Research, 26*, 29–37.

Fisher, R. J. (2001). The role of collaboration in consumers' in-store decisions. *Advances in Consumer Research, 28,* 251.

Fodness, D., & Murray, B. (1999). A model of tourist information search behavior. *Journal of Travel Research, 37,* 220–230.

Gardner, M. P., & Rook, D. W. (1988). Effects of impulse purchases on consumers' affective states. In: M. J. Houston (Ed.), *Advances in consumer research* (vol. 15, pp. 127–130). Provo, Utah: Association for Consumer Research.

Gilbert, D. C. (1991). An examination of the consumer behavior process related to tourism. In *Progress in Tourism, Recreation and Hospitality Management, 3,* 78–105.

Gitelson, R. J., & Crompton, J. L. (1983). The planning horizons and sources of information used by pleasure vacationers. *Journal of Travel Research, 23,* 2–7.

Gitelson, R. J., & Keresetter, D. L. (1990). The relationship between sociodemographic variables, benefits sought and subsequent vacation behavior: A case study. *Journal of Travel Research, 29,* 24–29.

Godbey, G., & Graefe, A. (1991). Repeat tourism, play and monetary spending. *Annals of Tourism Research, 18,* 213–225.

Graburn, N. H. H. (1977). Tourism: The sacred journey. In: V. Smith (Ed.), *Hosts and guests: The anthropology of tourism.* Philadelphia: University of Pennsylvania.

Granbois, D. H. (1968). Improving the study of customer in-store behavior. *Journal of Marketing, 32,* 28–33.

Gregory, R., Lichenstein, S., & Slovic, P. (1993). Valuing environmental resources: A constructive approach. *Journal of Risk and Uncertainty, 7,* 177–197.

Gross, B. L. (1994). Consumer responses to time pressure: A qualitative study with homeowners in foreclosure. *Advances in Consumer Research, 21,* 121–125.

Hawkins, S. A., & Hoch, S. J. (1992). Low-involvement learning: Memory without evaluation. *Journal of Consumer Research, 19,* 212–225.

Heilman, C. M., Bowman, D., & Wright, G. P. (2000). The evolution of brand preferences and choice behavior of consumers new to a market. *Journal of Marketing Research, 37,* 139–155.

Hendrick, C., Mills, M., & Kiesler, C. A. (1968). Decision time as a function of the number and complexity of equally attractive alternatives. *Journal of Personality and Social Psychology, 8,* 313–318.

Hornik, J. (1982). Situational effects on the consumption of time. *Journal of Marketing, 40,* 44–55.

Howard, J. A., & Sheth, J. N. (1969). *The theory of buyer behavior.* New York: Wiley.

Hu, Y., & Ritchie, J. R. B. (1993). Measuring destination attractiveness: A contextual approach. *Journal of Travel Research, 32*(Fall), 25–34.

Hyde, K. F. (2000). A hedonic perspective on independent vacation planning, decision-making and behavior. In: A. G. Woodside, G. I. Crouch, J. A. Mazanec, M. Oppermann & M. Y. Sakai (Eds), *Consumer psychology of tourism, hospitality and leisure.* New York: CABI Publishing.

Inman, J. J., & Winer, R. S. (1998). *Where the rubber hits the road: A model of in-store consumer decision making.* Report 98–122, Marketing Science Institute, Cambridge, MA.

Iyer, E. S. (1989). Unplanned purchasing: Knowledge of shopping environment and time pressure. *Journal of Retailing, 65,* 40–57.

Jacoby, J., Speller, D. E., & Berning, C. K. (1976). Brand choice behavior as a function of information load. *Journal of Consumer Research, 1*(1), 33–42.

Jeng, J. (1997). Facets of the complex trip decision making process. Paper presented at the Travel and Tourism Research Association's 28th annual conference, June 1997, Norfolk, Virginia.

Kalwani, M. U., & Silk, A. J. (1982). On the relationship and predictive ability of purchase intention measures. *Marketing Science, 1*, 243–286.

Kardes, F. R. (1994). Consumer judgment and decision processes. In: R. S. Wyer & T. K. Srull (Eds), *Handbook of social recognition*, (2nd ed.). Hove, UK: Lawrence Erlbaum Associates.

Katona, G. (1975). *Psychological economics*. New York: Elsevier.

Kelly, R. (1965). *An evaluation of selected variables of end display effectiveness*. Unpublished doctoral dissertation, Harvard University, Boston.

Klenosky, D. B., & Rethans, A. J. (1988). The formation of consumer choice sets: A longitudinal investigation at the product class level. *Advances in Consumer Research, 15*, 13–18.

Kollat, D. T., & Willett, R. P. (1968). Customer impulse purchasing behaviour. *Journal of Marketing, 6*(February), 21–31.

Leclerc, F., Schmitt, B. H., & Dube, L. (1994). Foreign branding and its effect on product perceptions and attitudes. *Journal of Marketing Research, 31*(2), 263–270.

Lilien, G., Kotler, P., & Moorthy, K. S. (1992). *Marketing models*. Englewood Cliffs, NJ: Prentice-Hall.

Manski, C. (1990). The use of intentions data to predict behavior: A best-case analysis. *Journal of American Statistical Association, 85*, 934–940.

Mayo, E. J., & Jarvis, L. P. (1990). *The psychology of leisure travel*. Boston: CBI Publishing.

Mazursky, D. (1989a). Past experience and future tourism decisions. *Annals of Tourism Research, 16*, 333–344.

Mazursky, D. (1989b). Temporal decay in the satisfaction-purchase intention relationship. *Psychology and Marketing, 6*, 211–322.

McFarlane, B., Boxall, P., & Watson, D. (1996). Past experience and behavioural choice among wildnerness users. *Journal of Leisure Research, 30*, 195–213.

McGoldrick, P. J. (1982). How unplanned are impulse purchases? *Retail & Distribution Management, 56*, 27–30.

McIntosh, R. W., & Goeldner, C. R. (1990). *Tourism: Principles, Practices, Philosophies*. New York: Wiley.

Mintzberg, H. (1978). Patterns in strategy formation. *Management Science, 24*, 934–948.

Mintzberg, H. (1994). *The rise and fall of strategic planning: Reconceiving roles for planning, plans, planners*. New York: The Free Press.

Mitra, A. (1995). Advertising and the stability of consideration sets over multiple purchase considerations. *International Journal of Research in Marketing, 12*, 81–94.

Mo, C., Howard, D. R., & Havitz, M. E. (1993). Testing an international tourist role typology. *Annals of Tourism Research, 20*, 319–335.

Morrison, A. (1996). *Hospitality and travel marketing*. Albany, NY: Delmar.

Morwitz, V. G. (1997a). Why consumers don't always accurately predict their own future behavior. *Marketing Letters, 8*, 57–70.

Morwitz, V. G. (1997b). It seems like only yesterday: The nature and consequences of telescoping errors in marketing research. *Journal of Consumer Psychology, 6*(1), 1–29.

Morwitz, V. G., & Schmittlein, D. C. (1992). Using segmentation to improve sales forecasts based on purchase intent: Which 'intenders' actually buy? *Journal of Marketing Research, 29*, 391–405.

Moutinho, L. (1988). Consumer behavior in tourism. *European Journal of Marketing, 21*(10), 5–44.

Otto, J. E., & Ritchie, J. R. B. (1996). The service experience in tourism. *Tourism Management, 17*, 165–174.

Parr, D. (1989). *Free independent travelers.* M.Sc. thesis, Lincoln College, Canterbury, New Zealand.

Payne, J. W., Bettman, J. R., & Johnston, E. J. (1987). Advertising strategy selection in decision making. Paper presented at the stellner conference on the uses of cognitive psychology in advertising and marketing, University of Illinois.

Pearce, P. L., & Caltabiano, M. (1983). Inferring travel motivations from travelers' experiences. *Journal of Travel Research, 22*, 25–30.

Perdue, R. R. (1986). The influence of unplanned attraction visits on expenditures by travel-through visitors. *Journal of Travel Research, 25*, 14–19.

Peter, J. P., & Olson, J. C. (1999). *Consumer Behavior and Marketing Strategy* (5th ed.). Boston: Irwin McGraw-Hill.

Peterson, L. (1987). Study confirms impulse buying on the rise, Promote, 6–10.

Plog, S. C. (1974). Why destination areas rise and fall in popularity. *The Cornell Hotel and Restaurant Administration Quarterly, 15*, 13–16.

Prasad, V. K. (1975). Unplanned buying in two retail settings. *Journal of Retailing, 51*, 3–12.

Raju, P. S. (1980). Optimum stimulation level: Its relationship to personality, demographics, and exploratory behavior. *Journal of Consumer Research, 7*, 272–282.

Rao, S. R., Thomas, E. G., & Javalgi, R. G. (1992). Activity preferences and trip planning behavior of the U.S. outbound pleasure travel market. *Journal of Travel Research, 30*, 3–13.

Ritchie, J. R. B. (1994). Research on leisure behavior and tourism – state of the art. In: R. V. Gasser & K. Weiermair (Eds), *Spoilt for Choice: Decision Making Processes and Preference Changes of Tourists – Intertemporal and Intercountry Perspectives.* Frankfurt: Kultur.

Roehl, W., & Fesenmaier, D. (1992). Risk perception and pleasure travel: An exploratory analysis. *Journal of Travel Research, 30*, 17–26.

Rook, D. W., & Fisher, R. J. (1995). Normative influences on impulsive buying behavior. *Journal of Consumer Research, 22*, 305–313.

Rook, D. W., & Garnder, M. P. (1993). In the mood: Impulse buyings' affective antecedents. In: J. Arnold-Costa & R. W. Belk (Eds), *Research in Consumer Behavior* (p. 6). Greenwich, CT: JAI Press.

Rook, D. W., & Hoch, S. J. (1985). Consuming impulses. *Advances in Consumer Research, 12*, 23–27.

Schul, P., & Crompton, J. L. (1983). Search behavior of international vacationers: Travel-specific lifestyle and socio-demographic variables. *Journal of Travel Research, 21*, 25–30.

Shapiro, S., & Krishnan, H. S. (1999). Consumer memory for intentions: A prospective memory perspective. *Journal of Experimental Psychology, 5*, 169–189.

Shoemaker, S. (1994). Segmenting the U.S. travel market according to benefits realized. *Journal of Travel Research, 32*, 8–21.

Snepenger, D. (1987). Segmenting the vacation market by novelty seeking role. *Journal of Travel Research, 26*, 8–14.

Stayman, D. M., & Deshplande, R. (1989). Situational ethnicity and consumer behavior. *Journal of Consumer Research, 16*, 361–371.

Stewart, S. I., & Vogt, C. A. (1999). A case-based approach to understanding vacation planning. *Leisure Sciences, 21*, 79–95.

Stigler, G. J. (1961). The economics of information. *Journal of Political Economy, 59*, 213–225.

Tsang, G. K. Y. (1993). *Visitor information network study: Visitors' information seeking behavior for on-site travel-related sub-decision making and evaluation of service performance.* Unpublished Masters of Commerce thesis, University of Otago, Dunedin, NZ.

Um, S., & Crompton, J. L. (1990). Attitude determinants in tourism destination choice. *Annals of Tourism Research, 17*, 432–448.

Vernplanken, B., Aarts, H., & van Kippenberg, A. (1997). Habit, information acquisition, and the process of making travel mode choices. *European Journal of Social Psychology, 27*, 539–560.

Warshaw, P. R. (1980). Predicting purchase and other behavior from general and contextually specific intentions. *Journal of Marketing Research, 17*, 26–33.

West, J. C. (1951). Results of two years of study into impulse buying. *Journal of Marketing, 15*, 362–363.

Weun, S., Jones, M. A., & Beatty, S. E. (1998). The development and validation of the impulse buying tendency scale. *Psychological Reports, 82*, 1123–1133.

Wicks, B., & Schuett, M. (1991). Examining the role of tourism promotion through the use of brochures. *Tourism Management, 12*, 301–313.

Williams, J., & Dardis, R. (1972). Shopping behavior for soft goods and marketing strategies. *Journal of Retailing, 48*(32–41), 126.

Woodside, A. G., & Jacobs, L. (1985). Step two in benefit segmentation: Learning the benefits realized by major travel markets. *Journal of Travel Research, 24*(1), 7–13.

Woodside, A. G., Trappey, R. J., & MacDonald, R. (1997). Measuring linkage-advertising effects on customer behavior and net revenue: Using quasi-experiments of advertising treatments with novice and experienced product-service users. *Canadian Journal of Administrative Sciences, 14*, 214–228.

Wright, P. L. (1974). The harassed decision maker: Time pressure, distraction, and the use of evidence. *Journal of Applied Psychology, 59*, 555–561.

Yiannakis, A., & Gibson, H. (1992). Roles tourists play. *Annals of Tourism Research, 19*, 287–303.

Young, M. R., DeSarbo, W. S., & Morwitz, V. G. (1998). The stochastic modeling of purchase intentions and behavior. *Management Science, 44*(2, February), 188–202.

Young, R. A., & Kent, A. T. (1985). Using the theory of reasoned action to improve the understanding of recreation behavior. *Journal of Leisure Research, 17*, 90–106.

Zalatan, A. (1996). The determinants of planning time in vacation travel. *Tourism Management, 17*, 123–131.

CHAPTER 9

A MODEL OF HUMOUR IN THE TOURIST EXPERIENCE

Elspeth Frew

ABSTRACT

The paper discusses humour and the tourist experience, with a particular focus on formal and informal humorous tourist experiences. The paper examines Stebbins' (1996) theory of social comic relief and applies the theory to the tourism sector. The paper provides a conceptual model of humour and the tourist experience by describing the three phases of the tourist experience in relation to humour, namely, before travel, during travel and after travel. The model refers to the role of humour in the tourist experience and the satisfaction levels tourists derive from their humour related travel experiences. The paper reflects on the importance of understanding the role of humour in the tourist experience, particularly in relation to the management of formal humorous experiences such as comedy festivals.

INTRODUCTION

Humour is universal, ubiquitous (Mahony & Lippman, 2001) and found in all cultures (Weisfeld, 1993). As such, humour is considered a genetic, biological characteristic of the human race (Fry, 1992). Humour is a form of communication where a complex mental stimulation amuses, or elicits the

Advances in Culture, Tourism and Hospitality Research, Volume 1, 257–272
Copyright © 2007 by Elsevier Ltd.
ISSN: 1871-3173/doi:10.1016/S1871-3173(06)01009-3

laughter reflex (Koestler, 1995). A sense of humour is the faculty of perceiving the ludicrous (Allen, 1990) and the "frequency with which the individual smiles, laughs, and otherwise displays amusement in a variety of
situations (Martin & Lefcourt, 1984, p. 147). As humour is part of every
social system and occurs in nearly every type of human interaction, analysis
can be conducted on how humour "influences each interaction pattern and
the social structure emerging from it" (Martineau, 1972, p. 103). In sociology, the humour literature can be split into two broad categories, namely
why individuals use humour, that is, motivationally/psychologically and, the
function humour has within a social setting (Lynch, 2002). From a sociological perspective, humour can assume different forms and "has different
functions in various structural settings" (Martineau, 1972, p. 114). For example, the use of humour creates many positive social outcomes such as
enhancing interpersonal relationships by reducing tension, acting as a social
lubricant, enhancing communication (Sultanoff, 2003) and, helping individuals cope with difficult emotional situations (Freud, 1928). However, a
thorough examination from a sociological perspective should consider humour from both extremes, namely as a "lubricant" where humour helps to
"keep the machinery of interaction operating freely and smoothly" (Martineau, 1972, p. 103) and, when humour is an "abrasive" resulting in "interpersonal friction and a juncture in the communication process which may
modify the character of the interaction" (Martineau, 1972, p. 103). Although many studies typically focus on the positive side of humour,
Gruner's (1997) superiority theory is one of the few perspectives focusing on
the darker side of humour by suggesting that humour always involves
gaining superiority over others. Similarly, Alexander (1986) suggests that
humour is often used to elevate the status of the joke-teller and to reduce
(either directly or incidentally) the status of the object or target of the joke.
Tragesser and Lippman (2005) also note that humour can either elevate
one's status by lowering another individual's status, such as when the lower-
status individual is the butt of the joke, or through solidifying bonds between in-group members, thus indirectly excluding and ostracising members
of the out-group. Therefore, any sociological study of humour should be
aware of both extremes, namely, the positive and negative influence that
humour can have on a social situation.

Management also considers humour (Barsoux, 1993) including hospitality
(Ball & Johnson, 2000) and leisure (Katovich, 1993; Stebbins, 1979, 1990).
In business, the use of humour allows managers to control certain situations, e.g., to make light of a serious situation, while humour in advertising
attracts attention and, makes adverts more likeable and more memorable

(Cline, Moses, & Kellaris, 2003). In the management area, humour can be deployed to influence, persuade, to motivate and to facilitate change (Barsoux, 1993) and, can lighten interviews, and negotiations, ease meetings and facilitate training (Ball & Johnson, 2000). In hospitality, Ball and Johnson (2000) consider how, when and why humour is deliberately used, by considering the role of humour between hospitality employees, between employees and managers and, between all staff and customers. Ball and Johnson (2000, p. 201) note that in hospitality, "humour is an essential ingredient in relieving a client's trauma and restoring him/her to a position of well-being". They suggest that humour increases the "fun factor" in hospitality situations and generates warmth, openness and trust. However, they also note that humour can be used as a defensive mechanism enabling one to cope with failure, criticism and stress and can act as an antidote to boredom and a release for frustration and tensions (Ball & Johnson, 2000). Research has shown that different types of humour exist, with Martin and Lefcourt (1983) describing proactive humour as the ability to produce humour in stressful situations, where the active creation of humour may have more impact on buffering stress and depression than just responding to humour. Consensual humour occurs when humour creates and reinforces "solidarity and intimacy in groups or interactive settings" (Stebbins, 1996, p. 4). Martineau (1972) summarises the social function of humour based on the type of humour used and, the outcome of the humour, namely; conflict, control, consensus or comic relief, whereby humour can create an outlet for group hostility and aggression, is a means to control undesirable behaviour, develops and maintains group cohesion, or provides relief from a tense situation. However, individuals must be careful when they deliberately use humour as they may inadvertently offend others and the situation may be made worse (Barsoux, 1993), with inappropriate humour in the service sector destroying rather than creating hospitality (Ball & Johnson, 2000). However, Stebbins (1996, p. 6) notes that as long as the humour is seen as appropriate, "telling jokes, making wisecracks, and spinning anecdotes can bring immense pleasure to the authors of such wit as well as their audiences". Fig. 1 illustrates the various uses and effect of humour within organisations.

Research into the impact of humour in society crosses many disciplines such as medicine (Fry, 1992), social psychology (Mahony, Burroughs, & Lippman, 2002), and, philosophy (Critchley, 2002). The field of gelotology is the scientific study of laughter. Such research has revealed that, when humour results in laughter, numerous physical benefits occur such as, the heart beating faster, an increase in circulation, a reduction in blood pressure, a

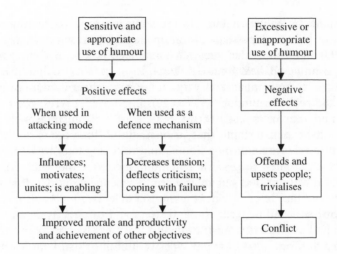

Fig. 1. Uses and Effects of Organisational Humour. *Source:* Ball and Johnson (2000).

change in hormones and immune elements in the bloodstream, some muscles become active and others relax, and, lung capacity and blood oxygen level improve (Strubbe, 2003). As Strubbe (2003, p. 134) notes, "for sedentary people and those confined to a bed or wheelchair, laughter can be a viable workout". Laughter has also been shown to change a person's mood and create a sense of well-being (Szabo, 2003). As a result, many health professionals now prescribe laughter therapy to help people cope with physical, mental and spiritual issues (Strubbe, 2003), recognising that humour is beneficial to a person's ability to cope throughout their life (Saper, 1990). Therefore, humour has "cognitive, emotional, physiological, and behavioural components and is important to human interaction and survival" (Solomon, 1996, p. 250).

APPLYING HUMOUR IN THE TOURISM SECTOR

Humour is considered in the realm of hospitality (Ball & Johnson, 2000) and, in leisure settings (Katovich, 1993; Stebbins, 1996). In the tourism literature, a range of authors have addressed particular aspects of humour. For example, Sweet (1989) considers the Pueblo Indians who performed humorous imitations of tourists as a means of helping the locals re-define their identity. Little (2003) also considers humour in a cultural context when he studied Maya women in Antigua and examined how they use humour to critique and undermine the tourism system in which they live and work. Wong (2001) considers the importance of humour used by tour guides to create a friendly and welcoming atmosphere among tour participants, while Mellinger (1994) investigated humour in relation to the content of historic photographic postcards of African Americans. Authors writing about their travel experiences often use humorous anecdotes to illustrate their adventures (see, for example Cahill, 2000; O'Reilly, Habegger, & O'Reilly, 2003) and this often serves to illustrate the cultural divide between the tourist and host. The research by Sweet (1989), Little (2003) and Wong (2001) closely relates to the use of humour in tourism as conceptualised below but no study has specifically examined the relationship between humour and the tourist during the three phases of the tourist experience, namely before travel, during travel and after travel.

Ball and Johnson (2000, p. 202) suggest that in tourism, the role of humour is far less central to the essential hospitality role of "converting strangers into friends". However, this paper suggests that humour in the tourism sector has indeed an important role to play in ensuring that the experience is a positive one for all involved namely, the tourist, the tourism employees and, the locals. Ball and Johnson (2000) suggest that humour offers the opportunity of adding value to the hospitality customers/guests experience and can appeal to most potential guests. This view is similar to the conceptualisation presented here in that humour, as a universal emotion, can enhance the travel situation and may help in understanding how tourists, tourism employees and locals cope with stressful tourism related situations. The principal objective of this paper, therefore, is to begin the process of addressing this gap in the literature by conceptualising humour and the tourist experience.

INFORMAL HUMOUR

Stebbins (1979, p. 7) describes humour used in social situations as social comic relief, which provides "a momentary humorous respite from the seriousness of lengthy concentration on a collective task, a respite that facilitates the completion of that task by refreshing the participants". Stebbins (1979) empirically tested his theory in a theatrical setting through the observation of actors rehearsing for a play. He suggests that social comic relief can occur when people are trying to maintain a "collective concentration in the pursuit of a goal" (1979, p. 102). However, in a later development of his theory, Stebbins suggests that the existence of social comic relief does not only occur during lengthy periods of concentration but also occurs in short-lived social situations. He uses the example of disabled people using social comic relief to "defuse situational awkwardness" (1996, p. 6). He also notes that as well as verbal comic relief, humour can be created through nonverbal or gestural expressions. This paper extends Stebbins' (1996) conceptualisation of social comic relief to the tourism sector by highlighting the potential of humour to diffuse awkward travel situations and, to help explain tourists' ability to handle the numerous difficult travel situations encountered during a trip away from home.

Tourists often spontaneously engage in humour with their travelling companions and, with the people they encounter during their tourist experience. This informal humour, in the form of proactive and consensual humour, has the potential to help the tourist do one, or more, of the following:

• Handle transport problems such as traffic jams, airport delays, cancellations and the vagaries of local transport;
• Cope with bad or extreme weather conditions;
• Endure the entertainment and/or accommodation at the tourist destination;
• Stomach particular types and quality of food; and
• Interact with local people and tourism employees.

Through the use of social comic relief by tourists in the form of proactive and consensual informal humour, the awkwardness, frustration and/or embarrassment of the tourist situation may lessen and, reinforce the social ties with others in the group. Humour in tourism, as in other social situations, may allow the tourist to gain control, by redefining the situation as less threatening (Solomon, 1996) and, that joking, may enable the tourist to redefine an embarrassing situation as "not serious" and thus under control (Goffman, 1967). Therefore, humour may be used in tourism to achieve cognitive control by helping the tourist restructure an aversive travel situation in their minds and creating a feeling of control (Solomon, 1996). While experiencing humour, emotional distress has been shown to dissolve and, although those feelings of distress may return, the experience of humour provides momentary relief (Sultanoff, 2003). In hospitality, humour is used as a form of communication between people involved in the production, delivery and receipt of hospitality and is a "fundamental element in the triadic relationship between hospitality managers, employees and customers" (Ball & Johnson, 2000, p. 209). This triadic relationship in hospitality

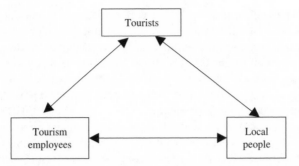

Fig. 2. The Triadic Humour Relationship between Tourists, Tourism Employees and Locals. *Source:* Adapted from Ball and Johnson (2000).

may be extended to tourism to conceptualise the use of humour among tourists, namely, during the triadic relationship between tourists, tourism employees and locals (see Fig. 2).

FORMAL HUMOUR

Comedy festivals, such as the Melbourne International Comedy Festival, the Edinburgh Festival Fringe and Montreal's Just for Laughs Comedy Festival, are well-established events, which help their respective cities develop and remain attractive tourist destinations. These comedy festivals are important cultural events and contribute substantially to the economic and social prosperity of the area due to the increase in visitation and the higher profile of the region during the period of the festival. As with other types of festivals, the associated increase in employment, the enhancement of a destination's image, the extension of the tourist season; and, the enhancement of community pride (Getz, 1997) all benefit the region. The size and longevity of these and other comedy festivals around the world, suggest that comedy is a popular art form among locals and visitors alike and one which can have many positive impacts on society. A comedy festival may provide the pull factor to tourists who are seeking the guarantee of laughter and fun. As humour is at the core of any comedy festival and, is pivotal in its survival, by attending such comedy events the tourists have the assurance of experiencing formal humour. Therefore, in contrast to the use of informal humour in tourism, formal humour is conceptualised as occurring when tourists purposely travel to visit "humorous events" such as comedy festivals and, to visit "humorous places" such as comedic TV and film locations. The shows at comedy festivals can feature domestic and/or international acts; established and/or new acts and, may represent a range of comedy genres, representing stand-up, theatre, cabaret, burlesque, music, visual and children's comedy. Theatrical, stand-up comedy and, by extension, comedy festivals provide a form of entertainment which is an alternative to theatre, films, and live and recorded music that is "affordable, available and acceptable to a sizeable public" (Stebbins, 1990, p. 17). The popularity of comedy festivals may be because people enjoy laughing and that "laughter brings relief from routine and discipline and unites those who share it" (Stebbins, 1990, p. 17) generating "a warm feeling of friendliness and good cheer" (Stebbins, 1990, p. 48). The comedy experiences during comedy festivals also represent a unique and popular art form which is readily acceptable and accessible to all in the local community (Glasgow International Comedy Festival, 2004). As such, comedy provides a relatively easy way for people to become involved in the appreciation of the arts compared with other performing arts such as classical music, ballet, and opera and, has the potential for longevity because of its popularity among all sections of society. If a comedy festival has been appropriately developed, any formal humour tourist attending the festival should have the opportunity to find something that appeals to their individual sense of humour. For example, experiencing a range of acts is possible at the Montreal Just for Laughs Festival, where tourists can undertake "a raucous series of close encounters with some of the world's best humorists: stand-up comics, clowns of every description, crafty illusionists, cutting-edge performance artists, and other wacky, in-your-face entertainers" (Henkin, 2002, p. 167). The Just for Laughs Festival provides a series of events reflecting the extensive range of potential audience members, namely:

> The Nasty Show (raunchy, vile humour), Queer Comics (gay humour), the Relationship Show (dating humour), Bubbling With Laughter (varied stand-ups), the Montreal Show (the city's own), the Really Late Show ("mind-blowing" midnight humour), the Bar Mitzvah Show (Jewish comics), New Faces of Comedy ("The funniest names in comedy you've never heard of!"), Britcom (British humour), O'Comics (Irish comics), and the Masters (veteran comics who are on the verge of rocketing to stardom) (Henkin, 2002, p. 167).

In other words, all types of formal humour tourists should be able to find a type of comedy to appeal to them at a comedy festival which reflects the fact that "different audiences have different stylistic and thematic preferences in comedy" (Palmer, 1994, p. 16). At a comedy festival, as with other performing arts festivals, the audience may need to be adventurous by attending shows of unknown performers and/or, they are willing to be challenged by attending shows which are controversial, topical, confronting and/or innovative. Particularly important for a comedy festival is to have adventurous audiences as the comedy shows often contain material which can challenge audience members when the performers discuss current events, political issues and controversial topics. In addition, some performers may use strong language, while others will use polite language and talk about agreeable topics but will still with an "attitude". The Melbourne International Comedy Festival (2004, p. 3) identified their audience as an:

> Open-minded, liberal thinking audience, with progressive personal values for whom the social aspect of the festival is highly important.

However, the content of a comedy festival will often reflect the local audience in the festival's local town or region, so the choice of shows being staged in a particular region should reflect the potential audiences in the area, namely, liberal or conservative individuals, families or young, single people. Thus a comedy festival, with its variety of comedy acts, may appeal to the formal humour tourist who is guaranteed laughter and fun by attending the event.

Within the tourism literature, the formal humour tourist can be described as engaging in special interest tourism which occurs when people travel because they "have a particular interest which can be pursued in a particular region or, at a particular destination" (Reed, 1980, p. 195). With special interest tourism, the traveller's motivation and choice of destination are primarily determined by a particular special interest (Hall, 1991). As a special interest traveller, a formal humour tourist may be similar to an "arts-core" tourist who travels and stays overnight so that they can "see a production because it is not available elsewhere or because it is of a high standard that cannot be seen elsewhere" (Hughes, 2000, p. 101). A special interest traveller therefore is seeking particular benefits and, as Kastenholz, Davis, and Paul (1999) note, segmentation based on benefits sought has generally been found to predict behaviour better than the other more descriptive variables such as demographics and geographics. The formal humour tourist experiences cultural tourism where they participate in new and deep cultural experiences of an aesthetic, intellectual, emotional or psychological nature (Reisinger, 1994). The concept of cultural tourism applies to the formal humour tourist as he or she may be searching for a "deep cultural experience of an ... emotional ... nature" (Reisinger, 1994, p. 24). The formal humour tourist, like any tourist, may experience a range of emotions during their travels, but the anticipation of pleasant emotions during their visit to a humorous event or place may encourage them to select these destinations over others. This concept is given support by Plutchik (2001, p. 347), who notes that an emotion is a "complex chain of loosely connected events that begins with a stimulus ... they are responses to significant situations in an individual's life, and often they motivate actions". Similarly, Gnoth, Zines, Lengmueller, and Boshoff (1999, p. 158) note that the 10 basic emotions of interest, joy, anger, disgust, contempt, distress, anxiety, fear, shame and guilt "contain information about a person's movement toward or away from an object". This is supported in leisure by Goossens (2000), who found that tourists are pushed by their emotional needs and pulled by the emotional benefits for leisure services and destinations and, that emotions and feelings about destination attributes probably motivate tourists to plan a trip. As service exchanges are fundamental to the tourism and hospitality industries, the moods, feelings and emotions of the participants are a crucially important part of the "exchange process" (Ball & Johnson, 2000, p. 206). In the tourism sector, the generation of pleasant emotions during formal humorous tourism activities may result in high satisfaction levels and, positive word of mouth recommendation about the experience and/or destination. Kastenholz et al. (1999, p. 354) note that personal recommendation is an important factor in helping to generate future visitation because "a satisfied guest is one of the destination's best assets". Similarly, Thrane (2002) found that in a festival context, attendees' overall satisfaction with a festival can exert a positive and direct influence on the intention to revisit and on the intention to recommend the festival to others. Therefore, the formal humour tourist, who attends a humorous event and/or a humorous place, may be a special interest tourist, with a particular interest in one aspect of culture, namely humorous places and/or events, which generates a range of positive, pleasant emotions.

CONCEPTUALISATION

Humour is therefore conceptualised as existing in two main areas of the tourist experience:

• As informal humour in the form of sharing jokes during difficult, awkward or frustrating travel situations; and
• As formal humour in the form of attendance at comedy festivals and/or at comedic TV and film locations.

This paper conceptualises humour and the tourist experience during the three phases of the tourist experience, namely, before travel, during travel and after travel. These three phases conceptualise the link between humour and the tourist in terms of travel motivations, experiences, satisfaction levels, and potential for repeat visits. In the development of the conceptual framework consideration is given to the following questions:

- What is the function of humour in the tourist experience?
- Is humour a motivator for travel?
- Can humour help individuals cope with difficult travel experiences?
- Can "humour tourists" be identified?
- Does the existence of humour during the tourist experience influence post-trip satisfaction levels?

Pre-Travel: In the pre-travel phase, humour may be a strong motivator for travel for the tourist as he or she may be motivated to travel to have fun and to laugh and, to share humorous experiences with family and/or friends. The existence of a range of attractive formal humorous events and places around the world may provide a travel pull for those tourists who want to guarantee their experience will generate laughter and fun.

During Travel: During the travel phase, the tourist may experience informal humour when sharing a joke with their travelling companions, with the tourism employees and/or, the local people they encounter. If the creation of the humour is the result of a stressful travel situation, this is known as proactive humour (Martin & Lefcourt, 1983). The tourist may also experience consensual humour when the humour has the effect of creating solidarity and intimacy in the group (Stebbins, 1996). Tourists may actively seek formal humorous experiences during travel in the form of attending "humorous events" such as comedy festivals and/or "humorous places" such as to visit the sites shown in TV sitcoms and/or comedic movies.

Post Travel: In the post travel phase, the tourist may experience benefits from the humorous experiences of their travel such as reduction of stress and increase in well-being, creating an overall improvement in mental and physical health. They may experience an enhancement in the social relationships with their travel companions and, with the social contacts in their home environments by recounting humorous holiday tales with their friends, family and work colleagues. Therefore, formal and informal humour tourists may experience physical, mental and social benefits. The tourist destinations also may receive long-term benefits due to positive word of mouth recommendation from the formal humour tourist and, the possibility of repeat visitation because of high levels of visitor satisfaction. The tourist who uses informal humour to handle difficult travel situations may recount their negative experiences to family and friends. However, if the

difficult travel situation had a subsequent satisfactory resolution (following
the use of proactive and consensual humour) then the tourist may ultimately
give the destination a positive word of mouth recommendation. Fig. 3

Pre-Travel   **Humour Related Motivation**

• To have fun and to laugh;
• To share humorous experiences with family and/or friends;
• To attend a comedy festival; and/or
• To visit a site featured in a comedic TV show and/or movie;

During Travel   **Humorous Experiences**

Informal humour
• Humour used as a coping mechanism during awkward travel situations
  (using proactive and consensual humour)
• Humour used as a means of reviving oneself (social comic relief)

Formal humour
Tourists visit the following humorous events and places:
• Comedy festivals and events; and/or.
• The sites featured in TV sitcoms and/or comedic movies.

Post Travel   **Personal Outcomes of Humour Related Travel**

Potential for tourists to experience the following:
• Reduced stress and increased well being, creating improved mental and physical health;
• Enhanced ability to cope with awkward travel situations (using proactive and consensual
  humour); and/or,
• Enhanced social relationships during and after travel
  e.g., by recounting humorous holiday tales with friends, family and work colleagues.

Tourism Outcomes of Humour Related Travel

Potential positive outcomes:
• High level of visitor satisfaction with visit;
• Repeat visitation;
• Good word of mouth recommendation; and/or,
• Positive promotion of destination.

Potential negative outcomes:
If destination and the tourist experience is the "butt" of humour:
• Negative promotion of destination; and/or,
• Poor word of mouth recommendation.

Fig. 3. Humour and the Tourist Experience.

conceptualises the link between humour and tourism in terms of travel motivations, experiences, satisfaction levels, and potential for repeat visits.

IMPLICATIONS

Future empirical research into the role of humour and the tourist experience could investigate each of the three identified stages of the humour related tourist experience, namely, pre-travel, during travel and post travel, as stand-alone projects or, as a three-stage project. The recognition of humour as an important factor in the tourist experience has implications for the tourist industry, particularly in relation to the management of "humorous events" such as comedy festivals, and "humorous places" such as comedic TV and film locations. If future empirical research supports the above conceptualisation and humour is shown to have a pivotal role in the motivation and ultimate satisfaction levels of tourists, then managers at tourist destinations would be wise to encourage the development of local humorous events such as the establishment or support of comedy festivals, stand alone comedy events, fun, light-hearted tourist activities and, the development and promotion of humorous places such as comedic TV and film sites. The development and extension of such humorous events and places may be useful for healthcare professionals who could encourage people suffering from a range of illnesses to visit the destination to allow them to engage in laughter because of all the positive physical benefits generated.

The positive economic and social benefits of festivals reflect the significance of festivals in general, and, comedy festivals in particular, and, reflect their potential to generate many visitors to the city or region. The popularity of these comedy festivals may reflect tourists' desire to find humour, fun and laughter in their travel experiences and emphasises the importance of more fully understanding those tourists' motivations and experiences. In addition, from a destination management perspective, the strategic provision of formal humorous travel experiences has the potential to enhance a region economically and socially and, to create high levels of post-trip satisfaction, repeat visits and positive word of mouth recommendation. This paper conceptualises the link between humour and the tourist experience. Clearly the field is worthy of further empirical research, with the objective of advancing the understanding of humour in the tourist experience.

REFERENCES

Alexander, R. D. (1986). Ostracism and indirect reciprocity: The reproductive significance of humor. *Ethology and Sociobiology, 7*, 253–270.

Allen, B. (1990). *The concise dictionary of current English.* Oxford: Clarendon Press.

Ball, S., & Johnson, K. (2000). Humour in commercial hospitality settings. In: C. Lashley, A. & Morrison (Eds), *In search of hospitality: Theoretical perspectives and debates* (pp. 199–216). Oxford: Butterworth Heinemann.

Barsoux, J.-L. (1993). *Funny business. Humour, management and business culture.* London: Cassell.

Cahill, T. (Ed.) (2000). *Not so funny when it happened: The best of travel humor and misadventure.* San Francisco: Travelers' Tales.

Cline, T. W., Moses, B. A., & Kellaris, J. J. (2003). When does humor enhance or inhibit ad responses? The moderating role of the need for humor. *Journal of Advertising, 32*(2), 31–46.

Critchley, S. (2002). *On humour.* London: Routledge.

Freud, S. (1928). Humor. *International Journal of Psychoanalysis, 9*, 1–6.

Fry, W. F. (1992). The physiologic effects of humor, mirth and laughter. *Journal of the American Medical Association, 267*(13), 1857–1858.

Getz, D. (1997). *Event management and event tourism.* New York: Cognizant Communication Corporation.

Glasgow International Comedy Festival. (2004). Web page http://www.glasgowcomedyfestival (Accessed 29/9/05).

Gnoth, J., Zines, A., Lengmueller, R., Boshoff, C. (1999). The relationship between emotions, mood and motivation to travel: Towards a cross-cultural measurement of flow. In: A. G. Woodside, G. I. Crouch, J. A. Mazanec, M. Oppermann, & M. Y. Sakai (Eds), *Consumer psychology of tourism, hospitality and leisure* (pp. 155–175). Oxon: CABI Publishing, CAB International.

Goffman, E. (1967). *Interaction ritual.* Chicago: Aldine.

Goossens, C. (2000). Tourism information and pleasure motivation. *Annals of Tourism Research, 27*(2), 301–321.

Gruner, C. R. (1997). *The game of humor: A comprehensive theory of why we laugh.* New Brunswick, NJ: Transaction.

Hall, C. M. (1991). *Introduction to tourism in Australia. Impacts, planning and development.* Melbourne: Longman Cheshire.

Henkin, S. (2002). In Montreal, comedy is serious business: The Just For Laughs Festival. *World and I, 17*(11), 67–68.

Hughes, H. (2000). *Arts, entertainment and tourism.* Oxford: Butterworth-Heinemann.

Kastenholz, E., Davis, D., & Paul, G. (1999). Segmenting tourism in rural areas: The case of north and central Portugal. *Journal of Travel Research, 37*(4), 353–354.

Katovich, M. A. (1993). Humor in baseball: Functions and dysfunctions. *Journal of American Culture, 16*(2), 7–15.

Koestler, A. (1995). Humour and wit. In: *New Encyclopaedia Britannica Macropaedia* (Vol. 20). London: Encylopaedia Britannica Ltd.

Little, W. E. (2003). Performing tourism: Maya women's strategies. *Signs: Journal of Women in Culture and Society, 29*, 528–533.

Lynch, O. H. (2002). Humorous communication: Finding a place for humor in communication research. *Communication Theory, 12*(4), 423–445.

Mahony, D. L., Burroughs, W. L., & Lippman, L. G. (2002). Perceived attributes of health-promoting laughter: A cross-generational comparison. *The Journal of Psychology, 136*(2), 171–182.

Mahony, D. L., & Lippman, L. G. (2001). Theme issue on humor and laughter: Guest editors' introduction. *The Journal of General Psychology, 128*(2), 117–118.

Martin, R. A., & Lefcourt, H. M. (1983). Sense of humor as a moderator of the relation between stressors and moods. *Journal of Personality and Social Psychology, 45*(6), 1313–1324.

Martin, R. A., & Lefcourt, H. M. (1984). Situational humor response questionnaire: Quantitative measure of sense of humor. *Journal of Personality and Social Psychology, 47*(1), 145–155.

Martineau, W. H. (1972). A model of the social functions of humor. In: J. H. Goldstein & P. E. McGhee (Eds), *The psychology of humor* (pp. 101–125). New York: Academic Press, Inc.

Melbourne International Comedy Festival (2004). Corporate report. http://www.comedyfestival.com.au/corporate/2005/content/stats.pdf (Accessed 29/9/05)

Mellinger, W. M. (1994). Toward a critical analysis of tourism representations. *Annals of Tourism Research, 21*(4), 756–779.

O'Reilly, S., Habegger, L., & O'Reilly, J. (Eds) (2003). *Hyenas laughed at me, and now I know why: The best of travel humor and misadventure.* San Francisco: Travelers' Tales.

Palmer, J. (1994). *Taking humour seriously.* London: Routledge.

Plutchik, R. (2001). The nature of emotions. *American Scientist, 89*(4), 344–355.

Reed, S. E. (1980). A prime force in the expansion of tourism in the next decade: Special interest travel. In: D. E. Hawkins, E. L. Shafer & J. M. Rovelstad (Eds), *Tourism marketing and management issues* (pp. 193–202). Washington, DC: George Washington University.

Reisinger, Y. (1994). Tourist–host contact as a part of cultural tourism. *World Leisure and Recreation, 36*, 24–28.

Saper, B. (1990). The therapeutic use of humor for psychiatric disturbances of adolescents and adults. *Psychiatric Quarterly, 61*(4), 261–287.

Solomon, J. (1996). Humor and aging well: A laughing matter or a matter of laughing? *American Behavioral Scientist, 39*(3), 249–271.

Stebbins, R. A. (1979). Comic relief in everyday life: Dramaturgic observations on a function of humor. *Symbolic Interaction, 2*(1), 95–103.

Stebbins, R. A. (1990). *The laugh-makers: Stand-up comedy as art, business and life-style.* Montreal: McGill-Queen's University Press.

Stebbins, R. A. (1996). Defusing awkward situations: Comic relief as an interactive strategy for people with disabilities. *Journal of Leisurability, 23*(4), 3–38.

Strubbe, B. (2003). Getting serious about laughter. *World and I, 18*(3), 132–137.

Sultanoff, S. M. (2003). Integrating humor into psychotherapy. In: C. E. Shaefer (Ed.), *Play therapy with adults* (pp. 107–143). NJ: Wiley.

Sweet, J. D. (1989). Burlesquing "the other" in Pueblo performance. *Annals of Tourism Research, 16*(1), 62–75.

Szabo, A. (2003). The acute effects of humor and exercise on mood and anxiety. *Journal of Leisure Research, 35*(2), 152–163.

Thrane, C. (2002). Music quality, satisfaction, and behavioral intentions within a jazz festival context. *Event Management, 7*(3), 143–150.

Tragesser, S. L., & Lippman, L. G. (2005). Teasing: For superiority or solidarity? *The Journal of General Psychology*, *132*(3), 255–266.

Weisfeld, G. E. (1993). The adaptive value of humor and laughter. *Ethology and Sociobiology*, *14*(2), 141–156.

Wong, A. (2001). Satisfaction with local tour guides in Hong Kong. *Pacific Tourism Review*, *5*(1), 59–67.

CHAPTER 10

ASSESSING ALL-INCLUSIVE PRICING FROM THE PERSPECTIVE OF THE MAIN STAKEHOLDERS IN THE TURKISH TOURISM INDUSTRY

Erdogan Koc

ABSTRACT

This study explores the influence of the wide spread adoption of all-inclusive pricing on various categories of businesses and the local government in the Turkish tourism industry. The study is based on interviews with key informants who represent local businesses of various sorts and the local government, which are collectively identified as the main stakeholders of tourism activity in Antalya region. As all-inclusive pricing system has a wide spread adoption in many destinations throughout the world, the interpretation of the findings and the main conclusions of the study may have implications for academicians and as well as practitioners in various other countries and destinations.

Advances in Culture, Tourism and Hospitality Research, Volume 1, 273–288
Copyright © 2007 by Elsevier Ltd.
ISSN: 1871-3173/doi:10.1016/S1871-3173(06)01010-X

1. INTRODUCTION

This paper investigates the influence of the all-inclusive inclusive pricing on the main stakeholders in the Turkish tourism industry. The interest for exploring this influence has been first triggered by various types of protests of all-inclusive pricing that have taken place in various Turkish holiday resorts by the participation of large numbers of local businesses. Moreover, the increasing number of statements and claims made by officials and tourism authorities expressing concerns about the wide spread adoption of all-inclusive pricing in Turkish tourism industry have also prompted the interest in the research. The concerns have mainly centered around the belief that although tourist numbers visiting Turkey have increased over the past years after the adoption of all-inclusive pricing, per person tourist spending has seen a steady decline. Therefore, based on these above reasons and the fact that tourism is an important industry for Turkey, as will be explained below, a deeper understanding gained from an investigation into the influences of all-inclusive pricing on various stakeholders may help policy-makers in their decision-making. Additionally, the potential findings of which may merge from this research may have policy implications not only for Turkey but also for many other counties as all-inclusive pricing is widely used in many destinations throughout the world.

Compared with other marketing mix elements, that is, product, place (making products available to the customers) and promotion (marketing communications), price appears to be the most significant of all, as it directly determines how much or how many of a particular or service product will be sold, if any (Kotler & Keller, 2006). This means that the pricing of a product or service has got serious implications not only for the producers and or marketers of various products and services as price influences their revenues and profits directly, but also for various stakeholders which may have interests in these transactions.

In Section 2, the significance of pricing as a marketing mix element for services marketing and particularly for tourism is analyzed. In Sections 3 and 4, all-inclusive pricing is explained and the importance of pricing is discussed from the viewpoint of Turkish tourism. Section 5 explains the research method. In Section 6, the findings are presented and interpreted, and final section concludes.

2. PRICING

The price of a product is the key element which influences a business firm's revenues and profits. The price of a product has also psychological impact on the consumers as by raising the price a business firm can emphasize the quality of a product or service and can attempt to increase the status and prestige associated with its ownership (Estalami & Maxwell, 2003; Hoffman, Turley, & Kelley, 2002). On the other hand, by lowering the price, a business firm can emphasize a bargain and can attempt to attract new customers or convince customers purchase, or purchase more of its products.

Pricing carries additional importance for services due to the fact that services are *perishable*, that is, they cannot be saved, stored, resold or returned. Spare seats on a package tour, a vacant room in a hotel, or any unsold tourism event, represent potential revenue that cannot be recovered. Hence, perishability increases tension for the managers to perform in tourism and hospitality sectors (Bowen, 1998). Services, and especially tourism operations, are usually characterized by high-fixed costs and sensitive profit margins. Irregularities in demand for services (Kotas, 1975, 1977), caused by factors such as seasonality, tend to make the management of tourism operations more difficult. Demand management and differential pricing become crucial tasks in the management of services. Additionally, perishability may cause service providers such as hotels and other establishments to resort to sales promotion campaigns more often, due to the pressure to make a sale, and this eventually may hurt the brand image, especially when these promotion campaigns are not used very appropriately.

As another service characteristic intangibility of services may cause further difficulties in pricing and marketing tourism and hospitality services. Unlike physical products, services cannot be seen, tasted, felt, heard or smelt before they are purchased. The traditional view of the main difference between products and services is based on the fact that goods are produced, services are performed (Baker, 1981). Goods products lend themselves to comparability more easily due to the tangible product attributes such as color, size, design and packaging. The lack of physical evidence that intangibility implies increases the level of uncertainty and hence the perception of risk which a consumer may feel when choosing between competing services (Palmer, 1994). This lack of physical evidence may cause difficulty for customers when evaluating services offered by competing companies. Thus, as a result of intangibility characteristic of tourism, price can become the primary tool for consumers to distinguish between competing products. Palmer (1994) states that the intangibility element results in using price as a basis for assessing quality by the customers, which may explain the increased price competition and low margins for various businesses within tourism industry. Customers may feel that the price of a service indicates certain elements of information about its quality and expected benefits. This phenomenon would seem to limit the ability of travel agencies or tour operators to create favorable associations with consumers for their products by other means. However, it could also be seen as an industry assumption, that is, seeing price as the most effective tool for differentiation, which has in fact reduced the search for other ways to differentiate service offerings.

Additionally, although the risk element on the part of the consumer is high for services in general, it could be said that decisions relating to tourism may cause higher levels of risk perception by consumers. When Goodall (1995) classified tourism as a high-risk purchase, he compared tourism with tangible products. There is a need to distinguish tourism from other services in terms of risk perception due to the following factors identified by Witt and Moutinho (1995):

- Tourism decisions involve committing large sums of money on something which cannot be seen or tested prior to purchase. Although tourism and travel activities of individuals may represent a relatively smaller proportion of time, they may involve large sums of expenditures. For instance, a week's holiday may represent less than two percent of time duration in a fifty two-week year. While the amount of money spent on this holiday may be as high as 10 percent or more of a tourist's annual income (Koc, 2004).
- Tourism decisions involve large emotional investments. Whole families look forward to and backwards from holiday activities, so the fear of failure is high, and the opportunity cost irreversible. If a holiday goes wrong, that may be it for another year.
- Holidays often involve encounters with the unknown in terms of destinations, accommodation, transport, etc.

Perceived risk motivates intensified information seeking and (if not properly reduced) erects a consumption barrier around the unacceptable alternatives (Witt & Moutinho, 1995), and hence makes the design of marketing communications messages a significant task in tourism.

3. ALL-INCLUSIVE PRICING

An all-inclusive package holiday, which is usually associated with 3S holidays, that is, sun, sea and sand holidays, is defined as a trip planned and paid for a single price in advance which covers commercial transportation and accommodation, meals and sightseeing, and sometimes with an escort or guide (Sheldon & Mak, 1987; Morrison, 1989). All-inclusive pricing system influences the all of the marketing mix elements, that is, pricing, product (designing of the holiday package), place (distribution/tour operators/travel agencies) and promotion (marketing communications). The all-inclusive pricing system was first used by Club Mediterranean in the 1960s and 1970s. French, Spanish, Greek, Italian and German tour operators have been pioneers in the establishment of the all-inclusive pricing system in the world.

The most frequently cited reasons for travelers purchasing all-inclusive package holidays are tour economics and overall convenience (Touché & Ross Company, 1975). However, more recent studies show that there are additional reasons for purchasing all-inclusive package holidays such as personal safety and overall risk minimization (Quiroga, 1990; Wong & Lau, 2001; Wong & Kwong, 2004).

Although certain advantages exist for various businesses in tourism sector which serve tourists, there are certain criticisms of the all-inclusive pricing system too. For instance, as mentioned earlier, in Turkey there were strong protests by local shopkeepers, restaurant owners, souvenir shops, etc. to stop all-inclusive pricing in some of the holiday resorts in 2003 and 2004. The owner and employees of these businesses expressed that they were disadvantaged as a result of the wide spread adoption of this pricing system. Protests included closing down of all shops for a day in some of the holiday resorts. Some of the main criticisms of the all-inclusive pricing system may include the following:

- All-inclusive pricing may attract tourists with lower holiday-spending budgets or customers who are not interested in making any additional expenditure in the holiday resort. The view that "although tourist numbers visiting Turkey have increased over the past years (after the widespread adoption of all-inclusive pricing) per person tourist spending has decreased" has been expressed by various officials and tourism authorities. However, research carried out in this field has shown that person tourist spending has not decreased over the years. In fact, per person tourist spending has increased in Turkey (Koc & Altinay, 2007).
- Frequent and common use of this system may create a "cheap destination" image, which may be difficult to reverse later. Turkish tourism establishments had to accept extremely low prices in 1990 and 1991 during the Gulf War enforced by large international tour operators (Koc, 2002). More than two decades after this event Turkey, as a destination has been unable to reverse its "cheap destination" image. Although to a large extent the quality of the package holidays in Turkey on is similar or even better than the holidays (mostly in better equipped and newly built accommodation establishments) in Greece, Portugal, Spain and Italy, the

prices of holidays in Turkey on average at least 25 percent cheaper than holidays in these countries (Tursab, 2005). The phenomenal growth of the numbers of international tourists visiting Turkey over the past decade can be at least partially attributed to the increasing awareness of comparative holiday prices among tourists. This brings forward the importance of creating and sustaining an appropriate destination image and destination personality which has become vital for effective product positioning (Hosany, Ekinci, & Uysal, 2006).

- As tourists visiting a destination through all-inclusive package holidays may feel reluctant to leave the accommodation establishment, and may prefer not to go out and spend money outside the hotel, local businesses may be disadvantaged. In fact, this reason has been the main focus of the criticisms of all-inclusive pricing in Turkey and other countries.

- Since prices are fixed per customer in the all-inclusive pricing system, and profit margins are narrow, holiday establishments may resort to various tactics to lower costs. This, in turn, may lead to a reduction in the quality of the service provided by the accommodation establishments.

- Additionally, all-inclusive pricing may have a negative influence on employees working in these accommodation establishments due to nonstop service provision in these accommodation establishments.

4. ALL-INCLUSIVE PRICING IN TURKEY

Turkey tourism has been one of the most significant industries, which fuels the growth of the economy over the past few decades. Between 1973 and 2003, the number of tourists visiting the country increased more than tenfold, and tourism revenues grew more than fiftyfold (Tursab, 2004). In 2004, Turkey earned $13 billion from 17.5 million tourists visiting the country, about a 25 percent increase over 2003 figures in terms of tourist numbers and about a 35 percent increase in terms of revenues. In 2003, in terms of the numbers of visitors, Turkey was the 14th largest tourism market in the world (1.82 percent of the whole world market), rising to the 12th rank when measured by tourism revenues (Tursab, 2005).

Forecasts show that the role played by the tourism industry in the economic development of Turkey will continue to grow. According to the World Tourism Organization (WTO) Turkish tourism is estimated to grow at an average of 5.5 percent every year by 2020 (World Tourism Organization, 1998). This growth rate of Turkish tourism is the fourth highest among all other European Union (EU) member states.

In developed countries tourism makes a major contribution to the diversification of the economy, and helps alleviate regional imbalances. On the other hand, in developing countries or newly developed countries, including Turkey, tourism provides an export opportunity which is subject to relatively high growth rates and is less constrained (e.g., greater price flexibility, self-determination and better employment opportunities) than the more traditional forms of export (Fletcher, 1995). It is important to note that tourism is an attractive industry for investment in developing countries (including Turkey) due to the low capital requirement and the shortness of the realization period for investments (Williams & Shaw, 1992).

As the pricing of holidays have important implications in terms of revenues and profits for all stakeholders including the central and local government, all-inclusive pricing system and its implications need to be studied from the perspectives of the stakeholders involved in this industry and for the whole society. Today, as much as 64.5 percent of all tourists visiting Turkey come to Turkey on all-inclusive package holidays (Tursab, 2004). As much as 80 percent of Russian citizens, who have been the fuel of the growth of tourism in Turkey over the past years, visited Turkey on all-inclusive package holidays.

5. METHOD

This study investigates the implications of all-inclusive pricing system based on the perceptions of the key informants working in the main stakeholders which include the accommodation establishments (that is, five- and four-star hotels that operate under the all-inclusive pricing system), transportation companies (airlines, in this particular case), local businesses (that is, local restaurants, souvenir shops, convenience stores, local suppliers of goods and services, etc.) and government (that is, central or local) (see Fig. 1). The key question of the research, which is how (whether positive or negative and to what extent) all-inclusive pricing influences the main stakeholders, has been investigated through interviews with the key informants.

The interviews with the key informants were carried out in July 2003 in Antalya (with key informants from accommodation establishments, local businesses and local government) and in Istanbul (with key informants from airline companies). Antalya region was especially chosen as it accounts for more than 30 percent (35.8 percent in 2002, 33.4 percent in 2003 and 34.5 percent in 2004) of all tourists visiting Turkey (Turkish Ministry of Culture & Tourism, 2005). The interviewees were asked to evaluate the present and

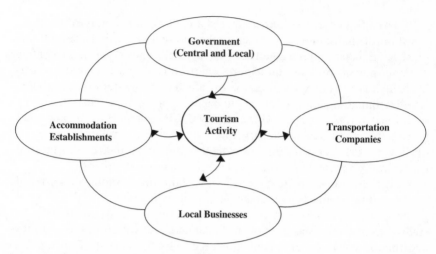

Fig. 1. The Main Stakeholders Influenced by All-Inclusive Pricing in Turkish Tourism.

future consequences of all-inclusive pricing from the perspective of their own businesses.

The key informant interviews include 42 people altogether from the following stakeholders: accommodation establishments (17) (8 of whom are from five-star hotels and 9 of whom are from four-star hotels), local businesses (18), transportation companies (3) and local government (4). Tour operators are not included among the main stakeholders in Turkey as a significant proportion of tourists come to Turkey through international tour operators established outside Turkey.

At the end of the interviews the key informants were asked to summarize their perceptions of the all-inclusive pricing system by rating the consequences of the system on a Likert scale from "very negative" to "very positive". Then each rating was given a value to calculate overall perceptions as follows: very negative (−2), negative (−1), neutral (0), positive (1) and very positive (2).

6. THE SUMMARY OF THE INFLUENCES OF THE ALL-INCLUSIVE PRICING ON THE STAKEHOLDERS

The findings of the research show that the perceptions of the stakeholders regarding the influences of all-inclusive pricing have been somewhat different. The interpretation of the findings points out a need for holistic approach in evaluating the influences of all-inclusive pricing for the destination as a whole. The existence of multiplicity of goals adds to the difficulty of conceptualizing the destination competitiveness concept (Crouch & Ritchie, 1999). The individual findings for each category of stakeholders are explained and analyzed below.

6.1. Accommodation Establishments

On the basis of perishable nature of tourism products explained above and the fact that tourism activity is highly seasonal (about 68 percent of tourists come to Turkey between 1 April and 30 September for sun and sea holidays) the perception of risk and pressure to make a sale in the Turkish hospitality sector is rather high.

The responses of key informants from both five- and four-star hotels were evaluated altogether, as no differences were observed in the interviews. The key informants in general believe that although all-inclusive pricing increases the level of the capacity use as it secures a certain number of tourists for the accommodation establishment, this pricing system has got negative influences on their profit margins. But contrary to this belief they had expressed satisfaction with the system. They stated that this was mainly due to the fact that there were not many options available for accommodation establishments as major international tour operators which send tourists to this region operated under this pricing system. They said that ideally things could have been better, but they were overall satisfied with the system. The key informants also expressed that many local businesses such as restaurants were blaming accommodation establishments for adopting all-inclusive pricing system, though the pricing system was in fact enforced on accommodation establishments by large tour operators which have strong bargaining power on accommodation establishments. The key informants put forward that many smaller accommodations establishments catering for the domestic tourism market also followed suit over the yeas and assumed all-inclusive pricing without such enforcement by large tour operators.

The key informants' final evaluations of the all-inclusive pricing system where they were asked to rate their overall perception of the all-inclusive pricing on a Likert scale (see Table 1 and Graph 1) revealed that they were happy to operate under this pricing system. The weighted average of their responses was 1.12 (out of a maximum of 2) indicating that the influence of the all-inclusive pricing system was positive.

Table 1. Key Informant Ratings of the Influence of All-Inclusive Pricing System.

Key Informants	N	Very Negative Responses (−2)	Negative Responses (−1)	Neutral Responses (0)	Positive Responses (1)	Very Positive Responses (2)	Total Weight	Total Weighted Average
Accommodation establishments	17	0	1	2	8	6	19	1.12
Local businesses								
Local suppliers of products and services	4	0	0	1	1	2	5	1.25
Restaurants	7	4	3	0	0	0	−11	−1.57
Souvenir shops	4	4	4	0	0	0	−8	−2.00
Convenience stores	3	0	2	1	0	0	−2	−0.67
Transportation Firms	3	3	0	2	0	0	1	0.33
Local government	4	4	0	0	0	4	8	2.00
Total	42	8	6	6	9	12	11	0.26

Among these cost-cutting practices the use of fewer numbers of staff, the use of lesser-qualified staff, the lowering of both the quality and the volume of foods and drinks served can be cited. The key informants also point out that the factors such as nonstop service provision by fewer number of and lesser-qualified staff and in return for no or very little tips under the all-inclusive pricing system may cause a decline in the satisfaction of staff, which in turn may lead to the reduction of the satisfaction of tourists. This finding is similar to Koc's (2006), which established that the adoption of all-inclusive pricing system with a cost-cutting orientation led to a dissatisfaction of both internal customers (employees) and the external customers (tourists).

6.2. Local Businesses

The influence of all-inclusive pricing on the local businesses can be analyzed under two different categories of businesses: (i) those who interact directly with tourists, that is, local restaurants, souvenir shops and convenience stores, and (ii) those who do not interact with tourists, that is, local suppliers of products and services. While the key informants from seven restaurants, four souvenir shops and three convenience stores stated that they have been negatively influenced, by all-inclusive pricing, the key informants from four local suppliers of products and services firmly stated that the influence has been somewhat positive (see Table 1 and Graph 1). The negative influence on restaurants, souvenir shops and convenience stores has been at varying levels. For instance, while the overall evaluations of key informants from souvenir shops indicated that the influence has been very negative (–2), the overall evaluations key informants from convenience stores was just negative (–0.67). However, it must be kept in mind that larger number of responses is required to make overall evaluations.

The first group of local businesses, that is, the local suppliers of food, drinks, other consumables and services sell their goods or services to local holiday establishments. The widespread adoption of all-inclusive pricing system has so far led to an overall increase in the tourist numbers staying in the accommodation establishments. The influence of the resulting increase in the capacity usage at accommodation establishments has been positive for the local suppliers of products and services. In fact, the satisfaction of the key informants in local businesses was even slightly higher than that of the key informants in the accommodation establishments.

On the other hand, the latter group, that is, the restaurants, souvenir shops and convenience stores sell their products and services directly to the

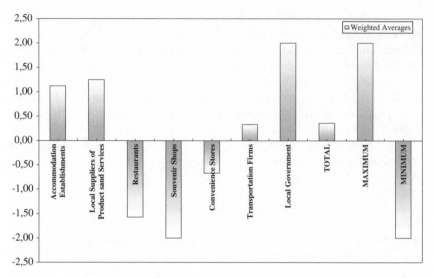

Graph 1. Key Informant Ratings of the Influence of All-Inclusive Pricing System.

tourists. With the increasing numbers of hotels adopting all-inclusive pricing, ranging from four- and five-star hotels to very small family establishments, increasing numbers of tourists spend most of their time in their accommodation and do not tend to go out and spend money in the local restaurants, souvenir shops and convenience stores. As tourists pay for a package holiday, which include all meals, drinks, etc. and usually in advance, they do not have the motivation to go out of the accommodation establishment and spend money on food, drinks, etc. Consequently, the owners of these local businesses who look forward to the summer season to earn money for the whole of the year find themselves in a situation where they incur losses year after year.

6.3. Transportation Companies

The key informants from transportation companies (airlines) have held the view that the influence of all-inclusive pricing has been neutral to slightly positive (see Table 1 and Graph 1). As in the case of the accommodation establishments, airlines were not happy about the squeeze on per person profit margin. Nevertheless, they expressed that the wide spread use of all-inclusive pricing has made a positive contribution in terms of increasing capacity use for airlines which influenced their overall profitably. They believed that this was important as due to the significant overhead cost involved. They expressed that it would be ideal to shift some of the demand for their services from the peak period to off-peak periods.

6.4. Government

The use of all-inclusive pricing has had a positive influence both on the central and local government in Turkey. As local governments receive a certain proportion of taxes collected in a particular region, and the level of employment increases in the region, they too have benefited from the widespread use of all-inclusive pricing system. The four key informants from the local government in Antalya evaluated the influence of all-inclusive pricing as very positive (see Table 1 and Graph 1). The phenomenal growth in tourism revenues over the past years in Turkey has already been explained above.

7. CONCLUSIONS

The findings showed that although there may be strong criticisms of the wide spread adoption of all-inclusive pricing by some of the stakeholders, the majority of the stakeholders appeared to be satisfied with adoption of this system. The growth in tourist numbers and expenditures over the past years appears to indicate that, in general, tourists find the all-inclusive pricing system attractive too. However, the interpretation of the findings points out a need for further research for providing better outcomes to help policy-makers in their decision-making processes. In the design of further research in addition to just extending the mere numbers of the stakeholder categories, a system enabling a more overall evaluation of the advantages and disadvantages can be installed. This can be made through assigning weightings according to the significance of each response received from each particular stakeholder for a better overall or holistic evaluation of the responses of the various stakeholders. Then, this evaluation may be used in measuring *deadweight loss*, which may help policy-makers to understand the total net loss or gain on the society. Moreover, in addition to the country multiplier value of Turkey, which is already available (calculated to be the highest in the tourism multiplier league in Fletcher's (1995) research), a regional multiplier value can be calculated for the Antalya region. Then, the multiplier values for the Antalya region and for the whole country can be used to make comparisons of the values between the pre-all-inclusive pricing and post-all-inclusive pricing periods.

Apart from its positive contribution to many of the stakeholders, all-inclusive pricing may play a useful role in establishing and maintaining a good brand image of Turkey as a destination region. As discussed above occasional problems relating to tourist dissatisfaction may occur in the all-inclusive pricing system due to the shortsighted cost-cutting practices of holiday establishments. However, individual tourists who visit Turkey on their own, without purchasing an all-inclusive package holiday, may be more prone to dissatisfaction. In the case of individual holidays tourists may be more often served badly and overcharged by taxi drivers, waiters in restaurants, shopkeepers, etc. If and when the same numbers of tourists visiting Turkey every year through all-inclusive package holidays choose to visit Turkey on individually organized holidays, a negative image of Turkey as a destination region may be more easily and quickly formed.

However, one still needs to be cautious when making policy statements in a highly dynamic market such as tourism, as consumer/tourist behavior can be quite volatile and may vary significantly in a few years or at least in a decade. Culligan's (1992) research pointed out to some of the changes taking place in the tourism market in terms of the preferences of tourists. Culligan (1992) suggests that the tourist's increasing desire for more novel, adventurous, and "authentic" forms of tourism experience is a function of the decline in *utility* associated with a decision to simply replicate previous experience: itself a function of an increasing ability of tourists to afford different forms of tourism. This means a move away from general interest tourism (GIT) toward special interest tourism (SIT) (Brotherton & Himmetoglu, 1997). Krippendorf (1987) argued that fundamental changes occurring in the tourism market in general are in line with the developments of new patterns of tourism consumption. He maintains that in the near future there will be a substantial decline in those tourists for whom *hedonism* is a dominant travel motive and for whom tourism is seen purely as a mechanism for recovery, that is, rest, and liberation, that is, escape from the ordinary. Instead, the travel market will place emphasis on the environmental and social context in which tourism occurs, and on the humanization of travel activities (Krippendorf, 1987).

By establishing that the seasonality of Turkish tourism is stochastic, that is, not deterministic, the findings of Koc and Altinay's (2007) study also support view that a need exists to create alternative tourism products in Turkey, and possibly in many other countries and destinations in more or less similar situation. Together with the move toward SIT, and the increasing tendency toward independent holidays coupled with the move away from sun and sea holidays, all-inclusive pricing system may not be as applicable as it is now for Turkish tourism in the coming decade or so.

REFERENCES

Baker, M. J. (1981). Services: Salvation or servitude? *Quarterly Review of Marketing, 6*(3), 7–18.

Bowen, D. (1998). *Consumer behaviour in tourism with specific reference to consumer satisfaction and dis-satisfaction on long-haul inclusive tours.* Unpublished Ph.D. thesis, Oxford Brookes University, Oxford.

Brotherton, B., & Himmetoglu, B. (1997). Beyond destinations – Special interest tourism. *Anatolia: An International Journal of Tourism and Hospitality Research, 8*(3), 11–30.

Crouch, G. I., & Ritchie, J. R. B. (1999). Tourism, competitiveness, and social prosperity. *Journal of Business Research, 44*(3), 137–152.

Culligan, K. (1992). *Developing a model of holidaytaking behaviour. Leisure and tourism futures conference proceedings.* London: The Henley Centre for Forecasting.

Estalami, H., & Maxwell, S. (2003). Introduction to special issue – The behavioral aspects of pricing. *Journal of Business Research, 56*(5), 353–354.

Fletcher, J. (1995). 'Economics and forecasting – economic impact'. In: S. F. Witt & L. Moutinho (Eds), *Tourism Marketing Management Handbook* (p. 457). Englewood Cliffs, NJ: Prentice Hall.

Goodall B. (1995). How tourists choose their holidays: an analytical framework. In: B. Goodall & G. Ashworth (Eds), *Marketing in the Tourism Industry – The Promotion of Destination Regions.* New York: Routledge.

Hoffman, K. D., Turley, L. W., & Kelley, S. W. (2002). Pricing retail services. *Journal of Business Research, 55*(12), 1015–1023.

Hosany, S., Ekinci, Y., & Uysal, M. (2006). Destination image and destination personality: An application of branding theories to tourism places. *Journal of Business Research, 59*(5), 638–642.

Koc, E. (2002). The impact of gender in marketing communications: The role of cognitive and affective cues. *Journal of Marketing Communications, 8*(4), 257–275.

Koc, E. (2004). The role of family members in the holiday purchase decision-making process. *International Journal of Hospitality and Tourism Administration, 5*(2), 85–102.

Koc, E. (2006). Order three advertisements and get one news story free: Public relations ethics and custom-made news features as advertisement incentives in Turkish print media. *Public Relations Review, 32*(39), 331–340.

Koc, E., & Altinay, G. (2007). An analysis of seasonality in monthly per person tourist spending in Turkish inbound tourism from a market segmentation perspective tourism management. *Tourism Management, 28*(1), 227–237.

Kotas, R. (1975). *Management accounting for hotels and restaurants.* Guildford: Surrey University Press.

Kotas, R. (1977). *Management orientation in the hotel and catering industry.* Guildford: Surrey University Press.

Kotler, P., & Keller, K. L. (2006). *Marketing management* (12th ed.). New Jersey: Prentice-Hall.

Krippendorf, J. (1987). *The holidaymakers: Understanding the impact of leisure and travel.* Oxford: Heinemann Professional Publishing.

Morrison, M. A. (1989). *Hospitality and travel marketing*. New York: Delmar Publishers.
Palmer, A. (1994). *Principles of services marketing*. London: McGraw-Hill.
Quiroga, I. (1990). Characteristics of package tours in Europe. *Annals of Tourism Research,* *17*(2), 185–207.
Sheldon, P. J., & Mak, J. (1987). The demand for package tours: A mode choice model. *Journal of Travel Research, 25*(3), 13–17.
Touché and Ross Company. (1975). *Tour wholesaler industry study*. New York: Touché Ross and Company.
Turkish Ministry of Culture and Tourism. (2005). Various tourism statistics. Available from http://www.kultur.gov.tr/. Accessed on 24.03.2005.
Tursab (Turkish Travel Agencies Association). (2004). Various tourism statistics. Available from http://www.tursab.org.tr/content/turkish/istatistikler/. Accessed on 29.12.2004.
Tursab. (2005). Various tourism statistics. Available from http://www.tursab.org.tr/content/turkish/istatistikler/. Accessed on 15.05.2005.
Williams, A. M., & Shaw, G. (1992). Tourism research – A perspective 'the horrible babel of tongues'. *American Behavioural Scientist, 36*(2), 133–144.
Witt, F. S., & Moutinho, L. (1995). *Tourism marketing and management handbook*. Hertfordshire: Prentice-Hall.
Wong, C. S., & Kwong, W. Y. (2004). Outbound tourists' selection criteria for choosing all-inclusive package tours. *Tourism Management, 25*, 581–592.
Wong, S., & Lau, E. (2001). Understanding the behaviour of Hong Kong Chinese tourists on group tour packages. *Journal of Travel Research, 40*(1), 57–67.
World Tourism Organization (WTO). (1998). *Tourism 2020 vision – Revised and updated 1998*. Madrid: World Tourism Organization.

CHAPTER 11

ADVANCING AND TESTING THEORIES OF HOW VISITORS ASSESS HISTORICAL DISTRICTS AS TOURISM DESTINATIONS WITH USE OF REPERTORY GRID ANALYSIS AND LADDERING ANALYSIS

Taketo Naoi, David Airey, Shoji Iijima and
Outi Niininen

ABSTRACT

The aim of this study is to discuss the complex nature of visitors' evaluation of historical districts as tourism destinations. Further this study proposes a theoretical framework and methods to elicit relationships between visitors' mental states and a district's features. The combination of repertory grid analysis and laddering analysis with use of photographs is discussed and demonstrated. These methods were applied to a sample of Japanese students, who were presented with photographs of a historical district in Takayama-shi, Japan. Results illustrate the efficacy of these methods in investigating the complex nature of visitors' evaluation of a

Advances in Culture, Tourism and Hospitality Research, Volume 1, 289–319
Copyright © 2007 by Elsevier Ltd.
All rights of reproduction in any form reserved
ISSN: 1871-3173/doi:10.1016/S1871-3173(06)01011-1

historical district as a tourism destination, shed light on issues raised by past studies and indicate the necessity of involving visitors' contextual and personal factors in the analysis.

Historical sites as tourism destinations are often not simple reflections of the past (Caffyn & Lutz, 1999; Johnson, 1999; Palmer, 1999), but necessarily incorporate contrived elements. How visitors evaluate a historical district containing these contrived elements is open to question. This study attempts to propose a theoretical framework and methods to investigate such an evaluation. Specifically this study explores relationships between visitors' mental states and the features of a historical district in order to understand the mixed nature of visitors' evaluation of such a historical district as a tourism destination.

THEORETICAL FRAMEWORK

This is part of a long-term study about visitors' evaluation of historical districts as tourism destinations and is a further development and application of theoretical frameworks and methods employed in a previous study at Rothenburg ob der Tauber in Germany (Naoi, Airey, Iijima, & Niininen, 2006). Further details about the theoretical framework presented here can be observed in this earlier study.

The Nature of Historical Districts as Tourism Destinations and Visitors' Evaluations

Commercialization is one of the issues that relate to visitors' evaluations of historical districts as tourism destinations. When developed into tourism destinations, historical districts are often transformed into commodified products (Adorno, 1991; Ashworth, 1991; Ashworth & Voogt, 1990, 1994; McKercher & du Cros, 2002; Sack, 1992). A number of authors have criticized such commercialization for transforming historical settings into superficial objects for the sake of tourism (Boorstin, 1964; Halewood & Hannam, 2001; Hewison, 1987; MacCannell, 1976; Mathieson & Wall, 1982; Walsh, 1992). However, some researchers have claimed that complete authenticity may not be a prerequisite to attract tourists (Ashworth &

Voogt, 1990; Caffyn & Lutz, 1999; Cohen, 1972). Indeed, visitors may differ in the levels of familiarity they demand (Cohen, 1972, 1979, 1988, 1995; Plog, 1974; Smith, 1989) and some visitors may require modern facilities (Ashworth, 1988; Ashworth & Tunbridge, 2000). Visitors may also vary in their demand for cultural experiences (McKercher & du Cros, 2002). For example, findings by Naoi et al. (2006) suggest that certain types of stores may be perceived as contributing to visitors' desire for local authenticity, for seeing something outside daily life or for experiencing things that would appeal to others.

Another issue is the existence of people at destinations. The presence of visitors has often been regarded negatively as a factor consuming both physical space (Misham, 1969) and perceptual value (Walter, 1982). In psychology also, *crowding* is viewed as a psychological stress that sometimes accompanies high-population density (Stokols, 1972), and has been regarded as related to deterioration in the desired tourist experience (Schreyer & Roggenbuck, 1978; West, 1982; Womble & Studebaker, 1981). Similarly, Urry (1990) also argues that a historical tourism object is basically regarded as the object of the *romantic gaze*, in terms of which solitude, privacy and a personal, semi-spiritual relationship with the object is appreciated.

By way of contrast, however, and recognizing the notion that a historical district could have been in the past or may still be a residential or commercial area, a historical district could be regarded as the object of the *collective gaze*, in terms of which the presence of other people is necessary to give atmosphere to the experience of a place. This is also supported in the field of psychology where some researchers have maintained that crowding in certain situations is perceived as exhilarating or arousing (Argyle, Furnham, & Graham, 1981; Hull, 1990) or as contributory to social affiliation (Ditton, Fedler, & Graefe, 1983, cited in Manning, 1985; Graham & Burge, 1984). The study by Zins (2001) indicates that the presence of other travelers might be perceived as relevant to fun, entertainment and excitement whereas Naoi and Iijima (2004) revealed relationships between the presence of others and a sense of activity in a historical district. Previous studies have also implied that the presence of others in a historical district might strengthen or weaken a sense of authenticity depending on the degree of preservation of the area (Naoi & Iijima, 2004), and that places where people are perceived to gather could be considered to satisfy visitors' desire to see something famous (Naoi et al., 2006).

With reference to these arguments, visitors' evaluations of historical districts as tourism destinations can be argued to relate to several evaluative dimensions, such as the place's spiritual value, or the sense of stillness or stimulation, according to visitors' mental states.

Much literature suggests that tourism destination image involves two components: cognitive components, which refer to beliefs and knowledge about an object/destination, and affective components, which concern feelings about or the affective quality of destination environments (Baloglu, 1999, 2000; Baloglu & McCleary, 1999a, 1999b; Beerli & Martin, 2004; Gartner, 1993; Pike & Ryan, 2004). Cognitive components could also relate to the physical features of a destination (Hanyu, 1993; Naoi et al., 2006). Some authors have pointed out that affective components are derived from cognitive components (Anand, Holbrook, & Stephens, 1988; Baloglu, 1999, 2000; Baloglu & McCleary, 1999a; Woodside & Lysonski, 1989) whereas others have suggested possible situations that do not require cognitive components as prior cognitions for affective responses (Solomon, Bamossy, & Askegaard, 1999; Zajonic, 1980).

A means-end chain model, which proposes attributes of an object as the means to achieve certain objectives, which are then the means for more ultimate objectives (Gutman, 1982), further illustrates the hierarchical relationships between cognitive and affective components and several types of mental states. Visitors' mental states can further vary in their degree of concreteness, and relationships between these are suggested. For instance, a *want* is usually regarded as a manifestation of a *need* while a *value* is defined as "a belief about a desirable end-state that transcends specific situations and guides selection of behaviour" (Schwartz & Bilsky, 1987, as cited in Solomon et al., 1999, p. 104). These arguments suggest hierarchical relationships between these components. The possible hierarchical relationships are illustrated in Fig. 1.

In tourism studies, these hierarchical relationships have been considered by authors such as Baloglu (1999, 2000), Baloglu and McCleary (1999a), and Beerli and Martin (2004), who used path analysis to investigate relationships between some variables, including motivations, and cognitive and affective components of destination image. Similarly, Prentice and Light (1994) applied the Manning-Haas hierarchy to investigate hierarchical relationships between benefits, experiences, activities and settings. Zins (2001) applied Association Pattern Technique (APT), in which subjects were required directly to indicate relationships between predetermined items, and direct ratings to explore relationships between attributes, consequences and values of visitors in general holiday-taking situations. However, these studies largely rely on predetermined variables rather than eliciting them by explorative methods. Fairweather and Swaffield (2001, 2002) applied Q

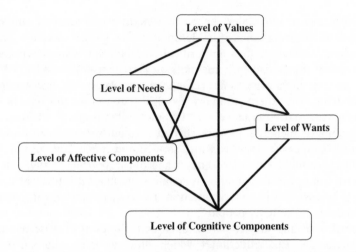

Fig. 1. The Possible Relationships between Visitors' Mental States and Cognitive/ Affective Components of a Historical District.

method with photographs to elicit the contents of visitors' experience in tourism destinations in New Zealand and compared them with their selection of photographs. Although their study illustrates the efficacy of the method in eliciting visitors' experiences and implying relationships between their experiences and the physical characteristics of places, further efforts seem necessary to investigate concrete relationships between the settings of a destination and visitors' mental states.

Proposed Methods

This study used a combination of *repertory grid analysis* and *laddering analysis* with use of photographs as stimuli to elicit the hierarchical relationships illustrated in Fig. 1. Repertory grid analysis is a method based on Kelly's (1955) *personal construct theory*, and attempts to reveal subjects' constructs, which are the actual discrimination that subjects make between phenomena (people or objects) in the environment, by providing subjects with several grids, each of which comprises a set of elements to be compared.

Laddering analysis builds on the means-end chain model (Gutman, 1982), and is useful in eliciting hierarchical relationships between attributes and various levels of abstract mental states. Cognitive components, affective components or mental states elicited by repertory grid analysis can be employed as the starting point of laddering analysis. Using laddering analysis, researchers ask subjects to think critically about relationships between the product's attributes and their mental states, by repeatedly asking "Why is that favorable/unfavorable/important for you?" questions. For instance, a subject, who says, "there are many people," may answer this type of question by saying that "it is active" or "I cannot walk around." When affective components or mental states are elicited through repertory grid analysis, *ladder-down* types of questions, which show, for example, how subjects think any objects should be in order to meet their objectives (Sanui, 1995), need to be asked. For instance, if an affective component like, "it is too crowded," is elicited, by asking this type of question, researchers may obtain responses like "there are too many people."

Instead of asking subjects vague open-ended questions, these two methods provide subjects with frames, which allow a complex human psychological structure to be extracted. These frames and almost the same controlled environments that these two methods offer to subjects also help to minimize biases resulting from researchers' subjectivity, their lack of experience or other uncontrollable factors. Laddering analysis, however, can be criticized as still being subject to researchers' subjectivity. Indeed, quantitative methods, such as APT, have been applied to obtain valid results within a theoretical framework of a means-end chain model in tourism (Zins, 2001). Although these quantitative methods are useful when variables have been well defined, more qualitative methods like repertory grid analysis or laddering analysis are preferable in the exploratory stage of a new area.

Repertory grid analysis has been used in earlier tourism studies. These have generally used the names of places for purposes of evaluation of museums and galleries (Coshall, 2000), countries (Embacher & Buttle, 1989; Gyte, 1988; Pearce, 1982), cities (Selby, 2004), specific tourism destinations (Pike, 2003; Walmsley & Jenkins, 1993; Young, 1995). Only a few (Botterill, 1989; Botterill & Crompton, 1987, 1996), use visual stimuli such as photographs. In a detailed investigation of relationships between the features of a historical district and visitors' mental states, the presentation to subjects of some signs of visual features such as photographs seem useful. The use of photographs is also expected to contribute to a high degree of reliability in their responses. As to the sample size, most of the previously mentioned past studies employed a small number of subjects ranging from 1 to 60. Although this certainly raises questions about the validity of the results, a small sample size for repertory grid analysis has been claimed to be sufficient for valid results (Young, 1995) or to be inevitable for practical reasons (Pike, 2003).

As for studies that employ laddering analysis, this method has been broadly applied in the fields of marketing (Gengler & Reynolds, 1995; Reynolds & Gutman, 1988) and architecture (Maki, 1994; Sanui, 1995). More specifically related to tourism, the work by Klenosky, Gengler, and Mulvey (1993) investigated skiers' evaluation of ski resorts with their names as stimuli while Klenosky (2002) used laddering analysis to investigate pull factors of potential spring break vacations for university undergraduates. Laddering analysis was also employed to assess the meaning of a museum visit as a cultural tourism activity (Jansen-Verbeke & van Rekom, 1996). Maruoka (1998) in the field of consumer behavior claims that 8–16 subjects per segment for laddering analysis is sufficient in a consideration of commonality of responses in group studies. The sample size of the previously mentioned three studies by Jansen-Verbeke and van Rekom (1996), Klenosky (2002), and Klenosky et al. (1993) ranges from 30 to 90.

IMPLEMENTATION, ANALYSES, AND RESULTS

The Selected Historical District

The historical district centers on Sanmachi in the middle of Takayama-shi, Gifu-Prefecture, Japan. The historical district, was selected as the study location because of the preserved historical environment, and its touristic and commercial characteristics.

This district is the remains of a part of the merchant's town (Takayama Municipal Committee of Education, 1994), which was established in the sixteenth century (JTB Toronto Office, n.d.). This district, with low-slung wooden streetscape (Monaghan, n.d.) and Edo-period merchants' houses with latticed bay windows and linked eaves (Takayama Municipal office, n.d.), offers preserved historical features as its main attraction. The district was designated a Preservation District of a Group of Important Historic Buildings in 1979 by the Agency for Cultural Affairs, Japan Ministry of Education, Culture, Sports, Science and Technology (The Agency for Cultural Affairs, n.d.).

Sanmachi is also well known as a tourism destination. The district is a part of the Tokai Region, one of ten themed regions designated by the Japan National Tourist Organization (Japan National Tourist Organization, 2000), and has also been chosen as a Japan Heritage Site by the country' largest tour operator (Japan Travel Bureau, 1999). According to recent statistics on domestic Japanese tourism, Takayama-shi attracted 2,524,035 tourists in 2002. This is the second largest number of the major tourism destinations in Gifu-Prefecture (The Japan Tourist Association, 2004). Such popularity is accompanied by a certain degree of commercialization of the district. The well-known *Lonely Planet* English-language guide to Japan describes the district as "lined with traditional shops, restaurants, museums and private homes" as well as sake breweries (Rowthorn et al., 2003, p. 275).

Repertory Grid Analysis and Laddering Analysis

Twenty-three settings within and around Sanmachi, Takayama-shi, were photographed under conditions varying mainly in the degree of conservation and in the prominence of stores. For each setting, several photographs were taken that vary in terms of the way people (no people, a few people, many people and so on) and vehicles appear. These criteria were based on the findings of Naoi et al. (2006), which show that settings in a historical district may be divided into residential and tourist/commercial settings according to the perceived presence of people and stores. In their study, vehicles (cars) were also identified as noticeable components that might have mixed effects (Naoi et al., 2006). In total, 58 photographs were selected as the stimuli. Descriptions of the 23 settings and 58 photographs are presented in Table 1.

The subjects for these interviews were 30 undergraduate students of Department of International Tourism, Okayama Shoka University, Japan (15 females and 15 males). Except one female, none of the others had visited Takayama-shi.

Each subject was presented with the 58 photographs and requested to classify them into five rows according to their own preference as places for sightseeing. The photographs were then placed in five rows in front of the subject so that their preference gradually decreased top to bottom. They were then asked the following five types of questions:

1. "What causes differences in your preference between the photographs in row 1 and row 2?" Then, the same question was asked for the differences between rows 2 and 3, and so on.
2. "Please state anything that causes differences in your preference between any rows."
   The procedure until "2" was also employed in Maki (1994).
3. "Please select the most preferable photograph for you. What makes the photograph the most preferable?"

Table 1.   Descriptions of the 58 Photographs of Takayama.

Number	Setting	Description 1 (Settings)	Description 2
1	1	A streetscape within a well-conserved area. Some plants and flowers are also noticeable	Without people (very few in the background)
2			With people
3	2	A streetscape within a well-conserved area	Without people (only one in the background)
4		Plants and flowers (especially morning glories) are very noticeable	With people
5			With a rickshaw
6	3	A streetscape with a shop and a private houses next to a well-conserved area	Without people
7		Some plants (especially pine trees) are noticeable	With people
8		TV aerials are also observable. A modern building is visible in the background	With a rickshaw
9	4	A streetscape with some private houses outside a well-conserved area. Some cars are parked	With people and a tour guide
10		Some plants (especially pine trees) are noticeable. Utility poles are also observed	Without people
11	5	A streetscape with a long established store (brewer) within a well-conserved area	With people
12		Some goods (local liquor) and flowers are observable outside the store	Without people
13	6	A streetscape with a long established store (brewer) outside a well-conserved area	With people
14		Some goods (local liquor) are observable outside the store	Without people
15		Utility poles and road signs are observed in the background	With a rickshaw
16	7	A streetscape with a long established store within a well-conserved area	Without people
17		Some flowers are also noticeable	With a rickshaw
18			With people (obviously a family with a child)
19	8	A streetscape with a long established store (brewer) next to a well-conserved area	With (very few) people

Table 1. (*Continued*)

Number	Setting	Description 1 (Settings)	Description 2
20		A modern building is observed in the background	With a rickshaw and a taxi
21	9	A streetscape with some stores next to a well-conserved area	Without people
22		Bicycles, a vending machine, and modern signboards (lettering) are observed	With people (probably a family with a child)
23		A modern building and an aerial are observed in the background	With a rickshaw
24	10	A streetscape within a well-conserved area Cars are parked. Some utility poles are observed in the background	Without people (very few in the background)
25			With people and a tour guide
26	11	A streetscape within a well-conserved area. Some bicycles are parked	Without people (very few in the background)
27		Some flowers are observed. An aerial is observed in the background	With a few people
28	12	A streetscape with stores (local crafts) within a well-conserved area	With a few people. A rickshaw in the background
29		Some bicycles are parked. A modern building is observed in the background	With people and a rickshaw
30	13	A souvenir shop just outside a well-conserved area with a few road signs visible	Without people
31			With many people
32			With a car
33	14	A streetscape with a store within a well-conserved area	With many people
34		Some flowers are observable	With a rickshaw
35		The street meets a wide road at the corner	With a few people in the background
36			With people. Also a coach in the background
37	15	A streetscape with a store within a well-conserved area	Without people (very few in the background)
38		White signboards with brushed black letters are noticeable. Pine trees are visible	With a few people in the foreground

Table 1. (*Continued*)

Number	Setting	Description 1 (Settings)	Description 2
39	16	A streetscape within a moderately conserved area	Without people (very few in the middle and background)
40		A shop with a red eave in the foreground and a pickles shop in the background	With people
41		A sign in the foreground states that the area is conserved under local regulations	With rickshaw
42	17	A shop (pickles shop) outside a	Without people
43		well-conserved area with a few vending machines, utility poles and adjacent modern buildings visible	With people
44	18	A streetscape within a moderately conserved area. A white eave is noticeable	Without people
45		Goods are displayed outside. A car is parked, and a ventilator is visible	With people
46	19	A streetscape outside a well-conserved area with a shop. A green flag clearly says that Japanese traditional sweets are sold	Without people (very few in the background)
47		Some road signs and utility poles are visible	With people
48	20	A streetscape in front of a shrine outside a well-conserved area with some signboards and utility poles	Without people (very few in the background)
49		The signs say that most of the shops sell Japanese traditional sweets	With people
50		A hill with green trees is observed in the background	With a rickshaw and a car
51	21	A streetscape in front of a shrine outside a well-conserved area with a liquor shop and utility poles	Without people (very few in the background)
52		A bicycle and some green trees are visible. A hill with green trees is observed in the background	With people. Also a car running
53	22	A streetscape with a wooden warehouse and a parking lot outside a well-conserved area	Without people

Table 1. (*Continued*)

Number	Setting	Description 1 (Settings)	Description 2
54		A car is parked, and plastic cases	With people
55		for beer are piled	With people and a rickshaw
56	23	A streetscape with a parking lot outside a well-conserved area	With people
57		Some cars are parked, and some utility poles are visible	Without people (very few in the background)
58			With people and a rickshaw

4. "Please select the least preferable photograph for you. What makes the photograph the least preferable?"

5. "Please state anything that causes differences in your preference among photographs in any single row."

Once a subject stated one component, ladder-up or ladder-down types of questions were then asked to extract relationships between components. Each set of interviews lasted from 40 minutes to 1 hour and 30 minutes. The components and the relationships that subjects stated were recorded in the shape of tree figure by each subject, and each subject's tree figure was later rewritten using terms commonly stated by the subjects. Both positive and negative relationships were recorded.

The triad method has commonly been applied in previous tourism studies (Botterill & Crompton, 1987, 1996; Coshall, 2000; Embacher & Buttle, 1989; Gyte, 1988; Pearce, 1982; Pike, 2003; Selby, 2004; Walmsley & Jenkins, 1993; Young, 1995). With this method, three elements (a triad) are presented to subjects, who are then asked to specify how two of them are alike and different from the third (Fransella & Bannister, 1977). However, for two reasons, this study did not use the triad method. First, in comparing three photographs, the participants would be more likely to focus on differences between them not related entirely to their preferences. If the comparison was not related to their preferences, the participants might experience difficulty in stating further ways in which photographs were perceived to be different from each other. Secondly, a historical district is a very complex and broad object compared to tangible products like cars. In this context, comparison between a broad range of photographs rather than between a limited number of photographs seemed to offer an efficient way of eliciting a large number of components and relationships between those components. Maki (1994) and Naoi et al. (2006) also utilized strategies similar to the ones employed here.

The authors attempted to classify the components extracted through repertory grid analysis and laddering analysis into five levels with reference to the theoretical framework set out above. These five levels comprise levels of cognitive components, affective components, wants, needs, and values. As for subjects' mental states, if subjects stated desires to do something with concrete objects (such as local food) or to do very particular activities (such as eating out), these statements were labeled as wants. If the activities were not very concrete (for example experiencing something outside daily life), the statements were classified as needs. More abstract components such as those that Gutman (1982) describes as "desirable end-states of existence, [that] play a dominant role in guiding choice pattern" (p. 60) and "a type of consequence for which a person has no further (higher) reason for preference" (p. 64) were planned to be categorized as values. As defined here values refer to end-states rather than means to achieve something and. as such were not extracted.

The authors then categorized the extracted components at each level into groups that shared similar meanings. Only grouped components that were mentioned by five or more subjects were used for the consecutive steps (see Table 2).

In addition to the five levels of components, what Horiuchi (1998) terms personal factors and contexts, were also extracted. According to Horiuchi (1998), consumption can be influenced by products' attributes, personal factors, and contexts. Product attributes are products' appearance or performance. Personal factors include characteristics, such as personality or lifestyle, which can be attributed to individuals rather than to their surroundings. Contexts refer to the environments that influence consumer behavior. These contexts could be physical, social, or temporal (Horiuchi, 1998). Among the extracted elements, two personal factors ("I dislike crowds" and "I like history/heritage") and one context related to social environment ("My daily life is tiring") were observed. Another contextual factor ("I have been to historical districts"), which is termed here personal history, was also extracted.

The reason why these personal factors and contexts were extracted could be that Takayama-shi is a domestic destination for the subjects. Photographed settings in Takayama-shi might somehow be similar to the settings of districts that the subjects might probably have visited or might be familiar with on TV and so on. This might have led the subjects to associate their evaluation of these settings with their usual preference for tourism destinations and contexts, such as their personal history or experience, in which their travel behaviors occur.

Table 2.   Extracted Components.

Elements	Frequency
(1) Cognitive components (48)	
C1: Rickshaws	27
C2: Cars	28
C3: Buses	11
C4: Taxies	6
C5: Car parks	7
C6: Bicycles	13
C7: Road signs	15
C8: Wearing fashionable clothes	5
C9: Carrying bags	13
C10: Carrying souvenir-like items	10
C11: Carrying cameras	6
C12: Carrying guide books/tourist maps, etc.	5
C13: Gathering	7
C14: Looking around restlessly	8
C15: Staring at something	5
C16: People	22
C17: Visitors	28
C18: A large number of visitors	18
C19: Families	8
C20: Guides	15
C21: Local people	9
C22: Signs	11
C23: Signs with a writing brush	7
C24: Colorful signs	6
C25: Modern signs	7
C26: A Curtain with a shop name on it	7
C27: Shops	15
C28: Souvenir shops	12
C29: Restaurants/cafes	9
C30: Traditional restaurants/cafes	15
C31: Traditional craft shops	6
C32: Local liquor shops/breweries	6
C33: Sunlight	8
C34: Old houses	19
C35: Wooden houses	5
C36: Houses with black timbers	7
C37: Old-fashioned lighting equipments	5
C38: Telephone masts/modern tall buildings	11
C39: Vending machines	8
C40: Yellow plastic containers for beer bottles	11
C41: Ordinary private houses	24
C42: The backside of houses	7
C43: Wide streets	8

Table 2. (*Continued*)

Elements	Frequency
C44: Narrow pavements	12
C45: Flowers	10
C46: Green plants	5
C47: Trees	8
C48: Hills	5
(2) Photography (1)	
A distance view	8
(3) Affective components (33)	
A1: Narrow	6
A2: Old-fashioned/old/historical	27
A3: Japanese-style	6
A4: Harmony with a historical district	21
A5: A sense of congruity	13
A6: Luxury	5
A7: Touristic	23
A8: Worth visiting	17
A9: Famous	18
A10: Main	5
A11: Interesting	10
A12: Relief ("This is the place for many people to visit. I am not odd to visit here.")	6
A13: Known only to those who appreciate its taste	8
A14: Places to visit only if time is available	5
A15: For local people	11
A16: Not normal-daily-life-like	24
A17: Unique/precious	22
A18: Fresh	5
A19: Available only in the area	5
A20: Special products available	6
A21: Commercial	7
A22: A sense of activity	25
A23: Cheerful	8
A24: Calm/restful	13
A25: Quiet	11
A26: Congested/crowded	5
A27: Dangerous (traffic)	14
A28: Good-looking	11
A29: Clean	6
A30: Elegant/tasteful	8
A31: Convenient	10
A32: Easy to understand	12
A33: Of high quality	5
(4) Wants (17)	
W1: Riding on a rickshaw	18

Table 2. (*Continued*)

Elements	Frequency
W2: Entering houses/buildings	5
W3: Worrying for other people/surroundings	7
W4: Queuing	6
W5: Walking	20
W6: Seeing scenery/townscape/houses	19
W7: Having a rest/break	5
W8: Shopping at the local shops	18
W9: Entering shops	10
W10: Buying items for myself	5
W11: Buying souvenir for friends/acquaintances	13
W12: Buying souvenir for my family	8
W13: Eating special food available only in the area	18
W14: Choosing shops from a range of alternatives	8
W15: Meeting new people	6
W16: Being explained/guided	8
W17: Visiting many places	7
(5) Needs (14)	
N1: Doing things freely/on my own pace	14
N2: Forgetting about time	5
N3: Seeing/visiting something famous	11
N4: Discovering something unique	6
N5: Seeing/visiting something known only to those who appreciate its taste	6
N6: Seeing the real local settings	6
N7: Knowing/learning something	10
N8: Actually visiting the sites	5
N9: Making good memories for myself/obtaining something as a memento	9
N10: Experiencing/obtaining something to tell/show others	11
N11: Relaxing/resting/slowing down	21
N12: Seeking something outside my daily life	10
N13: Escaping from my daily life	8
N14: Convincing myself that I have visited the right place	13
(6) Personality	
P1: I dislike crowds	6
P2: I like history/heritage	5
(7) Context (personal history)	
Con1: I Have been to historical districts	6
(8) Context (social environments)	
Con2: My daily life is tiring	9

Thereafter, a tree figure that shows hierarchical relationships between components was created for the whole group of subjects through the calculation of the frequencies of the relationships between components. In the study by Klenosky (2002), Klenosky et al. (1993), Naoi et al. (2006), and

Reynolds and Gutman (1988), both positive and negative, and direct and indirect relationships were counted. For example, if the following relationships as illustrated in Fig. 2 were extracted, this means, with the presence of cars (C2), a subject perceives a dangerous atmosphere (A27) and does not feel like going out for a walk (W5). As a consequence, the subject thinks that nothing famous will be found here (N3).

In this example, the relationships would be counted as in Table 3.

Identification of both direct and indirect relationships was attempted, but this created difficulties because too many indirect relationships were found. This is probably because the subjects were quite familiar with the settings of a Japanese historical district like the ones in Takayama-shi and could relate these to similar experiences of their own such as visiting a Japanese historical district like Kyoto on a school trip in the past or watching a historical soap opera filmed in Japanese historical settings. Probably for these reasons, the number of components extracted in this experiment was large, and subjects commonly stated many of these components. As a result, each subject's tree was very complicated. In this case, counting all the possible indirect relationships would prove to be extremely time-consuming. Moreover, a risk of over-estimating the strength of certain indirect relationships between two components exists when many routes exist between these components or/and when these components were connected through many other components.

Fig. 2. An Example of Relationships whose Frequencies to be Counted.

Table 3. Example of a Table to Count Frequencies of Relationships between a Pair of Components.

	A27				W5				N3			
	PD	PI	ND	NI	PD	PI	ND	NI	PD	PI	ND	NI
C2	1						1					1
A27						1						1
W5									1			

PD, Positive direct relationships; PI, Positive indirect relationships; ND, Negative direct relationships; NI, Negative indirect relationships.

In consideration of these issues, this study counts only direct (both positive and negative) relationships between components. In an attempt to minimize the risk of overlooking significant indirect relationships, two tree figures were created on the basis of different criteria. First, the frequencies of direct relationships between pairs of components were considered as the basis of the tree figure only when frequencies were five or more. The figure created according to this criterion is shown as Fig. 3. However, the number of relationships between higher levels (between affective components and needs/wants) was relatively small compared to the number of relationships between cognitive and affective components. Indeed, some pairs of components might be indirectly related to each other, but through different components. In this case, if two components are connected through other components that share, if not completely the same, then similar meanings, some may argue that the indirect significant relationships between the pair exist but were overlooked.

In response to this issue, the components in Table 2 were recategorized into a smaller number of groups to reflect the direct connections between components. First, all the direct relationships between affective components and needs/wants were scrutinized to see whether any significant relationships could be found by grouping components with similar meanings into one. As a result of this procedure, some needs/wants and affective components were recategorized. Thereafter, the same procedure of scrutiny was employed for all the direct relationships between cognitive components and regrouped affective components. These analyses generated Fig. 4, which includes components shown in Table 4. The direct relationships between a pair of components appear in Fig. 4 only when frequencies are five or more.

Eight cognitive components (C8, C9, C10, C11, C12, C13, C14, C15, and C19) were excluded from Fig. 4, as they merely related to the issue about what makes people look like visitors. During this scrutinizing process, the relationships between affective components and what could be called the combination of cognitive components ("A Shop with People" and "A Shop with No People") were detected. These two components imply that the combination of more than one cognitive component may relate to distinctive evaluations.

While the criterion for Fig. 4 seems likely to cover more relationships between components from the level of cognitive components to the higher levels than the criterion for Fig. 3, this criterion can admittedly be regarded as quite subjective compared to the one used to create Fig. 3. Furthermore, this criterion can be criticized on the basis that different relationships attributed to subtle differences between components in their meanings could

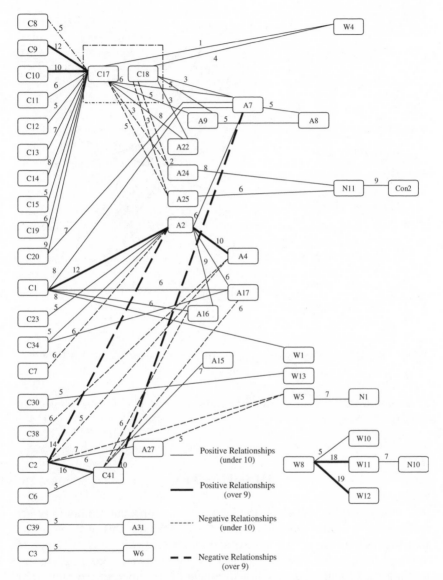

Fig. 3. Relationships between Cognitive/Affective Components and Mental States (1st Fig.).

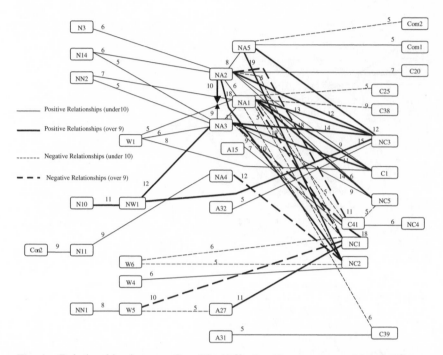

Fig. 4. Relationships between Cognitive/Affective Components and Mental States (2nd Fig.).

be compromised if components are categorized into a smaller number of groups.

DISCUSSION

This study aims to propose a theoretical framework and methods, rather than to draw conclusions to be generalized. However, this does not mean that the results cannot be analyzed and interpreted as a basis on which to appraise their usefulness. Such an analysis and interpretation is attempted on the basis of both Figs. 3 and 4, although Fig. 4 is considered more fully because this depicts more relationships, covering the level of cognitive components through to the level of mental states.

The results suggest possible mixed influences on evaluations of a historical district as a tourism destination. On the one hand, the presence of

Table 4. Recategorized Extracted Components.

Elements		Frequency
Cognitive aspects (11)		
C1	Rickshaws	27
NC1	Vehicles other than rickshaws (C2, 3, 4, 5, 6, 7)	30
NC2	People (mainly visitors) (C16, 17, 18)	29
NC3	Shops (C22, 23, 24, 26, 27, 28, 29, 30, 31, 32)	30
C20	Guides	15
C25	Modern signs	7
C38	Telephone masts/modern tall buildings	11
C39	Vending machines	8
C41	Ordinary private houses	24
NC4	Plants (C45, 46, 47, 48)	19
NC5	Old houses (C34, 35, 36, 37)	25
Affective aspects (9)		
NA1	Old (A2, 3, 4, 5)	28
NA2	Touristic/famous (A7, 8, 9, 10, 11, 12)	30
A15	For local people	11
NA3	Unique/not normal-daily-life-like (A16, 17, 18, 19, 20)	29
NA5	A sense of activity (A22, 23)	25
NA4	Calm/restful/quiet (A24, 25)	16
A27	Dangerous (traffic)	14
A31	Convenient	10
A32	Easy to understand	12
Wants (5)		
W1	Riding on a rickshaw	18
W4	Queuing	6
W5	Walking	20
W6	Seeing scenery/townscape/houses	19
NW1	Shopping (W8, 9, 10, 11, 12, 13)	23
Needs (6)		
NN1	Doing things freely (N1, 2)	15
N3	Seeing/visiting something famous	11
N10	Experiencing/obtaining something to show/tell others	11
N11	Relaxing/resting/slowing down	21
NN2	Seeking something outside my daily life (N12, N13)	16
N14	Convincing myself that I have visited the right place	13
Context (social environments) (1)		
Con2	My daily life is tiring	9
Combination (2)		
Com1	A shop with people	10
Com2	A shop with no people	9

people (NC2) may lead to both a touristic/famous (NA2) and an active atmosphere (NA5). Here, touristic atmosphere seems to contribute mainly to the achievement of seeing something famous (N3) and being convinced that the district is the right place to visit (N14). These results imply that a historical district as a tourism destination could be an object of the *collective gaze* (Urry, 1990). On the other hand, the presence of people (NC2) may relate to the lesser degree of quietness (NA4), and is perceived to prevent scenery watching (W6) and relaxing (N11). These results indicate the aspect of a historical district as the object of the *romantic gaze* (Urry, 1990). The presence of people (NC2) could also lead to the lesser degree of oldness (NA1), which is perceived to be an obstacle to the appreciation of something outside daily life (NN2). On the whole, the presence of people is implied to be perceived favorably or unfavorably depending on what visitors demand in a historical district. The presence of guides (C20) seems to relate to touristic atmosphere (NA2) and meet the desire to see/visit something famous (N3) and to be convinced that they are visiting the right place (N14).

Old houses (NC5) and shops (NC3) appear to be perceived as favorable in many respects. Both of them relate to touristic/famous (NA2), unique (NA3), old atmosphere (NA1), and, therefore, may fulfill both the desire to see/visit something famous (N3), be convinced that the right place is being visited (N14), taste something outside daily life (NN2), do shopping (NW1), and experience/obtain something to show/tell others (N10). However, the type of shops and houses seems to matter. Modern signs (C25) may have negative effects especially on desires to taste something outside daily life (NN2) in the district by relating to a new atmosphere (NA1). Ordinary private houses (C41) are associated with newness (NA1), an ordinary atmosphere (NA3) and a nontouristic atmosphere (NA2), and therefore, are perceived to prevent visitors from being convinced that they are visiting the right place (N14), from seeing/visiting something famous (N3), from tasting something outside daily life (NN2), from doing shopping (NW1), and from experiencing/obtaining something to show/tell others (N10). Telephone masts/modern tall buildings (C38) are also perceived to detract from the old atmosphere (NA1) and present difficulties in tasting something outside daily life (NN2). Furthermore, whether shops are observed with people influences the evaluation of them. While shops, particularly with people (Com1), seem to lead to an active (NA5) and a touristic atmosphere (NA2), which may result in opportunities to see/visit something famous (N3) and being convinced that they are in the right place (N14), shops with no people (Com2) indicate the opposite. On the whole, whether the effects of houses and shops are favorable is suggested to be determined by whether they are old- or new-looking.

Vehicles (NC1) may be perceived negatively in many ways. They are perceived as associated with newness (NA1), ordinary atmosphere (NA3), and danger (A27). Vehicles (NC1) may even relate to the perception that the district is minor as a tourism destination (NA2). As a result, vehicles seem to ruin almost all sorts of mental states, such as seeing/visiting something famous (N3), being convinced of visiting the right place (N14), seeking something outside daily life (NN2), doing shopping (NW1), experiencing/ obtaining something to show/tell others (N10), walking (W5), and doing things freely (NN1). However, rickshaws (C1), which are old-style carts pulled by hand to carry passengers, show completely different tendencies by relating to touristic (NA2), unique (NA3), and old atmosphere (NA1), and they seem to fulfill many mental states, such as seeing/visiting something famous (N3), being convinced that the visited place is right (N14), tasting something outside daily life (NN2), shopping (NW1), and experiencing/ obtaining something to show/tell others (N10). These results imply that, as Ooi (2002) found for trishaws in Singapore, rickshaws here might be perceived as the romantic presentation of a revised and animated past rather than a mode of transport.

Like other modern components, vending machines (C39) are also perceived to be new (NA1), and therefore, to be unfavorable for many mental states like seeing/visiting something famous (N3), being convinced that they have visited the right place (N14) and seeing something outside daily life (NN2). However, in terms of another affective component, convenience (A31), these machines may be contributory to a favorable evaluation.

Turning to the affective components more specifically, many of the extracted components correspond to three basic dimensions (staged-authentic, ordinary-unique, restful/relaxing-adventurous/exciting), which Sasaki (2000) conceptually proposed for evaluations of a tourism destination, but not necessarily in a straightforward manner. The dimension "ordinary-unique" was extracted very clearly (NA3). The extraction of this dimension also somehow corresponds to the findings of an empirical study about cultural attractions in Hong Kong by McKecher, Ho, and du Cros (2004), who found that, in the views of specialists in the local cultural management sector, one of the attributes that make cultural attractions popular is their uniqueness. The results also indicate the importance of "restful/relaxing-adventurous/exciting dimension" (NA4 and NA5).

The staged-authentic dimension was not clear in the results of this experiment, but was implied by the affective components like "touristic-not touristic" (NA2) or "old-new" (NA1), both of whose left-hand words relate positively to subjects' needs such as "seeing/visiting something famous" (N3), "being convinced that they have visited the right place" (N14) or "seeking something outside daily life" (NN2). These findings suggest the complex meanings of the concept of authenticity and a touristic atmosphere. In consideration of Urry's definition of authenticity as "the consistent relationship between the physical and built environments and a given historical period" (Urry, 1995, p. 190), the authenticity of the settings in this experiment could be perceived to relate to the congruity with oldness. That is, the more the settings in each scene were congruent with the old period the higher the level of authenticity the subjects perceived. Indeed, the findings show that these two concepts (NA1 and NA2) relate to each other. Furthermore, the touristic atmosphere (NA2) of the historical district may be perceived positively as such atmosphere is attributed to the fame of the object (N3) as well as its uniqueness (NA3) and outside-daily-life like taste (NN2). That is, the place can be unique and, at the same time, touristic in order to attract visitors. This assumption leads to the implication that the subjects perceived what MacCannell (1976) calls "staged authenticity." These results suggest that the concept of authenticity has a complexity that a simple single dimension cannot explain.

As for the subjects' mental states, many of the findings also accord with the past conceptual propositions concerning mental states of visitors to heritage sites. Novelty seeking (Nuryanti, 1996; Zeppel & Hall, 1991) appeared as "seeking something outside daily life" (NN2) in the results of this study. The quest for authenticity (Cohen, 1972; MacCannell, 1976; McIntosh & Prentice, 1999) was not clearly stated by the subjects. However, as previously argued regarding the relationship between authenticity and affective components extracted through this experiment, the fact that "to be convinced of visiting the right place" (N14) and "tasting something outside daily life" (NN2) seems related to unique (NA3) and old (NA1) atmospheres may imply that the desire for authenticity was perceived in the shape of other more concrete needs. In the same manner, nostalgia for the past (Halewood & Hannam, 2001; Timothy & Boyd, 2003; Zeppel & Hall, 1992) did not appear in this way, but as "seeking something outside daily life" (NN2). This was found to relate to the old atmosphere (NA1) and this is assumed to comprehend the concept of nostalgia for the past. Prestigious/status (Boniface, 1995; Zeppell & Hall, 1991) clearly appeared as "experience/obtain something worth telling others" (N10) in the results of this experiment. The desire to "see/visit something famous" (N3) in Fig. 4 also justifies the claim that tourism is the discovery of well-known things

(Brendon, 1991; Hashimoto, 1999) and supports the idea that visitors go to historic cities out of interest in seeing buildings or particular places that have a historic reputation (Newcomb, 1979). Social interaction (Zeppell & Hall, 1991), escape (Boniface, 1995; Zeppell & Hall, 1991), and learning about the past (Boyd, 2002; Confer & Kerstetter, 2000; Light, 1995; Prentice & Prentice, 1989; Richards, 2001; Thomas, 1989) were not observed in either Fig. 3 or Fig. 4, but did appear in Table 2 (W15, N13, and N7, consecutively). Among the extracted mental states, "desire to relax" (N11) is found to relate closely to the subjects' social context, which implies that their daily lives are tiring (Con2).

Turning to more detailed mental states, the importance of "walking" (W5) as in Figs. 3 and 4 was also supported by Orbasli (2000), who claims that the walkable environment in a historic city is one of its important attractions for visitors, and that such an environment provides visitors with an opportunity or a sense of discovery. The pleasure of walkable spaces could be reduced by vehicular traffic (Orbasli, 2000), which the results in Figs. 3 and 4 suggest.

CONCLUSIONS

Empirical investigation of relationships between visitors' mental states, and cognitive and affective features of a historical district with employment of well-structured methods is crucial for understanding of the complex nature of visitors' evaluation of such a district as a tourism destination. The combination of repertory grid analysis and laddering analysis could be useful to elicit those relationships, which have been theoretically argued, and have been awaiting empirical investigation.

Many of the results shed light on issues that have been raised by past studies. The mixed effects of the presence of people may relate to the concept of the collective and romantic gaze (Urry, 1990) while effects of shops, which are a reflection of commercialization, seem to vary according to their types. Modern objects like cars and vending machines are found to be perceived negatively in most cases, but the implication that effects of vending machines may be positive in terms of convenience may imply that many visitors demand contemporary facilities (Ashworth, 1988; Ashworth & Tunbridge, 2000). A sense of uniqueness, relaxation, excitement, and touristic atmosphere were found to be important affective components in visitors' evaluation as implied by past studies. The possible perceived compatible relationships between authentic and touristic atmosphere are interesting findings, which offer insights into the complex nature of authenticity. Among visitors' mental states argued as relevant to a historical district, novelty seeking, desire for prestigious/status, and discovery of well-known things clearly appeared whereas the quest for authenticity and nostalgia for the past are rather indirectly implied.

Elicitation of two personal factors, one personal history, one context and the relationship between "desire to relax" and the subjects' tiring daily lives suggests the necessity of investigating, not only visited environments, but also visitors' environment of residence, their personality and history. These findings and the process of creating tree figures also have implications that how much past direct or indirect experiences subjects have with the same or similar historical districts may require deliberation in the arguments about visitors' evaluation of a historical district as a tourism destination.

The hierarchical relationships extracted by the combination of repertory grid analysis and laddering analysis could help the management of a historical district because these relationships suggest how visitors commonly associate the physical elements of the district with their mental states. As the physical environments of a tourism destination are often very difficult to tailor-make, identification of existing physical elements that satisfy a certain number of visitors is essential. From the view of conservation also, the results obtained by repertory grid analysis and laddering analysis could be useful because managers of a historical district could find ways to relate the district's existing features to those mental states of visitors while securing an economically sustainable number of visitors. As a whole, the approaches of this study are useful in order to establish strategies for management and conservation of a historical district as a tourism destination. Although limited in the scope for generalization due to the small number of subjects, the methods employed in this study are argued to be reasonable and acceptable when the aim is to obtain fundamental data in order to propose theoretical frameworks for a newly explored area. This study could offer leads to future studies, which are expected to explore visitors' evaluative structures under a range of conditions, for example, with use of a survey of actual visitors.

ACKNOWLEDGMENT

This study is subsidized by The Yakumo Foundation for Environmental Science, to which the authors would like to express their gratitude. The authors are also very grateful to the undergraduate students of Okayama Shoka University for kindly participating in the interviews.

REFERENCES

Adorno, T. W. (1991). *The culture industry*. London: Routledge.

The Agency for Cultural Affairs. (n.d.). Retrieved February 4, 2003, from http://www.bunka.go.jp/pub/index.html

Anand, P., Holbrook, M. B., & Stephens, D. (1988). The formation of affective judgements: The cognitive-affective model versus the independence hypothesis. *Journal of Consumer Research, 15*(3), 386–391.

Argyle, M., Furnham, A., & Graham, J. A. (1981). *Social situations*. Cambridge, UK: Cambridge University Press.

Ashworth, G. J. (1988). Marketing the historic city for tourism. In: B. Goodall & G. Ashworth (Eds), *Marketing in the tourism industry: the promotion of destination regions* (pp. 162–175). London: Croom Helm.

Ashworth, G. J. (1991). *Heritage planning: The management of urban change*. Groningen, The Netherlands: Geopers.

Ashworth, G. J., & Tunbridge, J. E. (2000). *The tourist-historic city: Retrospect and prospect of managing the heritage city (advances in tourism research series)*. Oxford, UK: Pergamon.

Ashworth, G. J., & Voogt, H. (1990). *Selling the city*. London: Belhaven.

Ashworth, G. J., & Voogt, H. (1994). What are we doing when we sell places for tourism? *International Journal of Consumer Marketing, 6*(3/4), 5–19.

Baloglu, S. (1999). A path analytic model of visitation intention involving information sources, socio-psychological motivations and destination images. *Journal of Travel & Tourism Marketing, 8*(3), 81–90.

Baloglu, S. (2000). A path analytic model of visitation intention involving information sources, socio-psychological motivations and destination images. In: A. G. Woodside, G. I. Crouch, J. A. Mazanec, M. Oppermann & M. Y. Sakai (Eds), *Consumer psychology of tourism, hospitality and leisure* (pp. 63–90). Wallingford, UK: CABI.

Baloglu, S., & McCleary, K. W. (1999a). A model of destination image formation. *Annals of Tourism Research, 26*(4), 868–897.

Baloglu, S., & McCleary, K. W. (1999b). U.S. International pleasure travelers' images of four Mediterranean destinations: A comparison of visitors and nonvisitors. *Journal of Travel Research, 38*(2), 144–152.

Beerli, A., & Martin, J. D. (2004). Tourists' characteristics and the perceived image of tourist destinations: A quantitative analysis – A case study of Lanzarote, Spain. *Tourism Management, 25*(5), 623–636.

Boniface, P. (1995). *Managing quality cultural tourism*. London: Routledge.

Boorstin, D. J. (1964). *The image: A guide to pseudo-events in America*. New York: Atheneum.

Botterill, T. D. (1989). Humanistic tourism? Personal constructions of a tourist; Sam visits Japan. *Leisure Studies, 8*(3), 281–293.

Botterill, T. D., & Crompton, J. L. (1987). Personal constructions of holiday snapshots. *Annals of Tourism Research, 14*(1), 152–156.

Botterill, T. D., & Crompton, J. L. (1996). Two case studies exploring the nature of the tourist's experience. *Journal of Leisure Research, 28*(1), 57–82.

Boyd, S. W. (2002). Cultural and heritage tourism in Canada: Opportunities, principles and challenges. *Tourism and Hospitality Research, 3*(3), 211–233.

Brendon, P. (1991). *Thomas Cook: 150 years of popular tourism*. London: Curtis Brown Group.

Caffyn, A., & Lutz, J. (1999). Developing the heritage product in multi-ethnic cities. *Tourism Management*, *20*(2), 213–221.

Cohen, E. (1972). Toward a sociology of international tourism. *Social Research: An International Quarterly of the Social Science*, *39*(1), 164–182.

Cohen, E. (1979). A phenomenology of tourist experiences. *Sociology*, *13*(2), 179–201.

Cohen, E. (1989). Authenticity and commoditization in tourism. *Annals of Tourism Research*, *15*(3), 371–386.

Cohen, E. (1995). Contemporary tourism: Trends and challenges sustainable authenticity of continued post-modernity. In: R. Butler & D. Pearce (Eds), *Change in tourism: People, places and processes* (pp. 12–29). London: Routledge.

Confer, J. C., & Kerstetter, D. L. (2000). Past perfect: Exploration of heritage tourism. *Parks and Recreation*, *35*(2), 28–38.

Coshall, J. T. (2000). Measurement of tourists' images: The repertory grid approach. *Journal of Travel Research*, *39*(1), 85–89.

Ditton, R. B., Fedler, A. J., & Graefe, A. R. (1983). Factors contributing to perceptions of recreational crowding. *Leisure Sciences*, *5*(4), 273–288.

Embacher, J., & Buttle, F. (1989). A repertory grid analysis of Austria's image as a summer vacation destination. *Journal of Travel Research*, *27*(3), 3–7.

Fairweather, J. R., & Swaffield, S. R. (2001). Visitor experiences of Kaikoura, New Zealand: An interpretative study using photographs of landscapes and Q method. *Tourism Management*, *22*(3), 219–228.

Fairweather, J. R., & Swaffield, S. R. (2002). Visitors' and locals' experiences of Rotorua, New Zealand: An interpretative study using photographs of landscapes and Q Methods. *International Journal of Tourism Research*, *4*(4), 283–297.

Fransella, F., & Bannister, D. (1977). *A manual for repertory grid technique*. London: Academic Press.

Gartner, W. C. (1993). Image formation process. In: M. Uysal & D. R. Fesenmaier (Eds), *Communication and channel systems in tourism marketing* (pp. 191–215). New York: Haworth Press.

Gengler, C. E., & Reynolds, T. J. (1995). Consumer understanding and advertising strategy: Analysis and strategic translation of laddering data. *Journal of Advertising Research*, *35*(4), 19–33.

Graham, J. H., & Burge, R. (1984). Crowding perception determinants at intensively developed outdoor recreation sites. *Leisure Science*, *6*(2), 167–186.

Gutman, J. (1982). A means-end chain model based on consumer categorization processes. *Journal of Marketing*, *46*(2), 60–72.

Gyte, D. M. (1988). *Repertory grid analysis of image of destinations: British tourists in Mellorca*. Nottingham, UK: Nottingham Trent Polytechnic, Department of Geography.

Halewood, C., & Hannam, K. (2001). Viking heritage tourism: Authenticity and commodification. *Annals of Tourism Research*, *28*(3), 565–580.

Hanyu, K. (1993). The affective meaning of Tokyo: Verbal and nonverbal approaches. *Journal of Environmental Psychology*, *13*, 161–172.

Hashimoto, K. (1999). *Kankojinruigakunosenryaku: Bunkanourikataurarekata*. [Strategy for anthropology of tourism: how to buy and how to sell a culture.] Kyoto, Japan: Sekaishisosha.

Hewison, R. (1987). *The heritage industry: Britain in a climate of decline*. London: Methuen.

Horiuchi, K. (1998). Proposed research framework for factors and scales of product hedonic values. *Japanese Association of Industrial/Organizational Psychology Journal, 11*(2), 135–146.

Hull I V, R. B. (1990). Mood as a product of leisure: Causes and consequences. *Journal of Leisure Research, 22*(2), 99–111.

Jansen-Verbeke, M., & van Rekom, J. (1996). Scanning museum visitors: Urban tourism marketing. *Annals of Tourism Research, 23*(2), 364–375.

Japan National Tourist Organization. (Ed.). (2000). *Sekai to Nihon no Kokusaikankoukouryu no Doukou: Kitai no Takamaru Wagakuni no Hounichi Kankou.* [*Trends of international tourism exchanges between the world and Japan: Hopeful Japanese inbound tourism.*] Tokyo: Kokusai Kankou Service Centre.

The Japan Tourist Association. (2004). *Heisei 14 Nendo Zenkoku Kankoudoukou.* [Trends in tourism throughout Japan 2002.] Tokyo: Japan Tourist Association.

Japan Travel Bureau. (1999). *Utsukushii Nippon: Ichido ha Otozuretai Nippon no Kankoushigen.* [*Beautiful Japan: Japanese tourism heritage that should be visited at least once.*] Tokyo: Japan Travel Bureau.

Johnson, N. C. (1999). Framing the past: Time, space and politics of tourism in Ireland. *Political Geography, 18*(2), 187–207.

JTB Toronto Office. (n.d.). *JTB Toronto Office Tour Packages.* Retrieved December 8, 2003, from http://www.jtbi.ca/jtbi_html/html/culture/architect/architect_map.html

Kelly, G. A. (1955). *The psychology of personal constructs.* New York: Norton.

Klenosky, D. B. (2002). The "pull" of tourism destinations: A means-end investigation. *Journal of Travel Research, 40*(4), 385–395.

Klenosky, D. B., Gengler, C. E., & Mulvey, M. S. (1993). Understanding the factors influencing ski destination choice: A means-end analytic approach. *Journal of Leisure Research, 25*(4), 362–379.

Light, D. (1995). Heritage as informal education. In: D. T. Herbert (Ed.), *Heritage tourism and society* (pp. 117–145). London: Mansell.

MacCannell, D. (1976). *The tourist: A new theory of the leisure class.* Los Angeles: University of California Press.

Maki, K. (1994). *Unpublished doctoral dissertation,* Tokyo: Tokyo Institute of Technology.

Manning, R. E. (1985). Crowding norms in backcountry settings: A review and synthesis. *Journal of Leisure Research, 17*(2), 75–89.

Maruoka, Y. (1998). *Laddering-hou no genzai: chosa-houhou, bunseki-shuhou, kekka no katsuyou to kongo no kadai.* [The currently employed laddering analysis: Research methods, analyses, applications of the results, and issues for future studies.] *Marketing Science, 7*(1.2), 40–61.

Mathieson, A., & Wall, G. (1982). *Tourism-economic physical, and social impacts.* London: Longman.

McIntosh, A. J., & Prentice, R. C. (1999). Affirming authenticity: Consuming cultural heritage. *Annals of Tourism Research, 26*(3), 589–612.

McKercher, B., & du Cros, H. (2002). *Cultural tourism.* New York: The Haworth Hospitality Press.

McKercher, B., Ho, P. S. Y., & du Cros, H. (2004). Attributes of popular cultural attractions in Hong Kong. *Annals of Tourism Research, 31*(2), 393–407.

Misham, E. (1969). *The cost of economic growth.* Harmondsworth, UK: Pergamon.

Monaghan, K. (n.d.). *Takayama: The town that time forgot.* Retrieved December 8, 2003, from http://www.intrepidtraveler.com/travels/takayama.html

Naoi, T., Airey, D., Iijima, S., & Niininen, O. (2006). Visitors' evaluation of an historical district: Repertory grid analysis and laddering analysis. *Tourism Management, 27*(3), 420–436.

Naoi, T., & Iijima, S. (2004). Effects of the presence of other people on visitors' evaluation of a historical district. *Proceeding of the 14th international research conference of the council for Australian University tourism and hospitality education,* Brisbane, Australia.

Newcomb, R. (1979). *Planning the past; historical landscape resources and recreation: Studies in historical geography.* Hamden, CT: Dawson/Archon Books.

Nuryanti, W. (1996). Heritage and postmodern tourism. *Annals of Tourism Research, 23*(2), 249–260.

Ooi, C. S. (2002). *Cultural tourism and tourism cultures: The business of mediating experiences in Copenhagen and Singapore.* Copenhagen: Copenhagen Business School Press.

Orbasli, A. (2000). *Tourists in historic towns: Urban conservation and heritage management.* London: E & FN Spon.

Palmer, C. (1999). Tourism and the symbols of identity. *Tourism Management, 20*(3), 313–322.

Pearce, P. L. (1982). Perceived changes in holiday destinations. *Annals of Tourism Research, 9*(2), 145–164.

Pike, S. (2003). The use of repertory grid analysis to elicit salient short-break holiday destination attributes in New Zealand. *Journal of Travel Research, 41*(3), 315–319.

Pike, S., & Ryan, C. (2004). Destination positioning analysius through a comparison of cognitive, affective, and conative perceptions. *Journal of Travel Research, 42*(4), 333–342.

Plog, S. C. (1974). Why destination areas rise and fall in popularity? *Cornell Hotel and Restaurant Administration Quarterly, 14*(4), 55–58.

Prentice, R. C., & Light, D. (1994). Current issues in interpretative provision at heritage sites. In: A. V. Seaton (Ed.), *Tourism, the state of the art* (pp. 204–221). Chichester, UK: John Wiley & Sons.

Prentice, M., & Prentice, R. (1989). The heritage market of historic sites such as education resources. In: D. Herbert, R. Prentice & C. Thomas (Eds), *Heritage sites: Strategies for marketing and development* (pp. 143–190). Hants: Avebury.

Reynolds, T. J., & Gutman, J. (1988). Laddering theory, method, analysis, and interpretation. *Journal of Advertising Research, 28*(1), 11–31.

Richards, G. (2001). The market for cultural attractions. In: G. Richards (Ed.), *Cultural attractions and European tourism* (pp. 31–53). Wallingford, UK: CAB International.

Rowthorn, C., Ashburne, J., Atkinson, D., Bender, A., Benson, S. S., & McLachlan, C. (2003). *Lonely planet: Japan* (8th ed.). Melbourne, Australia: Lonely Planet Publications Pty.

Sack, R. D. (1992). *Place, modernity and the consumer's world.* Baltimore, MD: Johns Hopkins University Press.

Sanui, J. (1995). *User needs no Kashika Gijyutsu.* [Methods for visualization of user needs.] *Kigyo Shindan. [The Assessment of Enterprises.]* (January), 31–38.

Sasaki, T. (2000). *Ryokosha Kodo no Shinrigaku.* [The psychology of tourists behavior.] Osaka, Japan: Kansai University Press.

Schreyer, R., & Roggenbuck, J. W. (1978). The influence of experience expectations on crowding perceptions and social-psychological carrying capacities. *Leisure Sciences, 1*(4), 373–394.

Schwartz, S. H., & Bilsky, W. (1987). Toward a universal psychological structure of human values. *Journal of Personality and Social Psychology, 53,* 550–562.

Selby, M. (2004). Consuming the city: Conceptualizing and researching urban tourist knowledge. *Tourism Geographies, 6*(2), 186–207.

Smith, V. L. (1989). *Hosts and guests: The anthropology of tourism* (2nd ed.). Philadelphia: University of Pennsylvania Press.

Solomon, M., Bamossy, G., & Askegaard, S. (1999). *Consumer behaviour: A European perspective.* New York: Prentice-Hall Europe.

Stokols, D. (1972). On the distinction between density and crowding: Some implications for future research. *Psychological Review, 79*(3), 275–277.

Takayama Municipal Commitee of Education. (1994).*Takayama no bunkazai.* [Cultural assets of Takayama.] Takayama, Japan: Takayama Municipal Committee of Education.

Takayama Municipal Office. (n.d.). Retrieved February 4, 2003, from http://www.hida.jp/english

Thomas, C. (1989). The role of historic sites and reasons for visiting. In: D. T. Herbert, R. C. Prentice & C. J. Thomas (Eds), *Heritage sites: strategies for marketing and development* (pp. 62–93). Aldershot, UK: Gower.

Timothy, D. J., & Boyd, S. W. (2003). *Heritage tourism.* Harlow, UK: Prentice-Hall.

Urry, J. (1990). *The tourist gaze.* London: Sage.

Urry, J. (1995). *Consuming places.* London: Routledge.

Walmsley, D. J., & Jenkins, J. M. (1993). Appraisive images of tourist areas: Application of personal constructs. *Australian Geographer, 24*(2), 1–13.

Walsh, J. (1992). *The representation of the past.* London: Routledge.

Walter, J. A. (1982). Social limits to tourism. *Leisure Studies, 1*(3), 295–304.

West, P. C. (1982). Effects of user behaviour on the perception of crowding in recreation settings: An urban case-study. *Leisure Sciences, 9*, 87–99.

Womble, P., & Studebaker, S. (1981). Crowding in a national park campground: Katmai National Monument in Alaska. *Environment and Behavior, 13*(5), 557–573.

Woodside, A. G., & Lysonski, S. (1989). A general model of traveler destination choice. *Journal of Travel Research, 27*(4), 8–14.

Young, M. (1995). Evaluative constructions of domestic tourist places. *Australian Geographical Studies, 33*(2), 272–286.

Zajonic, R. B. (1980). Feeling and thinking: Preferences need no inferences. *American Psychologist, 35*(2), 151–175.

Zeppel, H., & Hall, C. M. (1991). Selling art and history: Cultural heritage and tourism. *Journal of Tourism Studies, 2*(1), 29–45.

Zeppel, H., & Hall, C. M. (1992). Review: Arts and heritage tourism. In: B. Weiler & C. M. Hall (Eds), *Special interest tourism* (pp. 47–68). New York: Halsted Press.

Zins, A. (2001). Two methods to the same end: Hierarchical Value Maps in Tourism – comparing the association pattern technique with direct importance ratings. In: A. Mazanec, G. I. Crouch, J. R. B. Ritchie & A. G. Woodside (Eds), *Consumer psychology of tourism, hospitality and leisure*, (Vol 2, pp.123–151). Wallingford, UK: CABI Publishing.

SET UP A CONTINUATION ORDER TODAY!

Did you know that you can set up a continuation order on all Elsevier-JAI series and have each new volume sent directly to you upon publication? For details on how to set up a **continuation order**, contact your nearest regional sales office listed below.

To view related series in Business & Management, please visit:

www.elsevier.com/businessandmanagement

The Americas
Customer Service Department
11830 Westline Industrial Drive
St. Louis, MO 63146
USA
US customers:
Tel: +1 800 545 2522 (Toll-free number)
Fax: +1 800 535 9935
For Customers outside US:
Tel: +1 800 460 3110 (Toll-free number).
Fax: +1 314 453 7095
usbkinfo@elsevier.com

Europe, Middle East & Africa
Customer Service Department
Linacre House
Jordan Hill
Oxford OX2 8DP
UK
Tel: +44 (0) 1865 474140
Fax: +44 (0) 1865 474141
eurobkinfo@elsevier.com

Japan
Customer Service Department
2F Higashi Azabu, 1 Chome Bldg
1-9-15 Higashi Azabu, Minato-ku
Tokyo 106-0044
Japan
Tel: +81 3 3589 6370
Fax: +81 3 3589 6371
books@elsevierjapan.com

APAC
Customer Service Department
3 Killiney Road #08-01
Winsland House I
Singapore 239519
Tel: +65 6349 0222
Fax: +65 6733 1510
asiainfo@elsevier.com

Australia & New Zealand
Customer Service Department
30-52 Smidmore Street
Marrickville, New South Wales 2204
Australia
Tel: +61 (02) 9517 8999
Fax: +61 (02) 9517 2249
service@elsevier.com.au

30% Discount for Authors on All Books!

A 30% discount is available to Elsevier book and journal contributors on all books *(except multi-volume reference works)*.

To claim your discount, full payment is required with your order, which must be sent directly to the publisher at the nearest regional sales office above.